A SACRED CITY

MANCHESTER
1824

Manchester University Press

MANCHESTER MEDIEVAL STUDIES

SERIES EDITOR   Professor S. H. Rigby

The study of medieval Europe is being transformed as old orthodox-
ies are challenged, new methods embraced and fresh fields of enquiry
opened up. The adoption of interdisciplinary perspectives and the
challenge of economic, social and cultural theory are forcing medieval-
ists to ask new questions and to see familiar topics in a fresh light.
    The aim of this series is to combine the scholarship traditionally
associated with medieval studies with an awareness of more recent
issues and approaches in a form accessible to the non-specialist
reader.

MANCHESTER MEDIEVAL STUDIES

A SACRED CITY
CONSECRATING CHURCHES AND REFORMING SOCIETY IN ELEVENTH-CENTURY ITALY

Louis I. Hamilton

Manchester University Press

Manchester and New York

*distributed in the USA exclusively
by Palgrave Macmillan*

The right of Louis I. Hamilton to be identified as the author of this work has been asserted by him in accordance with the Copyright, Designs and Patents Act 1988.

Published by Manchester University Press
Oxford Road, Manchester M13 9NR, UK
and Room 400, 175 Fifth Avenue, New York, NY 10010, USA
www.manchesteruniversitypress.co.uk

Distributed in the United States exclusively by
Palgrave Macmillan, 175 Fifth Avenue, New York,
NY 10010, USA

Distributed in Canada exclusively by
UBC Press, University of British Columbia, 2029 West Mall,
Vancouver, BC, Canada V6T 1Z2

British Library Cataloguing-in-Publication Data
A catalogue record for this book is available from the British Library

Library of Congress Cataloging-in-Publication Data applied for

ISBN   978 0 7190 8026 5   *hardback*

First published 2010

The publisher has no responsibility for the persistence or accuracy of URLs for any external or third-party internet websites referred to in this book, and does not guarantee that any content on such websites is, or will remain, accurate or appropriate.

Typeset
by Servis Filmsetting Limited, Stockport, Cheshire
Printed in Great Britain
by TJ International Ltd, Padstow

For Lydia

CONTENTS

TABLES AND FIGURES

Tables

Figures

ACKNOWLEDGEMENTS

As I consider how this work arrived finally at its conclusion, I am reminded of medieval pilgrimage narratives where many strangers appear miraculously to provide the pilgrim essential assistance, or who turn out to be the journey's object in disguise. The record certainly reveals an itinerary dotted with countless generosities and kindnesses large and small; I hope the final product does them justice. The research for this book was supported in part by a Fulbright Fellowship (1998–99) and writing was completed thanks to a Postdoctoral Associate Professorship in Medieval History at Rutgers University (2003–2005), an Andrew W. Mellon Fellowship at the Pontifical Institute of Mediaeval Studies, Toronto (2005–2006), and a junior sabbatical granted by Drew University (2008). I am profoundly grateful to Susan L. Boynton who read the entire draft manuscript and offered innumerable insights and boundless enthusiasm. I also owe a great debt to Richard F. Gyug, my dissertation director, who read and offered comments on multiple subsequent revisions. Portions of the work were generously commented on by Brenda Bolton, Stefano Riccioni, Didier Méhu and Joseph Goering. I am deeply grateful for their efforts and friendship. The comments of Stephen Rigby and the anonymous readers of Manchester University Press were particularly helpful, generous and insightful and improved the work. It has been a pleasure working with them. Karl Morrison has been a genuine support, both during my time at Rutgers and subsequently, and I have learned much from him about the Middle Ages (as have so many). Robert Dodaro, OSA, has also offered much direction and encouragement over many years, helping to create opportunities for me to pursue research in Europe and the Americas. The research for this project benefited from many conversations with and the extensive comments and observations of Jennifer Harris, Dorothy Glass, Laura Gathagan, Valerie Ramseyer, Greti Dinkova-Bruun, Fred Unwalla, Lucy Donkin, Roger Reynolds, D. Medina Lasansky and Elizabeth Parker. Virginia Brown did me the extreme kindness of lending and copying materials for me; this will not surprise those who knew her. I am also grateful for the generous support and encouragement of James K. McConica, CSB, OC. Kathy Juliano and

Ernest Rubinstein of Drew University's Rose Library have been tremendously helpful in their efforts to borrow or acquire books and articles that always seem to be rush-ordered (and returned late). My parents, Richard F. and Marie I. Hamilton, have learned the subtle art of gentle and supportive inquiry into the book's progress over many years. Lydia G. Hamilton has read through and edited the entire manuscript, offered endless support and many critiques, sacrificed much, endured the anxieties and encouraged the joys of the process as only she can. This book is dedicated to her.

ABBREVIATIONS

AASS	*Acta sanctorum quotquot toto orbe coluntur*, ed. Johannes Bollandus et al., 69 vols (Antwerp, 1643-1940).
CCL	*Corpus Christianorum, series Latina* (Turnhout, 1954-).
CCCM	*Corpus Christianorum, Continuatio Mediaevalis* (Turnhout, 1971-).
DMA	*Dictionary of the Middle Ages.*
Forcella	Forcella, Vincenzo, *Iscrizioni delle chiese e d'altri edificii di Roma dal secolo XI fino ai giorni nostri* (Rome, 1869-84).
Jaffé	Jaffé, Philipp and Wilhelm Wattenbach et al., *Regesta pontificum romanorum ab condita ecclesia ad annum post Christum natum MCXCVIII*, 2 vols (Leipzig, 1885).
MGH	*Monumenta Germaniae Historica* (Berlin, 1877-).
MGH LdL	*Monumenta Germaniae Historica, Libelli de Lite imperatorum et pontificum* (Hanover, 1891-97).
MGH SS	*Monumenta Germaniae Historica, Scriptores in folio.*
MPG	*Patrologiae cursus completus, series Graecae*, ed. J.P. Migne et al., 161 vols (Paris, 1857-87).
PL	*Patrologiae cursus completus, series Latine*, ed. J.P. Migne et al., 221 vols (Paris, 1844-64).
PRG	Romano-Germanic Pontifical.
RIS	*Rerum italicarum scriptores: raccolta degli storici italiani dal cinquecento al millecinquecento*, ed. Lodovico Antonio Muratori et al. (Città di Castello, 1900-).
RPXII	Roman Pontifical of the twelfth century.

Introduction: a sacred city

And then coming to the door of the church . . . [the bishop] says 'Open'. Then the door having been opened, [the bishop], entering alone with the clergy, says, 'Peace to this house.'

Response: 'Upon your entrance. Amen.'

The Roman Pontifical, Ordo XVII[1]

Among those [travelling with Bruno of Toul as Leo IX to Rome] was a handmaid of God of religious life, who . . . admonish[ed] him . . ., 'As soon as you place your first step inside the doors of the church of the prince of the apostles, do not forget to use these divine words, 'Peace be on this house and on all those who dwell in it.'

Life of Leo IX[2]

On 2 October, 1049, less than a year after being appointed as pope, Leo IX consecrated the church of St Remigius in Rheims. It was a rare act for a Roman pontiff. In the previous forty years, his predecessors had only dedicated two churches.[3] It was also a major liturgical event with the archbishops of Rheims, Trier, Lyons, and Besançon; John, Bishop of Portuensis; Peter, a Roman Deacon and Prefect of the city; the bishops of Senlis, Anjou, and Nevers; the abbot and monks of St Remigius, as well as the secular clergy of the city present. Apart from clergy, the church was filled to capacity with men and women, townspeople (*oppidani*) and citizens (*cives*), and others from across Gaul.[4] Moreover, the spectacular dedication was followed by 'the crucial innovation' of the reform papacy: an assembly of bishops from outside the Roman ecclesiastical province and the imperial territories, under the leadership of the Pope, whose decrees were expected to be binding in all of Latin Christendom.[5] That synod

1

met in the newly consecrated space of St Remigius and issued canons that contained the essential themes of the emerging eleventh-century reform: prohibitions against simony, clerical marriage and 'sodomy', clerical military activity, theft from the poor, and the holding of ecclesiastical offices or altars by the laity.[6] The attendees swore to these canons before the relics of St Remigius.[7] Leo seems to have declared the *pax Dei* here as well.[8] Such important canons aimed at the very heart of the religious and political customs that dominated Europe, pronounced before large gatherings of clergy and laity, had an electrifying effect on Latin Christendom. As Uta-Renate Blumenthal has observed, 'Under Leo IX, almost overnight, the papacy became a living and ever-present reality for all Christians.'[9]

The synod marked a shift in the broader nature of a more diffuse reform movement that began in Latin Christendom prior to the year 1000. Driven in part by millennial hopes for the second coming of Christ, in part by a perceived social instability, and in part by demographic expansion in population and wealth, a series of important religious innovations and transformations swept across tenth-century Europe. The first of these was in response to the perception of social instability, the movement known as the Peace of God (*pax Dei*). In the last quarter of the tenth century, a series of large local gatherings, often out of doors, were convened by bishops (often in conjunction with local secular leaders). These meetings were with the express purpose of binding knights (*milites*) and armed peasants under oath, sworn on relics and at the pain of excommunication, that they would refrain from breaking into or stealing from churches, from stealing from the poor (as at Rheims above), or from attacking the clergy and other non-combatants. The movement began in the Auvergne, the south central region of modern France, and spread across Europe in the eleventh century. It also took on more complex forms in leagues of local lords who agreed to enforce the Peace and in what came to be known as the Truce of God. The Truce of God extended the Peace temporally (and liturgically) by asserting that there were certain times when warfare was prohibited. This was liturgical in the sense that the times deemed inappropriate for Christians to fight one another were Sundays, holy days, and ultimately Fridays, and the entire season of Lent. Moreover, these same synods increasingly came to insist upon the reform of the clergy as well, turning their attention to clerical celibacy and the enforcement of excommunication.[10] At the same time, monastic communities were expanding: for our purposes the most important are those of Cluny, Montecassino, and Fonte Avellana. The first of these, dedicated to Saints Peter and Paul at Cluny, was founded in 910 by William of Aquitaine with the surprising

proviso that it would be subordinate to no one other than St Peter's successors in Rome. In north central Italy, in the middle of the tenth century, a hermitage was formed in a valley known as Fonte Avellana. That hermitage, dedicated to St Andrew, soon came to be known for the rigour of its monastic discipline. At the same time, the very seat of Latin monasticism, Benedict's monastery at Montecassino, was re-established after a period of Arab raids had left it in ruins. These three monastic communities would gain a reputation for independence, for the rigour of their discipline, and for learning. They attracted pious donations and formidable leaders in impressive quantities. Three of those abbots would become important papal reformers: Peter Damian (Cardinal and prior of Fonte Avellana, d. 1072), Desiderius, Abbot of Montecassino (who became Pope Victor III, 1085–1087), and Odo of Cluny (who became Pope Urban II, 1088–1099). There emerged a growing desire to have all clerics live more like monks, in celibacy, community, and with devotion to correct liturgical practice, and monastic ideals and leadership would transform the Latin Church. With the election of Leo IX, the papacy came to the fore in promoting these ideals. This was Leo's real innovation at Rheims.

It has long been understood that the synod at Rheims was precedent-setting in terms of the reform agenda and in creating a new, active papacy. Less attention has been paid to how the seemingly chance request for the Pope to dedicate the church was to set a precedent for the liturgical practice of the reforming era and for the role of liturgy in the reforms.[11] Historians who have considered the dedication have considered it in more isolated contexts. Particular attention has been given to the dedication of Cluny by Urban II in 1095 and how that dedication created a sacred zone around the abbey church. That has, in turn, been considered as a means of asserting social control (using methods borrowed from anthropology).[12] For this reason, Urban II's itinerary has also received close attention. The presentation of the dedication in the pontificals (the liturgical texts used by bishops during the rite) has also been seen as a mechanism for asserting the authority of the bishop.[13] Other approaches to the dedication have been largely rooted in intellectual history and have considered the commentaries on the dedications apart from the practice; nor have these closely considered the eleventh-century materials.[14] Thus, the larger eleventh-century context for these dedications has not been systematically considered. Dedications became the subject of much exegesis, commentary and canon law among the reformers. The act of consecrating a church was filled with symbolic opportunities for the reformers and for local communities: it could signify the rebuilding of the Church, purging the

Temple, the purity of the Heavenly Bride and the restored heavenly city of Jerusalem. The possibilities go on. Church dedications often drew large crowds – crowds that were, in the eleventh century, becoming increasingly self-conscious participants in the life of the city (for example the townsfolk and citizens present at Rheims and in the Peace movements).[15] Such occasions were natural moments to explain the significance of the dedication rite. In turn, those explanations could be, and often were, challenged.

Leo IX's consecration at Rheims set a powerful precedent, but it was not an event with a single universal meaning readily grasped by all. It would take a full generation of papal reformers and their supporters to come to terms with the rite and to learn how to coordinate its use effectively to the purposes of the reform. Leo himself clearly was responding to an opportunity at Rheims, as it was the Abbot of Rheims who appears to have initiated the idea that Leo dedicate the church. Leo also set a precedent in the number of churches he consecrated as Pope: fifteen.[16] Such dedications were often accompanied by the granting or confirming of privileges, and so could reshape the social landscape or reinforce lines of allegiance.[17] As such, Leo's dedications were intensely conservative; one-third of Leo's dedications were of churches associated with Leo's own family, and one church had direct imperial links.[18] In this sense, Leo's dedications reinforced the familial dominance of ecclesiastical structures that his own canons and the emerging literature on the significance of the dedication rite would begin to undermine.

The dedication did not take place in a vacuum. The larger context of the dedication at Rheims, and of the dedications to be examined in detail, was one of rapidly expanding population across Latin Christendom and particularly in its urban centres; as a result, churches were being built and rebuilt. These forces were fostering independent urban political authority on the Italian peninsula; albeit largely inchoate in the eleventh century, this is the era of the 'nascent Italian commune', and our records reveal associations of 'citizens' coming together to affect religious and civic life.[19] To complicate the matter further, it was a period of great religious reform with monastic centres such as Cluny, Fonte Avellana, and Montecassino, and with early support from the German emperors. The reform initially sought to 'purify' the clergy along monastic lines and later to create an independent and ecclesiastically dominant papacy.[20] To name these monasteries and offices, Cluny, emperor, pope, is to expose that there can be no distinction between reforms that were 'properly' religious, political, or social in our period. The intertwined nature of these types of authority is clearly visible in the debate over liturgical meaning that has

come to define the period: the investiture controversy. As it developed in the late eleventh and early twelfth century out of the earlier reforms, the investiture controversy became a debate (often bloody) over who (lay or ecclesiastical lord – emperor, king, bishops or pope) could properly lead the rites in general, and what parts of the rites in particular – consecration, investment with pallium, ring, staff, etc. – that made a bishop, and what those ritual actions and objects signified. In the vast literature on the period, the liturgical dimension has been overshadowed by the rivalry between emperor and pope that has given this period the alternate title of the 'Gregorian' reforms.

In the midst of these religious reforms, social transformations and political conflicts, new churches were being built and old churches reno-vated, reflecting the new wealth, population and ideals of Christendom. These churches, in turn, were increasingly being consecrated by bishops. That rite, in the words of one hymn often associated with the dedication, transformed the church building into the 'Blessed city of Jerusalem, called the vision of peace, which is constructed in heaven from living stones . . . newly come from heaven'.[21] That space – now a sacred city – was the centre of worship and the resting place of the holy dead; it could become the locus of religious and communal identity, or not.[22] This book is about that liturgical rite, the dedication of a church, during the eleventh and twelfth centuries, primarily on the Italian peninsula.[23] It was a period deeply concerned to explain, reform and regulate a variety of liturgical practices, especially those concerned with consecration, from the Eucharist to the investment of bishops. What did the liturgy mean and for whom; and how was that liturgical meaning created and received? The liturgy for the dedi-cation has received far less attention than other contemporary disputes over consecrations (of the Eucharist or of bishops or even of cemeteries). At the time, however, the dedication or consecration (to use only its most common names) of a church was described as a sacrament and later, in Gratian's canon collection, it became the framework for the discussion of the sacramental life of the Church. It was a rite that clearly mattered to the people of the eleventh century to an extent that modern scholars have not yet fully appreciated. The dedication rite became significant for the reforming papacy in the late eleventh century, and the reformers attempted to shape its meaning – these two facts (a significant rite and the desire to shape it) regularly resulted in conflict.

In order to understand these three phenomena (significance, control and conflict), the liturgy itself must be understood, both in its broad his-torical outline and in the particular versions of the liturgy available for the

dedication of a new church in eleventh- and early twelfth-century Italy. It is important to begin with an appreciation of the symbolic richness of the dedication rite. These rites clearly attempted to create an ideal eschatological community within the mundane community (the sacred space that the 'Peace of God' was intended to uphold), and sought to establish a series of relationships between bishop, clergy, lay ruler and congregation. It is, however, the overall symbolic richness of the rite that must be appreciated here, as it is exceedingly difficult to move from the prescriptive liturgical sources to a reliable description of any particular dedication. Comparing a number of extant liturgical manuscripts from northern and southern Italy demonstrates the incredible variety of possibilities within the rite. Local custom, the site of the church itself, variety within the extant manuscripts, and our inability to know which texts were used where, all urge caution when attempting to place the rite in its context. Local topography and the location of these churches points to the need for a flexible approach to the practice of the rite. If the full details of the liturgical experience are not known, it is impossible for us to assign any single meaning to the rite. The first chapter, therefore, offers very few and only the broadest 'outsider' interpretations of the liturgy itself, since the manuscript evidence suggests the great variety and richness of the liturgy without fully revealing which liturgies were used where and when.[24] Ritual theory must be used here, but should be applied with great caution.[25] At the same time, the variety of liturgical forms available, the act of preserving those forms and the richness of the liturgies all suggest the symbolic capacity of the liturgy and the appeal of that richness to those who preserved its diversity. That the liturgy was both symbolically rich and capable of being altered to local needs indicates its broad and multi-layered appeal, not only to the educated elite who would debate its meaning, but also to the laity who would crowd the event.

That crowd is the subject of the second chapter. It is essential to understand whether or not that crowd was present at these liturgies (or if they are to be understood as a literary device) and, if they were present, what their behaviour meant. The sources suggest that people were shaped by the rite: they hoped for cures or the miraculous, they commemorated important events on the feast of the dedication, or the rite may have enhanced their sense of local prestige, etc. There is much evidence that people sought out this liturgical moment and expected something of significance to take place. However, given that it would be in the interest of hagiographers and chroniclers to promote the popularity of their local patron saint and his or her church, and that these crowds are often quite

generically described, it is appropriate to question to what extent these crowds were real. While all of our sources are composed by clerics, they do not present an undifferentiated portrait of the dedication event itself or of the attendant crowds. Their descriptions reveal the important elements of the 'emerging crowd' of eleventh- and twelfth-century Italy. Eleventh-century texts increasingly present us with active crowds of people: crowds that demand or object to religious reform, and that support or co-opt activities within their communities that had previously been the domain of the political elite. The behaviour of these crowds set precedents essential for the independent civic activities of the later communes, and were also integral to both the eleventh-century reforms and later heretical and orthodox religious movements.[26] The records of dedications reveal not only the urban and rural ruling classes, bishops, monks and lesser clerics but also the *boni homines* ('good men'), merchants, women and children. Some are named or otherwise further identified. The chronicles describe tensions within dedications and evidence for violent crowds and conflicts between bishop and *cives* and/or monastery. In short, the activities of the crowd do not always reflect the ambitions of those leading the liturgy. Rather, there were a variety of forces at work within the event of the dedication. First, there is the appeal of the dedication liturgy and the importance of the sanctified space that drew the crowds and promised a variety of signs and healings. Second, this often combined with changes within the Italian cities to make the consecration of a new church a contested event between episcopal and monastic households, the *cives* and dominical authorities, papal and imperial supporters. These groups allied with one another as the situation allowed. Observation is a form of participation and, in turn, shapes the liturgy and its significance. These crowds and the variety of their responses to the dedication – from simple attendance, to pious theft and miraculous claim or murderous and destructive rioting – gave meaning to the rite. Their response endorsed, rejected or offered an alternate understanding of the significance proposed by the clerical elite who led the rite. Third, while the pro-papal reformers had begun to promote the liturgy as a means to assert papal authority and reform ideals within Italy and the broader Church, it is clear that the event was also of concern to local bishops and abbots who saw the dedication event as shaping their religious identity and authority, and felt the need to support or resist these dedications. Thus, the clerical effort to explain the liturgy is the subject of the final chapters.

From the papacy of Leo IX to that of Paschal II, a wealth of materials was produced to articulate the meaning of the dedication of churches.

That this discussion of the consecration of a church would have implications for the effort to create a sacred community, a reformed Church, or that it would be an extension of the debate over consecrating people (emperors, kings and bishops) and the significance of their symbols of authority (the ring and staff at the heart of the investiture controversy) has been little considered.[27] It is in the context of these debates over symbolic meaning and ecclesiastical reform that the eleventh- and early twelfth-century commentaries on the dedication should be understood. These commentaries include the sermons of Peter Damian (1007–1072), the canon collection of Anselm of Lucca (c.1036–1086) and the commentaries of Bruno of Segni (c.1048–1123). These were composed within the context of the dedicatory activities of the reforming papacy, especially the major itineraries of Urban II and Paschal II. When traced in this manner, there emerges an expanding argument that the consecration of churches reflected the sacrality and centrality of the Church of Rome and its leadership. Seemingly abstract exegesis on the heavenly city or the definition of the word 'church' versus that of 'synagogue' are revealed as fraught with tensions when placed into this context. The dedication of a church, in the hands of the reformers, became an argument for a clear, Rome-centred ecclesiology. The itinerant papacy, even when these itineraries were necessitated by their inability to control their episcopal see, became an opportunity to spread the message of reform and the ideals of the reformers, and to punctuate papal authority via elaborate liturgies such as the consecration of churches. The popes of the eleventh century chose and explained their liturgical moments with increasing sophistication. At the end of this creative period, Bruno of Segni and Pope Paschal II first promoted then debated the meaning of the elaborate ritual life that would characterise the twelfth-century papacy.[28]

In this period of expanding urban centres, changing political structures and religious expectations, invariably crowds and controversies followed the dedication. The power of the event, of the space, the persons and the liturgy itself to draw crowds, with the rite's rich but ambiguous symbolic gestures and activities, its promise to set a space apart governed by a different set of social norms (the 'Peace of God'), to make a place sacred, all fuelled conflict over the rite and over who controlled the sacred space.[29] As symbols gain significance they become volatile, they need to be defended or attacked; they cannot be ignored. So it was with the consecration of sacred space. Even as the reformers invested more meaning into the rite, dedications became moments of communal unrest. At the moment of the most effective use of the rite (the papacy of Paschal II) their explanation of

the rite could be and, it is suggested, was undermined by one of its great architects, Bruno of Segni.

If the eleventh-century debates teach us one thing, it is that the dedication had no static significance; it had no inherent social function.[30] Rather, it was attractive: it was a rich liturgy for which people assigned or accepted meaning. Since the dedication was rich enough to attract and permit multiple explanations, inevitably there ensued different, even conflicting, understandings or valuations (good or bad) of the rites.[31] As the context changed across the peninsula and the eleventh century, the significance of the ritual activity changed (here a sign of sanctity, there a statement of defiance), sometimes only subtly, and so needs to be understood afresh.[32] Different people in different contexts assign, accept or reject different meanings.[33] From the famous bishops at the head of the liturgy to the observing crowd whose names are now mostly lost to us, all transformed the event more or less by their words and actions, and more or less deliberately. In turn, the dedication of churches shaped them, their communities and the eleventh century.

Notes

1   Michel Andrieu, *Le Pontifical Romain au Moyen-Âge*, 4 vols (Louvain, 1931–61): t. 1, *Le Pontifical Romain du XIIe siècle*, 180.

2   *Sancti Leonis Vita*, PL 143, 488a. See I.S. Robinson, *The Papal Reform of the Eleventh Century: the Lives of Leo IX and Gregory VII* (Manchester, 2004), 131–2.

3   Phillip Jaffé and Wilhelm Wattenbach et al., *Regesta pontificum romanorum ab condita ecclesia and annum post Christum natum MCXCVIII*, 2 Vols (Leipzig, 1885) [Jaffé], 3969 and 4027 (April 24).

4   Anselm, *Historia dedicationis ecclesiae S. Remigii*, PL 142, 1424–5.

5   I.S. Robinson, *The Papacy, 1073–1198: Continuity and Innovation* (Cambridge, 1990), 122.

6   PL 142, 1431, 1437. Peter Damian will dedicate his *Book of Gomorrah* to Leo IX around this time. Uta-Renate Blumenthal, 'Eine neuer Text für das Reimser Konzil Leo IX. (1049)?', *Deutsches Archive für des Mittelalters* 32(1) (1976), 23–48.

7   Charles A. Frazee, 'The Origins of Clerical Celibacy in the Western Church', *Church History* 41(2) (June 1972), 149–67, at 162.

8   Robinson, *Papacy*, 326.

9   Uta-Renate Blumenthal, *The Investiture Controversy: Church and Monarchy from the Ninth to the Twelfth Century* (Philadelphia, 1988), 73.

10 See the helpful overview in Kathleen G. Cushing, *Reform and the Papacy in the Eleventh Century: Spirituality and Social Change* (Manchester, 2005), 39–54.

11 For the essential materials see the essays and extensive bibliography of Didier Méhu (ed.), *Mises en scène et mémoires de la consécration de l'église dans l'occident médiéval* (Turnhout, 2008).

12 Barbara Rosenwein, *Negotiating Space: Power, Restraint, and Privileges of Immunity in Early Medieval Europe* (Ithaca, 1999); Didier Méhu, *Paix et communautés autour de l'abbaye de Cluny, Xe–XVe siècle* (Lyon, 2001); Dominique Iogna-Prat, *Order and Exclusion: Cluny and Christendom face Heresy, Judaism and Islam (1000–1150)*, trans. Graham Robert Edwards (Ithaca, 2002); Jennifer A. Harris, 'Building Heaven on Earth: Cluny as *Locus Sanctissimus* in the Eleventh Century', in Susan Boynton and Isabelle Cochelin (eds), *From Dead of Night to End of Day: the Medieval Customs of Cluny* (Turnhout, 2005), 131–51.

13 Eric Palazzo, *L'Évêque et son image: l'illustration du pontifical au Moyen Âge* (Turnhout, 1999).

14 Brian Vincent Repsher, *The Rite of Church Dedication in the Early Medieval Era* (Lewiston, NY, 1998); Christina Whitehead, 'Columnae . . . sunt episcopi. Pavimentum . . . est vulgus: The Symbolic Translation of Ecclesiastical Architecture in Latin Liturgical Handbooks of the Twelfth and Thirteenth Centuries', *The Medieval Translator/Traduire au Moyen Age* 8 (2003): 29–37; Ruth Horie, *Perceptions of* Ecclesia: *Church and Soul in Medieval Dedication Sermons* (Turnhout, 2006). The exception is István Bejczy, 'Kings, Bishops, and Political Ethics: Bruno of Segni on the Cardinal Virtues', *Mediaeval Studies* 64 (2002): 267–86.

15 R.I. Moore, 'Family, Community and Cult on the Eve of the Gregorian Reform', *Transactions of the Royal Historical Society*, 5th Ser., 30 (1980), 49–69.

16 R. Crozet, 'Etudes sur les Consécrations Pontificales', *Bulletin Monumental* 104 (1946): 5–46, at 16–24.

17 Rosenwein, *Negotiating Space*. Especially significant is her chapter on Cluny and its sacred ban enforced by Urban II's dedication and discussed below in chapter 4; Rosenwein, *Negotiating Space*, 156–83.

18 Crozet, 'Etudes', 17–20, 23–4.

19 Philip Jones, *The Italian City-State: From Commune to Signoria* (Oxford, 1997), 150.

20 Cushing notes the emphasis on purity, and its emphasis in Leo's dedication, in her *Reform and the Papacy*, 125. Other essential works on the eleventh-century reform include Augustin Fliche, *La Réforme grégorienne*, 3 vols (Louvain, 1924); Gerhart Ladner, *Theologie und Politik vor dem Investiturstreit: Abendmahlstreit/ Kirchenreform, Cluni und Heinrich III* (Brünn, 1936); Walter Ullman, *The Growth of Papal Government in the Middle Ages; A Study in the Ideological Relation of Clerical to Lay Power* (London, 1965 [1955]); Giovanni Miccoli, 'Chiesa Gregoriana: Ricerche sulla Riforma del secolo XI', *Storici antichi e moderni* 17 (Florence, 1966); H.E.J. Cowdrey, *The Cluniacs and the Gregorian Reform* (Oxford, 1970); Rudolf Hülls, *Kardinal, Klerus und Kirchen Roms, 1049–1130* (Tübingen, 1977); Heinrich Dormeier, *Montecassino und die Laien im 11. und 12. Jahrhundert* (Stuttgart, 1979); Cowdrey, *The Age of Abbot Desiderius: Montecassino, the Papacy, and the Normans in the Eleventh and Early Twelfth*

Centuries (Oxford, 1983); Colin Morris, *The Papal Monarchy: The Western Church from 1050 to 1250* (Oxford, 1989); and Cowdrey, *Pope Gregory VII (1073-1085)* (Oxford, 1998).

21 *Analecta Hymnica Medii Aevi*, ed. C. Blume and G.M. Dreves (Leipzig 1886-1922; repr. Frankfurt am Main 1961), 55 vols, v. 51, 110-11.

22 Foundational to understanding the role of cult centres in civic life was Bernhard Töpfer, 'The Cult of Relics and Pilgrimage in Burgundy and Aquitaine at the Time of the Monastic Reform', trans. János Bak and Thomas Head, in Thomas Head and Richard Landes (eds), *The Peace of God, Social Violence and Religious Response in France around the Year 1000* (Ithaca, 1992), 41-57, esp. 45-8. Originally published as 'Reliquienkult und Pilgerbewegung zur Zeit der Klosterreform im burgundisch-aquitanischen Gebeit', in Hellmut Kretzschmar (ed.), *Vom Mittelalter zur Neuzeit: Zum 65. Geburtstag von Heinrich Sprömberg* (Berlin, 1956), 420-39. Töpfer, however, writing in post-war Germany, saw the medieval world in twentieth-century terms: 'Clearly the main task of the [Church] was to implant its ideology among the masses and secure control over them.' Saint's cults were the means to that end: ibid., 41-57. More recent approaches that reveal more integrated, complex and precise relationships include Augustine Thompson, *Cities of God: the Religion of the Italian Communes, 1125-1325* (State College, 2005); and Diana Webb, *Saints and Cities in Medieval Italy* (Manchester, 2007).

23 This book originated in my dissertation, revised and expanded subsequently: Louis I. Hamilton, 'The Power of Liturgy and the Liturgy of Power in Eleventh- and Twelfth-Century Italy' (PhD diss., Fordham University, 2000).

24 For an overview of a variety of approaches to sacred space, approaches that this work seeks to bridge, see Harris, "Building Heaven on Earth,", 131-51; Sarah Hamilton and Andrew Spicer, 'Defining the Holy: the Delineation of Sacred Space', in Andrew Spicer and Sarah Hamilton (eds), *Defining the Holy: Sacred Space in Medieval and Early Modern Europe* (Aldershot, 2005), 1-23.

25 Philippe Buc, *The Dangers of Ritual: Between Early Medieval Texts and Social Scientific Theory* (Princeton, 2001). For my response to Buc and his critics via the dedication rites, see Louis I. Hamilton, 'Les Dangers du ritual dans l'Italie du XIe siècle: entre textes liturgiques et témoignages historiques', in Méhu (ed.), *Mises en scène*, 159-88.

26 R.I. Moore, *The First European Revolution, c.970-1215* (Oxford, 2000).

27 Most importantly reviewed by Roger E. Reynolds, 'Liturgical Scholarship at the Time of the Investiture Controversy: Past Research and Future Opportunities', *Harvard Theological Review* 71 (1978): 109-24. Enrico Cattaneo, 'La liturgia nella riforma gregoriana', in *Chiesa e Riforma nella Spiritualità del sec. XI: Convegni del Centro di Studi Sulla Spiritualità Medievale VI, 1-16 Ottobre 1963* (Todi, 1968), 169-90. Portions of this discussion appear in Louis I. Hamilton, 'To Consecrate the Church: Ecclesiastical Reform and the Dedication of Churches', in Christopher M. Bellitto and Louis I. Hamilton (eds), *Reforming the Church* (Aldershot, 2005), 105-37.

28 On twelfth-century papal ritual, see Nine Robijnte Miedema, *Die 'Mirabilia Romae': Untersuchungen zu ihrer Überlieferung mit Edition der deutschen und*

niederländischen Texte (Tübingen, 1996); Mary Stroll, *Symbols as Power: The Papacy following the Investiture Contest* (Leiden, 1997); Susan Twyman, *Papal Ceremonial at Rome in the Twelfth Century* (London, 2002); Dale Kinney, 'Rome in the Twelfth Century: *Urbs fracta* and *renovatio*', *Gesta* 45(2) (2006), 199–220; Kinney, 'Fact and Fiction in the *Mirabilia Urbis Romae*', in Éamonn Ócarragáin and Carol Neman de Vegvar (eds), Roma Felix – *Formation and Reflections of Medieval Rome* (Aldershot, 2007), 235–52. More broadly see Charles Homer Haskins, *The Renaissance of the Twelfth Century* (Cambridge, MA, 1927); Robert L. Benson et al., *Renaissance and Renewal in the Twelfth Century* (Oxford, 1985).

29 On the Peace and social change, see R.I. Moore, 'Postscript: The Peace of God and the Social Revolution,' in Head and Landes, *Peace of God*, 308–26. On the Peace and Truce of God in Italy see Hartmut Hoffmann, *Gottesfriede und Treuga Dei*, MGH Schriften 20 (Stuttgart, 1964), esp. 81–7; Roger E. Reynolds, 'Odilo and the *Treuga Dei* in Southern Italy: A Beneventan Manuscript Fragment', *Mediaeval Studies* 46 (1984): 450–62 (note plate between 444 and 445); and John Howe, *Church Reform and Social Change In Eleventh-Century Italy: Dominic of Sora and His Patrons* (Philadelphia, 1997).

30 I owe much to the work of the late Catherine Bell, *Ritual: Perspectives and Dimensions* (Oxford, 1997) and *Ritual Theory, Ritual Practice* (New York, 1992). These studies helped me conceive of a method to move from the compelling nature of the rites to the efforts to explain their meaning and to control that meaning.

31 On the Petrobusian rejection of sacred space altogether in France, see Iogna-Prat, *Order and Exclusion*, 108–9.

32 C. Clifford Flanigan, 'The Apocalypse and the Medieval Liturgy', in Richard K. Emmerson and Bernard McGinn (eds), *The Apocalypse in the Middle Ages* (Ithaca, 1992), 333–51 at 342: '[S]ince rituals are among the most permanent institutions in a society's history, they often continue in use long after the dominant discourses to which they were originally tied have lost their hegemonic powers. *Thus rituals abide, but their interpretations are subject to constant change.*' Emphasis mine.

33 Peter Burke states the problem clearly: 'The stumbling-block for historians who try to come to terms with the ideas of structuralists is their willful lack of concern with change, local context and individual intentions', in his *The Historical Anthropology of Early Modern Italy: Essays on Perception and Communication* (Cambridge, 1987), 5.

1

The liturgies for the dedication of a new church

O how awful is this place, surely it is none other than the house of God and the gate of heaven.

Walk, o saints of God, enter into the city of the Lord, indeed a new church is built for you, where the people ought to adore the majesty of the Lord.

Antiphons from the Romano-Germanic Pontifical[1]

A careful examination of the liturgy (or better, liturgies), its history, and its common features in eleventh- and twelfth-century Italy provides an understanding of its symbolic possibilities.[2] The emphasis must be placed on the potential of the rite while resisting assertion of a single overarching meaning for the rite, since doing so would conceal its local flexibility and wide variance in form in eleventh- and twelfth-century Italy. It is only once these possibilities are appreciated that the historian can begin to comprehend this liturgy's appeal (see Chapter 2) and therefore what was at stake in debating its meanings and contesting its practice (see Chapters 3 to 5).

From its earliest recorded appearances the dedication liturgy held within it eschatological and ecclesiological import.[3] Eusebius of Caesarea (d. AD 339) placed a brief discussion of the dedication of churches and a long sermon on the significance of church ornamentation at the outset of Book 10 in his *Ecclesiastical History*. These church dedications provided the transition between the triumph of Constantine over his enemies and the legislation permitting Christianity. They represented a new unity among people in the world and a Divine Spirit in the Church worshipped in better rites by better priests.[4] Eusebius described the church of the Holy Sepulchre as a 'new Jerusalem' ornamented with jewels, echoing Revelation 21.[5] The dedication of a church also marked the opening of the

synod at Antioch in AD 349 according to both the history of Socrates and that of Sozomen (d. c.450).[6] That a dedication rite emerged so quickly after the legalisation of Christianity with these two meanings (an emphasis on the church as Heavenly Jerusalem and the dedication as a marker of a Council) may suggest that some form of rite preceded AD 313.[7]

While these earliest accounts do not mention the presence of relics, evidence for the practice of placing the bodies of the saints in the churches, or building on the sites of their graves, appears soon after.[8] The presence of the relics would heighten the significance of the dedication ceremony by making the church a centre of the cult of the saint and an eschatological space wherein the faithful worshipped God in the presence of the saints. In 787, the Second Council of Nicaea made the practice of placing relics into dedicated altars normative, and the custom emerged of including the consecrated host along with or instead of the relics.[9] On the Italian peninsula this new practice served the additional purpose from the eighth century of protecting the bodies of the saints from depredation, and was an important feature of the papal building campaigns of the Carolingian era.[10] Not only was the dedication thus connected to the violence of the eighth century, but it received further significance during the Peace movements throughout the tenth and eleventh centuries that emphasised the inviolable nature of the sanctified church.[11]

The Romano-Germanic Pontifical (PRG), a mixture of the Roman and Gallican rites, was formed in the Carolingian period and was a reflection both of the Carolingian effort to create greater ecclesiastical uniformity and of admiration of Roman precedence.[12] The PRG, containing (as all pontificals contain) the rites of bishops but also of abbots with episcopal privileges, came into existence in the middle of the tenth century and into prominence in Italy by the end of the same century.[13] It was still being copied in the twelfth century even as the later Roman Pontifical was circulating.[14] At least one extant copy of the PRG was produced in the fourteenth century, which hints at both its long-term appeal and the ongoing diversity of practice.[15] In the second half of the eleventh century there were two broad forms of Latin pontificals in circulation in Italy, the PRG and the Roman Pontifical.

Two characteristics are worth noting: first, the arrival and dissemination of the PRG and its liturgical forms coincided roughly with that of the Peace movement; and second, it contained more elaborate versions of the rite than had been previously practised on the peninsula.[16] Thus, the more elaborate ritual may have reflected a need for a greater sense of the sacrality of the space now protected by the Peace of God. At the very least

it is clear that the Peace movement provided the context for the emerging liturgy, and the eschatological nature of both the Peace movement and the dedication rite would have reinforced one another.[17] That is, the increased sense of the church as a sacred space in the presence of the eschatological community would have lent force to the compulsion to retain it inviolate. In turn, the ideals of the Peace promoted the sense of the church as a space apart from the ordinary, a point that the PRG intended to be stated expressly to the lay lord(s) present at the dedication by the bishop.[18]

Indeed, in its broad outline the PRG reinforced many common themes of turn-of-the-millennium eschatology and of the Peace movement. But the PRG was largely a construct of the modern critical redactor, and local variations on the liturgy must be considered typical. Variations specific to given pontifical manuscripts or families of manuscripts could vary the possible meanings of the liturgy. Local variations even within the limited confines of southern Italy were significant. For example, the eleventh-century Cassinese pontifical of Desiderius has more occasions for the bishop to process around the exterior of the Church in sight of the congregation than does *Ordo XXXIII*, found in a tenth-century Cassinese manuscript (compare Table 1, Col. I, 2 and 15 and Col. V, 4 and 12, as done by clerics). One Benevantan Pontifical limited the bishop's initial circuits around the exterior of the church to two (Table 1, Col. II, 4), while another had the bishop complete three circuits around the exterior (Table 1, Col. III, 3); one central Italian Pontifical contained no exterior circuits and another has three initially, followed later by a single circuit (Table 3, Col. I and II, 2, 15). If these exterior circuits were an important moment for lay participation as witnesses, their singing of the *Kyrie* also heightened their participation. This occurred in only two of the southern Italian rites (see Table 2) and one of the central Italian rites (see Table 3, Col. II, 15). Only three of the eighty-six antiphons found in the five southern Italian rites of Table 1 were shared by all. Only an additional six antiphons were contained in a majority of the five manuscripts (see Table 2). The rite varied significantly in Southern Italy, and varied still more across Italy.

Thus, an examination of the rite for the dedication in the PRG is an examination only of the outline of a ritual that had many local permutations, more or less significant. It is difficult to connect a specific liturgical book to a specific ritual event. While the itinerant papacy helped to spread the Roman Pontifical, this does not necessarily mean that the copied text was the one used locally.[19] It is not known if the Desiderian pontifical (see Table 1) was used at the dedication of Desiderius' rebuilt Saint Benedict

at Montecassino; while it might be surmised, there is no definitive evidence. This is not to be overly pessimistic, but cautious about our ability to assess what happened at these rites. An examination of the PRG in its most general outline reveals the symbolic potential of the rite. The PRG contained certain essential themes of religious and social import: primarily that in creating the church as a Heavenly Jerusalem, an ideal sacred city within the earthly city, it also asserted a specific, sacerdotal political order. While this was its potential meaning, it remained only a potential within the liturgy, and its significance could and did change according to its context and its exegete. The meaning of the liturgy could also change as regional variations emphasised or omitted dimensions of the rite. Several of these possibilities will be examined later in the chapter.

An overview of the liturgy as contained in the PRG

The liturgies available on the Italian peninsula for the dedication of a church varied in specifics but all were elaborate. The liturgy for the dedication was an intensely physical one, filling the nose with incense; the ears with the echoing thuds of the bishop's staff against the empty church's doors and with the singing of antiphons; the mouth with the taste of the consecrated bread and, perhaps, wine; and the eyes with the images of a community arrayed in its finest, relics in reliquaries, new liturgical vestments and tools and, just before Mass, the splendors of a church fully illumined for the first time.

This liturgy was symbolically rich and, in particular, *Ordo XL* (the most studied of the *ordines*) provides a sense of its potential grandeur (Table 1, Col. IV). It was preceded by an evening vigil with the relics to be deposited in the new church. In the morning the bishop and his clerics approached the tent containing the relics and invoked the litany of saints. This was followed by prayers for freedom from temptation, and for salvation, prayers for peace, forgiveness of sins and the fruitfulness of the earth. Prayers for the 'lord apostle' and all clerics were followed by a prayer for the Church, and for 'this house, a royal hall', that it might be worthily consecrated. This elaborate opening was concluded with the *Agnus dei* and *Kyrie*.[20] Thus, from the very outset, the *PRG* emphasised the eschatological, the peaceful and a priestly-royal authority, typified by the common antiphon (see Table 2), 'Rise o saints from your dwellings, sanctify the place, bless the people, guard us, sinning people, in peace'.[21]

After the exorcism of salt and blessing of water, the relics were placed on a bier and carried to the church, accompanied by censors and candle-

bearers, there the bishop knocked on the door three times and recited the Psalm:

> Lift up your gates o ye princes, and rise eternal doors, and the King of Glory will enter.

A deacon inside replied,

> Who is this King of Glory?

The bishop,

> The Lord strong and mighty, the Lord powerful in battle (Ps. 23 [Ps. 24: 7–8]) (Table 1, Col. IV, 4).

In *Ordo XL*, the bishop then circled the church three times (this might be reduced to two circuits as in Table 1, Col. II, 4), sprinkled the walls of the church with holy water, and repeated the prayers at the doors. Before knocking on the doors a final time, the bishop's prayers again invoked the saints and the peace:

> Omnipotent and merciful God, who bestowed such grace on your priests before all others, that whatever is done worthily and perfectly by them, may be believed to be done by you, we ask your immense mercy that everything which in a moment we will visit, you will visit, whatever we are about to bless, you will bless, and let there be at the introit of our humility, by the merit of your saints, the flight of demons and the entrance of the angel of peace.[22]

When the bishop knocked on the doors a third time, the doors were opened from within, and he entered, saying three times, 'Peace to this house'. After he had entered the church the doors were shut behind him, and the litany of saints was repeated.[23] (Table 1, Col. IV, 5). *Ordo XL* left the congregation and some of the clergy outside still singing. However, prior to the bishop entering the church, *Ordo XL* had engaged the congregation with six antiphons; other pontificals have as few as three prior to the entrance of the bishop and as many as eight.

Now inside, the bishop blessed the interior of the church, its ornaments, vestments and utensils while the relics remained outside with the clergy and the laity who continued to sing. This interior blessing included the abecedarium, that is, the tracing of the Greek and Roman alphabets in a cruciform pattern through the nave of the church (Table 1, Col. IV, 7 and absent only from Table 3, Col. 1). With this the antiphon was sung, 'O how fearful is this place, surely it is not other than the house of God

17

and the gate of heaven'.[24] This was followed by the exorcism of the salt and water, the blessing of the interior and a prayer that the church might be made pure and holy.[25]

The blessing of the interior culminated in the unction of relics and fragments of the Eucharist and their deposition into the altar, and the blessing of liturgical utensils. The deposition of relics is the universal element of the dedicatory rites of the eleventh century. Here the prayers hearken to the Old Testament precedents and to the Temple in Jerusalem in particular; referencing Abraham's sacrifice of Isaac, Jacob's construction and unction of the pillar at Bethel, the Temple cult and Melchizedek.[26] *Ordo XL* reinforced this Old Testament precedent in an antiphon referencing Moses' construction of an altar (Table 1, col. IV, 16q).[27] Thus, the consecration of the altar provided a locus for the Christian cult, while it placed apostolic and priestly authority into a continuum with Old Testament precedent. These prayers also included a strong prayer bolstering apostolic doctrinal authority:

> God, who upon the mystical rock of apostolic power principally built your Church having promised that the gates of hell shall never prevail against it, remove from it all errors, Peaceful One, so that whoever raises the presumption of falsity against it might be conquered by the spirit of truth.[28]

After exiting the church, the bishop blessed the door and lintel saying,

> May you be an entrance of salvation and peace . . . a peaceful door through [Christ] the door . . .

and further

> God [bless] this house of prayer . . . so that the help of your defence may be felt by everyone here invoking your name.[29]

The bishop, clergy and congregation processed with the relics around the exterior of the church singing antiphons that emphasised the new church as the eschatological Jerusalem. As the congregation, priests and bishop processed with the relics, the bishop prayed, 'Walk, saints of God, to the destined place which was prepared for you from the beginning of time.'[30] While 'the people with the women and children' sang *Kyrie eleison*, the clerics responded with the antiphon 'The streets of Jerusalem will rejoice, and all its districts will sing songs of joy'. Later in the procession the theme was continued by the clergy: 'Walk, saints of God, enter into the city of the Lord, indeed a new church is built for you, where the people ought to

adore the majesty of the Lord.'[31] And again, 'I have sanctified Jerusalem, says the Lord, and I will give my saints a kingdom and a chosen tabernacle which I have prepared in the fragrance of perfume.'[32]

That the church became a new Jerusalem, indeed, *the* new Jerusalem, is evident from its heavenly citizens; but the congregation was also encouraged to think of themselves as the citizens of Jerusalem processing in joy through its streets, their city. Thus, by linking the antiphons to the action of the community processing with relics, the two groups became linked and the two cities fruitfully confused. The connection was most explicit in the antiphon sung after the relics had been sealed in the altar: 'Beneath the altar of the Lord you have taken your seat, intercede for us to the Lord who has chosen you.'[33] This was a reference to Revelation 6: 9-11, where the martyrs, situated underneath the heavenly altar, prayed for revenge upon those who persecuted them. Their prayers were carried to God by the angelic censers (Rev. 8: 3). These references placed the church community within the eschatological liturgy and the community of saints.[34]

At the end of the procession, the bishop instructed the faithful on the peace of the Church, tithing and the celebration of the anniversary of the dedication, and announced to whom the church was dedicated. He then instructed the 'lord and constructor' of the church on its endowment and on honouring its clergy. He demanded (*postulans*) that the lord confirm these, and the lord was to 'declare publicly' that he would act accordingly.[35] At this point, the lord who built the church having been publicly subordinated to it, all entered the church, the relics were deposited and the first Mass was said in the church. The deposition of relics emphasised the church as the Heavenly Jerusalem, the deposited saints' relics as the citizens of the heavenly city and the congregation's welcome of Jesus into the city of Jerusalem.[36] An antiphon (*Urbs beata Hierusalem*) commonly found in Italian manuscripts of the tenth and eleventh century that may have been sung at the dedicatory Mass (and more certainly on the anniversary), declared that the Heavenly Jerusalem itself was made of the living stones of the saints.[37] In these moments the liturgy described the sacred political community and its relation to the earthly one of the church being dedicated. Finally, the Mass was celebrated and the octave commenced.

This brief synopsis makes clear that the dedication was a rite that contained a wealth of possible implications for the community of this new church. It engaged all of the senses of the participants in physical movement, darkness and light in the new church, concealment and revelation of the altar, the smell of incense, and possibly the taste of the consecrated bread and wine. It was also a moment of confrontation between

ecclesiastical and lay lords, whereby the bishop asserted his authority. It was a moment where sacerdotal authority itself was asserted and the Peace of the Church established. It also created an eschatological city (i.e., the church itself) within the earthly city and placed the assembled community in relation to both. In this latter characteristic the rite continued to reflect the eschatological ideal found in the earliest evidence for the dedication.

The intensity of this experience must have been remarkable, especially in the many smaller town and villages that were not episcopal seats. In those places, the arrival of the bishop with his clerics and choir to carry out such a luxuriant, song-filled ritual would have been an unparalleled experience. (Even the briefest of the central Italian liturgies has thirteen antiphons.) In larger towns or episcopal seats, perhaps the pomp was less unique and so less awe-inspiring, but the culmination (though not necessarily the completion) of the local effort (either as patron or labourer) to construct a new church could have made the ceremony compelling.

This general outline of the rite was not followed everywhere, probably not even in all the places where the appropriate texts were available (as Tables 1 and 2 make clear). The symbolic possibilities of the liturgy were heightened or shifted by the significant variations possible within the liturgy itself. This may well have included, at one extreme, the complete absence of a dedication for the many smaller chapels or encastled altars or churches of eleventh-century Italy.[38] At some sites, where churches were built onto marvelous and defensible cliff edges, as at St Thomas in Vallemaio (dedicated by Bruno of Segni in 1111), the procession around the church would have been either impossible or all the more dramatic, as at Santissima Trinità in Cava (dedicated by Urban II in 1092). External circuits would have been impossible at an important shrine such as Monte Gargano where the church was built into the side of the mountain. In other cases, the external circuits would have become as extravagant and labourious in the extreme as they would have at Santi Quattro Coronati in Rome if Paschal II processed up and down the Coelian Hill when dedicating it in 1116 (a circuit of about 300 metres up and down the steep hill).

The precise liturgical form used to dedicate most churches cannot be known, nor to what extent it was followed, nor how effectively its instructions were implemented. It is reasonable to assert, however, that this liturgy in some form was most likely to have been used, though what tropes or local idiosyncrasies altered that most probable form remain unknown. While the eleventh and twelfth centuries were a period of increasing liturgical uniformity, this was far from a period of homogeneity in the liturgy.[39] This is, perhaps, especially true of the dedication rite. The

hybridization of the earlier Frankish and Roman rites in the PRG resulted in only a limited uniformity of the ritual of dedication.[40]

In order to briefly illustrate the possible dedication liturgies available in southern and central Italy, Table 1 reproduces and expands slightly on the work of Roger Reynolds.[41] Table 1 presents dedication liturgies available in the manuscripts of southern Italy from the late tenth to early twelfth centuries. These, in fact, all could be found either in Montecassino or in Benevento and, indeed, are related pontificals, with the first three associated with the liturgical expansion under the Gregorian papacy.[42] Benevento is less than seventy miles from the Abbey. The first three columns are of the eleventh and twelfth centuries (possibly thirteenth). The first column belongs to Montecassino and was produced during the abbacy of Desiderius (1058–1087); the last two years of his tenure he was also Pope Victor III (1085–1087). This form of the liturgy would become normative in the Roman liturgy of the twelfth century.[43] The Macerata and Casanatense Pontificals are from Benevento and are twelfth- and possibly thirteenth-century respectively.[44] The fourth and fifth columns are taken from the PRG, based on Montecassino 451; it contains two *ordines* (*Ordo XXXIII* and *Ordo XL*) for the dedication.[45] In their edition, Vogel and Elze compared Montecassino 451 with pan-European manuscripts deemed exemplary of the earliest PRG.[46]

While a different liturgy might be copied out at a given monastery or church, it is not certain that only the most recently copied manuscript was used. Thus, older manuscripts offered a range of liturgical possibilities in a given locale and might also have been incorporated into the newer liturgy if it was copied locally.[47] The liturgies began differently, most notably for the congregation; exterior circuits could range from none (Table 1, Col. V., 4), to two (Col. II, 4), to three (Cols I, 2; III, 3; and IV, 4). This would have had the effect of emphasising, or not, the symbolic baptism of the church important in the earlier commentaries.[48] At the same time, the number of antiphons sung prior to the bishop's entrance into the church ranged from as few as four (Cols I, III, and IV) to as many as eight (Col. II). From the perspective of the congregation left outside after the bishop enters the church, this would have marked a significant change in their participation as observers of the liturgy. All but the Desiderian pontifical (Col. I) included the antiphon, *Tollite portas*. Its absence would have rendered Damian's sermon on the dedication discussed below (Chapter 3), for example, much more difficult to follow, if not irrelevant, as he spent some time considering the princes referenced in the antiphon.

Once inside, three of the *ordines* have the bishop asperse the altar seven times (Cols III, 8; IV, 10; and V, 10), while two do not have such aspersions. After the aspersion of the interior, one of the *ordines* had the bishop leave the church to sprinkle the exterior another three times (Col. III, 10) only to have the bishop exit later to anoint the walls (Col. III, 18). This addition could reflect Norman influence and may have added emphasis to the sacred Peace of the Church.[49] Another *ordo* had the bishop send 'two or three clerics' to complete only one circuit around the church (Col. V, 12), while the other three did not contain this step. Again, the presence or absence of this step would have altered the visual participation of the laity and the possible allusion to the baptism of the church structure. Therefore, while the liturgy spoke of the *populus* and their participation directly, the immediacy of that participation varied depending on the version of the liturgy available and how closely it was followed. The liturgy in the pontifical of Desiderius (Col. I) had the bishop anoint the altar and church only after the relics had been processed around the church and installed in the altar (Col. I, 18–19). The other liturgies anointed the altar and church before the relics were installed (Cols II, 14–15; III, 16–17; IV, 16–17; V, 17–18). The latter liturgy might have placed greater emphasis on the saint's cult than the Desiderian liturgy that seems to have emphasised the structure itself. Table 1 only begins to point to the diversity of ritual experiences presented by the dedication: variation in liturgical hymns, tropes and site-specific alterations in the liturgy (as has already been suggested) further variegated the experience.[50] Tropes of the *Terribilis locus est* from mid-twelfth-century Piacenza, for example, emphasised the church both as the native home (*patria*) of angels, as the ladder to heaven, the bride of Christ and the mediatrix of the faithful, as well as being the Heavenly Jerusalem.[51]

While variance was considerable, the *sine qua non* of the consecration was the anointing of the altar and deposition of relics within it. This act would have made the altar the centre of a local or even pan-European cult.[52] The deposition, however, only pointed to the enormous range of possible meanings for the liturgy. In a city such as Rome, the deposition of relics might recall the translation of relics from the catacombs to the intramural churches by Paschal I (817–824), or the entombment of Christ. It might also have referred to the relics of the apostles in the altar of St Peter's, and thus their martyrdom and its consecration of the soil of Rome. If the first or last were correct, then the ritual might have taken on a decidedly pro-papal overtone.[53] Or it might not. It might have been perceived as a reminder of Christian heroism against sinful earthly rulers

via its reference to the martyrs of Revelation, as will be suggested in the Desiderian church of St Angelo in Formis, outside of Capua (see Chapters 3 and 5).

The late eleventh century was an age of great architectural revival and the nature of the building itself must have transformed the meaning of the rite for its participants.[54] The altar itself might have reflected these possibilities. A porphyry sarcophagus, such as that at S. Bartolomeo on the Isola Tiberina (of Carolingian origin and rededicated in 1113),[55] might have recalled the purple of royalty, or of Constantine, or of the papacy, or of martyrdom.[56] The classical sarcophagi used for other altars might have reminded people of the ancient Church, or the triumph over paganism, or the tomb of Christ.

Away from Rome, what resonance did these images have? Ancient architectural fragments taken from Rome and used elsewhere (as at Montecassino, and discussed in Chapter 3) might have greater capacity to recall antiquity than at Rome, where monuments had been used as scrap construction material since at least the time of Theodosius.[57] Without reference to Christian antiquity, the dedication might call to mind one's baptism, and inspire a commitment to those vows or to membership in the Christian community.[58] Thus, while the meanings of this ritual need to be examined, the reality of conflicting and competing meanings must be remembered. The historical record tempts us to privilege one voice (such as that of a clerical specialist) that might speak more clearly than others. Rather, that clerical specialist is best understood to be asserting one meaning among competing meanings. If that asserted interpretation were clear to all or understood in advance uniformly, its assertion would be insignificant and unnecessary.

To further compound the possibilities, the liturgy for the dedication was beginning to change in the later part of the eleventh century. This liturgical reform was promoted by Gregory VII (1073–1085) and produced the so-called Roman Pontifical of the twelfth century (RPXII); Table 1, Col. I (the Desiderian pontifical Barb. Lat. 631) is the early exemplar.[59] The late eleventh and early twelfth century was a period of gradual change that further compounded divergence into the fifteenth century at least.[60] Thus, our sense of which liturgy may have been used, for any given dedication from Gregory's reign through the rest of our period of study, is even more limited. The Desiderian version of the RPXII from the late eleventh century (Table 1, Col. I) may represent the form used by Bruno of Segni and Paschal II at the height of the debate over the meaning of the liturgy (see Chapter 5).[61] It should be noted that the RPXII exists in

perhaps even greater flux than the PRG and does not form a more consistent pattern until the reforms of the thirteenth century.[62]

The *RPXII* rite for the dedication would have offered ample reason for reconsidering the meaning of the liturgy. The materials eliminated from the PRG (Table 1, Cols IV and V) to form the RPXII (Table 1, Cols I, II and III) disclose a rational pattern. First, more material is deleted than is added, suggesting a desire to abbreviate the liturgy from around thirty steps to closer to twenty-five steps. (Although steps were added in later copies, Cols II and III, they remain shorter overall.)[63] Second, the initial litany of saints is dropped in the Desiderian pontifical (Table 1, Cols IV, 2, and V, 2 have no parallel in Cols I and III, but are retained in II, 2).[64] Third, of the four prayers dropped from the blessing of salts and of water, three asked for protections against monstrosities and phantasms while those that are retained contain no such requests.[65] Fourth, three sections are dropped that might have even more directly addressed the Peace of the Church, including, surprisingly, the direct address of the lord constructor by the bishop.[66] The fifth (and largest) primary category of deletions concerned the anointing and incensing of the altar, and blessing of individual vestments.[67] The Desiderian pontifical eliminated the initial anointing of the altar (Table 1, Cols IV, 16 and V, 17), though the Beneventan pontificals reinserted these (Cols II, 14 and III, 16). These editorial changes seem to have had the overall effect of reducing the sacral quality of the building itself and seem to reflect less anxiety for the Peace of the Church. This is surprising in the socially and politically volatile climate of the late eleventh century, and perhaps explains in part why these changes spread so inconsistently in the twelfth century (as evidenced in Cols II and III).

Reducing the emphasis on the cult of the saints and the sacral quality of the building, per se, might have lent greater emphasis to those blessing and dedicating the building. Indeed, some of the additional material supports such a conclusion. It should be noted that two of the added sections bolster the cults of the saints and Peace of the Church. However, the antiphon added commands the saints rather than invoking them (as did the litany or the *Sancti dei*, Col. IV, 26), 'Move, O saints, from your dwellings, hasten to the places prepared for you' (Col. I, 13).[68] The materials concerning the Peace likewise emphasise the clergy who sing 'He will be to me a lord in God, and the stone I have built will be called the house of God, and the whole world will give to me a tithe, and I will offer a peace offering to you'. The sense of the church as the eschatological Jerusalem was also not forgotten by the revised liturgy.[69] But this was a church built by the clergy, as an additional clerical response makes plain:

'Bless, O Lord, this house which I have built to your name.'[70] Indeed, the Desiderian pontifical spent the least amount of time outside of the church prior to the consecration, and, in that regard, most quickly isolated the congregation from the clergy (a pattern not sustained in later forms, Cols II and III). Thus, while critical elements of the Peace were retained, the popular role was reduced and the emphasis subtly shifted to the clergy themselves. This reflected the legal desire on the part of the Gregorians to control church construction (see Chapter 4) though hardly the political reality (as discussed in Chapters 4 and 5).

This brief discussion is intended to emphasise the possibilities of the rite. This rite was not a staged production with a fixed conclusion. The discussion is intended to also make plain why the dedication came under scrutiny during the late eleventh and early twelfth centuries, a period of religious and liturgical reform, and increased church construction. The dedication, ostentatious in obscurities of meaning and idiosyncrasies of practice, and purple in its pomp, was a ready and flexible medium for those interested in motivating personal, institutional or religious ideological allegiance. The multivocality of symbolic meaning made symbols ambiguous, but it also made them powerful. This complexity and uncertainty of meanings created an opportunity for those seeking power, healing, reform or renewal.[71] The dedication liturgy was used to all of these ends in late eleventh- and early twelfth-century Italy. Its broad import was the result of its symbolic richness and flexibility, combined with the rapid religious and social transformations taking place in Europe.

Older approaches to the liturgy in general and the dedication in particular have emphasised the linear progression to more normative, ordered forms, from local particularity to Roman standards.[72] There is much to recommend such an overall pattern, but, as liturgists know, and as with much of history, it was far from a direct and uniform transition. While the Romano-Germanic liturgy was increasingly prevalent at the time of the Gregorian reform and often introduced as part of those reforms, the more significant period of normalisation began with the mendicant orders.[73] Even at that late date, however, mediaeval liturgists were struck by the wealth of diverging practices across Europe.[74] Liturgists have in recent years turned their attention toward local variance and its persistence.[75] This trend has allowed liturgists and non-specialists alike to begin to examine the social import of mediaeval religious ritual. Surprisingly, however, this broader interest has been primarily among students of the later Middle Ages.[76] This is all the more surprising considering the intense interest the Gregorian reform has continued to generate among historians

and the large number of liturgical treatises written by the eleventh- and twelfth-century reformers.[77] This historiographic gap is unfortunate given that so much of the controversy surrounding the late eleventh-century reforms revolved around a liturgy, in fact a liturgy of consecration: the consecration of a bishop and his investment with the symbols of episcopal office.[78]

Table 1 Comparison of southern Italian dedication liturgies and the critical edition of the Romano-Germanic Pontifical. This table demonstrates the amount of liturgical variation possible even within a very limited geographic area

I Roman Pontifical of Desiderius[a]	II Macerata Pontifical (from Benevento)[b]	III Casamatense Pontifical (provenance: Benevento)[c]	IV Montecassino 451, Ordo XL (ed. Vogel and Elze)[d]	V Montecassino 451, Ordo XXXIII (ed. Vogel and Elze)
1 Blessing of the 'Gregorian' water (salt, ash and wine) outside of church, with litanies	1 Preparation of the Gregorian water, with litanies			
		1 Vesting of clergy a Zachee festinans	1 Vesting of clergy	1 Vesting of clergy
	2 Litany at site of relics		2 Vigil, litany inside tent with relics	2 Litany inside tent containing the relics
	3 Procession with relics a Surgite sancti b Cum iocunditate c Zachee festinans		3 Procession with relics a Surgite sancti b Cum iocunditate	3 Procession with relics a Cum iocunditate
		2 Assembly at the church		

27

Table 1 (continued)

I Roman Pontifical of Desiderius[a]	II Macerata Pontifical (from Benevento)[b]	III Casanatense Pontifical (provenance: Benevento)[c]	IV Montecassino 451, Ordo XL (ed. Vogel and Elze)[d]	V Montecassino 451, Ordo XXXIII (ed. Vogel and Elze)
2 Triple circuit around exterior of church, Bishop knocks on door each circuit a *Fundata est V. Venientes* b *Benedic domine V. Domine si* c *Tu domine universorum V. Tu elegisti*		3 Triple circuit around exterior of church, Bishop knocks on door each circuit b *Tollite portas Ps. Domini est terra*	4 Triple circuit, aspersion of walls, Bishop knocks on door each circuit c *Tollite portas Ps. Domini est terra* d *In circuitu tuo V. Magnus dominus* e *Fundata est V. Benedic domine*	4 Three knocks on door, antiphon and response three times, no circuits b *Tollite portas*

	4 Three knocks on door separated by two circuits around exterior of church **d** *In circuitu V. Lux perpetua* **e** *Fundata est V. Venientes*			***c*** *Dominus virtutum*
3 Entrance **d** *Pax huic*	**5** Entrance **f** *Tollite portas* **g** *Pax huic* **h** *Pax eterna*	**4** Entrance **c** *Pax huic* **d** *Benedic domine Ps. Fundamenta*	**5** Entrance **f** *Pax huic*	**5** Entrance **d** *Pax huic*
4 Litany and prostration	**6** Litany and prostration	**5** Litany and prostration	**6** Litany and prostration	**6** Litany and prostration
5 Inscription of Greek and Latin alphabets in ash on floor **e** *O quam metuendus Ps. Benedictus*	**7** Inscription of Greek and Latin alphabets in ash on floor **i** *O quam metuendus Ps. Benedictus*	**6** Inscription of Greek and Latin alphabets in ash on floor **e** *Fundamentum Ps. Fundamenta* **f** *Hec Aula Ps. Magnus dominus*	**7** Inscription of Greek and Latin alphabets in ash on floor **g** *O quam metuendus Ps. Benedictus*	**7** Inscription of Greek and Latin alphabets in ash on floor
6 Preparation of Gregorian water		**7** Preparation of Gregorian water	**8** Preparation of Gregorian water	**8** Preparation of Gregorian water

Table 1 (continued)

I Roman Pontifical of Desiderius[a]	II Macerata Pontifical (from Benevento)[b]	III Casanatense Pontifical (provenance: Benevento)[c]	IV Montecassino 451, Ordo XL (ed. Vogel and Elze)[d]	V Montecassino 451, Ordo XXXIII (ed. Vogel and Elze)
7 Consecration of altar **f** *Asperges me ysopo Ps. Miserere*	**8** Consecration of altar **j** *Asperges me ysopo Ps. Miserere*		**9** Consecration of altar	**9** Consecration of altar
		8 Aspersion of altar (7 times) **g** *Asperges me ysopo Ps. Miserere*	**10** Aspersion of altar (7 times) **h** *Asperges me ysopo Ps. Miserere*	**10** Aspersion of altar (7 times) **e** *Asperges me ysopo Ps. Miserere*
8 Aspersion of interior (three circuits) **g** *Haec est domus Ps. Laetus sum* (repeat) **h** *Qui habitat Ps. Qui habitat*	**9** Aspersion of interior (three circuits) **k** *Asperges me ysopo* **l** *Tu domine universorum Ps. Exurgat* **m** *Haec est Domus Ps. Qui habitat*	**9** Aspersion of interior (three circuits) **h** *Sanctificavit dominum Ps. Deus noster* **i** *In dedicatione Ps. Laudate* **j** *Qui habitat Ps. Qui habitat*	**11** Aspersion of interior (three circuits) **i** *Similabo eum* **j** *Exurgat deus* **k** *Tu domine universorum V. Tu, domine* **l** *Qui habitat Ps. Hec est*	**11** Aspersion of interior (three circuits) **f** *Exurgat Deus* (same Ps.) **g** *Qui habitat* (same Ps.)

9 Aspersion of interior (length and width) i *Domus mea V. Narrabo*	10 Aspersion of interior (length and width) n *Domus mea V. Narrabo*	10 Aspersion of exterior (3 circuits) k *Asperges Ps. Miserere* l *Exurgat Deus Ps. Exurgat* m *Fundamenta templi Ps. Fundamenta*	12 Aspersion of interior (length and width) m *Domus mea V. Narrabo cum Gloria patri*	12 Two or three clerics exit church to asperse exterior (1 circuit)
10 Prayers of consecration	11 Prayers of consecration	11 Reentry n *Benedic domine Ps. Magnus domine*	13 Prayer of consecration	13 Aspersion of interior (length and width) h *Domus mea V. Narrabo cum Gloria*
11 Proceeds to altar	12 Proceeds to altar o *Introibo Ps. Iudica me*	12 Aspersion of interior (length and width) o *Benedictus est Ps. Benedictus*	14 Proceeds to altar n *Introibo Ps. Iudica me*	14 Prayers of consecration
		13 Prayers of consecration		15 Proceeds to altar
		14 Proceeds to altar p *Introibo Ps. Iudica me*		

Table 1 (continued)

I Roman Pontifical of Desiderius[a]	II Macerata Pontifical (from Benevento)[b]	III Casanatense Pontifical (provenance: Benevento)[c]	IV Montecassino 451, Ordo XL (ed. Vogel and Elze)[d]	V Montecassino 451, Ordo XXXIII (ed. Vogel and Elze)
j Introibo Ps. Iudica me				i Introibo Ps. Iudica me
12 Preparation of mortar	13 Preparation of mortar p Dirigatur domine	15 Preparation of mortar q Ecce tabernaculum Ps. Laudate deum	15 Preparation of mortar	16 Preparation of mortar
	14 Anointing of altar with oil and chrism q Mane surgens r Erexit lapidem s Unxit te Ps. Eructavit	16 Incensing and anointing of altar with holy water and oil r Dirigatur domine s Erexit Iacob Ps. Quam amabilia t Mane surgens Ps. Deus Noster u Vidit Iacob Ps. Fundamenta	16 Incensing and anointing of altar with oil and chrism o Erexit Iacob Ps. Quam dilecta p Mane surgens Ps. Fundamenta q Edificavit Moyses Ps. Deus noster r Unxit te dominus Ps. Eructavit	17 Incensing and anointing of altar with oil and chrism j Edificavit Moyses Ps. Deus noster k Ecce odor Ps. Fundamenta
15 Anointing of interior walls with chrism t Sanctificavit Ps. Deus		17 Anointing of interior walls with chrism (in 12 places)	17 Anointing of interior walls with chrism (in 12 places)	18 Anointing of interior walls with chrism (in 12

noster	v *O quam metuendus Ps. Magnus deus*	s *Sanctificetur hoc templum* t *Sanctificavit dominus* u *Lapides pretiosi Ps. Lauda Ierusalem*	places)
16 Return to altar u *Aedificavit Moyes* v *Ecce odor*	**18** Anointing of exterior with chrism w *Lapides pretiosi Ps. Lauda Ierusalem* **19** Reentry	**18** Return to altar	**19** Return to altar
17 Prayers before the altar, unction and blessing of altar cloths, etc.	**20** Prayers of consecration before the altar	**19** Incensing altar v *Ecce odor filii Ps. Fundamenta* **20** Prayers of consecration before altar w *Confirma hoc Deus*	**20** Incensing altar l *Confirma hoc* **21** Prayers of consecration before the altar
		21 Blessing of linens, ornaments, vestments, tools, etc.	**22** Blessing of linens, ornaments, vestments, tools,

Table 1 (continued)

I Roman Pontifical of Desiderius[a]	II Macerata Pontifical (from Benevento)[b]	III Casanatense Pontifical (provenance: Benevento)[c]	IV Montecassino 451, *Ordo XL* (ed. Vogel and Elze)[d]	V Montecassino 451, *Ordo XXXIII* (ed. Vogel and Elze)
			(Blessing of a portable altar)	etc. (Blessing of a portable altar)
		21 Procession toward the relics	22 Exits church to tent where relics had been previous evening, changes vestments	23 Procession out of church, prayers at doors
13 Next to relics k *Movete sancti* l *Ecce populus*	18 Bishop receives relics outside w *Ingredimini benedicti* V. *Sancti dei* x *Sancti et Iusti* y *Benedicta gloria*	22 Return procession with relics x *Surgite sancti* y *Sanctum et verum*	23 Prayers outside of doors, blessing doors	24 Return procession with relics to altar
14 Procession with relics m *Cum iocunditate* n *Ambulate sancti* o *Surgite sancti* p *Ambulate sancti*				

34

15 Circuit outside of church with relics **q** *Erit mihi dominus V. Si reversus* **r** Populus: *Kyrie*			**24** Processes around exterior of church with people, women and children **x** *Kyrie eleison* **y** *Ambulate, sancti Dei*	**25** Installation of relics in altar **m** *Exultabant*
16 Entrance with relics **s** *Pax eterna* **t** *Ingredimini*	**19** Entrance with relics **z** *Ingredere benedicte*	**23** Entrance with relics **z** *Ingredere benedicte*	**z** *Plateae Hierusalem* **aa** *Custodit dominus animas* **bb** *In sanctis gloriosus* **cc** *Ambulate, sancti Dei* **dd** *Sanctificavi Iherusalem* **25** Addresses people, lord and constructor	
17 Installation of relics in altar **u** *Exultabunt*	**20** Installation of relics in altar **z** *Exultabunt sancti Ps. Cantate*	**24** Installation of relics in altar **aa** *Exultabunt sancti Ps. Cantate*	**26** Entrance with relics **ee** *Ingredimini, benedicti* **ff** *Sancti Dei* **gg** *Benedicta gloria* **hh** *Exultabunt sancti Ps. Cantate* **27** Installation of relics in altar **ii** *Sub altare Ps. Exultabunt*	

Table 1 (continued)

I Roman Pontifical of Desiderius[a]	II Macerata Pontifical (from Benevento)[b]	III Casanatense Pontifical (provenance: Benevento)[c]	IV Montecassino 451, *Ordo XL* (ed. Vogel and Elze)[d]	V Montecassino 451, *Ordo XXXIII* (ed. Vogel and Elze)
sancti Ps. Cantate	**aa** *Sub altare*	**bb** *In celestibus Ps. Beati immaculati*		*sancti Ps. Cantate domino*
v *Sub altare*	**bb** *Circumdate Syon*	**cc** *Sub altare*		**n** *Sub altare*
w *Dirigatur domine*	**cc** *In velamento clamabunt*	**dd** *Corpora sanctorum cum Gloria patri*		
18 Anointing of altar with oil and chrism			**28** Anointing of altar with chrism	**26** Anointing of altar with chrism
x *Erexit Iacob Ps. Quam dilecta*			**jj** *Corpora sanctorum*	
y *Mane surgens Ps. Deus noster*				
z *Ecce odor Ps. Fundamenta*				
19 Anointing of interior of church with chrism				
aa *Hec est domus Ps. Letatus*				

20 Return to and incensing of altar
bb *Hedificavit Moyses*
21 Prayers of consecration
bb *Confirma hoc deus*
22 (Blessing of a portable altar)
23 Blessing of linens, etc.
cc *Corpora sanctorum*
24 Vesting of altar

21 Blessing of paten, etc.

25 Vesting of altar
ee *Ornaverint faciem*
ff *Circumdate Syon*

29 Vesting of altar
kk *Circumdate Syon*
ll *In velamento*
mm *Omnis terra adoret*

27 Vesting of altar

Table 1 (continued)

I Roman Pontifical of Desiderius[a]	II Macerata Pontifical (from Benevento)[b]	III Casanatense Pontifical (provenance: Benevento)[c]	IV Montecassino 451, Ordo XL (ed. Vogel and Elze)[d]	V Montecassino 451, Ordo XXXIII (ed. Vogel and Elze)
dd *Circumdate* *Syon Ps.* *Mirabilis deus*		26 Illumination of church gg *Ab oriente* hh *Confirma hoc Deus*	30 Illumination of church nn *Terribilis locus est*	28 Illumination of church
25 Mass	22 Mass	27 Mass	31 Mass	29 Mass

[a] Table 1 is based on Reynolds, 'Les Cérémonies liturgiques', in *La Cathédrale Bénévent*, 170–72, 189–93; and Vogel and Elze (eds), *Le Pontifical romano-germanique*. I would like to thank Roger Reynolds for reviewing this table. Column 1 is Vatican, Biblioteca Apostolica Vaticana, Barberini Latinus 631; see Gyug, 'The Pontificals of Monte Cassino', 413–39.

[b] Macerata, Biblioteca Comunale 'Mozzi-Borghetti' 378; see Gyug, 'A Pontifical of Benevento', 355–423.

[c] Rome, Biblioteca Casanatense, 614.

[d] Montecassino, Archivo della Badia, 451.

Table 2 Alphabetical list of antiphons from Table 1 with relevant step of dedication from Table 1

Antiphon	Desiderian	Macerta	Casanatense	Montecassino, Ordo XL	Montecassino, Ordo XXXIII
Ab oriente			26gg		
Ambulate sancti	**14n; 14p**			24y; **24cc**	
Asperges me hysopo		9k			
Asperges me hysopo Ps. Miserere	7f	8j	8g; **10k**	10h	10e
Benedic domine Ps. Fundamenta		4d			
Benedic domine Ps. Magnus domine			11n		
Benedic domine V. Domine Si	2b				
Benedicta gloria		18y	12o	26gg	
Benedictus est Ps. Benedictus					
Circumdate Syon		20bb	25ff	29kk	
Circumdate Syon Ps. Mirabilis deus	24dd				
Confirma hoc deus			26hh	20w	20l
Corpora sanctorum	23cc			28jj	
Corpora sanctorum cum Gloria patri			24dd		
Cum iocunditate	14m	3b		3b	3a
Custodit dominus animas			16r	24aa	
Dirigatur domine	17w	13p			
Dominus virtutum					4c
Domus mea V. Narrabo	9i	10n			
Domus mea V. Narrabo cum Gloria patri				12m	13h

Table 2 (continued)

Antiphon	Desiderian	Macerta	Casanatense	Montecassino, Ordo XL	Montecassino, Ordo XXXIII
Ecce odor		16v			
Ecce odor Ps. Fundamenta	18z			19v	17k
Ecce populus	13l				
Ecce tabernaculum Ps. Laudate deum			15q		
Erexit Iacob Ps. Quam amabilia			16s		
Erexit Iacob Ps. Quam dilecta	18x			16o	
Erexit lapidem	15q	14r			
Erit mihi dominus V. Si reversus	17u				
Exultabunt sancti Ps. Cantate		20z	24aa	26hh	25m
Exurgat Deus				11j	11f
Exurgat Deus Ps. Exurgat			10l		
Fundamenta templi Ps. Fundamenta			10m		
Fundamentum Ps. Fundamenta			6e		
Fundata est V. Benedic domine		4e		4e	
Fundata est V. Venientes	2a				
Hec aula Ps. Magnus dominus			6f		
Hec est domus Ps. Letatus		9m			
Haec est domus Ps. Laetus sum	8g				
Haec est domus Ps. Qui habitat	19aa				
[H]edificavit Moyses	20bb	16u		16q	
[H]edificavit Moyses Ps. Deus Noster					17j

In celestibus Ps. Beati immaculati			24bb		
In circuitu V. Lux perpetua		4d			
In circuitu V. Magnus deus					
In dedicatione Ps. Laudate			4d	4d	
Ingredere benedicti			9i		
Ingredimini	16t		23z	26ee	
Ingredimini benedicti V. Sancti dei		18w	18w		
In sanctis gloriosus				24bb	15i
Introibo Ps. Iudica me	11j	12o	14p	14n	
In velamento clamabunt		20cc		29ll	
Kyrie	15r			24x	
Lapides pretiosi Ps. Lauda Hierusalem			18w	17u	
Mane surgens		14q			
Mane surgens Ps. Deus noster	18y		16t	16p	
Mane surgens Ps. Fundamenta					
Movete sancti	13k				
Omnis terra adoret				29mm	
O quam metuendus Ps. Benedictus	5e	7i	17v	7g	
O quam mentuendus Ps. Magnus deus			25ee		
Ornaverint faciem					
Pax eterna	16s	5h			
Pax huic	3d	5g	4c	5f	
Plateae Hierusalem				24z	5d
Qui habitat Ps. haec est				111	

Table 2 (continued)

Antiphon	Desiderian	Macerta	Casanatense	Montecassino, Ordo XL	Montecassino, Ordo XXXIII
Qui habitat Ps. Qui habitat	8h		9j		11g
Sancti dei		18x		26ff	
Sancti et Iusti				17t	
Sanctificavit dominus				24dd	
Sanctificavi Hierusalem		15t	9h	17s	
Sanctificavit Ps. Deus noster					
Sanctificetur hoc templum			22y		
Sanctum et verum				11i	
Similabo eum	17v	20aa	24cc		
Sub altare	14o				25n
Sub altare Ps. Exultabunt		3a	22x	3a	
Surgite sancti				30nn	
Terribilis locus est		5f			4b
Tollite portas			3b	4c	
Tollite portas Ps. Domini est terra		9l		11k	
Tu domine universorum Ps. Exurgat					
Tu domine universorum V. Tu, domine					
Tu domine universorum V. Tu elegisti	2c	14s			
Unxit te Ps. Eructavit			16u	16r	
Vidit Iacob Ps. Fundamenta			1a		
Zachee festinans		3c			

Table 3 Comparison of eleventh-century Italian rites. Cols 1 and 2 being Central Italian, cols 3 and 4 Cassinese

BAV, Vat. Lat. 4770, s. XI[a]	MS Harley 2906, s. XI[b]	Roman Pontifical of Desiderius (Vaticanus Barberini Latinus 631)	Montecassino 451, *Ordo XL* (ed. Vogel and Elze)
1 Litany a *Surgite sancti* b *Ecce populus* 2 Procession a *Cum iocunditate* b *De hierusalem* c *Ambulate sancti* d *Ingredimini* e *Ad honorem*	1 Blessing of the 'Gregorian' water (salt, ash, and wine) outside of church 2 Triple circuit around exterior of church, Bishop knocks on door each circuit a *Fundata est V. Venientes* b *Benedic domine V. Domine si*	1 Blessing of the 'Gregorian' water (salt, ash, and wine) outside of church, with litanies 2 Triple circuit around exterior of church, Bishop knocks on door each circuit a *Fundata est V. Venientes* b *Benedic domine V. Domine si*	1 Vesting of clergy 2 Vigil, litany inside tent with relics 3 Procession with relics a *Surgite sancti* b *Cum iocunditate* 4 Triple circuit, aspersion of walls, Bishop knocks on door each circuit c *Tollite portas Ps. Domini est terra*

Table 3 (Continued)

BAV, Vat. Lat. 4770, s. XI[a]	MS Harley 2906, s. XI[b]	Roman Pontifical of Desiderius (Vaticanus Barberini Latinus 631)	Montecassino 451, *Ordo XL* (ed. Vogel and Elze)
		c *Tu domine universorum V. Tu elegisti*	d *In circuitu tuo V. Magnus dominus*
			e *Fundata est V. Benedic domini*
3 Entrance	3 Entrance	3 Entrance	5 Entrance
	d *Pax huic*	d *Pax huic*	f *Pax huic*
	4 Litany	4 Litany and prostration	6 Litany and prostration
	5 Inscription of Greek and Latin alphabets in ash on floor	5 Inscription of Greek and Latin alphabets in ash on floor	7 Inscription of Greek and Latin alphabets in ash on floor
	e *O quam metuendus Ps. Benedictus*	e *O quam metuendus Ps. Benedictus*	g *O quam metuendus Ps. Benedictus*
4 Preparation of Mortar			
	6 Preparation of Gregorian water	6 Preparation of Gregorian water	8 Preparation of Gregorian water
	7 Consecration of altar	7 Consecration of altar	9 Consecration of altar
	f *Asperges me ysopo Ps. Miserere*	f *Asperges me ysopo Ps. Miserere*	10 Aspersion of altar (7 times)
6 Aspersion of altar			h *Asperges me ysopo Ps. Miserere*

8 Aspersion of interior (three circuits)
g *Haec est domus Ps. Laetus sum* (repeat)
h *Qui habitat Ps. Qui habitat*

9 Aspersion of interior (length and width)
i *Domus mea V. Narrabo*

10 Prayers of consecration
11 Proceeds to altar
j *Introibo Ps. Iudica me*
12 Preparation of mortar

8 Aspersion of interior (three circuits)
g *Haec est domus Ps. Laetus sum* (repeat)
h *Qui habitat Ps. Qui habitat*

9 Aspersion of interior (length and width)
i *Domus mea V. Narrabo*

10 Prayers of consecration
11 Proceeds to altar
j *Introibo Ps. Iudica me*
12 Preparation of mortar

11 Aspersion of interior (three circuits)
i *Similabo eum*
j *Exurgat deus*
k *Tu domine universorum V. Tu, domine*
l *Qui habitat Ps. Hec est*

12 Aspersion of interior (length and width)
m *Domus mea V. Narrabo* cum *Gloria patri*
13 Prayers of consecration
14 Proceeds to altar
n *Introibo Ps. Iudica me*
15 Preparation of mortar
16 Incensing and anointing of altar with oil and chrism
o *Erexit Iacob Ps. Quam dilecta*
p *Mane surgens Ps. Fundamenta*
q *Edificavit Moyses Ps. Deus noster*
r *Unxit te dominus Ps. Eructavit*

Table 3 (continued)

BAV, Vat. Lat. 4770, s. XI[a]	MS Harley 2906, s. XI[b]	Roman Pontifical of Desiderius (Vaticanus Barberini Latinus 631)	Montecassino 451, *Ordo XL* (ed. Vogel and Elze)
			17 Anointing of interior walls with chrism (in 12 places)
			s *Sanctificetur hoc templum*
			t *Sanctificavit dominus*
			u *Lapides pretiosi* Ps. *Lauda Ierusalem*
			18 Return to altar
			19 Incensing altar
			v *Ecce odor filii* Ps. *Fundamenta*
			20 Prayers of consecration before altar
			w *Confirma hoc Deus*
			21 Blessing of linens, ornaments, vestments, tools, etc.
			(Blessing of a portable altar)
7 Priest, Cantors bring relics to door exterior singing litany			

8 Bishop opens door

13 Exits church to tent where relics had been previous evening, enters
k *Ecce populus*
14 Procession with relics
m *Cum iocunditate*

15 Circuit outside of church with relics
n *Sanctos portamus*
o *Kyrie* (women and children)
p *Domum tuam quaesumus*
q *Ingredimini*

13 Next to relics
k *Movete sancti*
l *Ecce populus*
14 Procession with relics
m *Cum iocunditate*
n *Ambulate sancti*
o *Surgite sancti*
p *Ambulate sancti*

15 Circuit outside of church with relics
q *Erit mihi dominus V. Si reversus*
r *Populus: Kyrie*

22 Exits church to tent where relics had been previous evening, changes vestments

23 Prayers outside of doors, blessing doors

24 Processes around exterior of church with people, women and children
x *Kyrie eleison*
y *Ambulate, sancti Dei*
z *Plateae Hierusalem*
aa *Custodit dominus animas*
bb *In sanctis gloriosus*
cc *Ambulate, sancti Dei*
dd *Sanctificavi Iherusalem*
25 Addresses people, lord and constructor

Table 3 (continued)

BAV, Vat. Lat. 4770, s. XI[a]	MS Harley 2906, s. XI[b]	Roman Pontifical of Desiderius (Vaticanus Barberini Latinus 631)	Montecassino 451, *Ordo XL* (ed. Vogel and Elze)
	16 Entrance with relics, displays relics between people and altar r *Exultabant sancti Ps. Cantate*	16 Entrance with relics s *Pax eterna* t *Ingredimini*	26 Entrance with relics ee *Ingredimini, benedicti* ff *Sancti Dei* gg *Benedicta gloria* hh *Exultabunt sancti Ps. Cantate*
9 Places relics on altar f *Ambulate Sancti*			
10 Installation of relics in altar g *Sub altare*	17 Installation of relics in altar u *Sub altare* v *Exultabunt sancti* w *Ascendit fumus* x *Erexit Iacob V. Quam dilecta*	17 Installation of relics in altar u *Exultabunt sancti Ps. Cantate* v *Sub altare* w *Dirigatur domine*	27 Installation of relics in altar ii *Sub altare Ps. Exultabunt*
11 Anointing of altar with chrism	18 Anointing of altar with oil and chrism y *Mane surgens Ps. deus noster* z *Ecce odor Ps. fundamenta*	18 Anointing of altar with oil and chrism x *Erexit Iacob Ps. Quam dilecta* y *Mane surgens Ps. deus noster* z *Ecce odor Ps. fundamenta*	28 Anointing of altar with chrism jj *Corpora sanctorum*

12 Vesting of altar

19 Anointing of interior of church with chrism
aa *Hec est domus Ps. Letatus*
20 Return to and incensing of altar
bb *Hedificavit Moyses*
21 Prayers of consecration
bb *Confirma hoc deus*
22 (Blessing of a portable altar)
23 Aspersion, incensing, anointing altar with chrism
24 Blessing of linens, etc.
cc *Corpora sanctorum*
dd *Gloria*
25 Incensing [of altar]
ee *Circumdate Syon Ps. Mirabilis deus*

19 Anointing of interior of church with chrism
aa *Hec est domus Ps. Letatus*
20 Return to and incensing of altar
bb *Hedificavit Moyses*
21 Prayers of consecration
bb *Confirma hoc deus*
22 (Blessing of a portable altar)

23 Blessing of linens, etc.
cc *Corpora sanctorum*

24 Vesting of altar
dd *Circumdate Syon Ps. Mirabilis deus*

29 Vesting of altar
kk *Circumdate Syon*
ll *In velamento*
mm *Omnis terra adoret*

Table 3 (continued)

BAV, Vat. Lat. 4770, s. XI[a]	MS Harley 2906, s. XI[b]	Roman Pontifical of Desiderius (Vaticanus Barberini Latinus 631)	Montecassino 451, Ordo XL (ed. Vogel and Elze)
13 Aspersion of church			
14 Illumination of church			30 Illumination of church
h *Terribilis locus est*			nn *Terribilis locus est*
15 Mass	26 Mass introit	25 Mass	31 Mass
	ff *Terribilis locus est*		
	gg *Domus mea*		

[a] This was created in part using Thomas Davies Kozachek, 'The Repertory of Chant for Dedicating Churches in the Middle Ages: Music, Liturgy and Ritual' (PhD diss., Harvard University, 1995), 362–4. It is not clear why his index of antiphons does not include *Ad honorem* (Vat. Lat. 4770, Table III, col. 1, 2e).

[b] London, British Library. MS Harley 2906 as presented in Kozachek, 'Repertory of Chant', Appendix III, 370–4.

Notes

1 Cyrille Vogel and R. Elze (eds), *Le Pontifical romano-germanique du dixième siècle: Le Texte* [PRG], Vol. 1, *Studi e testi*, v. 226 (Vatican City, 1963), 40:127, 169; and 40: 148, 173, compare with 40: 26, 136.

2 For possible southern Italian liturgies of the twelfth century, and for an excellent summary of the different liturgies for the dedication, see Roger E. Reynolds, 'Les Cérémonies liturgiques de la cathédrale de Bénévent', in Thomas Forrest Kelly' (ed.), *La cathédrale de Bénévent*, (Ghent, 1999), 167–205, esp. 189–94.

3 Flanigan, 'Apocalypse and the Medieval Liturgy', 332–4.

4 Eusebius, *Historia Ecclesiastica*, ed. Gustave Bardy, *Sources Chrétiennes*, Vols 31, 41, 55 and 73 (Paris, 1952–60) Bk. X, cc. III–IV (at III, 3).

5 Ibid., Bk. X, c. IV, 70. Repsher, *The Rite of Church Dedication*, 15.

6 Socrates Scholasticus, *Ecclesiastical History*, in Günther Christian Hansen (ed.), *Socrates Kirchengeschichte* (Berlin, 1960), Bk. 8, 2, 97. Hermiae Sozomeni, *Historia Ecclesiastica*, Bk. III, 5; MPG LXVII, 1041.

7 Relatively few attempts have been made to trace the origins of the rite prior to Eusebius and such work is speculative. G.B. DeRossi, 'Degli Alfabeti che il Vescovo scribe sulla Croce Decussata ne Consecrare le Chiese', in *Bulletino di Archaeologia Cristiana* (1881): 140–95. Brian Repsher, 'The Abecedarium: Catechetical Symbolism in the Rite of Church Dedication', *Mediaevalia* 24 (2003): 1–18.

8 Constantine's Church of the Holy Sepulchre is in many ways the norm in negative plate, where the relic is the lack of a body. On the history of the transition from celebrating rites at the tombs of Martyrs to incorporating them into Church architecture see Robert A. Markus, *The End of Ancient Christianity* (Cambridge, 1990), 142–9; the articles collected in André Vauchez, *Lieux sacrés, lieux de culte, sanctuaires, approches terminologiques, méthodologiques, historiques et monographiques* (Rome, 2000). In sixth-century Rome, a dedication may or may not have included the deposition. Repsher, *Rite of Church Dedication*, 17–18.

9 Thaddeus S. Ziolkowski, *The Consecration and Blessing of Churches: A Historical Synopsis and Commentary* (Washington, DC, 1943), 14–15 remains the standard account.

10 Richard Krautheimer, *Rome, Profile of a City* (Princeton, 1980), 112–20. Patrick Geary, *Furta Sacra: Thefts of Relics in the Central Middle Ages* (Princeton, 1978), 114, 136.

11 Hans-Werner Goetz, 'Protection of the Church, Defense of the Law, and Reform: on the Purposes and Character of the Peace of God, 989–1073', Head and Landes, *Peace of God*, 259–79.

12 PRG, Vol. 3: *Introduction générale et Tables*; Andrieu, *Pontifical romain*, 4.

13 PRG, Vol. 1: xi–xiii.

14 Sarah Hamilton, *The Practice of Penance, 900–1050* (Woodbridge, Suffolk, 2001), 220–3.

15 Bamberg, Staatsbibliothek, Cod. Lit. 56; Hamilton, *Practice of Penance*, 222.

16 Thomas Head and Richard Landes, 'Introduction', Head and Landes, *Peace of God*, 3–9. Also in *Peace of God*, also suggesting the relation to the movement in Italy, Frederick S. Paxton, 'History, Historians and the Peace of God', 21–40, at 34, Amy G. Remensnyder, 'Pollution, Purity, and Peace: An Aspect of Social Reform in the Late Tenth Century', 280–307, at 295.

17 Briefly touched upon in Daniel F. Callahan, 'The Peace of God and the Cult of the Saints in Aquitaine in the Tenth and Eleventh Centuries', in Head and Landes, *Peace of God*, 165–83, at 172–3.

18 PRG XL, 128–9, 169.

19 Vogel, *Medieval Liturgy*, 251.

20 PRG, XL, 128.

21 Ibid., 131.

22 Ibid., 133; compare with Repsher, *Rite of Church Dedication*, 244.

23 PRG XL, 133–5.

24 Ibid., 136. On the abecedarium, see Repsher, 'The Abecedarium'.

25 PRG, XL 143.

26 Ibid., 161 (note the reference to Jacob, Gen. 28: 11–17, contains the antiphon), 150–1, 157, 162.

27 Edificavit Moyses altare domino Deo. Ibid., 144.

28 Ibid., 150.

29 Ibid., 168.

30 Ibid.

31 Ibid., 169.

32 Ibid.

33 Ibid., 137, 171.

34 In continuity with the earliest forms of the rite as discussed above, but with new significance in this latter period, see Flanigan, 'Apocalypse and the Medieval Liturgy'.

35 PRG XL, 128–9, 169.

36 Ibid., 170.

37 Urbs beata Hierusalem, dicta pacis visio, Quae construitur in caelis vivis ex lapidus, Et angelis coronata ut sponsata comite. *Analecta Hymnica* 51, 110–11. This hymn was known at Montecassino, Farfa, Rome, Verona and Nursa.

38 Further considered in Chapter 4. Aldo A. Settia, '"Ecclesiam Incastellare". Chiese e Castelli in Diocesi di Padova', in *Chiese, Strade e Fortezze Nell'Italia Medievale*, Italia Sacra, Studi e Documenti di Storia Ecclesiastica 46 (Rome, 1991), 67–97.

39 In the period of greatest standardisation, the thirteenth century, via the mendicant orders, local variance continues to be normative; S.J.P. Van Dijk, *The Origins of the Modern Roman Liturgy: The Liturgy of the Papal Court and the Franciscan Order in the Thirteenth Century* (Westminster, MD, 1960).

40 Ibid., 190.

41 Reynolds, 'Les Cérémonies liturgiques', 192–3.

42 Richard F. Gyug, 'The Pontificals of Monte Cassino', *L'Età dell'abate Desiderio*, Atti del IV Convegno di studi sul medioevo Meridionale (Montecassino

- Cassino, 4–8 ottobre, 1987) (3 Vols), ed. Faustino Avagliano and Oronzo Pecere (Montecassino, 1992), Vol. 3, 413–39.

43 Andrieu, *Pontifical romain*, t. 1, 1–19, 61–71. Gyug concludes that Cassino became the sources for the Roman Pontifical, 'Pontificals of Monte Cassino', 439.

44 See the complete chart in Reynolds, 'Les Cérémonies liturgiques', 191–2.

45 Vogel and Elze, *Pontifical romano-germanique*, Vol 1, 82–9, 124–78.

46 These include several others of Italian origin: Rome, Biblioteca Vallecelliana D. 5; Lucca, Biblioteca Capitolare 607; Pistoia, Biblioteca Capitolare 141; and Rome, Biblioteca Alexandrina 173.

47 As exemplified in the Pontifical of Kotor (Leningrad, Biblioteki Akademii Nauk, F. no 200), Gyug, 'Pontificals of Monte Cassino', 420–1.

48 As for the *Quid Significent*, see Repsher, *Rite of Church Dedication*, 1998).

49 Reynolds, 'Les Cérémonies liturgiques', 191. Troping, including that within the dedication liturgy, also appears to have reflected or influenced the Peace of God in Aquitaine; Callahan, 'The Peace of God and the Cult of the Saints', in Head and Landes, *Peace of God*, 165–83, esp. 180–1, ss. f–i. With the dedication, as with other liturgies, it was the appearance of permanence more than an unchanging reality that lent it authority. Roy Rappaport cautions that rituals that become overly referential to the immediate social, psychic or physical (too 'indexical') lose authority, while those that create a sense of permanence ('canonical') retain their authority. Roy A. Rappaport, 'Veracity, Verity, and *Verum* in Liturgy', *Studia Liturgica* 23 (1993): 35–50.

50 On liturgical diversity in penitential rites, see Hamilton, *Practice of Penance*, 136–72.

51 Brian Møller Jensen, *Tropes and Sequences in the Liturgy of the Church in Piacenza in the Twelfth Century, An Analysis and an Edition of the Texts.* Texts and Studies in Religion, 92 (Lewiston, 2002), 353–7.

52 As in Burgundy and Aquitaine; Töpfer, 'The Cult of Relics', in Head and Landes, *Peace of God*, 45–8. See the example of the dedication of Montecassino below in Chapter 2.

53 Dorothy Glass, 'Revisiting the "Gregorian Reform"', in C. Hourihane (ed.), *Romanesque Art and Thought in the Twelfth Century* (Princeton, 2008), 200–18; Glass, *Studies on Cosmatesque Pavements* (Oxford, 1980); Hélène Toubert, 'Le Renouveau paléochrétien à Rome au début du XIIe siècle', *Cahiers archéologiques fin de l'Antiquité et le Moyen Âge* 20 (1970), 99–154; themes touched upon also by Christopher Walter, 'Papal Political Imagery in the Medieval Lateran Palace', *Cahiers archéologiques fin de l'Antiquité et le Moyen Âge* 20 (1970), 155–76; E. Kitzinger, 'The Gregorian Reform and the Visual Arts: A Problem of Method', *Transactions of the Royal Historical Society*, 5th ser., 22 (1972): 87–102.

54 The current trend, begun by Richard Krautheimer and Dorothy Glass and continued by Hélène Toubert, is to view the artistic and architectural revival of the eleventh century as an extension of reforming ideologies. Hélène Toubert, 'Didier du Mont-Cassin et l'art de la réforme grégorienne: l'iconographie de l'Ancien Testament à Sant'Angelo in Formis', in Hélèn Toubert, *Desiderio di Montecassino e l'arte della riforma gregoriana* (Montecassino, 1997), 17–106;

Lucinia Speciale, 'Montecassino, Il classicismo e l'arte della Riforma', in Toubert, *Desiderio di Montecassino*, 107–46; Glenn Gunhouse, 'The Fresco Decoration of Sant'Angelo in Formis' (PhD diss., Johns Hopkins University, 1992); Lucinia Speciale, *Montecassino e la Riforma Gregoriana, L'Exultet Vat. Barb. Lat. 592*, Studi di Arte Medievale 3 (Rome, 1991); Hélène Toubert, *Un Art dirigé: Réforme grégorienne et iconographie* (Paris, 1990); Cowdrey, *Desiderius*, 1–45; Richard Krautheimer, *Rome: Profile of a City, 312–1398* (Princeton, 1980), 170. On S. Angelo in Formis and the Byzantine question, see Herbert Bloch, *Monte Cassino in the Middle Ages*, 3 Vols (Cambridge, MA, 1986), 60–5.

55 Ann Edith Priester, 'The Bell Towers of Medieval Rome and the Architecture of *Renovatio*' (Ph.D. diss., Princeton University, 1990), 73, n. 28.

56 As when Paschal II discovered the urns containing remains of the martyrs at Santi Quattro Coronati.

57 Theodor Mommsen and Paul Krueger (eds), *The Digest of Justinian*, trans. Alan Watson, 4 Vols (Philadelphia, 1985), 43: c. 6. 3; c. 8. 2 (17).

58 Repsher, *Rite of Church Dedication*, 205–13.

59 Vogel, *Medieval Liturgy*, 249.

60 'All surviving copies [of the 12th-c. Roman Pontifical] diverge to such a degree that there could not have been a common Roman archetype', Vogel, *Medieval Liturgy*, 249.

61 Vatican City, Biblioteca Vaticana, codex Barberini lat. 631. See Vogel, *Medieval Liturgy*, 250; Andrieu, *Pontifical romain*, t. 1, *Le Pontifical romain du XIIe siècle*.

62 Vogel, *Medieval Liturgy*, 252.

63 Some 80 sections from the PRG are removed or abridged in the RPXII, while the RPXII adds material to some 24 sections. By sections I refer to the divisions in the Vogel-Elze and Andrieu editions. These are somewhat artificial, but they reveal the pattern.

64 Sections 1–3 of the PRG, that portion of section 23 of the PRG containing the litany is dropped from section 17 of the *RPXII*.

65 *PRG* ss. 29, 31, and 33.

66 That is PRG s. 130, but also ss. 124 and 134.

67 These are PRG ss. 51, 53–7, 65–72, 76–122.

68 RPXII s. 42. RPXII s. 45 invokes the peace and echoes PRG 126 with the people, women and children singing *Kyrie eleison*.

69 RPXII ss. 73–6.

70 RPXII s. 11, Benedic, domine, domum istam quam aedificavi nomini tuo.

71 David I. Kertzer, *Ritual, Politics, and Power* (New Haven, 1988), 11; citing Gilbert Lewis, *Day of Shining Red: An Essay on Understanding Ritual* (Cambridge, 1980), 9.

72 Douglas L. Mosey, 'Allegorical Liturgical Interpretation in the West 800 AD To 1200 AD' (PhD diss., University of Toronto, 1985); Vogel, *Medieval Liturgy*, 1–5; Aimé-Georges Martimort et al., *L'Eglise en prière: introduction à la liturgie* (Paris, 1961), 34–43; Ludwig Eisenhofer, *The Liturgy of the Roman Rite* (New York, 1961), 430–4; T. Klauser, *A Short History of the Western Liturgy* (Oxford,

1979); R.W. Muncey, *A History of the Consecration of Churches and Churchyards* (Cambridge, 1930); Ziolkowski, *Consecration and Blessing of Churches*; John Wordsworth, *On the Rite of Consecration of Churches* (London, 1899).

73 Van Dijk, *Origins of the Modern Roman Liturgy.*

74 Guillelmus Durandus (d. 1296), *Rationale divinorum officiorum*, trans. John Mason Neale and Benjamin Webb in their *The Symbolism of Churches and Church Ornamentation* (London, 1906), 7.

75 E.g., Richard F. Gyug, 'The Milanese Church and the Gregorian Reform', *Scintilla* 2–3 (Toronto, 1985–86): 29–65; the essays collected in *La Cathédrale de Bénévent* as well as those in *Liturgie et musique (IXe–XIVe s.)*, Cahiers de Fanjeaux: Collection d'histoire religieuse du Languedoc au XIIIe et au début du XIVe siècles 17 (Toulouse, 1982); Margot Fassler, *Gothic Song: Victorine Sequences and Augustinian Reform in Twelfth-Century Paris* (Cambridge, 1993); Craig Wright, *Music and Ceremony at Notre Dame of Paris, 500–1550* (Cambridge, 1989); Chrysogonus Waddell, 'The Reform of the Liturgy from a Renaissance Perspective', in R.L. Benson and Giles Constable (eds), *Renaissance and Renewal in the Twelfth Century* (Cambridge, MA, 1982), 88–112. Sarah Hamilton dedicates two chapters to the topic, *Practice of Penance*, 104–72.

76 Eamon Duffy, *Stripping of the Altars: Traditional Religion in England, c.1400–c.1580* (New Haven, 1992); John Bossy, 'The Mass as a Social Institution, 1200–1700', *Past and Present* 100 (1983): 29–61; Miri Rubin, *Corpus Christi: the Eucharist in Late Medieval Culture* (Cambridge, 1991).

77 Reynolds, 'Liturgical Scholarship at the Time of the Investiture Controversy', 109–24; H.E.J. Cowdrey, 'Pope Gregory VII and the Liturgy', *Journal of Theological Studies* 55 (2004): 55–83; and Daniel S. Taylor, 'Bernold of Constance, Canonist and Liturgist of the Gregorian Reform: An analysis of the Sources in the *Micrologus de ecclesiasticis observationibus*' (PhD diss., University of Toronto, 1995).

78 Although important work has been done on liturgy and sacral kingship: Ernst Kantorowicz, *Laudes Regiae: A Study in Liturgical Acclamations and Medieval Ruler Worship* (Berkeley, 1946); H.E.J. Cowdrey, 'The Anglo-Norman Laudes Regiae', *Viator* 12 (1981): 37–78; Percy Ernst Schramm, *Herrschaftszeichen und Staatssymbolik: Beiträge zur ihrer Geschichte vom dritten bis zum sechszehnten Jahrhundert*, MGH Schriften 13 (1–3) (Stüttgart, 1954–1956).

2

'Turba concurrit': attending the ritual and its meanings

> It is fitting that such a large throng of people gathers from everywhere at the dedication of churches.
>
> Bruno of Segni[1]

Historians have tended to discuss power in regard to the physical space of churches in three general categories: the meanings of the symbols they contain, their unique status as sacred spaces, and their location within the local topography broadly understood (political, social or physical).[2] This chapter considers these same categories, but from a different perspective: the experience of the contemporary observer. That observer, or more properly the participant in the liturgy, walked the topography, engaged and was moved variously by images and symbols, and responded or did not to the unique sacrality of the church building. Within this context the dedication of a new church existed always as an ephemeral, experiential reality. The liturgical texts themselves varied, as discussed in the previous chapter, and did not reflect the inevitable transformation that would have occurred when they were read and their instructions followed more or less well. Therefore, this chapter takes us from the possibilities of the rite (Chapter 1) to the experience of the rite. The liturgy was transformed by any number of contextual realities as it was put into practice. Not the least of these transforming forces was the act of observation that was always, even in its most passive, a type of participation. The participants in the rite and their behaviour helps explain the meaning of the rite even as it shaped the rite and its significance. The behaviour and experience of individuals and of crowds provide clues as to why they attended and what they might have come to expect, and were certainly led to expect, at the dedication. That is to say, there is sufficient evidence to suggest why the rite mattered to contemporaries.

The first part of this chapter describes what can be known about who attended eleventh-century dedications and, to the extent possible, how participants attempted to shape the form and meaning of the rite. The second part of this chapter considers how people appear to have been shaped by dedications. Both of these categories reveal the meaning and import of the rite, in part, for those who participated in it and, in part, for those who recorded the event. This approach reveals both the broad social spectrum present at the dedication and something of the attractive and transformative force at work within the event. Later chapters will return to particular examples to consider further how the participants attempted to, and did, shape that liturgical experience and its meanings in the context of the more formal clerical efforts to shape ritual meaning. It is the power, the variety of formative effects, of the liturgical experience that caused it to be worthy of contest and control, that is, to become the object of power. Therefore, the crowd and how they may have been shaped by the event must first be examined before the effort to give meaning to the rite can be understood.

Crowded dedications

Some time in the late eleventh century Bruno, bishop of Segni and Roman Cardinal, observed that it was 'fitting that such a large throng should gather from everywhere at the dedication of churches'. The dedication reminded Bruno of Noah's ark and even of the Church itself. A bishop and cardinal observing the presence and commenting on the significance of large boisterous crowds is worthy of our close attention because the 'emerging crowd' of eleventh-century Italy is essential to our understanding of the nascent communal movement, the urban dynamic between bishop and *popolo*, the heresies of the twelfth and thirteenth centuries, and the reforming and imperial papacies. For R.I. Moore and many subsequent historians, this crowd has also become the subject of much debate. In 1977 Moore described the *Origins of European Dissent* and pointed to the eleventh-century crowd as formative of subsequent mediaeval history. Most importantly, he pointed to the crowds in Milan and Florence who, described as Patarines, demanded the reform of the bishops and clergy. In this they were supported by popes Alexander II and Gregory VII.[3] Later, Moore described the eleventh century as a period when the 'crowd' emerged in European history and became actors, shaping history in their own right. For Moore the crowd that emerged in the eleventh-century was composed of the disenfranchised in opposition to the violent military

elite.[4] Thus the eleventh-century crowd, for Moore, assembled to oppose a variety of dominant groups both religious and lay. In 1987, Moore considered the extension of these processes as the *Formation of a Persecuting Society* whereby a series of categories (such as Jews, heretics, sodomites, lepers) emerged in the twelfth century, and partly in the eleventh, as a means of subordinating and controlling segments of the population by an emerging mediaeval bureaucracy.[5] Moore's thesis was opposing a trend that saw the cult of the saints as promoting civic identity and so essential to the communal movements that emerged in the late eleventh and early twelfth centuries. In these approaches, while conflict with particular bishops remains part of the narrative, the emphasis was placed on the positive dynamic between community and cult.[6] Diana Webb has argued, based on Tuscan sources, that the eleventh-century crowd was described largely as an undifferentiated host of 'the faithful'. Only in the early twelfth century does she see the civic actors of the emerging commune as truly present.[7] Webb along with Paolo Golinelli and George Dameron present a more symbiotic relationship between emerging commune and episcopal power than does Moore.[8] Recently, that thesis has been examined further by Maureen Miller in *The Bishop's Palace*. Miller asserts that the emergence of the bishop's palace was an extension of the bishop's increased reliance 'on the coercive use of spiritual authority to retain status and public influence'.[9] Thus, her critique of Moore's *Persecuting Society* was that it failed to precisely locate the increased persecution of the later Middle Ages in episcopal power in particular, rather than in increasing bureaucratic power in general.[10] This approach, while an effort to reintegrate the bishop into later communal history, simultaneously suggested an understanding of the Italian city as a polarised society of battling forces, the dominical elites versus the greater part of society, the bishops versus the communes. A brief consideration of two of the earliest and relatively well-known examples of communal movements, those of Milan and Lucca, suggests the complex dynamic between reform and *cives* and helps explain the increasingly volatile dynamic of later eleventh-century dedications. They suggest that these simple categories of opposition are not particularly helpful.

The so-called *pataria* of Milan emerged after the death of the Archbishop Aribert and the imperial appointment of Guido of Velate (1045–1071).[11] Guido was widely perceived as having bought his office (a charge that was almost certainly accurate given that this was standard practice in Milan and most eleventh-century churches), and no improvement over his much disliked predecessor.[12] A wide cross-section of the

population resisted his consecration; he was refused acclamation, and the cathedral clergy abandoned him at the altar. Guido persisted and was able to secure papal approval by 1050, calming the resistance to his appointment. In 1056, though, Guido lost a critical ally with the untimely death of the emperor Henry III and, in the same year, he also gained a powerful critic. The deacon Ariald had been preaching the need to purify the clergy in the Milanese countryside and arrived in Milan sometime in 1056. His preaching inflamed the widespread discontent with Guido and with archiepiscopal and imperial dominion in Milan. Later in 1056 or early 1057 the Patarine movement commenced in earnest.[13]

On 10 May 1057, during the solemn procession for the feast of San Nazario (a Milanese martyr), the Patarines clashed with the supporters of Archbishop Guido. By the end of the summer Ariald and his supporters appealed to Rome for permission to choose a new bishop. This precipitated the arrival of a papal legation later in the same year. The legates were none other than the bishop of Lucca, Anselm da Baggio (the future Pope Alexander II) and the Roman monk, Hildebrand (the future Pope Gregory VII). The legation negotiated a truce, leaving Guido in office but condemning his simony.[14] The truce would not last. Ariald soon began to focus on the problems of simony and nicolaitism (clerical marriage or concubinage) within the Milanese clergy more broadly. In the meantime a synod at Rome had endorsed the use of 'liturgical strikes' against simoniac or nicolaitan clerics.[15] This encouraged the laity to support reforming clerics and avoid the sacraments of those deemed impure, and may have exacerbated tensions in Milan. The bishop's supporters attempted to murder the Milanese cleric Landulf, a member of an aristocratic family and a strong supporter of Ariald. They managed instead to destroy a vineyard and desecrate a chapel of Ariald's north of Milan (donated to Ariald by a Milanese knight).[16] For our purposes this act of desecration is worth noting, especially since Landulf was supposed to have preached that the sacraments of the Bishop and his supporters were 'dog's dung' and their churches were 'cow-stalls.'[17] This anxiety over the purity of sacred space as it related to the consecration of the Eucharist, and the exchange of desecration for a charge of desecration, reflected the conflict over consecration (discussed in Chapters 4 and 5).[18] That is, the charge against the Milanese archbishop and his simoniac clergy was that they desecrated the sacrament by their sins (simony and/or nicolaitanism) and the response from the bishop's supporters was, in part, to attack the sacred space of his critics and so to undermine, in turn, their sacral authority and their sacraments. In 1059 another mission from Rome arrived, this time with Peter

Damian at its head accompanied by Anselm da Baggio. Damian was met with a violent and dangerous crowd of clergy and laity who pressed their cause against the Archbishop, 'Everything I might say,' he worried in a letter, 'seemed to point to my death.'[19] Damian was shocked to learn that nearly all the clerics admitted to having paid for their office. But Damian and Anselm were able to negotiate a truce requiring offending clerics to renounce their sin. The situation in Milan remained violent (Ariald was assassinated in 1066) until 1072 when the Patarines and their supporters chose an archbishop to displace the imperially confirmed and openly simoniac Goffredus of Castiglione. Gregory VII's confirmation of the Patarine-supported Atto marks the traditional beginning of the Investiture Controversy. In the Patarine crisis the lines of allegiance ran across the city and cannot be described as an episcopacy opposed by a 'popular communal' movement; as contemporaries themselves understood the matter, 'One household was entirely faithful, and the next entirely faithless; in a third, the mother believed with one son, while the father disbelieved with another. The whole city was thrown into disorder and strife.'[20]

A similar if opposite relationship occurred in Lucca, when the reformer Anselm II of Lucca (the nephew of Alexander II) was forcibly removed from the city by the cathedral clergy in conjunction with a mixture of local supporters. Their opposition to the reforming bishop was, in part, because of his efforts to compel the canons to hold their property in common and, in part, because of his support for Matilda of Canossa.[21] In both cases, the pro-reforming Patarines and the anti-reforming canons of Lucca, the net result was our earliest examples of communal activity in Italy.[22] In the former case reformers, the reforming papacy and their ideals both fostered and attempted to mediate a crisis between bishop and urban collective activity. In the latter case of Lucca, the reforming ideal lacked essential popular support and the reformers were perceived as too closely connected to the dominical authority of Canossa.

It is in this nexus of competing interests and concerns that the crowds described as assembling for these dedications should be considered. The dedications of eleventh-century Italy took place within a context of an emerging communal movement, as well as within a movement of broad religious and social reform. While not an identifiable religious movement as the Patarines or later Cathars, or an overtly political assembly, these dedications were the (relatively) more ordinary experiences of liturgical assembly that had both religious reforming and socially transforming import. The use of liturgical strikes to support (or oppose) the reforming cause in a context concerned with the purity of the clergy and of sacred

space reveals the connection between sacred and civic life. In a sense, these dedications ought to be considered among the religious and communal activities that fostered the development of the commune proper.[23]

Bruno of Segni's 'large throng of people . . . at the dedication of churches' was not simply a device or topos.[24] First, Bruno's claim is made in a commentary on the symbolism of the dedication, his *Sententiae* (*De laudibus ecclesiae*, see Chapter 5). His clerical audience would have known what to expect at such an event and the veracity of Bruno's claims. Since his exegesis of the liturgy in this text depended upon a comparison to the crowded Noah's ark, it would have undermined his image if the crowds existed only in his mind and not on the ground. Bruno's off-hand remark about the presence of large crowds at church dedications ought to be read as one he considered obvious and unassailable, and crowded dedications, therefore, to be common. Second, and more importantly, our sources testify to a diverse crowd at the dedication, not unlike the cross-societal crowds of Milan, and one that becomes increasingly volatile after the reign of Gregory VII.

It is possible in many instances to know what the large, turbulent and pressing eleventh-century crowd that Bruno presumed so natural to the liturgy for the dedication looked like. There exists a range of evidence, largely from monastic, cathedral or later communal chronicles, but also from *vitae* and diplomatic sources that suggest not simply a formulaic crowd, but a complex and changing one.[25] Evidence from approximately fourteen dedications describes the attendant crowds on the Italian peninsula in the eleventh century in the period roughly 980–1116. A summary of that evidence follows and is further summarised in Appendix A: Italian dedications with named participants. This evidence demonstrates the social spectrum of participants found at dedications in eleventh-century Italy. The variety of sources and language suggests a non-formulaic description of the event. Nor does it particularly suggest that the make-up of the crowd changed in the eleventh century, even as their behaviour became more potentially explosive.

In the 980s at Chiusa, at the dedication of its monastery the prerequisite bishop and all the clergy and the people, an innumerable multitude of people from diverse cities, towns and villages, as well as the local lord participated.[26] In 1036, at the dedication of S. Salvatoris at Monte Amiata, there were multiple bishops as well as the Patriarch of Aquileia accompanied by a retinue of clerics 'and other good men'. These last were called *viri boni*, a category essential to twelfth- and thirteenth-century communal and heretical movements.[27] Between 1038 and 1050 there were a range of

churches dedicated as an extension of Vallembrosia. In 1038 participants included bishops, cardinals and the not-yet emperor Henry and his wife.[28] There were also 'noble and faithful men';' 'others' engaged in the process of construction (and so presumably consecration) of dependent churches.[29] Likewise, construction attracted the marginalised, including the poor and the infirm. In 1070, Alexander II dedicated the cathedral of St Martin in Lucca before an 'infinite multitude of clerics' including French clergy. What is more, the eleventh-century sermon that records the event admonished its listeners that *plebs* were to celebrate the feast day, while *citizens* of Lucca were to observe the octave.[30] This suggests the presence of both plebs and *cives* at the dedication.

The dedication of the new basilica of St Benedict at Montecassino on 1 October 1071[31] was witnessed by many of the greatest figures of eleventh-century Italy: Alexander II (1061–1073), Archdeacon Hildebrand, soon to become Gregory VII, and Abbot Desiderius himself, later Victor III (1086–1087). In addition there were another three cardinal bishops, nine archbishops, thirty-four bishops and at least three cardinal priests.[32] A large number of Normans also participated in the dedication. It is interesting to note here the apparent absence of anyone apart from the ruling elite. But the author, Leo Marsicanus, also failed to mention the presence of ordinary clergy. Since it seems unlikely that at least some ordinary clergy would not have attended along with the Pope, Archdeacon and forty-six bishops, it may be inferred that he preferred to bedazzle his readers with the magnates present at the dedication and chose to ignore more ordinary attendants. Thus, while this dedication can provide only limited evidence for participants, it is helpful in two ways: one, as a warning that our sources are biased in their description of the crowd; and, two, in reiterating the lack of formulae in these descriptions. In fact, elsewhere Leo was at pains to point out that even the people of Cassino carried the columns to help in the construction of the basilica in a kind of ritualised volunteerism imitated in later sources.[33] The orchestrated volunteerism reveals the presence of Cassinese children and suggests that such an enormous event would likely attract a crowd for a variety of possible material and spiritual reasons.

1089 saw the dedication of the church of S. Nicola at Bari by Urban II. This was the peaceful conclusion of one of the most celebrated events in Europe of its day: the theft and translation of the relics of Saint Nicholas of Myra by merchants from Bari.[34] There exist multiple sources for the event and the earliest is perhaps the Russian account, the so-called *Legend of Kiev*.[35] However, another account reveals the tension surrounding the

event, the merchants insisting upon close control of the relics.[36] Urban, 'his bishops and his ecclesiastical cohort' were present, and these were followed by a great multitude that came to venerate and kiss the relics and reliquary. Afterward Urban, the bishops and 'all the citizens' orchestrated a large festival, which concluded with gifts to the poor.[37] That crowd would most certainly have included the society formed by those who stole the relics, their financial supporters and their social network. These included *nobiles homines* or *boni viri, presbyteri, clerici, filii clericorum, mercatores* and *marinerii*.[38] A letter from Urban to the new bishop, Elias, suggested the presence also of the recently reconciled Counts Roger and Boemond, successors of Robert Guiscard.[39]

All the Venetians joined together, clergy and laity, *plebs* and doge to rediscover the remains of San Marco, and restored and dedicated his church in either 1089 or 1094 according to the Doge Andrea Danduli. While composed a century after the event, Danduli's *Chronica* does fit contemporary patterns.[40] The central tympanum of S. Marco, also later, but possibly reproducing a previous fresco, presented only the elites of this crowd (doge, archbishop, bishop and lay aristocracy, including women and children) and may represent the eleventh-century dedication.[41] Indeed, the inscription 'The *plebs* deposit [St Mark] here and honour him with worthy praise and hymns, so that he might serve the Venetians and govern the earth and the sea', seems to reference exactly what is depicted by the laity, especially the women and children (impressively arrayed), crowded at the entrance of the church singing the *Kyrie*.[42] That is, it gave prominence to the lay participation by depicting their one act during the consecration, standing outside and singing the hymn.

In 1092, at Cava, Urban II dedicated the new church of Santissima Trinità. In addition to the abbot Peter and the monks, Duke Roger, cardinals, princes and people from every jurisdiction were also present. The abbots were given the right to appoint notaries, judges and vassals, and this might suggest the presence of people of a status to hold those offices.[43] In 1099, 'not only the clergy' but the plebs, prelates, citizens and soldiers, in the absence of a bishop, demanded (*una vox, unus clamor*) the renovation of the cathedral in Modena.[44] In addition, the Countess Matilda rejoiced upon hearing the idea (which may imply that her approval had been sought out by the laity).[45] The citizens and the people helped to select the location of the new basilica and at the blessing of the foundation a 'multitude of men and women' processed to the site. The new basilica was to be duly consecrated by Paschal II in 1106, with Matilda of Canossa at the head of her army, and the bishop Dodo also

present. Word of the imminent consecration spread not only through the city but the surrounding countryside, and bishops, clerics, abbots, monks, knights and 'an infinite crowd of people' of both sexes crowded 'every doorway and window'.[46] The crowd was so large that they had to reassemble at another site where they received instruction before the rite took place.[47] Apparently a dispute arose between the bishops and the 'citizens' concerning the exhumation and examination of the relics of San Geminiano. Matilda deferred to Paschal who, upon his arrival, selected a compromise delegation of six knights and twelve (*bis seni*) citizens to witness the exhumation.[48] As at Bari, there was a crisis between the bishop and the citizens resolved by the visiting Pope. A similar crowd of 'the plebs', Countess Matilda, the Bishop Bernard and Roman cardinals were present when Paschal II dedicated the cathedral at Parma in the same year (1099). As will be discussed in Chapter 5, this consecration reconciled the city of Parma to the papacy after they had supported a rival claimant to the papal throne and challenged Bernard, Paschal's appointed bishop. The 'citizens' of Parma are supposed to have requested this reconciliation.[49]

In 1106, Bruno of Segni, then a monk at Montecassino, dedicated a chapel to St Nicholas, attached to the church of St Angelo in Formis – a Cassinese monastic dependency. Other participants can only be assumed, but the event was observed, in a sense, by the Archbishop of Capua, Sennes, who sent an armed group of men from Capua to destroy the chapel and steal the relics. In 1108, having successfully resolved the dispute in Montecassino's favour, Bruno and Paschal II would dedicate the church of St Benedict *in* Capua. It seems clear that the intended audience was the Archbishop Sennes and his supporters.[50] Bruno of Segni also dedicated the church of St Thomas in Vallemaio on 13 April 1111; he would have been attended by his then fellow monks of Cassino and apparently at least one 'raving woman' (*arreptitia mulier*), sick with an unclean spirit.[51] In 1115 Paschal II, accompanied by cardinals, archbishops, bishops and twenty abbots dedicated the church of S. Vincenzo al Volturno.[52] In 1116 Paschal dedicated the church of S. Maria in Monte, outside of Bologna, accompanied by the local lord who built the church, the archbishop of Bologna and the bishops of Immola, Ferrara and Modena.[53]

What can be learned from this crowded litany? First, the liturgy attracted a large and varied group of people; for our Italian liturgies at least, there does not appear to be a simple generic description of the crowd. Second, these crowds could cut across the social spectrum, from the very margins of eleventh-century society (*plebs, mulier, marineri*) to its most elite (emperors, dukes, bishops, lords and their retinue).[54]

Third, the sources reveal the emergence of the civic actors who appear to be regularly at odds with one another in the twelfth and thirteenth centuries: the 'good men', bishops and canons of urban affairs; as well as the plebs, princes and monks often from the countryside. Thus, it is already clear from this simple catalogue that the crowds who gathered in the eleventh century for the dedication were not gathered in polar opposition to 'elites', whether ecclesiastical or lay, at least not initially and never uniformly; nor was there a simple urban versus rural dynamic. Rather, these major communal events attracted the full community: marginal peoples and ruling elites at times in direct contact with one another, at times in unity, at times in conflict. Starting in the reign of Urban II there is increased evidence that the dedication provoked tensions within the communities that gathered to celebrate them. These tensions, however, cannot be described as urban–rural or ecclesiastical-lay oppositions.

Experiencing the dedication

Having seen that the liturgy was participated in by a wide range of people, and that it was a rich and complex experience, it remains to suggest what significance the liturgy may have held for these participants. It is easiest, as always, for us to examine the ways in which the liturgy directly shaped the clergy, although the chroniclers implied or directly stated a variety of meanings for the participants in the dedication. These suggest ways in which others, from the nobility to people on the margins, may also have been affected by the liturgy. Five categories for which there exists textual evidence are apparent. The first category is the moral significance of the liturgy: it was a source of obligation and responsibility, clerics and rulers were obliged to renew churches both by the examples of their predecessors and the demands of the laity. They were also expected, in the eleventh century, to exhibit a commitment to the liturgy and to conform to appropriate forms of conduct. Moreover, the dedication had a place within the hagiographical ideal that suggested not only a model for the clergy but something of the charisma necessary for the successful reformer. Second, some clerics came to think in terms of, and promote, a series of liturgical metaphors based on the dedication rite. Third, the aesthetics of the liturgy were observed and commented on, and contained an eschatological force. Fourth, the liturgy created a series of expectations within participants; or, more precisely, our textual evidence encouraged readers to expect something significant to take place because of the liturgy. These might

be understood as an extension of the eschatological nature of the newly consecrated space; it had a miraculous power in its own right. Fifth, the dedication helped shape a community's identity, as the dedication became a feast within the calendar, and possibly an occasion to consider the history of the community. These categories overlapped with one another and reinforced each other; for example, the record of miraculous events at the dedication could both strengthen the reforming ideal via the *Vita* of a reforming saint and strengthen the sense of communal (whether monastic or urban) identity through a chronicle.

Moral meanings

The construction and dedication of churches was an important duty for ecclesiastical leaders of the period. This is not only evinced by the growth of the ecclesiastical building industry and the many major dedications beginning in the latter half of the eleventh century, but also by the literary records left by these reformers. (See Appendix B – Pontifical dedications.)

As early as 1038 the dedication of churches appears as part of a process of clerical reform. At Vallembrosia, the dedication was associated with a perceived increase in the prestige of the clerical office. This greater sacrality, according to the *Vita sancti Iohannis Gualberti*, caused priests to stop saying the Mass if they thought they were ordained in simony or by a simoniac, likewise if they had a concubine or other serious sin.[55] This, in turn, provoked the local nobility to offer land and support for the creation of new monasteries.[56] Thus, the dedication was presented in the *Vita sancti Iohannis Gualberti* as a key part of the dynamic of encouraging the moral reform of the clergy and enhancing clerical prestige.

The construction and dedication of churches was part of Desiderius' monastic ideal for himself, and of his understanding of the *imitatio Benedicti*. The famous *Codex Benedictus* (Vat. lat. 1202), was one of the many brilliant productions of the abbey's scriptorium during Desiderius' tenure as abbot, and was also considered to have been a possible medium for promoting (or at least reflecting) contemporary reform efforts.[57] The codex contained the lives of Benedict, Maurus and Scholastica, and emphasised their role as builders of churches, thus honouring Desiderius as a worthy successor. Its initial folios paired a poem in honour of Desiderius (fol. 1r) with an illumination of him presenting the codex to Benedict, seated before what appears to be the new basilica (fol. 2r); the caption above Benedict read 'With these buildings, father, accept many wonderful books.'[58] These two folios served to heighten the connection between

Desiderius and Benedict, the former becoming a worthy successor of the latter, whom he honoured with both a dedication (Benedict's seat) and the commissioned codex. Desiderius was laudable, in part, because he has led a liturgical revival at Montecassino. He was also praised for the construction of the basilica and its ornamentation in the initial dedication of the manuscript.[59] Thus, as a rebuilder of Montecassino, Desiderius became a worthy successor of Benedict, its founder. The codex continued to emphasise Desiderius' *imitatio Benedicti* through its illuminations.

Parallel images of collapsing walls (fols 36r and 151v) heightened the miraculous association with church construction and dedication. At folio 36r there were six images divided into two columns depicting the encounter between Florentius and Benedict at Subiaco. Florentius attempted to poison Benedict and ultimately Benedict left Subiaco. After his departure, Florentius was killed through the collapse of the balcony on which he was standing. This miraculous structural failure was depicted with Florentius pitching head first amid the crumbling balcony at the bottom left of folio 36r. It was followed at folio 39v and 40r with the narrative of Benedict's foundation and the dedication of Montecassino, likewise divided into six images in two columns. Folio 39v began where 36r left off; here in the top left, however, it was an idol being toppled by Benedict that pitches forward in the manner of a person, head first, arms outstretched and knees bent, recalling the death of Florentius at folio 36r. Benedict destroyed the altar in the temple in the next image (top right, 36r).[60] No sooner was the idol destroyed than the bishop was depicted consecrating the new altar with oil poured from a bottle with his hand in a gesture of prayer in the middle left image. Benedict stood at the ready in the middle right image and began preaching to well-dressed laity in the bottom left image. The construction theme was continued in the last three images on folio 40r when a monk was gravely injured during construction of the monastery and healed by Benedict. The collapse of this wall, however, was depicted as the work of Satan.[61] Thus, the example of Benedict was that the construction and destruction of ecclesiastical structures were part of the larger struggle against the enemies of the Church: here Satan, idols and Florentius.

A parallel miracle was accomplished by Benedict's disciple Maurus when he founded a new monastery. At folio 151v, divided into four scenes, a construction worker was seriously injured while erecting the walls for Maurus' new church in the top left and was subsequently healed at Maurus' hands in the top right image.[62] Desiderius' *Codex Benedictus*, therefore, not only revealed the Benedictine exemplum of miraculous

construction but described it as the role of Benedict's successor Maurus. Thus, it revealed the normative ideal of monastic building even as it demonstrated Desiderius' successful *imitatio Benedicti*. These events would provide the framework for the narrative of a miraculous cure at Montecassino by Peter Damian while the basilica was under construction, but prior to its dedication. Damian, through Desiderius' basilica, also became a second Benedict (or rather fourth, after Desiderius and Maurus). When Desiderius requested another cure, Damian replied, 'They have here the most holy Benedict who, if he wished, could confer to him the recovery of his health. Who am I?' Benedict smiled on Damian's humility and the cure was accomplished.[63]

Such miraculous legacies provided divine sanction, not only to the well-established cult, but also to the re-establishment of that cult with the reconstruction of the basilica. It was a divine endorsement of the monastic lives and ideals of Desiderius and Damian. In turn, these events served to re-emphasise Desiderius' *imitatio Benedicti* in constructing and dedicating his basilica; Damian was likewise imitating Benedict through the miracle of healing. As monastic reading, these miraculous narratives fostered Benedict as an ideal for the community to imitate and also held up Damian and Desiderius as ideal successors of Benedict. They were among the many such miraculous stories that helped to contribute to heightened expectations at the dedication, not least of all among the monastics who sought to follow their founder in holiness and who would have been regularly exposed to these texts as part of their daily readings.

Another example likewise suggested this sense of abbatial responsibility after Desiderius: the Cassinese foundation of San Benedetto in Capua. This church was dedicated in 1108 by Paschal II and Bruno of Segni, then abbot of Montecassino, bishop and cardinal in the midst of some controversy. The inscription on the church is telling, reinforcing the notion that the successors of Desiderius saw the building and consecration of churches as part of their monastic obligation.

> Desiderius, known as Victor, bishop and abbot
> Began this work; Oderisius, best abbot,
> Completed it, o Benedict, decorating it to your honour.[64]

Thus, at the dedication of 1108, four Cassinese abbots were presented as defined by the project, Benedict, Desiderius, Oderisius and Bruno. In fact, it has been suggested that fragmentary frescoes of monks still visible within the church were part of a larger depiction of the monastic succession at Montecassino.[65]

Allegory

This moral sense that a worthy cleric was identifiable by the act of constructing and dedicating churches was reinforced within clergy and laity by an increasing number of allegorical associations with the dedication. These allegorical associations suggest a relationship between patterns of thought and liturgical experience. Even as Peter Damian, Bruno, Oderisius and Desiderius deliberately acted in imitation of Benedict (and thereby gained legitimacy as monastic reformers) by means of church dedications, so too did the dedication shape their own religiosity. This is most clear in the case of Damian for whom the dedication was an important metaphor for exploring the mystery of the incarnation and Mary's role in it.[66] In a variety of sermons and liturgical hymns on the Virgin, Damian consistently drew upon the image of the consecration of a church to capture the solemnity, the sacrality of the incarnation.[67] Damian compared the dedication of the Temple with the incarnation. He amplified the value of the supernatural dedication of the incarnation, by contrasting it with the fabulous, but comparatively mundane, dedication of Solomon's Temple. Damian expected his audience to imagine the dedication of Solomon's Temple and, by comparison with the elaborateness of that rite, comprehend how they ought to respond to the incarnation. That is, he expected them to be able to conjure the joy of an elaborate religious rite in order to understand the appropriate response to the incarnation.

> For if Solomon with the Israelite people celebrated with such magnificent and copious sacrifices the dedication of the Temple made from stone, then what joy, and how much joy ought the nativity of the blessed Mary bring to Christian people? In her womb, as the truly most sacred temple, God himself descended, and even thought it worthy to take up human nature from her, and to live visibly with people.[68]

He added that as the Temple was consecrated ground, so much more sacrosanct was the incarnation, and so much more worthy of wonder.[69]

The image of the incarnation as dedication is still further expanded and more strikingly articulated in Peter Damian's devotional work. In his prayer *Ad deum filium* he addressed Mary as the temple of the living God, and begged Christ to make him (Peter) like Mary. On its most basic level the prayer suggested not only that Mary was a temple consecrated by and to Christ, but that the individual Christian could become likewise dedicated. This prayer was most clear if the one praying, or reading, had in mind the image of the deposition of relics in a consecrated altar, just

as Christ is deposited within the Christian, who is made holy (that is, consecrated). As relics, even Eucharistic fragments, placed within an altar became a living presence within a church, so too that same power could come to dwell within the Christian. God is portrayed as a dominant Lord taking possession of the soul through the dedication.

> Come, O Lord Jesus, come into me sweet dweller. Your scent conquers every fragrance; your sweetness transcends . . . the honeycomb and every honey. Come, I beseech you, and, thus, protect me entirely by your law; a tyrant might think he holds himself in no way with the rest, but dedicate me completely as your temple, because you are my God and my Lord, who with the Father and the Holy Spirit lives and reigns for ever and ever.[70]

This was a prayer to be made into a church. The one praying begged to become consecrated, to become like Mary, or like consecrated altars, with Christ and the saints dwelling in them.[71] The liturgical metaphor was heightened by the sensual elements of *odor* and *suavitas* that were intended to recall, it seems, the incensing of the altar, and the consecrated wine. This was not an abstract request for indwelling; the liturgical element lent to it a corporeal reality. The one praying was asking to become fully caught up in the cult – that is, to become inseparable from the act of worshipping God. The liturgical metaphor was deepened by the reference to the threatening tyrant, as the liturgy referred to the church both as the city and the house of God with its own legal prerogatives.[72] So, too, the consecrated self belonged to God.

This metaphor was continued in Damian's *Rhythmus super salutatione angelica*, a poetic meditation on the *Ave Maria*. Here, he incorporated an additional Eucharistic element: Mary not only was dedicated by Christ but was also the source of heavenly manna. In essence, Christians became daughter churches of the Marian Abbey (dedicated by Christ) through the 'deposition' (i.e., the reception) of the Eucharist.[73]

> Your fruit, o Lady, is the fruit of heaven.
> By it angels and the company of saints are fed:
> Contemplation of Christ is the food of those
> Who walk on the path of his commands.
> The King of kings entered the little home of the womb,
> Whose tabernacle he dedicated to himself:
> Sheathing there the sword,
> With which he laid low the enemy
> And Manna most sweet, with which he fed the faithful.[74]

Mary was the tabernacle dedicated by Christ to himself, and she was the sheath of the sword that defeated the enemy and the sweetest manna that fed the faithful.[75] This striking choice of language might, at first, appear to be simply unfortunate, but it built on the image of the temple as the house of God and the dedication hymns that revered the church as God's house and a door of heaven (*Terribilis locus est* . . .). The sheathing of the sword was also a reminder of the peace of the Church established in the dedication. Moreover, the hymn drew on the dedication liturgy by treating Mary as an altar. A church was dedicated by the deposition of relics and Eucharistic fragments in its high altar, followed by a Mass at that altar. Likewise, Mary was dedicated (in the sense of consecrated) by the incarnation: Christ deposited within her. Mary then became the source for the Eucharist (as was the altar), the 'Manna most sweet' which the faithful eat.

That Damian would try to articulate here and elsewhere in hymn and prayer these central mysteries of Christianity (the incarnation and the Eucharist) through the metaphor of a dedication bespeaks the profundity of the dedication liturgy. It also implies that Damian believed that his audience might find those mysteries more understandable and even more affecting through comparison with the dedication. Overall, the intense sensuality of all of these prayers, with their emphasis on smell (*odor, aromata*), taste (*fructus, suavitas, favos, mella, manna*), and mystical indwelling (*veni dulcis habitator in me, condens ibi gladium*) were most probably the product of their liturgical setting. As prayer they reinforced the immediacy, the physicality of the liturgy, especially the dedication. Thus, the dedication rite informed Damian's prayers and theology (see Chapter 3; the imagery was also very much a part of Damian's rhetoric of reform).

This same formative effect of the liturgy can be seen in more simple ways. At the dedication of Chiusa in the 980s the bishop along with 'the people' saw something like a comet and responded in liturgical language, 'O how fearful is this place! Truly this is done by God and it is wonderful in our eyes. This is that burning bush in which Moses saw the Lord, this is another mount Synai, [where] the burning law is taken up through the disposition of the angels.'[76] That the bishop responded, or was supposed to have responded, to a natural event in terms of the liturgical antiphon, and in turn echoed the giving of the law present at the dedications of Montecassino and antiphon (*terribilis locus est*) suggested that the clergy (either the bishop or the clerical chronicler) viewed their own world in liturgical patterns. Or, at least, that they thought the world could be understood by such patterns.

Likewise formed by the liturgy in general and committed to the

dedication in particular was Anselm of Lucca. His anonymous *Vita* has been described as a 'manifesto of the Gregorian reform'; it originated within Anselmian circles and was written for his cause for canonisation (1087).[77] It also represented an ideal Gregorian bishop, an ideal that the reformers were themselves creating for one another.[78] His devotion to the liturgy in general and the dedication in particular was an important element of the anonymous *Vita*, and liturgies provided the locus for most of his living miracles. This was directly commented upon by his biographer, who made it clear that Anselm's meticulous liturgical practices were a taxing expression of his deeply felt piety.

> In consecrating churches or altars he bellowed completely as if entirely filled by the spirit, because he always did whatever was ecclesiastical with a burning love of devotion. We all wondered at the insurmountable power of his simplicity, because, having exhausted ourselves, alone he laboured within; so that having come to the solemnity of the Masses, suddenly he was entirely streaming with tears.[79]

Solus laborabat and *totus lacrymis manabat* were parallel constructions intended to make clear to the reader that it was Anselm's effort alone that brought him to tears. In the context of the dedication liturgy that it described, it was Anselm's struggles (the very physical liturgy itself) that resulted in his unique and secret religious experience within the church.[80] When the congregation was permitted to enter the church for Mass (the laity was waiting outside during the interior rite of consecration), they discovered Anselm in tears. As the locus of Anselmian miracles, the dedication rite was perceived by his hagiographer as giving Anselm's sanctity its charismatic force. This has two implications. First it means that it was Anselm's devotion that moved others to an emotional response (wonder) to the liturgy. In particular, it was the bishop's 'burning love of devotion' that resulted in his bursting into tears after the climax of the dedication (that is, possibly, the deposition of relics, unctioning of the altar or illumination of the church) just prior to the Mass. Second, his commitment to, and moving practice of, the liturgy were among the elements that made him worthy of a cult. This liturgical devotion was presented by the hagiographer as a sign of Anselm's holiness.

Expectations and the miraculous

Anselm's devotion to the liturgy for the dedication drew him in to ecstatic vision of the Virgin while dedicating an altar to her honour.

> He very often saw noteworthy visions, of which it is appropriate to mention some. Once, when in the church of Saint Paul in Mantuan territory, near the episcopal house, he was consecrating an altar in honour of Saint Mary, he saw her with his very own eyes on the very altar during the solemnity of the consecration.[81]

It is impossible to say whether it was the affective force of the dedication liturgy, the association of the dedication, the Virgin, and the incarnation already suggested by Damian, or Anselm's devotion to Mary, or his devotion to the liturgy itself that prepared him for this vision in the mind of the hagiographer. It would seem to have been a combination of his devotion to Mary and his love of the liturgy, as Anselm continued to have visions at the feast of the Purification.[82]

His *Life* presented Anselm as strongly committed to proper liturgical practice and, therefore, an appropriate reformer. Anselm made sure to use proper, authoritative texts in the liturgy, as prescribed by the papacy and 'the fathers'. The liturgy established his orthodoxy:

> He permitted only the writings of orthodox fathers to be read in church, just as holy authority has taught. He tried to observe order and concord in both song and readings, just as the holy fathers established. He did not allow any apocrypha into the office of the Church, just as the most blessed Pope Leo commanded, but for reading privately at table or at meeting, he did not reject it completely. Indeed, he has taught us to sing the Psalms cautiously and even meditatively, otherwise he rebuked [us] sharply.[83]

This passage also reflected Anselm's concern to familiarise himself with proper liturgical precedent; it was his awareness of such precedence, as well as his adherence to it, that stood out in the mind of the hagiographer. Anselm's interest in such liturgical authorities in terms of the reform is the subject of a later chapter, but it is important to recognise here that it was considered by his hagiographer a part of his sanctity and part of the validity of his own sacramental activity.

The sacraments moved Anselm to tears, and his own humility in their presence compelled him typically to stand (thus denying himself the episcopal prerogative of being seated) during the sacraments in general and always during the Mass. This ceremonial humility and emotional response were connected directly to his perceived sanctity.

> God knew that I seemed to be myself full of the Spirit from seeing Anselm, and he, as if forgetting me, seemed to me like an angel. During

the divine mysteries he rarely or never sat. He never finished the solemnity of the Mass without tears, as we could see.[84]

That Anselm's devotion was compelling to those who attended his services is also clear. More generally, his saintly devotion to the Mass encouraged several clerics to steal the water Anselm had used to wash his hands before the consecration in what the *Vita* claims was a successful search for a miraculous cure. Indeed, it was such liturgical decorum and the consequent miraculous verification that created loyalties, not only to individuals, but also to the ideals of the reform itself. Thus, after his death one woman even felt obliged to search for someone else who worshipped as worthily as Anselm. Popular loyalty was with clerics whose liturgies were deemed worthy. It was precisely this sort of 'sciopero liturgico', the refusal of the laity to attend the services of unworthy clergy, that often lent decisive support to the reformers in the face of serious imperial or local noble opposition.[85] The extensive list of those at the exposition of Anselm's corpse and his funeral, as well as those who visited his tomb shortly after his deposition, reflected the bonds he was able to create among the Italian (especially female) nobility.[86]

This type of expectation of the miraculous may be further substantiated by Bruno's only living miracle of healing at the dedication of the church of St Thomas the Apostle at Vallemaio.[87] This dedication is interesting because of its unexceptional setting: Vallemaio is a small town perched on a peak in the hills due south and across the Liri River from Montecassino, in the *terra Sancti Benedicti*. As bishop of Segni and abbot of Montecassino, Bruno arrived to dedicate the new church of St Thomas on 13 April 1111. Some ninety-five miles north, in Rome, the defining crisis for the twelfth-century Church was unfolding, the fateful confrontation between the Emperor Henry V and Paschal II. The dedication ritual would have required Bruno to process through the streets of Vallemaio to the church and to circle the building three times. If Bruno completed the full liturgy at Vallemaio, he would have done so pressed into steep narrow streets, just over an arm's length across, and he would have had to circle a church that had steep drop-offs on two sides.

Bruno may well have employed the full liturgy, and such a display for this tiniest of village churches would have been awe-inspiring. Bruno, Cardinal, Bishop of Segni, Abbot of Montecassino, in his episcopal finest, surrounded by an entourage of monks, elaborately garbed in vestments – perhaps the very tricoloured vestments that Desiderius had made for the dedication of Montecassino – would have processed up the twisting

street toward the church. The clerical retinue would have packed into the narrow streets of Vallemaio, censors swinging, lamps burning, and the crowds, residents and visitors filling the doors and windows, pressed in on either side. One 'raving woman' (*arreptitia mulier*) managed to gain access to the water Bruno used to asperse the church and altar during the consecration. She drank these waters and the unclean spirit left her, never to return.[88] Miracles were likewise associated with the dedication of S. Paolo in Mantua, S. Nicola in Bari, and San Marco in Venice. That these may have the ring of topoi to them is to the point: these events were moments of reputation for great possibility, a possibility that drew crowds and created opportunities.[89] The expectation of the miraculous itself has an eschatological dimension to it, as these were moments when the believer perceived or was asked to perceive the divine presence within the liturgy and its accoutrement.[90] The eschatological dimension of the church, that is, the church as the Heavenly City, was emphasised and represented in eleventh-century ecclesiastical art.

Aesthetics and eschatology

Bruno of Segni also participated, as part of the entourage of Urban II, in the dedication of Santissima Trinità at Cava in 1092. Bruno had the privilege of consecrating the abbot of Santissima Trinità on the same day (which suggests something of Bruno's growing importance).[91] The liturgy moved the anonymous narrator of the dedication, who described it as being conducted with 'magna pompa' and 'magnifica pompa':

> Truly such was the magnificent pomp of the consecration that the most charming odours were burnt continuously, the most sweet harmony was heard, the modulations of organs and flutes, at the most pleasant intervals, so that they were heard, not in the manner of ears, but, reason being amazed, they excited even souls to piety and religion.[92]

The experience of the liturgy had a nearly miraculous (*mira ratione*) quality to it, similar to Leo's amazement at Montecassino.[93] The paving of Montecassino was so beautiful that it seemed to Leo a field of flowers. Many stood in wonder at the sight, and some could scarcely comprehend it.[94] Similarly 'wonderful' was the church of St Nicholas in Bari where the saint accomplished miracles 'like a fountain flowing without end'.[95] In these examples, as was the case with the comet at Chiusa, or the prayers of Damian, the beauty of the liturgy and its setting compelled the viewer to wonder at the power of God. It affirmed the church's place within the

liturgical calendar, as a holy entity, and as a New Jerusalem. Indeed, the presence of relics of Jesus and the saints confirmed that this was the New Jerusalem.[96]

This sense was broadcast to the larger community through eleventh-century mosaics, frescoes and paving in broad motifs common to the Italian religious art and architecture of the period. First, the church became an eschatological city within the earthly city and the eschatological city was not uncommonly presented to the viewer in some form.[97] The role of the Law as at Chiusa and Montecassino discussed above was also emphasised.[98] Along with this the theme of just judgement was also presented. In these images a political and communal ideal was put forward that could assert and challenge a variety of local political entities.

Communal identity

Even as an idealised communal identity was promoted, local identities were fostered in the dedication. Bruno, Anselm and Peter, who had such powerful experiences of the dedication themselves, would in turn have informed others' understanding of the liturgy. Several examples illustrate the sort of effect the dedication rite may have had on local communities or individual religious. It is reasonable enough to assume that the dedication would become the basis for the formation of chronicles, as the construction of a new church was an event of such relative rarity and monumental effort. For the monasteries at Chiusa (the narrative was composed between 1058 and 1061), Cava (ded. 1092) and Montecassino (dedicated in 1071); for the basilicas at Lucca (ded. 1070) and Modena (ded. 1106); or for the church in Monte Amiata (ded. 1036), the dedication was an event of great pride and marked, if not the beginning of each community's narrative chronicle, one of its earliest extended literary descriptions.[99] For Montecassino, in addition to a chronicle, this meant creating a variety of texts that might be used as separate readings for the dedication or its anniversaries.[100] Such texts would honour, and establish as an ideal worthy of imitation, the abbot (or bishop) who built the church and/or renewed its furnishings. Thus, these events could help to create a sense of local identity and history. This identity would be reinforced annually at the feast of the dedication of that church, when the narrative description of its construction, its patrons, and consequent miracles might be reread or reconsidered.

The feast day would require the reorganisation of the local liturgical calendar to incorporate the memory of the dedication and to commemorate

the saints housed in the new church.[101] These liturgical texts might be entirely rewritten (as at Lucca), or the calendar appended to these liturgies might be altered to emphasise the celebration of the dedication and its concomitant saint's cult. The distinction between the extent of the feast of the dedication in Lucca between city and countryside could foster civic pride. As at S. Nicola, it might be the occasion for public feasting.[102]

The dedication could also lend further impetus for an updating of liturgical texts, and, in turn, might require seeking out new and more authoritative sources for those religious books, as in Lucca, Montecassino and Piacenza.[103] The dedication at Montecassino resulted in the production of new manuscripts that emphasised the themes of *renovatio* and reform flowering rapidly on the Italian peninsula.[104] This textual production would extend the significance of the dedication to the feasts or occasions on which the general literal production of such a *renovatio* would be read. Thus, the dedication could imply religious and intellectual renewal, exchange and cohesion (through the borrowing and copying of texts).[105]

In the case of Santa Maria in Pallaria in Rome (a dependency of Montecassino), its eleventh-century liturgical calendar was used to record the conversion of five monks in two different years on the feast of the church's dedication – i.e., on the thirteenth Kalends of July, the date of the dedication of their monastery, the monks made their professions.[106] For Santa Maria the anniversary of the dedication marked a double communal memory: its founding and construction, and its renewal through the addition of new converts. For these individual converts, as well, the feast day of the dedication would be a day of special memory, an occasion to think about their own conversions in light of the history of their community and its renewal. In a complex way, their dedication to the monastic life reinforced the foundation and dedication narratives of the community as a whole, and was literally inscribed into the liturgical calendar and by extension into the history of the community.[107]

The dedication exerted a kind of charisma that drew to itself broad elements of society who wanted to enjoy spectacle and feasting, to celebrate their particular history, to see or experience the miraculous, to witness the Divine made manifest, to fulfil their religious duty or to engage in profound liturgical prayer. The elaborate rites of dedication, therefore, fostered and took place in an emotional and communal atmosphere. This context made them both the object and the expression of the community's various political tensions as well as religious ambitions. Despite a limited historical record there remains much evidence that the liturgy helped shape the religious lives of a broad variety of people. While there must have been

exceptions to the way the rite was executed and without discounting the emphases of regional architecture and art, or of specific sermons, certain patterns most certainly would have emerged. First, it is clear that across the eleventh century the dedication attracted crowds made up of the full spectrum of the urban and rural leadership, as well as the more ordinary plebs. Second, that crowd became conflicted in the later eleventh and early twelfth century. Third, the crowd expected something dramatic to take place, and contemporaries recorded a variety of transforming dimensions to the dedication from religious and social change, to affecting aesthetics, to visions and healing. Chapter 1 discussed a wide variety of possible meanings expressed through the liturgy for the dedication and its relationship with contemporary art forms; these complex religious and political messages were being presented to large and diverse crowds with some effect. Chapters 3–5 examine the ways in which the papal reformers attempted to direct those meanings toward their own objectives. They attempted to canalise the meanings of the dedication into a pro-papal message. This effort both reached its height and began to collapse during the reign of Paschal II.

In a period when communal life of clerics was the rallying cry of a variety of religious reformers, the liturgy called together a wide array of people and began to subtly suggest to them a variety of ways to think abstractly about the city around them and how they might live within it. The liturgy did so more and more frequently as the eleventh century progressed. Thus the liturgy created, almost inadvertently, a kind of for-mation of the participant that lent itself to communal civic-mindedness. Those 'good men' who would form the communes were exposed to lessons from the liturgy whose implications would extend well beyond the eleventh century. It makes sense, therefore, that the kinds of contro-versy that engaged the crowd in the eleventh century reveals an array of liturgical questions: the sacramental worthiness of priests in the case of the Patarines, the proper appointment and consecration of bishops in the investiture contest, the relationship between bishops and canons and the enforcement of the common life (in Capua, Lucca, Rome and elsewhere), and the meaning of the dedication of churches. All of these ostensibly liturgical questions were questions of sacral lordship as they relate to the bishop and his household. Urban life as well as religious and political ideals were shaped by these rites.

Methods that limit the significance of the liturgy to its social function overlook this essential prerequisite.[108] If mediaeval people did not find the liturgy affective, they would not have tried to control it, contest its

meaning or direct its power. Our eleventh-century Italians did all of these things because of the importance of this liturgy in their lives. The liturgy for the dedication was symbolically rich and meant many things to many people: it was a moment of intense prayer, of communal recollection, of healing, of communal strife or reconciliation, and was a metaphor for the ideal Christian community. It was precisely this broad range of possible meanings that made the liturgy powerful. Once this is appreciated, the binary oppositions of committal elite versus plebs, of bishop versus citizen, should become more complex. Both groups were shaped by, contested the meaning of and patterned their lives around, the liturgy and liturgical spaces. That the struggles for power in the twelfth and thirteenth centuries would be articulated in this same language, therefore, is not only logical, it is clear witness to the formative power of the liturgy.

Notes

1 Bruno of Segni, *Libri sententiarum*, PL 165, 879c.

2 Examples include, respectively, Toubert, 'Didier du Montcassin'; Goetz, 'Protection of the Church', in Head and Landes, *Peace of God*, 259–79; Maureen Miller, *The Bishop's Palace: Architecture and Authority in Medieval Italy* (Ithaca, 2000), 123–69.

3 *Origins of European Dissent* (NY, 1977, repr. Toronto, 1994), 54–5. Moore was partly preceded in this by G. Volpe, *Movimenti religiosi e sette ereticali nell società medievale italiana* (Florence, 1922). On the controversies in Florence see George Dameron, *Episcopal Power and Florentine Society* (Cambridge, MA, 1991), 53–4. On the Patarines in Milan, see Olaf Zumhagen, *Religiöse Konflicte und Kommunale Entwicklung: Mailand Cremona, Piacenza und Florenz zur Zeit der Pataria* (Weimar, 2002); Cinzio Violante, *La Pataria Milanese e la riforma ecclesiastica* (Rome, 1955) and Violante, *La Società Milanese nell'età precomunale* (Bari, 1953). P. Toubert, 'Hérésies et réforme ecclésiastique en Italie au XIe et au XIIe siècles: A propos de deux études récentes', *Revue des études italiennes*, nouv. série VII (Paris, 1961), 58–71 and repr. in Toubert, *Études sur l'Italie médiévale (IXe–XIVe s.)* (London, 1976).

4 Moore, 'Family, Community and Cult', 49–69.

5 R.I. Moore, *The Formation of a Persecuting Society: Power and Deviance in Western Europe, 950–1250* (Oxford, 1987 and Malden, MA, 2007).

6 Paolo Golinelli, Indiscreta sanctitatis, *studi sui rapporti tra culti, poteri e società nel pieno medioevo* (Rome, 1988), continuing his earlier work on northern Italian civic cults. Golinelli, *Città e culto dei santi nel Medioevo italiano* (Bologna, 1996); G. Passarelli (ed.), *Il santo patrono nella città medievale: il culto di s. Valentino nella storia di Terni* (Rome, 1982); *La coscienza cittadina nei Comuni italiani del duocento*, Covegni del Centro di Studi sulla Spiritualità Medievale, 11 (Todi, 1972).

7 Diana Webb, *Patrons and Defenders: The Saints in the Italian City States* (London, 1996), 33–4. It is clear, as Webb suggests and from the evidence I present in this chapter, that the dynamic of the crowd, rather than the makeup of the crowd, is shifting in the later eleventh century. See Webb, *Patrons and Defenders*, 54. See also Maureen Miller, *The Formation of a Medieval Church: Ecclesiastical Change in Verona, 950–1150* (Cornell, 1993), 99–116.

8 'It is very difficult indeed to disentangle the issues of lay investiture, clerical marriage, simony, and the struggle between empire and papacy. However, it is evident that we can get a full understanding of eleventh-century church history only by studying first the local origin of the disputes over clerical marriage or the involvement of the churchmen in the monetarized economy', Dameron, *Episcopal Power*, 188.

9 Miller, *Bishop's Palace*, 5.

10 Ibid., 6. See my review of Miller in *The Bryn Mawr Medieval Review* (March, 2002).

11 The essential accounts remain Violante, *Pataria Milanese; Società Milanese*; and his, 'I laici nel movimento Patarino', in *I laici nella "societas christiana" dei secoli XI e XII*, Atti della terza settimana internazionale di studio, Mendola, 21–27 agosto 1965, Publicazioni dell'Università Cattolica del S. Cuore, Contributi – serie terza, Miscellanea del Centro di studi medioevali, V (Milan, 1968), 597–687. Repr. in Cinzio Violante, *Studi sulla cristianità medioevale: Società, istituzioni, spiritualità* (Milan, 1972). Paolo Golinelli, intr. and tr., *La Pataria, lotte relgiose e sociali nella Milano dell'XI secolo* (Milan, 1984).

12 The problem of the validity of simoniac sacraments and the Patarenes is considered in Louis I. Hamilton, 'Sexual Purity, "The Faithful", and Religious Reform in Eleventh-Century Italy: Donatism Revisited', in Kim Paffenroth et al. (eds), *Augustine and Politics* (Lanham, MD, 2005), 237–59.

13 A most clear summary is provided by Paolo Golinelli, *La Pataria, lotte religiose e sociali nella Milano dell'XI secolo* (Milan, 1984), 11–22. Brian Stock, *The Implications of Literacy: Written Language and Models of Interpretation in the Eleventh and Twelfth Centuries* (Princeton, 1987), 153–240.

14 Golinelli, *La Pataria*, 13.

15 Giuseppe Fornasari, *Medioevo riformato del secolo XI: Pier Damiani e Gregorio VII* (Naples, 1996), 31–49; Fornasari, 'S. Pier Damiani e lo "sciopero liturgico"', *Studie Medievali*, ser. 3 an. 17, f. 2 (1976), 815–32; Ernst Werner, 'Pietro Damiani ed il movimento popolare del suo tempo', *Studi Gregoriano* (1975), 289–314; Constanzo Somigli, 'San Pier Damiano e la Pataria', *San Pier Damiano nel IX centenario della morte (1072–1972)*, 4 Vols, Centro studi e ricerche sulla antica provincia ecclesiastica ravennate (Cesena, 1972), Vol. 3, 193–206.

16 Andrea Strumi, *Vita sancti Arialdi*, ed. F. Baethegen, MGH 30 (Berlin, 1929), cc. VIII–IX.

17 Arnulf, *Gesta archiepiscoporum Mediolensium*, ed. L.C. Bethmann and W. Wattenbach, MGH 8 (Hanover, 1826), iii. II, 19.

18 On purity and the Pataria see Hamilton, 'Sexual Purity', esp. 240–9.

19 Peter Damian *Die Briefe des Petrus Damiani*, ed. Kurt Reidel, 4 Vols, MGH (München, 1983–93), 3, 65, 26.

20 Andrea, 10, 1057. See H.E.J. Cowdrey, 'The Papacy, Patarenes and the Church of Milan', *Transactions of the Royal Historical Society*, ser. 5, 18 (1968), 25–48, at 33.

21 Kathleen G. Cushing, *Papacy and Law in the Gregorian Revolution: the Canonistic Work of Anselm of Lucca* (Oxford, 1998), 55–63; Cosimo Damiano Fonseca, 'Il movimento canonicale a Lucca e nella diocesi lucchese tra XI e XII secolo', in Cinzio Violante (ed.), *Allucio da Pescia (1070 c.a.–1134): Un santo laico dell'età postgregoriana. Religione e società nei territori di Lucca e della Valdinievole*, Pubblicazioni del Dipartimento di Medievistica dell'Università di Pisa, 2 (Rome, 1991), 147–57.

22 See Zumhagen, *Religiöse Konflikte*.

23 This has been suggested for the similar, albeit later, Spanish evidence concerning the dedication and political assembly, Adam J. Kosto, 'Reasons for Assembly in Catalonia and Aragón, 900–1200', in P.S. Barnwell and M. Mostert (eds), *Political Assemblies in the Earlier Middle Ages* (Turnhout, 2003), 133–50, on dedications at 136–9, on their relationship to Peace assemblies, at 146. Dameron, *Episcopal Power*, 188 also emphasises the local nature of reform and their relation to early assemblies. Recently providing the local Lombard and imperial context for the Pataria is Zumhagen, *Religiöse Konflikte*, 8–25.

24 Bruno of Segni, *Libri sententiarum*, PL 165, 879c.

25 On the use of this evidence see Geary, *Furta Sacra*, 108–9.

26 *Chronica monasterii sancti michaelis clusini*, ed. G. Schwartz and Elisabeth Abegg, MGH 30, t. 2, (Leipzig, 1936), 962–3 at 963.

27 *Notitia dedicationis ecclesiae Sancti Salvatoris in Monte Amiata*, ed. P. Schramm, MGH t. 30, pt. 2 (Leipzig, 1934), 971.

28 *Vita sancti Iohannis Gualberti*, ed. F. Baethgen, MGH t. 30, pt. 2 (Leipzig, 1934) s. 23, 1086.

29 Ibid., s. 25, 1086.

30 Lucca, Biblioteca Capitolare codex P. † as transcribed in Pietro Guidi, 'Per la storia della cattedrale e del Volto Santo', *Bolletino Storico Lucchese* (1932), 169–86 at 182–6.

31 Essential works with further bibliography are Herbert Bloch, *Monte Cassino*; Cowdrey, *Desiderius*; and Pierre Toubert, 'Pour une histoire de l'environnement économique et social du Mont-Cassin (IXe–XIIe siècles)', *Comptes rendus de l'Académie des Inscriptions et Belles-Lettres, nov.–déc. 1976* (Paris, 1976), 689–702.

32 Leo Marsicanus, *Narratio De Consecratione et Dedicatione Ecclesiae Casinensis*, ed. T. Leccisotti, 'Il racconto della dedicazione dell basilica desideriana nel codice Cassinese 47', *Miscellanea Cassinese* 36 (1973) 215–23, at 219–23. See Bloch, who doubts that Peter Damian was present, *Monte Cassino*, 118–21.

33 *Chron. Cas.*, MGH SS 34, 3.26, 25–30.

34 As described also at length in Orderic Vitalis, *The Ecclesiastical History*, ed. Marjorie Chibnall, 6 Vols (Oxford, 1973),Vol. 4, 54–7.

35 Gerardo Cioffari (ed. and trans.), *La Leggenda di Kiev: La traslazione delle reliquie di S. Nicola nel racconto di un annalista russo contemporaneo* (Bari, 1980).

36 J. McGinley and H. Mursurillo, trans., 'An Anonymous Greek Account of the Transfer of the Body of Saint Nicholas from Myra in Lycia to Bari in Italy', *Bolletino di S. Nicola*, N. 10, Studi e testi (Bari, October 1980), 3–17.

37 Cioffari, *Leggenda di Kiev*, 117–25.

38 See the analysis of these in Francesco Babudri, 'Sinossi critica dei traslatori Nicolaiani di Bari', *Archivio storico Pugliese*, an. 3 (1950), 3–94, esp. 63–94.

39 *Codice Diplomatico Barese*, 19 Vols (Bari 1897), I, n.33, 61–3.

40 Danduli, *Chronica*, RIS XII, t. 1, 219.

41 Thomas E.A. Dale, 'Inventing a Sacred Past: Pictorial Narratives of St Mark the Evangelist in Aquileia and Venice, ca. 1000–1300', *Dumbarton Oaks Papers* 48 (1994): 53–104, at 91–93. Against the argument of Otto Demus, *The Mosaics of San Marco in Venice*, 2 Vols (Chicago, 1984), 201–2.

42 Dale, 'Sacred Past,' 93. Dale misses this liturgical act and argues, following Demus, that the laity are emerging from the church, a possible reading but one that makes less liturgical sense and less sense of the inscription.

43 *Historia consecrationis sacri monasterii Sanctissimae Trinitatis Cavensis solemniter factae a beatae memoriae Urbano papa secundo, Anno Domini MXCII die quinta Septembris*, RIS 6, pt. 5, 45, 14–20; 47, 8–11. As in Bari, this dedication is also for an important abbot and appears to reunify the members of the local community gathered for the event (at ibid., 47, 8–11). Gerardo Ciofarri, *Storia della Basilica di S. Nicola di Bari*, I: *L'Epoca Normanno Sveva* (Bari, 1984); Simeone Leone, 'La data di fondazione della Badia di Cava', in Simeone Leone and Giovanni Vitolo (eds), *Minima Cevensia: studi in margine al ix volume del* Codex Diplomaticus Cavensis (Salerno, 1983), 45–59. On the legal class, see Michela Sessa, 'La condizione giuridica della donna nel sec. XI', in Alfonso Leone (ed.), *Appunti per la storia di Cava* (Cava dei Terreni, 1983), 15–20.

44 Quo terrore permoti non tantum ordo clericorum, sed et universus quoque eiusdem ecclesie populus inter se vicissim conferre ceperunt quid consulendum quidve sit inde agendum. Tandem divina disponente providentia, unito consilio non modo clericorum . . . sed et civium universarumque plebium prelatorum seu etiam cunctorum eiusdem ecclesie militum una vox eademque voluntas, unus clamor idemque amor totius turbe personuit: iam renovari, iam rehedificari, iam sublimari debere tanti talisque patris nostri ecclesiam. *Relatio aedificationis ecclesiae Mutinensis*, ed. H. Bresslau, MGH t. 30, pt. 2 (Leipzig, 1934), s. 1, 1310–11.

45 *Relatio aedificationis*, MGH t. 30, pt. 2, s. 1, 1311.

46 Ibid., s. 2, 1311.

47 Ibid., s. 3, 1312.

48 Ibid., ss. 3–4, 1312–13.

49 Donizio, *Vita Comitissae Mathildis*, Bk II, xvii, 246, ed. and tr. by Ugo Bellocchi and Giovanni Morzi, *Matilda e Canossa: Il poema di Donizone*. Deputazione di storia patria per le antiche provincie modenesi, Monumenti, t. XXIV (Modena, 1984). First the saner part of the plebs, then the greater part of the citizens request

this reconciliation in the *Vita prima et secunda Bernardi episcopi Parmensis*, ed. P. Schramm, MGH t. 30, pt. 2 (Leipzig, 1934), 1317.

50 On the question of audience in regard to S. Angelo in Formis, see Hamilton, 'Desecration and Consecration in Norman Capua, 1062–1122: Contesting Sacred Space during the Gregorian Reforms', *Haskins Society Journal* 14 (2005): 137–50.

51 *Vita Brunonis*, AA SS 31, t. 4, 483a. It should be noted that this water might have been used in a variety of ways: to bless the church, to wash Bruno's hands during the Eucharist or for Bruno's bath. The construction implies the first.

52 *Chronicon Vulternense del Monaco Giovanni*, ed. Vincenzo Federici, Fonti per la storia d'Italia, Vols. 58–60 (Rome, 1925), at Vol. 58, 20–1, and noted by Paschal when granting privileges to the monastery at Vol. 60, doc. 86, 170.

53 *Cronica gestorum ac factorum memorabilium civitatis Bononie*, ed. H. Bursellis, RIS 23, 2, 13, 4–8. He goes on to point out in 1106: Fuerunt et ablatae a iuris-dictione Ravennatis archiepiscopi per Paschalem secundum civitates Aemiliae, scilicet Bononia, Mutina, Regium, Parma et Placentia, ibid., 12, 35–6.

54 This supports Howe's analysis of Dominic's liturgies. Howe sees the lesser peoples as essential to Dominic's success. He objects to Moore's re-emerging populus 'as a reaction of disenfranchised people, those without political power, against the *milites*, the violent military elite'. This is not the case with Dominic: 'he received enthusiastic support from the comital elite, the solid citizens of the *castelli*, and the socially marginal'. Howe, *Church Reform*, 117–18. This closer relationship would also support Webb's observation that 'the laymen who began to rule [the city state] in the course of the twelfth century were the political heirs of the bishop and his entourage. They were not infrequently to be found at odds with their bishops; but the role that they were now claiming committed them to an interest in the civic cult. They had to learn to share the public responsibility for obtaining celestial guarantees of the city's well-being; this and their increasing involvement, collectively, in the management of the fabric of the cathedral and other urban churches, and individually as patrons and benefactors of those same churches, meant a continuing involvement with the saints whose names were invoked and whose relics lay within the city and its locality', Webb, *Patrons and Defenders*, 54.

55 *Vita Gualberti*, ss. 23–4, 1086.

56 Ibid., s. 25: Per idem tempus ceperunt ad tantum patrem concurrere de diversis partibus viri nobiles et fideles. Alii ei offerebant loca cum suplicatione nimia ad edificanda cenobia . . .

57 Paul Meyvaert (ed.), *The Codex Benedictus: An Eleventh-Century Lectionary from Monte Cassino, Vat Lat 1202*, Codices e Vaticanis Selectis Quam Simile Expressi Iussu Ioannis Paulus PP II Consilio et Opera Curatorum Bibliothecae Vaticanae Volumen L (New York, 1982). On the issue of this codex and the contemporary reforms see ibid., 70–1, 84; H.E.J. Cowdrey, 'Pope Gregory VII (1073–85) and the Liturgy', *Journal of Theological Studies* 55(1) (2004): 55–83; Lucinia Speciale, 'Montecassino e la Riforma Gregoriana, L'Exultet Vat. Barb. Lat. 592', *Studi di Arte Medievale* 3 (Rome, 1991).

58 Cum domibus miros plures, pater, accipe libros.

59 Ratio nequit intima reri/ Nequit os labiumque fateri/ Sacra vascula quanta paravit/ Quibus et lapidum decoravit./ Ibi sardius et chrisoprassus/ Nitet ac speciosa smaragdus/ Simul emicat his amethistus/ Radiat pretiosa iacynthus./ Varias quoque Grecia vestes/ Dedit artificesque scientes/ Tribuit sua marmora Roma/ Quibus est domus ista decora; Vatican City, Biblioteca Apostolica Vaticana, Vaticanus Latinus 1202, fol. 1r. Note that the first letter of each stanza (here in bold type) of the full poem would spell out Desiderius Abbas.

60 This is the altar within the same temple, not the destruction of another temple as Meyvaert states, *Codex Benedictus*, 68.

61 The caption of the middle right image depicting the accident reads, Dixit. Structa ruunt. Sathanas abit. Orbuit unum.

62 'The illustration shows the high wall from which the foreman is falling . . . Other workers appear on the ledge with the foreman above. All are clearly secular; the central figure holds a hammer, and none of them expresses the slightest concern'; Meyvaert, *Codex Benedictus*, 85. This illumination parallels that of Benedict destroying the idol, and has many parallels in mediaeval art and architecture: see Michael Camille, *The Gothic Idol, Ideology and Image-making in Medieval Art* (Cambridge, 1989), 3 and 59. Camille understands these to be linked to social transformation, ibid., 7–9.

63 John of Lodi, *Vita sancti Petri Damiani*, PL 144, 114–46, at 141–2.

64 M. Monachus, *Sanctuarium capuanum* (Naples, 1630), 165. See Lucinia Speciale and Giuseppina Torriero Nardone, 'La Basilica e gli affreschi desideriani di S. Benedetto di Capua', in Avagliano, *Desiderio di Montecassino e l'arte*, 147–88, at 153. Speciale and Nardone do not suggest any construction that might have precipitated the 1106 dedication. If there were none, this would suggest that the motive for Paschal's 1108 dedication was the perceived importance of a papal dedication. It would be unsurprising if Oderisus' dedication of 1090 preceded the actual completion of the work, but less common to rededicate a church so soon. Bloch does not mention Oderisius' dedication. Bloch, *Monte Cassino*, 236.

65 Speciale and Nardone, 'La Basilica e gli affreschi', 177–9.

66 Metaphors shape thought even as they illustrate ideas: see Ian Barbour, *Myths, Models and Paradigms: A Comparative Study in Science and Religion* (San Francisco, 1974), 12–13, 120–1. The poetic language of prayer not only creates the imagery of contemplation, but shapes the nature of that contemplation. See for example Mary J. Carruthers, *The Book of Memory: a Study of Memory in Medieval Culture* (Cambridge, 1990), 229–41. See also the discussion of *Sapientia* and *Lumen* and the transformation of the self in Ivan Illich, *In the Vineyard of the Text: A Commentary on Hugh's* Didascalicon (Chicago, 1993), 17–26. Thus, it would be inaccurate to create too sharp a distinction between the language of prayer, the meaning of prayer and the religiosity of the one praying.

67 On his Marian devotion, see Owen J. Blum, *St Peter Damian: His Teaching on the Spiritual Life* (Washington, DC, 1947), 157–62.

68 Damian, *Sermones*, 45, 39–45.

69 Ibid., 45–9.

70 Damian, PL 145, 921–2.

71 On the significance of the presence of relics see Geary, *Furta Sacra*, 32–8.

72 PRG, 40:127–9.

73 Compare with Damian, *Sermones*, 24, 52–6.

74 Damian, PL 145, 940c: Fructus tuus, domina, fructus est coelorum./ Quo pascuntur angeli, coetusque sanctorum:/ Christi meditatio cibus est eorum/ Qui per viam ambulant eius mandatorum./ Ventris habitaculum Rex regum intravit/ Cujus tabernaculum sibi dedicavit:/ Condens ibi gladium, per quem hostem stravit/ et manna dulcissimum, quo fideles pavit.

75 There is an element of the eschatological here as well as that of the bride-of-Christ imagery, a union of imagery that was being brought together in the eleventh-century reform; see Ann Matter, *Voice of My Beloved* (Philadelphia, 1990), 106–11.

76 MGH 30, 963, 25.

77 On the anonymous *Vita Anselmi* see, E. Pásztor, 'La "Vita" anonima di Anselmo di Lucca, Una rilettura', in Violante, *Sant'Anselmo Vescovo*, 207–22. The problems of the *vitae* of Anselm have received much attention: see the summary of these in Cushing, *Papacy and Law*, 4. The central arguments are contained in Paolo Golinelli, 'Dall'Agiografia all Storia: Le "Vitae" di Sant'Anselmo di Lucca', in *Sant'Anselmo, Mantova, e la Lotta per Le Investiture*, Atti del convegno internazionale di studi (Mantova 23–24–25 maggio 1986), ed. Paolo Golinelli (Bologna, 1987), 27–79; and Pasztor, 'Una fonte per la storia dell' età gregoriana: la *Vita Anselmi episcopi Lucensis*', *Bolletino dell'istituto storico italiano per il medio evo e archivio Muraturiano* 72 (1960): 1–33.

78 For an examination of the hagiographical material composed by reformers, especially Bruno of Segni, see P. Toubert, 'Essai sur les modèles hagiographiques de la réforme grégorienne', in *Les structures du Latium médiéval – Le Latium méridional et la Sabine du IXe à la fin du XIIe siècle*, Bibliothèque des Ecoles françaises d'Athènes et de Rome, fasc. 221 (Rome, 1973), 806–40.

79 *Vita Anselmi episcopi Lucensis*, ed. R. Williams, MGH SS 12 (1856), 29.

80 See also Palazzo, *L'Évêque et son image*, the last chapter being on the dedication and its role in creating the authority of the bishop.

81 *Vita Anselmi*, 37. Hildegard of Bingen's visions were likewise shaped by the dedication, most overtly at Hildegardis, *Scivias*, ed. Adelgundis Führkötter, OSB and Angela Carlevaris, OSB, CCCM 43–43A, pt. 3, vision 5, ss. 20–1, and s. 25; references to the liturgy for the dedication are made another twelve times: see the 'Index Locorum Liturgiae', in idem, 664–5.

82 *Vita Anselmi*, 37.

83 Ibid., 31.

84 Ibid., 31.

85 Pásztor, 'La "Vita" anonima di Anselmo di Lucca', 217. In Milan widespread resistance emerged in the mid-eleventh century to an unworthy bishop and was encouraged by Hildebrand and Alexander II: see Violante, *Pataria Milanese*; Ernst Werner, *Pauperes Christi, Studien zu Sozial-Religiösen Bewegungen im Zeitalter des Reformspapsttums* (Leipzig, 1956).

86 *Vita Anselmi*, 44–9.

87 On Vallemaio see Bloch, 'Valle Frigida', *Monte Cassino*, 180, n. 14.

88 *Vita Brunonis*, 483a, see above note 51.

89 Barbara H. Rosenwein, 'Worrying About Emotions in History,' *American Historical Review* 107(3) (June 2002): 821–45, where note 70 points to William Reddy, *Navigation of Feeling*; *The Invisible Code*, 'Reddy revels in sources that are stereotypical, the kinds of materials that other historians might reject or query as "insincere". Arguing that sincerity itself is culturally managed, Reddy sees "official" representation of emotions as effective, if imprecise, shapers of individual representations', 839, note 70.

90 Benedicta Ward, *Miracles and the Medieval Mind, Theory, Record and Event, 1000–1215* (Philadelphia, 1982), 3–4.

91 *Historia consecrationis*, RIS 6, pt. 5, 47.

92 Ibid., 47; and 45 for 'magna pompa'.

93 Leo, *Narratio*, 219.

94 Ibid.; *Chron. Cas.* MGH SS 34, 3.28, 14–32.

95 Cioffari, *La Leggenda di Kiev*, 114–15, 138.

96 See for example the long list of relics from Jerusalem (primarily of the passion, but also of prophets and of Mary), and of the saints at the dedication of S. Salvatoris. *Notitiae dedicationis ecclesiae Sancti Salvatoris in Monte Amiata*, MGH t. 30, pt. 2, 972. On Damian's sermons conflating the earthly city and the allegorical city see Webb, *Patrons and Defenders*, 47–8.

97 As at S. Clemente, Rome, see Stefano Riccioni, *Il Mosaico Absidiale di S. Clemente a Roma:* Exemplum *della chiesa riformata* (Spoleto, 2006).

98 S. Matteo in Salerno; inscription from Montecassino, statement from Chiusa MGH 30, 963.

99 *Chronica monasterii Sancti Michelis Clusini*, MGH SS 30, 959–70; *Notitiae dedicationis ecclesiae Sancti Salvatoris in Monte Amiata*, MGH SS 30, 971–2; *Relatio aedificationis ecclesiae cathedralis Mutinensis et translationis Sancti Geminani*, MGH SS 30, 1308–13; *Historia consecrationis sacri monasterii Sanctissimae Trinitatis Cavensis*, RIS 6, pt. 5, 39–48; Lucca, Bibl. cap., cod. P. †, fol. 132 (sec. XII), in Guidi, 'Per la storia della cattedrale'. There are another thirty-two examples in Germania and Gaul, exclusive of narratives of translations of relics that may or may not have implied a dedication, also given in MGH SS 30. This is only a cursory survey, but it is clearly a significant phenomenon.

100 Cowdrey, *Desiderius*, 20, 75–9.

101 An especially complete example of this is Lucca; see Grégoire, 'Liturgia e agiografia a Lucca durante gli episcopati di Giovanni II (1023–1056), Anselmo I (1056–1073) e Anselmo II (1073–1086)', in Violante, *Sant'Anselmo Vescovo*, 273–82.

102 During the debate over the simony of Grosulanus (1105) in Milan, relics were discovered and a feast resulted (which included a market); while there appears to be no dedication, the annual feast seems to have elements of a triumphal entry (with palm branches and chanting holy holy), RIS V, 3 pp 20–1.

103 For Piacenza see Jensen, *Tropes and Sequences*.

104 These would include Vat. Lat. 1202; Vat. Barb. Lat. 592; Montecassino, Biblioteca dell'Abbazia 98, and 99; see Meyvaert, *Codex Benedictus*, fols 70-1, 84.

105 On Montecassino, see Bloch's discussion of Montecassino and its dependencies in *Monte Cassino*, 40-112. On the creation of textual communities see Stock, *Implications of Literacy*.

106 Vat. Lat. 378, fol. 33v. Half of the folio is a palimpsest and the following notes are inserted in that space at, 'martyri iaosyderea regnam migraver[am] In hispani civitate alaca sanctorum mar[tyrorum] siriaci et paule virginis/ *B. xiii kal iul Dedicatio Huius Ecclesie sce Marie in Palladio Mediolani nativitate sanctorum mar[tyrorum] gervasii et protasii*, qui beatissimi per decem an[nos]'. [Emphasis mine.] These additions are in twelfth-century hands distinct from the book hand (XI s.) That the addition was made in the twelfth century may be confirmed by the presence of the Abbot R. of Montecassino and the Prior B. of S. Maria. The abbot has been identified as Rainauld Colementanus (1137–1166). Bloch, *Monte Cassino*, 321-2; Pietro Egidi, *Necrologi e libri affini della provincia Romana, Fonti per la storia d'Italia* 44 (Rome, 1908), 105-6; A. Wilmart, OSB, 'La Trinité des Scots à Rome et les notes du Vat. lat. 378', *Revue Bénédictine* 41 (1929), 226-8. I would like to thank Stefano Riccioni for his assistance with this material; my transcription of 33v follows:

+Ego frater Mainardus promitto stabilitatem meam et conversionem morum meorum et obedientiam secundum regulam sancti Benedicti in monasterio Sancte Marie de Palladio et Sancti Sebastiani martyris [et Sancti Zotici martyris [in left margin]], tempore domini Rainaldi casinensis abbatis et Sancte Romane Ecclesie cardinalis in presentia fratris Martini preposti.

+Ego [——] sancte marie palladio et sancte sebastiani martyris et sancti zotici martyris tempore domini Rainaldi casinensis abbatis et sancte romane ecclesie cardinalis presentia fratris Martini preposti in presentia casinensis fratrem videlicet [——] sul [——] et fratris o[——] et fratris cono[——].[This section appears to be a deliberate palimpsest.]

Ego frater Odersius Subdiaconus promitto stabilitatem meam et conversionem morum meorum et obedientiam secundum regulam Sancti Benedicti in monasterio Sancte Marie de Palladio et Sancti Sebastiani martyris et Sancti Zotici martyris. Tempore domini Rainaldi casinensis abbatis et Sancte Romane Ecclesie cardinalis in presensentia fratris Martini preposti in presentia fratris nostri videlicet Vinhelmi et Petri et andre [in a distinct hand]

[in left hand margin:] +Ego frater Petrus promitto stabilitatem meam et conversionem morum meorum et obedientiam secundum regulam sancti Benedicti in monasterio Sancte Marie de Palladio et Sancti Sebastiani martyris tempore domini Rainaldi casinensis abbatis Sancte Romane Ecclesie cardinalis presentia fratris Martini preposti.

[At foot of folio]+Ego frater Iohanis Capuane civitatis promito stabilitatem meam et conversionem morum meorum et obedientiam secundum regulam Sancti Benedicti Monasterio, Sancte Marie de Palladio et Sancti Sebastiani martyris et Sancti Zotici martyris in tempore Rainaldi casinensis abbatis et sancte romane ecclesie cardinalis in presentia fratris B cappellanis domini preposti et

rectoris de Palladio et dedit unam equam pro redemptione animae mee et vita corporis videlicet dominus Manardus et W et scientes plures omnes videlicet Leo et Sasanu et Galterus et Bernardus.

107 For a contemporary example of the integration of liturgy and communal history in the monastery, see Susan L. Boynton, *Shaping a Monastic Identity: Liturgy and History at the Imperial Abbey of Farfa, 1000–1125* (Ithaca, 2006).

108 On this problem, see Hamilton, 'Les Dangers du ritual'. While most mediaevalists who employ anthropolgical methods consider themselves post-functionalist and indebted to the work of Clifford Geertz, even as magesterial a work as Iogna-Prat's *Order and Exclusion* states as its objective 'to provide a social history, to study the rules by which medieval society functioned': Iogna-Prat, *Order and Exclusion*, 4. This results in a tendency to privilege binary oppositions in the meaning of ritual ('white churches and black chateaux'), to read ritual as existing primarily to assert social rules: *Order and Exclusion*, 171. These oppositions are only a portion of the meaning, and privileging them risks our ability to appreciate the attractive force of the ritual and the capacity for its meaning to be repeatedly reshaped. See Gabrielle Spiegel's review of Buc, *Dangers of Ritual, American Historical Review* 108(1) (2003), 148–9.

3

Peter Damian: from mystical to political allegory

Rejoice Venice, . . . just as the mother of cities, Rome, is raised above every kingdom . . . in Peter, so even you, as if her distinguished daughter will be glorified in Christ through Mark.

Peter Damian[1]

The dedication liturgy could draw together many people from a broad spectrum of mediaeval society in the late eleventh and early twelfth centuries. From the most ordinary of the laity to their lay overlords, from humble monks to the highest levels of the clerical elite, mediaeval people felt drawn to the moment of the dedication, and it became significant in their lives. This did not go unobserved by the religious leaders of the period who were themselves formed by the increasing number of dedications and anxious to explain to the populace, as well as to one another, the import of the rite. One of the earliest of these eleventh-century commentators scrutinised and shaped the event's reform and political significance.

Some historians studying the dedication and its exegesis have maintained that the interpretation of the rite's significance reached a creative peak during the Carolingian reforms and remained largely static thereafter.[2] Such a conclusion might at first appear warranted from a textual standpoint since the *Quid significent duodecim candelae*, a Carolingian commentary on the dedication *ordo*, provided the commentary structure for Damian and Bruno's exegesis of the dedication, and was both widely circulated and broadly influential.[3] However, such claims mask the great import and expressive capacity of the liturgy, and the fluidity with which its meaning changed over time. This becomes clear when commentaries of the late eleventh and early twelfth century, in particular those of

Peter Damian, Humbertus of Silva Candida, Anselm of Lucca and Bruno of Segni, are considered within the milieu that produced them.[4] This chapter is concerned with the earliest reforming commentaries of Peter Damian and Humbertus, as well as the indirectly represented ideas of Desiderius of Montecassino and Alfanus of Salerno.

Though it is not known where Peter Damian delivered his one extant sermon on the dedication, the sermon was very likely known to Desiderius and Montecassino at the time of the church's consecration in 1071, and would have provided an important precedent for the meaning of the rite.[5] This sermon demonstrates a keen awareness of the pressures of eleventh-century Italian society. It may have been that Damian, rhetorically trained at Ravenna, was influenced by the strong Byzantine use of political iconography.[6] It is clear, however, that Damian incorporated contemporary socio-political concerns into his exegetical compositions.[7]

The career of Peter Damian, from hermit to cardinal bishop of Ostia, is itself emblematic of the transformation of the eleventh-century reform efforts from personal to institutional.[8] It is worth reviewing it in outline.[9] Having studied at Faenza and Parma, and pursued a career as a rhetorician at Ravenna, Damian, caught up in the religious zeal of the era, joined a hermitage at Fonte Avellana around 1035 or 1038. For Damian, the religious life was a life of travel in Italy, preaching a spiritual *renovatio*. In 1043, he was elected prior of Fonte Avellana. In 1053 he wrote his *Liber gratissimus* arguing in favour of the validity of the sacraments of simoniacal clergy.[10] Stephen IX (1057–1058) consecrated Damian as cardinal and bishop of Ostia, possibly in 1057, as a way of drawing the prior into the work of the Roman Curia. As an itinerant monastic reformer, Damian would have known at first hand the relationship between personal reform and the structures that controlled the Italian peninsula. In particular, he would have observed that the structures girding ecclesiastical and secular authority (especially monasteries and churches) were often themselves the fruit of the spiritual *renovatio* sweeping Italy. Monastic reformers were essential to the increasingly centralised power structures, especially of southern Italy.[11] Indeed, the establishment of new monastic houses, or the expansion of older ones, had a similar socio-economic effect to that of secular *incastellamento*.[12]

This is the context in which the dedication of a new church and its commentaries must be understood. From the beginning of the reign of Gregory VII (1073–1085) to the end of the reign of Paschal II (1099–1118), according to papal registers and inscriptions, twelve churches or altars were dedicated in Rome by the eleventh-century popes. These figures

compare with one dedication in Rome in the first seventy years of the century.[13] These numbers are even more impressive if one considers that Gregory VII (1073-1085) and Urban II (1088-1099) spent large portions of their papacy in exile, or as virtual prisoners within the city, and that the city was regularly in a state of political and military turmoil throughout the last quarter of the eleventh century.[14] Thus, although the number of dedications seems small, they are significant relative to both precedent and circumstance. When the papal reformers were finally back in control of the city under Paschal II (1099–1118), there was a renewed burst of church building and dedications. The dedications of the late eleventh and early twelfth centuries were part of a larger process transforming the broadly diffused religious zeal of the late tenth and early eleventh century into concrete institutional reform.[15] The interest in episcopal dedication and the increasing number of dedications also reflected a reforming effort to both assert the bishops' authority within their episcopates and to compel bishops to complete their ecclesiastical duties. As has been observed broadly in southern Italy, new churches were rarely dedicated from the ninth to the eleventh century and religious structures were centred on local lords.[16] Even as the reform shifted on the eleventh-century Italian peninsula from monastic to episcopal leadership, from the personal to the institutional, the exegesis of the rite of dedication shifted from its moral to its allegorical meaning.[17] Exegesis of the dedication was transformed in eleventh-century Rome in the same manner as Scriptural exegesis was being transformed by the reformers: toward increasingly 'political' allegory.[18] Thus, even as the reformers shifted their emphasis, the exegesis of the dedication moved from the personal moral significance to its broader political/ecclesiological significance.

In this context, consecration came under increased scrutiny. The most famous example of that debate over consecration was in the Berengarian controversy over the Eucharist. In essence, however, the debate over investiture was also a question of consecration, not only in terms of sacral kingship but most directly over who had authority over and who created consecrated people: bishops, priests and lesser clerics. The earliest articulations of this broader problem of consecration came from Peter Damian and Humbertus of Silva Candida. Humbertus (c.1000/05–1061) was a monk in the Lorraine until brought to Rome by Leo IX and made cardinal bishop by early 1051. He articulated the Roman position of Petrine supremacy against the patriarch of Constantinople and was an essential part of the legation to Constantinople that ultimately excommunicated the Patriarch.[19] Between 1057 and his death in 1061 Humbertus

composed his most famous work, the *Libri tres adversus simoniacos*. He took up an extreme and essentially donatist position in the *Libri tres* arguing that the consecrations by simoniac bishops were invalid and needed to be done again.[20] This position marks the most radical – but ultimately rejected – position of the reforming party. It was the extension of a rigorous ecclesiology that rejected lay control over the Church and its foundations.[21] He rejected both simoniacs' consecrations of individuals and also their dedication of churches. In the third book, written perhaps as early as 1058, he shifts his focus from simony per se to its sources in princely control of the Church. This book marked an essential shift in the reform.[22] In the chapter entitled 'On the priestly dignity of the old law and the presumption and punishment of the kings of Judah and Israel', Humbertus conflated a series of Old and New Testament texts to assert the clerical privilege of dedication. He observed that it was to Aaron and his sons that the task of dedication of the tabernacle, altar and its utensils by aspersion with hyssop properly belonged.[23] He cited Hebrews 9: 19–22, somewhat incongruously, as a proof text for the appropriateness of this arrangement. It remained the task of the Levites and not the princes to serve in the Temple, and he offers the cautionary tale of the punishment of King Uzziah (2 Chron. 26: 17–21) who dared to approach the altar with incense. Further, he offered the example from 1 Maccabees 4: 42–58, where the sanctuary of the Temple, the altar and all of its utensils are rededicated after having been profaned by idols. This was to serve, at least metaphorically, as an example of how to approach the Church having been profaned by the sacrilege of simony according to Humbertus.[24] Thus, by the middle of the eleventh century, the language was in place for the reformers to consider the dedication of churches as an extension of the history of Old Testament priesthood and of the Temple and, as a result, as part of the effort to assert priestly over royal prerogatives. In short, the dedication was becoming another front in the fight against simony.

At this same time, even as Humbertus emphasised the purity of the Church space and the contamination of simony, Damian was moderating his position on clerical purity and the legitimacy of the sacraments.[25] Nonetheless, he too understood the dedication within the context of the current debate over ecclesiology. Damian's preaching on the dedication of a church was the fullest expression of his original thought on the significance of the dedication liturgy. The precedents readily available to Damian for understanding the rite included the Carolingian commentary *Quid significent duodecim candelae* in the PRG, which was present both

in eleventh-century Rome and at contemporary Montecassino.[26] This text emphasised the moral – what mediaevals called the tropological – sense of the liturgy. That is, the *Quid significent* explored the relationship between the liturgy and the progress or conversion of the soul toward God. The *Quid significent* compared the dedication to a baptism, and then used that as an opportunity to instruct the clergy and, perhaps, the laity in the rudiments of conversion, instruction, initiation and repentance within the Christian community.[27] It served to affirm the ecclesiastical and social cohesion within the Carolingian reform.[28] Bede's sermon on the dedication was also available to Peter Damian; like the many sermons available in the collections of eleventh-century Rome (if not also at Fonte Avellana), it emphasised the moral meaning of the rite.[29]

Damian's sermon, even if not delivered at Montecassino, was almost certainly known to Abbot Desiderius by 1071.[30] It is difficult to imagine Desiderius not being aware that Damian considered the dedication of importance to the central religious questions of the day, since Damian had articulated that belief publicly as early as the 1050s. Damian's *Liber gratissimus*, written in 1052, lists the abusive episcopal practice dedicating churches for profit among the sins of simony.[31] In his *De sacramentis per improbos administratis* (1067) it is clear that simony tainted dedications as it had other moments of consecration.[32]

Even more than an occasion for simony or abuse, Damian had begun to understand the dedication as an important basis for Petrine authority and papal prerogative. Three sermons on the feast of St Mark, delivered at Venice, became an occasion for Damian to discuss the pre-eminence of Rome through reference to Mark's dedication of a church in Alexandria. Damian attempted to draw upon both the Venetian devotion to St Mark and the significance of the dedication to promote Venetian loyalty to Rome. In these sermons Damian traces Roman prestige in Mark's dedication of a church in Alexandria:[33]

Saint Mark, having been made bishop, founded the Church of Alexandria and he, after he erected [the church] upon the rock of which Christ is the singular architect, he faithfully dedicated it to the name of his glorious teacher. Whence it came to be that the church was called by the designation 'apostolic seat', not as much on account of Mark as of the blessed Peter, just as if Peter himself held the episcopal *cathedra* by himself. And, therefore, by the distinguished designation of heavenly key bearer, in the entire sphere of countries that Church holds the second throne after Rome. And although at Antioch, where the name of the Christian religion began, Peter himself produced the

first fruits of faith through himself, the see of Alexandria obtained the higher rank.[34]

Mark, despite his own authority as an Evangelist, deferred to the authority of Peter. Although Mark established the *cathedra* at Alexandria he did so only through Peter, as Peter's disciple.[35] Thus, Mark's foundation and dedication of a Church at Alexandria reaffirms, rather than challenges, Rome's Petrine pre-eminence.[36] Damian added that since Alexandria was Mark's way of dedicating (here with the force of consecrating) the East, Venice was Mark's dedication of the West.[37] If this serves to exalt Venice, Damian quickly reasserts Rome's predominance.[38] 'Rejoice, therefore, Venice, and, exulting in the Lord, applaud . . . Wherefore, just as the mother of cities, Rome, is raised above every kingdom of the earth in Peter, so even you, as if her distinguished daughter, will be glorified in Christ through Mark.'[39] Thus, Roman prerogative and pre-eminence, and the significance of Roman reform, were bound to the dedication by Damian. Damian asserts that the dedication of a church can reveal its status. Nor would this have been lost on the Venetians, who were self-conscious of their dedication to Mark and displayed (at least in the later eleventh century) a keen awareness of how the dedication created prestige.[40] Damian would also invoke Rome's consecration at the martyrdom of Peter and Paul ('the Roman Church was consecrated by their blood') in the midst of the Patarine controversy, over the claims of the Milanese Church.[41] This metaphor will be more fully developed by Anselm of Lucca.

While Damian does not comment on the dedication liturgy per se in his Venetian sermons, he does draw upon the liturgy in oblique ways. Damian's peculiar use of *insignis* and *insignitia*, here translated as 'singular' and 'distinguished', is worth noting. Their meanings include ideas of honour or pre-eminence, of being decorated, or of the ornaments that honour. The root of both these word is *signum*; the prefix *in* completes the literal sense of being 'under a sign'. In this broad sense Damian was drawing upon the religious images/signs that decorate a church and distinguish it as sacred, and the cultural emblems that mark the body as belonging to a given elevated rank. As the dedication liturgy illuminates the church, blesses its walls, liturgical tools, vestments, and altar(s) and marks them by the sign of the cross as holy, so also can the dedication distinguish the spiritual and social rank of the church. Urban II would later employ this meaning directly.[42] Damian returned to these same themes of ornamentation and religious and social order when sermonising directly on the dedication.

The dedication of churches and *renovatio*

Although the exact occasion for Peter Damian's sermon remains elusive, internal evidence allows for generalisations about the nature of its circumstance and points us to its broader import.[43] There is substantial evidence to suggest that it was delivered on the occasion of a major dedication. Briefly: Damian referred to the new church as a basilica, and allegorised the new church as a 'library of divine law', 'a school of spiritual study' and 'a city of letters'.[44] These suggest that the sermon was delivered at the dedication of either a major monastic or episcopal church, as in the dedication at Montecassino in 1071 with which Damian's sermon shared many themes. It may have been at one of the dedications in the crypt of St Cecilia, the dedication of St Odilo in Gaul, or that of the Farfa in 1060, or it may have been a significant dedication now lost to us.[45]

While the exact moment of the sermon is unknown, it is appropriate to consider it in light of other contemporary dedications. Desiderius and Damian were in regular contact during the construction of Montecassino's basilica, and Damian's sermon on the dedication was, perhaps, already in the monastery library. Desiderius himself understood the dedication allegorically and in terms of the reform movement. Indeed, as Leo's description of the new basilica makes plain, Desiderius saw the dedication as a kind of reconstruction of Rome's past; specifically, the Christian Rome of Constantine.[46] Thus, inscribed in the apse of the new basilica were the verses calling for reform, but inasmuch as the text echoed the corresponding text at Constantine's basilica of St Peter in Rome, the reform was to declare a return to the glory of Constantinian Rome.[47]

> This House is as Sinai bearing the sacred law
> As the law establishes, which was here put forth one day
> Hence the law has gone forth, which leads minds from destruction
> And having been made public, it has given light to all regions of the world.[48]

For Desiderius, the dedication of his new basilica at Montecassino had, in a sense, an evangelical element to it: the church was to become a force for the spreading of the gospel and the conversion of the world, the bearing of the new law to the nations.[49] The author of those verses, Alfanus, Archbishop of Salerno and monk of Montecassino (d. 1085), reiterated this theme while praising the monks of the great monastery. Cassino is 'the hall of God, another Mount Sion . . . the mountain where the Law of God

is written'.[50] Likewise, he composed verses in honour of the church of St John the Baptist in Cassino that echoed those at the Abbey:

> This House is as Sinai bearing the sacred law
> As the law establishes, which was here put forth one day
> So that, with you leading, the fatherland obtained for the just is received.
> Here Father Desiderius built this hall for you.[51]

This sense of the new law had a practical political aspect to it as well. The famous frescoes of Desiderius' church at S. Angelo in Formis have been studied as an extension of the papal reforms.[52] This argument has been defended through allegorical readings of the frescoes of Old Testament righteous warriors, and so by extension to the papal calls for Christian military expansion. Moreover, it has been suggested that both the church's Roman form and the frescoes' direct imitation of Roman artistic exemplars served to heighten the emphasis on the Roman norm.[53] This may well be the case. However, what remains most clear in the frescoes, and perhaps the most striking symbol for contemporaries, is the presence (in the fresco of the central apse) of Desiderius holding his little Romanesque church.

In fact, the placid scene belies the local tensions centred on Cassinese expansion in the area. The dispute between Cassino and Capua centred initially around the donation of a run-down little church three miles outside of Capua on Monte Tifata. The property had been purchased from the Archbishop by the Norman prince of Capua, Richard. In 1063, Richard granted both the church of St Angelo in Formis along with land for its support, and the church of St Angelo Odaliskos in Capua itself to Montecassino.[54] This donation endowed the abbey with a significant presence within the seat of Capua. Such prominence was immediately perceived as a problem by Archbishop Hildebrand of Capua since the Normans, under Richard of Aversa, were directly attacking the familial power of the Capuan Archbishop and, through Desiderius of Montecassino, the papacy was aligning itself with the insurgent Normans against older Capuan institutions.[55]

In that same year, 1063, the Lombard families of Capua (among these the family of Hildebrand of Capua) revolted against Richard and forced him out of the city. It would take him two years to regain control of the city of Capua, and even then he no longer resided there. Regardless of this, he did pursue a more aggressive policy of donating land and wealth to the Capuan dependencies of Montecassino (St Benedetto, St Angelo in Formis, St Angelo Odaliskos, and St Rufo).[56] This tension, however, cannot be explained simply in terms of Lombard institutions in

opposition to Norman ones.[57] Instead there was a more complex triangle of donations. Richard's monastic policy supported the male Cassinese dependencies. This contrasted with an urban burgess donation pattern that appears to have preferred the Cathedral. The urban nobility, on the other hand, preferred the nuns of S. Maria in Capua, a Lombard foundation, the wealthiest female monastery in the principality, and famously relentless in their opposition to Cassinese control.[58] These point to a number of independent donation strategies within the city of Capua to support Capuan institutions, though not necessarily exclusively Lombard in motive, nor strictly urban versus rural. These donations do suggest a unique preference for Cassinese dependencies by the Norman princes of Capua.

Given the contemporary tensions between Cassinese and Capuan clerics, that image of Desiderius presenting St Angelo to the angelic assembly before the enthroned Christ may have been potent enough to remind the viewer of the thread leading back, certainly to Montecassino, but perhaps also to Desiderius' allies in the eternal city.[59] The frescoes' donation portrait placed the Abbot of Montecassino (and later Pope Victor III) in the centre of an extended allegory of just rulership, and most plainly placed the living abbot in the midst of the heavenly court beneath the enthroned Christ. In this manner the frescoes of St Angelo reinforced the propriety of Montecassino's leadership in the region. The just judgement of God within salvation history was presented throughout the church, from the expulsion of Adam and Eve from Eden to the final judgement scenes, to the heavenly court. These scenes of the heavenly court with Christ seated in judgement framed and dominated the church, as they were the subject of the frescoes in the apse and rear wall of the church. On the walls of the nave, parallel Old and New Testament images emphasised scenes of just and unjust rulers through portraits of David and Solomon as well as the torture of the martyr St Pantaleon and the crucifixion. Of the identifiable rulers depicted in the frescoes, Desiderius (the only living ruler) alone was presented within the central apse's representation of the heavenly court. This heavenly court was comprised of Desiderius and the archangels. The central archangel, Michael, was himself an object of important local cults, especially for the Normans. Thus, the placement of Desiderius suggests that he was himself a just earthly ruler, perhaps even the most important of the earthly rulers depicted, and certainly the latest in a lineage of just rulership. The central apse fresco left no question as to Desiderius' importance. In fact the most important of the examples of just earthly rulers were David and Solomon, whose location (in the entablature

above the capitals supporting the wall of the nave) suggested their support for and subordination to Desiderius' rule and building. Moreover, in the frescoes Desiderius became the successor of Solomon and so, not only promulgator of a new law, but also the builder of the new Temple. In this way, the art of St Angelo echoed the inscription at Montecassino: Desiderius' churches were sources for the new law.[60] They employed a metaphor for justice with significance for the very real debates over rulership in the eleventh century, debates that would erupt in violence and desecration in Capua (as discussed in Chapter 5).

It was this last theme of just rulership and the new law that Desiderius shared with Damian's sermon at the dedication. Both of these reformers attached the theme of spreading the law to a specific event in salvation history. It was this connection that lent force to their understanding of the event. Montecassino can help explain Damian's sermon. First, both interpreted the dedication in a typological manner, that is, in terms of biblical precedent, thus placing a local event, the dedication of this new church, into the larger context of the history of God's people. They then cast their congregation's vision forward and interpreted the dedication anagogically, in terms of the divine plan, the ultimate future of the Church. (The heavenly Church is the subject of the anagogical meaning.) The typological interpretation became an *exemplum* to which their behaviour ought to conform, the tropological meaning.[61] In Damian's hands the dedication of a new church became an important moment in the progress of salvation history.

For Damian, ultimately the liturgy of the dedication called to mind two great events in the history of God's people: the attack on Jericho (Joshua 6: 3–5) and the command to rebuild the Temple (Haggai). These two events provided the link between the tropological (moral) and the anagogical (future heavenly) meanings: a renewal of God's Church on earth, its evangelical mission to bring God's law to the world, and the coming of the Heavenly Jerusalem. Damian prefaced that discussion for his audience, however, by drawing a sharp distinction between those who live under the old law, and those who live under the new. He reminded his listeners (and his later readers) of the difference between a church and a synagogue. A synagogue was a mere congregation while an *ecclesia* was a convocation; brute animals might congregate, but to be convoked belongs to those with reason.[62] The former saw only externalities, while the reasoned penetrated mysteries and recognised in the liturgy and themselves, as the Church, a sacrament of divine power, and not, as it appeared to the foolish, only a child's game.[63]

It is very likely that Damian did not here intend any actual synagogue. Rather, this was the language adopted by the papal reform party following Damian's lead after the schism of 1061. At that time, imperial supporters had charged that papal reformers were being too liberal in asserting the scriptural basis for sacerdotal authority. The pro-imperial reformers insisted on a more literal reading of the Old Testament to demonstrate that kings were meant to have authority over priests. Damian, in response to these arguments, had already insisted upon a more mystical (here sacramental) reading of scripture, or as Robinson and Smalley have described it, 'political allegory', in order to defend the *novus ordo* of the cardinalate, and denounce the literal reading of the scriptures as a product of the 'old law'.[64] By referring his listeners to the new and old laws he has placed them in the frame of *renovatio* and reform exegesis with which they had become increasingly familiar. In so doing, he prefaced the parallel drawn between the liturgy for the dedication and its Old Testament precedent (Exodus 40: 1–15). While the dedication might seem to have reaffirmed the Old Testament order on its surface, Damian went on to explain, in reality it established the new law of the Spirit.

Mystical and political allegory in Peter Damian's sermon on the dedication

Damian's sermon followed the fourfold exegetical method typical of mediaeval scriptural commentators. In the mediaeval sense, it was an *exegesis* of the liturgy of the dedication. In addition, the structure of the sermon followed the unique commentary style of the *Quid significent* (i.e., an article-by-article commentary on the dedication rite). To begin with the typological sense: the initial sprinkling of the church in the name of the Trinity recalled for Damian the Israelites' exodus through the desert, the bitterness of the water they found and how it was made sweet by the staff of Moses. So, too, the old law, served carnally, was bitter, but was now made sweet by the Cross which offered spiritual understanding and grace.[65] As the elements of the Greek and Latin alphabet were written on the floor of the new church, so did this new basilica inscribe the new law in the hearts of the congregation.[66] The dedication set the Christian community apart as the bearers of the new divine law, even as it placed that community within the Old Testament story.[67]

The turn to the heart became a call for conversion (the tropological), not just of the individual but of the entire community. The basilica represented the secret heart, the book of God on which heavenly commands

are written, a bookcase of law, a school of spiritual study and a true city of letters.[68] This new church, then, was to be the library of the Word of God, a community living under God's precepts (here the anagogical sense). It was to be an ideal Church, each member in conversation with God.[69] Each member was truly in direct communication and society with God when they were in the church participating in its rites, in prayer and in the readings from the New Testament. Once again, Damian has reconnected his congregation with the ancient Israelites in the desert, speaking with God on his holy mountain. From the outset, then, Damian established a pattern of interpretive movement from the typological to the tropological to the anagogical: from the Old Testament precedent, to a call for personal reform, and a hoped-for, idealised Church of the reformed. With each return to these themes he reinforced and expanded the image of the fully realised Church.

The typological context for Damian's seven circuits around the altar of the new basilica, blessing its walls in dedication, was the seven circuits the priests and people of Israel made around the city of Jericho. The force of this Old Testament metaphor, and Damian's introductory image of the new church as a city of God's Word, would seem to direct him to interpret this new basilica as a type of promised land, or new Jerusalem, but Damian resisted the obvious and chose a bolder interpretation. The basilica's altar, standing for Jericho, was the entire unconverted world, the priests were not carrying the ark of the covenant but rather the Church itself, and the horn blast of the preaching of 'the doctrine of truth' by the preachers of the holy Church sapped the walls that are the exalted and the haughty, of infidelity, pride and objections.[70] Rather than turning this individual church into a metaphorical heaven, Damian identified it as part of a larger effort to convert the entire world. This was reminiscent of Desiderius' view of the importance of his basilica: making the law known to all.[71] Damian's new church would only become the promised land when it was consecrated; in turn it became a stepping stone in the conversion of the world; this church, as Desiderius', was to bear the light of the new law to all the world.

The message, so eloquently but subtly delivered in the image of Jericho, must not be overlooked. For it is here that Damian's sermon took a turn away from the moral and toward mystical allegory. The gospel for the dedication was the story of Zaccheus (Luke 19: 1–10). When Jesus, upon entering Jericho, met the wealthy tax collector Zaccheus and offered to dine with him in his home, Zaccheus promised to give half of his possessions to the poor and repay by fourfold those whom he had defrauded.

To which Jesus replied, 'Today salvation has come to his house, because he too is a son of Abraham.' Thus, in the minds of his audience, Christ's entry into Jericho and meeting with Zaccheus could have had two ready associations: first, a message for the wealthy of a community, certainly present at the dedication; second, the question: who is a child of Abraham? Damian would have been emphasising these two associations by allegorising the walls of Jericho as the exalted and the esteemed. In short, Damian's message on this occasion was a strong one: not only did he expand the image of the dedication in order to incorporate the conversion of the entire earth, but he identified the obstacles to this conversion as being the exalted and the esteemed (*elati quilibet atque sublimes*).[72] He had begun to employ a kind of mystical allegory of ecclesio-political significance. The dedication of a basilica would have been crowded, certainly with local magnates, and, depending on its importance, potentially regional or pan-European lay and ecclesiastical leaders (as at Montecassino). In other words, by declaring the exalted and esteemed an obstacle to the fulfilment of the Church's mission, Damian was criticising the most powerful portion of his congregation. In an era receptive to an ideology placing kings, and perhaps lesser leaders, closer to God, Damian would have been inverting his audience's expectations.[73] In the context of the liturgy, to become true sons of Abraham in order to enter into the promised land of salvation, the wealthy and powerful must purge themselves of their injustices. In Damian's sermon, they must humble themselves before Christ.[74] The mystical had become political.

Damian then commented on the liturgy in a manner that reflected contemporary reform concerns. When the bishop, having circled the church, rapped three times on its door and proclaimed the Psalm, 'Raise your gates, princes, and be lifted up, ancient doors, so that the King of Glory may enter',[75] Damian confronted a moment rife with the tensions between the authority of the bishops (as vicars of Christ) and secular authority. By claiming that the walls were the 'exalted and the esteemed' he had unmistakably associated these with the princes of Psalm 23 (24) (above). By declaring them an obstacle to the true Church, torn down by preaching (an episcopal responsibility), he was, in essence, asserting the primacy of sacerdotal over lay authority. Damian's sermon, here, marked a break with the Carolingian interpretation of the liturgy, moving to a broader appreciation of its power. The *Quid significent* had interpreted the bishop rapping on the doors of the new church as a reminder of his apostolic position and episcopal responsibilities.[76] Damian, instead, used the occasion so as to deliver a powerful warning to the social elite.

Damian heightened this sense of social reversal through his interpretation of the anointing of the altar. He began with the conventional interpretation of the Church as being made of living stones.[77] Like Jacob anointing the foundation stone of Bethlehem, so, too, the unction of the altar made the church 'undoubtedly the house of God'.[78] Moreover, this represented the anointing of the body of Christ, the universal Church. The altar represented Christ, and was the head of the church, while the building was made of living stones, the 'inferior members' of the body of Christ.[79]

At this point, however, Damian went further than his predecessors. He claimed that everyone who was connected by genuine faith to Christ acquires the dignity of a royal priesthood: anointed as priests, since they received the oil of the Holy Spirit *in regeneratione* (i.e., baptism), and as kings because they bore the standard of the cross on their foreheads.[80] He pointed his listeners to the words of Peter (I Peter 2: 9) and the song of the saints in Revelation (5: 10): 'You have made us a kingdom and priests for our God and they will reign upon the earth.' This call was made more immediate by the object *nos* instead of *eos*.[81] The challenge, then, was directed toward Damian's present, rather than being confined to the biblical past. It was Damian's listeners who have been made into the new kingdom, a new priesthood.[82]

In short, Damian had taken the occasion of the dedication to deliver a strongly personal but also eschatological message. Having distinguished the Christian community from the original Israelites, he offered a radical vision of 'the true Church'. This Church, a Church of living stones whose members were all anointed as priests and kings, was tearing down the walls of the exalted and the proud, the unfaithful and the resistant, and converting the entire world *in hoc tempore*.[83]

Damian issued a subtle message with serious import for his listeners; he questioned their role within the Church and its mission. Having laid down this challenge, he stepped back. He told his audience that he wanted to 'touch lightly' on the significance of various liturgical elements 'of profound mystery'.[84] For several minutes of preaching, he moved from one element of the liturgy and the church to the next, saying a few words about each. There is a sense of inventory, or cataloguing, in many dedication commentaries, and here Damian's sermon took on those qualities.[85] At the same time, however, the section was centred on many of the same motifs already examined.

Damian paused and apologised to his listeners lest he burden their charity with an excess of detail. The water and wine intermingled at the consecration represented the Old and New Testaments. As Christ turned

water into wine at the marriage feast (John 2: 1–9), so, too, the law was instantly changed in our hearts.[86] This reading of the wedding at Cana derived, most likely, from Augustine's commentary on the passage.[87] Likewise, the salt represented the bitter old law made sweet by the spiritual understanding of the gospels.[88] Thus, Damian continued his strategy of pulling his congregation from Old Testament precedent to the present events of the dedication, and then distinguishing the Christian community by pointing to the new, interior law. He pointed to the elements of that interior life – purity, humility and, above all, charity – by means of the ornaments of the church and tools of the liturgy. The hyssop represented faith as it purified our secret heart (*pectoris arcana*). That faith purified the heart (*corda*) was an allusion to Acts 15: 9, but the shift from *cor* to *pectus* might point to another source for Damian's attachment of purity to hyssop.[89] Ashes represented humility.[90]

Of the three dimensions of the interior law, the most important for Damian was charity. The fervour of charity was represented through an enigmatic red fragment (*speciem rubei fragminis*), which reminded the faithful of Adam, who was made from red earth, representing both humility and charity. This charity must not be allowed to grow lukewarm.[91]

Damian now directed his gaze to the building itself: what, he asks, was the sacramental significance of this church, which we both are, and dedicate?[92] Pausing, he offered a brief, cautionary allegory on the importance of cementing and fortifying a stone structure that, on the volatile Italian peninsula of the late eleventh century, would have been appreciated by all.[93]

> Moreover, you will observe, dearest ones, that this basilica is made from stones and cement; but if the wall of a rampart, itself standing on high, is assembled with stone alone, and they were not held together by a lime and sand paste, then, at an attack of any violence at all, whatever was constructed would inevitably be destroyed.[94]

Damian used the striking image to great effect. What was the temple of God, if not the people of God? What were the stones, if not humans? What was the mortar, if not the sticky coagulate of charity? Not everyone so called belongs to Christ, not everyone who has the society of the Church was truly a member of the ecclesiastical body.[95] 'Charity alone', Damian warned, distinguished those who belong to Christ from those who belong to Antichrist.[96]

Damian delivered a message that appears especially directed toward social and ecclesiastical elites. (The dedication rite expected the lay lord

and builder of the church to be addressed directly.) The castles, towers, monasteries and churches, the domains of the powerful elite that provide safety in a violent world were held together by mortar. Likewise, the Christian community was held together by charity; fraternity depended upon it. It was charity that allied one with Christ and made one a member of his mystical body. Overtly, therefore, Damian was warning his audience that without charity they were outside the Church, of the Antichrist, and, so, condemned. Indeed, the biblical imagery that Damian employed of the proud as builders of towers was also the language employed by the Milanese *pataria*.[97] Damian knew their critiques and how these could rapidly be transformed into civil strife and violence at first hand, having been nearly attacked by a mob while in Ambrose's city in 1059.[98] In fact, he had used similar language in his own exhortation to the Roman Prefect Cencius, warning him against the infernal building programmes of Richard, abbot of St Vanne.[99] The language of vain builders was, therefore, a contemporary critique of an episcopate rooted in the military aristocracy.

Damian's rhetorical observation that the walls of the church could be easily overthrown without charity points directly to the transformation of the personal charismatic leadership of reform (of which Damian's early career was emblematic) into the kind of institutional charisma such as the building of a church that helped his contemporaries control the Italian peninsula.[100] Damian's metaphor was a thinly disguised social threat: without charity the structures that provide security would fail and collapse. In a culture accustomed to thinking about society as a body whose members must act in a unified manner, where social disruption was therefore often understood to reflect the moral disorder of society, Damian need not have overstated his threat.[101] He simply needed to remind his listeners of the defensive structures, including the basilica, that surrounded them and to connect that timely reminder to the imagery of the union of the church (*ecclesiae societatem*), and the unity of the ecclesial body (*ecclesiastici corporis . . . unitatem*).[102] Thus, Damian impressed upon the congregation the present and eternal value of Christian charity.

The final movement of Damian's sermon was structured around the more conventional theme of the people of God as the temple of God. This conventionality was recast by Damian as a discussion of temple pollution and restoration. Damian prefaced this exploration of ecclesiastical reform based on Old Testament imagery by characterising the Antichrist and heretics as slavish, carnal and literal in their following of the law.[103] Damian continued to be concerned to distinguish the new Israelites from the old. The last lines of the sermon were, 'I will walk among them, and I will live with

them, and I will be their God'. This was a Pauline paraphrase of Leviticus, the very old law Damian had condemned all along. Even as he drew on Old Testament imagery to assert the unity of the Church as the people of God, and to assert the need for reform within that Church, Damian distinguished the new reformed community from the community of the old law.

The distinction between the old and new law became all the more important as Damian concluded with a more conventionally hierarchical view of the reform Church, even as he called for its reform. Before closing he raised the possibility that the consecrated church might become contaminated, either by bloodshed or some grave crime, and need to be reconsecrated by the 'highest priest'.[104] Likewise, an individual became the temple of God at baptism, and, so, might become contaminated, a contamination that could be cleansed by the clergy:

> If we are stained by the leprosy of serious guilt, mother Church is to be immediately approached, and the pontiff beseeched, so that the temple of our soul, which is considered violated and even destroyed by inhuman crime, may be renewed again through the office of priestly authority and the remedy of appropriate satisfaction.[105]

Earlier, Damian was willing to assert the royal priesthood of all believers to deliver a strong warning to the magnates of the community; here he emphasised the role of the office of the priest and the episcopal structure as the basis of individual spiritual reform, and thus reasserted sacerdotal authority. Damian was no longer interested in social inversion as a tool for ecclesiastical completion or for entering the promised land *in hoc tempore*. Here, the priestly office became a sure conduit for divine power and, by implication, the priest became an icon for Christ. There was no doubt that this restoration of the spiritual temple, which was rendered through the office of the visible priest, was fulfilled on the inside through the effect of divine virtue and power. 'Christ, who is the true king and the priest, renews and reforms into [something] better, through the largess of grace, what he finds destroyed and collapsed in humanity through the artifice of the evil spirit.'[106]

The realisation of the Christian community came about through the action of the priest, acting as intermediary for Christ. The consecration of this church became a call to rededicate the spiritual, interior temple. In this way Damian had become, as the one dedicating and preaching, one of the priests carrying the ark of the Church around the walls of hypocrisy and infidelity, sounding the horn of preaching.[107] Clerical authority was on the move to undermine the ramparts of the powerful.

As at the restoration of the Temple in Jerusalem in the time of the prophet Haggai, the new, renewed Temple was greater than the first. Christ was the royal priest who would restore the temple to even greater grace.[108] Damian called his listeners to reform the temple of their souls by seeking forgiveness at the hands of their pontiffs. More than restoring his listeners, the pontiffs could bring them into full union with Christ.[109] This was the fulfilment of the Christian life, and, by extension, an eschatological vision of the Christian community. Damian immediately pointed to the significance of the restoration of the Temple for the Israelites, 'and all desired things will come to the people together, and I will fill this house with glory, says the Lord of hosts'.[110] The passage linked ecclesial unity with the restoration of the sacred site.

Cardinal and Bishop Damian concluded the sermon with an examination of various sins and their remedies. Eliminate vice, he admonished his congregation, and it would be replaced with the ornaments of *virtutes*.[111] The image was a striking one, with many levels of meaning similar to the *insignitia* of his Venetian sermon. The image hinged on the mediaeval word *virtus*; as Damian used it here, it had a double force. In the first place, it was an active message, with a passive response: eliminate vice, and virtue replaced it. But the image was of the redecoration of a church in ruins, the re-ornamentation of a neglected structure. In this sense, *virtus* implied a miraculous force, or divine characteristic, where the individual became a reflection of a church, ornamented with icons. In late eleventh-century Rome, it would be an apt image indeed. As one banished the ugliness of vice, a church was ornamented with icons and sacramental objects that brought one closer to God. It was an image of the perfection and interiorisation of Christian cult, of the relation between grace and free will, as experienced in that perfected cult.

The last few moments of the sermon centred on the specifics of the interior life. Depraved aspirations, rage and anger, luxury, vain thoughts, envy, libidinousness and fornication: these vices must be eliminated because they destroyed the temple of the heart.[112] It was the bishop, the pontiff, who was the primary tool at the disposal of sinners for combating this corruption.[113] The pontiffs of the Church, or rather 'that pontiff who holds principally the power of restoration', were at the very centre of the restoration of this new, interior cult of the temple. The pontiffs were the new priestly class of a restored temple.

Damian concluded, aptly, by returning to Leviticus by way of St Paul. He warned his listeners that the new Israel followed a renewed, interiorised cult. With the restoration of this cult, God and his people dwelt

together. 'Our mind ought not be an oven of obscene luxury, or a cesspool of carnal passion, nor a pig's wallow of vice, but let it be, with God's help, a hall of spiritual virtues, which the celestial inhabitant might deign to visit, and inhabit the temple of a heart dedicated to him.'[114] Damian had turned to the old law, as restated by Paul, to summarise this vision of the fulfilled Christian community. He referred to this Pauline paraphrase of Leviticus, thus sanitised, simply as the words of the prophet: 'I will walk among them, and I will live among them, and I will be their God.'[115]

The sermon, taken as a whole, emphasises the restoration of God's people. It was an eschatological, fulfilled vision of the Church. It was a vision of a Christian community in full union with God. It moved from a discussion of the fulfilled community, bound together by the interior law of charity, to a discussion of the individual Christian as temple of God. If, in the former discussion of the Christian community, Damian was more willing to overturn social expectations, that was because he was delivering a pointed warning to the magnates of Italian society about the need for charity within Christian society.[116] If the latter utilised a more conventional metaphor it did so to emphasise pontifical authority in cleansing the corrupt body. The sermon was consistent in presenting the priests of the Church as leading the effort to reform the Church and draw it into its fulfilled state. Indeed, by the end of the sermon Damian had strongly affirmed the power of the priestly class, and the central role of the episcopate, the pontiffs, in restoring each individual Christian soul as a place of worship. It presented a strong model of sacerdotal authority in Christian society.

Thus, Damian and Desiderius incorporated the novel strategy of applying a mystical allegory of political import to the exegesis of the dedication rite. These reformers began to change how the dedication was viewed in eleventh-century Italy and would do so at a time of intensive church building and dedication within the city. The generation that followed these ecclesiasts capitalised on these novel meanings of the dedication liturgy. Damian did not live to see Hildebrand succeed Peter. Gregory VII's innermost circle would lead the effort to expand the pro-papal, pro-reform import of the liturgy. Anselm II, exiled bishop of Lucca, Gregory's staunchest clerical ally and spiritual advisor to Matilda of Tuscany (Gregory's most committed military ally), was set the task of compiling the precedents to defend the Gregorian model of the papacy. Anselm would use architectural and dedicatory metaphors to assert the specifically papal prerogative within the Church. Under Anselm's direction these legal texts would claim papal authority over all dedications, in fact, all consecrations.

Anselm's collection of canons would also use the imagery of the dedication rite to reinforce the basis for papal authority.

Notes

1 Damian, *Sermones*, 16, 7.114–20.
2 Repsher, *Rite of Church Dedication*, 36, characterising a variety of later exe-
getes, including Damian, claims, 'These later writers are only continuing in
the tradition of interpretation that reached its fullest expression in the ninth
century'. This is the underlying assumption in Lee Bowen, 'The Tropology
of Mediaeval Dedication Rites', *Speculum* (1941): 469–79. See also Daniel J.
Sheerin 'Dedication "Ordo" Used at Fulda, 1 Nov., 819', *Revue Bénédictine*
(1982): 304–16. A reading of Carolingian ecclesiastical architecture aware of
contemporary iconographic controversy is provided by Susan A. Rabe, 'The
Mind's Eye: Theological Controversy and Religious Architecture in the Reign
of Charlemagne', in Lizette Larson-Miller, *Medieval Liturgy: A Book of Essays*
(New York, 1977), 235–66. Dominique Iogna-Prat implies the same while rightly
pointing to the new context for the commentaries in the eleventh century,
although he does not here consider the eleventh-century in detail, 'Lieu de culte
et exégèse liturgique à l'époque carolingienne', in Celia Chazelle and Burton Van
Name Edwards (eds), *The Study of the Bible in the Carolingian Era* (Turnhout,
Brepols, 2003): 215–44, 242–3.Horie, *Perceptions of* Ecclesia, ignores the eleventh century.
3 PRG, 1: [xxxv].
4 On the importance of contemporary context in understanding liturgical significance, see Flanigan, 'Apocalypse and the Medieval Liturgy', 333–51 at 342.
5 Cowdrey, *Desiderius*, 36 n. 157. Part of this sermon is still preserved in
an eleventh-century manuscript from Montecassino: Biblioteca dell'Abbazia
359, fols 79r–83r. Two complete twelfth-century versions are also extant:
Vatican City, BAV, Chigianus A. V. 145, fols 8r–10r, and Florence, Biblioteca
Laurenziana, Acquisti e doni 84, fols 50r–2r. See Lucchesi's remarks in Damian,
Sermones, xviii and 420. There do not seem to have been any significant dedications at Ostia during Damian's episcopate. Internal evidence, discussed below,
suggests the sermon was delivered at a major dedication, but is not definitive.
Damian is known to have dedicated at least one monastic church, but any one
of the monastic communities he founded is a possibility for the sermon. See
Damian, *Sermones*, 72, at 1.1–6, 3.43–6, and 4.57 for the most suggestive passages
concerning the occasion of the sermon.
6 For an excellent example of political iconography and exegesis see Leslie
Brubaker, *Vision and Meaning in Ninth-Century Byzantium: Image as Exegesis
in the Homilies of Gregory of Nazianus* (Cambridge, 1999), esp. 147–200.
7 I.S. Robinson, '"Political Allegory" in the Biblical Exegesis of Bruno of Segni',
Recherches de théologie ancienne et médiévale 50 (1983), 69–98.
8 For a parallel example see Howe, *Church Reform,* on Dominic of Sora.

9   See the 'Select Bibliography' in Peter Damian, *Letters 1–30*, trans. Owen J. Blum, OFM (Washington, DC, 1989), xi–xviii. For a brief summary of the important events of his life, see ibid, 3–11. Giovanni Lucchesi, 'Per una vita di San Pier Damian', *San Pier Damian nel ix centenario della morte (1072–1972)*, 4 Vols (Cesena, 1972–3), 1: 26–8; and 'Il Sermonario di S. Pier Damian come monumento storico agiografico e liturgico', *Studi Gregoriani* 10 (1975): 7–67, esp. 12–13, 31–6.

10 Kennerly M. Woody, 'Damian and the Radicals' (PhD diss., Columbia University, 1966).

11 As Howe observes, *Church Reform*, 23.

12 Patricia Skinner, *Family Power in Southern Italy* (Cambridge, 1995), 170–72. So too the Abbey of Santissima Trinità in Cava near Salerno, the dedication of which by Urban II in 1092 will be discussed in the next chapter. See Valerie Ramseyer, *The Transformation of a Religious Landscape: Medieval Southern Italy, 850–1150* (Ithaca, 2006).

13 See Table 5. These numbers are conservative with named dedications, not all construction. Works consulted include Walther Buchowiecki, *Handbuch der Kirchen Roms: Der Romische Sakralbau in Geschichte und Kunst von der altchristlichen Zeit bis zur Gegenwart* (Vienna, 1967–74); Vincenzo Forcella, *Iscrizioni delle chiese e d'altri edificii di Roma dal secolo XI fino ai giorni nostri* (Rome, 1869–84); Paul F. Kehr, *Regesta Pontificum Romanorum*, Vol. 1: *Roma* (Berlin, 1961 [1906]); Richard Krautheimer, *Corpus basilicarum christianorum Romae: The Early Christian Basilicas of Rome (IV–IX Cent.)* (Vatican City, 1937–77), 5 Vols; Christian Hülsen, *Le chiese di Roma nel medioevo* (Florence, 1927); and Ferruccio Lombardi, *Roma: Chiese, Conventi, Chiostri. Progetto per un inventario, 313–1925* (Rome, 1993). On S. Clemente see Leonard E. Boyle, 'The Date of the Consecration of the Basilica of San Clemente', *San Clemente Miscellany II: Art and Archaeology* (Rome, 1978), 1–12 (reprint of *Archivium Fratrum Praedicatorum* 30 (1960): 417–27); and Federico Guidobaldi, *Il Complesso Archeologico di San Clemente: Resulti degli scavi più recenti e riesame dei resti architettonici* (Rome, 1978). For a broader list, including construction and possible dedications see Hamilton, 'Power of Liturgy', Appendix A.

14 See esp. 'Rome and the Patrimony of St Peter', in Robinson, *The Papacy*, 17–21; Blumenthal, *Investiture Controversy*, 64–98, 113–26; and Gerd Tellenbach, 'La Città di Roma dal IX al XII secolo Vista dai Contemporanei d'Oltre Frontiera', in *Studi Storici in Onore di Ottorino Bartolini* (Pisa, 1972) 679–734.

15 Gerd Tellenbach, *The Church in Western Europe from the Tenth through the Twelfth Century* (Cambridge, 1993), 140–1.

16 Ramseyer, *Transformation of a Religious Landscape*, 46–54, 61–4.

17 This relationship between the political and religious landscape is clearly articulated in Howe, *Church Reform*, xiii–xxiii, 160–1.

18 See Robinson, 'Political Allegory', 76–8, 84–6; and Beryl Smalley, *The Becket Conflict and the Schools: A Study of Intellectuals in Politics* (Oxford, 1973). The term 'political allegory' does not come from Damian, who refers to the mystical or sacramental meaning. It bears re-emphasising that 'political' as used here is a

strictly modern idea, and risks creating distinctions between the proper subject of religion and that of politics that Damian would not have recognised.

19 Margit Dischner, *Humbert von Silva Candida: Werk und Wirkung des lothringischen Reformmönches* (Novotny, Starnberg, 1996); J.T. Gilchrist, 'Humbert of Silva-Candida and the Political Concept of *Ecclesia* in the Eleventh Century Reform Movement', *Journal of Religious History* 2 (1962–1963): 13–28; Walter Ullmann, 'Cardinal Humbert and the *Ecclesia Romana*', *Studi Gregoriani* IV (1952), 111–27.

20 See Hamilton, 'Sexual Purity', 237–59. Blumenthal, *Investiture Controversy*, 75–6.

21 Elaine Golden Robison, 'Humbert of Silva Candida', *DMA* 6, 329–30.

22 Blumenthal, *Investiture Controversy*, 87–9.

23 *Humberti Cardinalis Adversus Simoniacos*, LdL 2, 214, 10–15.

24 Ibid., 222–3.

25 Having read Augustine more closely it seems: Hamilton, 'Sexual Purity', 249–53.

26 Vogel, *Medieval Liturgy*, 237–9. The PRG contains commentaries on liturgies as well as didactic texts. It may have served as a handbook of correct practice. See PRG, 3: 32, 50–1. The extant Roman and Cassinese copies of the *Quid significent* are Montecassino, Biblioteca dell'Abbazia 451, fols 22r–33v; Rome, Biblioteca Vallicelliana D. 5, fols 18v–27v. See Andrieu, *Ordines Romani* 1: 176–7, 184. Bruno of Segni and Peter certainly had contact with the text at Montecassino, if not at Rome.

27 See Repsher, *Rite of Church Dedication*, 194–233, for a detailed discussion. More poetic, though similar, is Bowen, 'Tropology of Mediaeval Dedication Rites', 470. Christopher A. Jones, 'The Book of Liturgy in Anglo-Saxon England', *Speculum* 73 (1998): 659–702, though also considering them as a largely undifferentiated whole offers a more subtle appreciation of the early commentaries.

28 Repsher, *Rite of Church Dedication*, 232–3.

29 Collections containing Bede are Vatican City, BAV, S. Pietro C 103 and C 105; see Paola Supino Martini, *Roma e l'Area Grafica Romanesca (Secoli X–XII)* (Alessandria, 1987), 59, citing Bede, Homilia 21, *In Dedicatione Ecclesiae* (PL 94: 244A–C, 245C–46A, and 248D–49A). The Roman Homiliary included Sermons 47 and 49 of Eusebius 'Gallicanus' on dedications (ed. Iohannes Leroy, *Corpus Christianorum Latina* [CCL] 101A [Turnhout, 1971], 555 and 573), and 227 of Cesarius of Arles (ed. D. Germanus Morin, CCL 104 [Turnhout, 1953], 897–900) for the feast of the dedication. The homiliaries of St Peter's and of Eginon of Verona most likely also contained these homilies. The Roman Homiliary of Agimond (copies of which were made in eleventh-century Montecassino and ninth- or tenth-century Rome) also contained Sermons 158 and 19 of Cesarius on dedications, as does the Homiliary, Vatican City, BAV, Vat. lat. 3828. The Homiliary of Paul the Deacon added Bede's homilies 24, 25 both on the dedication (ed. D. Hurst, CCL 122 [Turnhout, 1955], 358–78), and 66 (PL 94: 439–41). Among manuscript collections are Vatican City, BAV, Chigianus P VIII (s. XI), fols 283v–5v contains Cesarius, Sermo 227 and Bede, Homilia 66 (interestingly

followed by a Life of St Nicholas); Reg. lat. 496 (s. XI, French), fols 114r–22v contains two dedication sermons: Cesarius, Sermo 227, Bede, Homilia 66, and another unidentified homily on the dedication attributed to Bede beginning 'stetit itaque rex'; Vat. lat. 8563 (s. X–XI), fols 247r–57v contains Bede, Homiliae 24, 25 and 66. Vat. lat. 5055 has a brief commentary at fol. 43v with 'de xiii [*sic*] crucibus in dedicatione ecclesiae' in rubrics (its ecclesiology is that of Christ as bridegroom) and takes a sermon for the feast of the dedication from Jerome's *Tractatus in Psalmos 137* (ed. D. Germanus Morin, CCL 78 [Turnhout, 1958], 39) at 59r. While both Peter Damian and Bruno of Segni could have consulted any of these it seems clear that the exemplar they had before them (and deviated from) was the *Quid significent*, as it is unusual in its structure (being a direct commentary on the Pontifical).

30 See note 4 above.

31 Damian, *Die Briefe*, n. 40, 437, 4–9.

32 Ibid., n. 146, 535, 11–14.

33 Krautheimer, 'Iconography of Medieval Architecture'; Töpfer, 'The Cult of Relics and Pilgrimage', 45–8. A careful cataloguing of dedications has been done for Cornwall and Devon and provides guidance for the relationships between those churches; Nicholas Orme, *English Church Dedications, With a Survey of Cornwall and Devon* (Exeter, 1996).

34 *Sermones*, 14, 145–55.

35 Ibid., 16, 1.12–16.

36 See Jerome, *De viris illustribus* I, PL 23, 638–9.

37 *Sermones*, 15, 5. 97–102. Hic vero de quo nunc agitur sanctus evangelista Marcus de Alexandria transuectus est, Deo misericorditer disponente, Venetiam, ut qui tunc totum orientem velut aureus lucifer illustraverat, nunc per plagas occidui climatis praesentiae suae radiis enitescat. *Per Aegyptum quippe sibi dedicat ortum, per Venetiam tenet occasum.* [Emphasis mine.]

38 Damian grants Peter the title of evangelist; ibid., 16–19.

39 Gaude igitur et exultans in Domino plaude, Venetia . . . Quamobrem, sicut mater urbium Roma super omnia regna terrarum sublimatur in Petro, sic et tu, velut eius *insignia* filia, per Marcam gloriaris in Christo. *Sermones*, 16, 7.114–120.

40 The dedication of the church graces the central tympanum of the rebuilt S. Marco (dedicated in the last two decades of the eleventh century). While the current mosaics are later in date they are considered representative of the eleventh-century original. Dale, 'Inventing a Sacred Past', 90. The Venetian doge and chronicler Andrea Dandolo was also aware of Damian's historical writing and his repute. RIS 12, nos 1–4.

41 Damian, *Die Briefe*, n. 65, 233 B 34. See also Josef Szövérffy, 'The legends of St Peter in Medieval Latin Hymns', and 'Der Investiturstreit und die Petrus-Hymnen des Mittelalters' (esp. 53–6), in *Religious Lyrics of the Middle Ages* (Berlin, 1983).

42 *Historia Consecrationis*, RIS 6, pt. 5, 47–8.

43 Richard Hodges, *Light in the Dark Ages: The Rise and Fall of San Vincenzo al Volturno* (Ithaca, 1997). Chris Wickham, 'Il problema dell'incastellamento

nell'Italia centrale: l'esempio di San Vincenzo al Volturno', in Federico Marazzi ed., *San Vincenzo al Volturno: Cultura, istituzioni, economia* (Abbazia di Montecassino, 1996). Ramseyer, *Transformation of a Religious Landscape*, 158–92.

44 *Sermones*, 72, 3.43–7.

45 For the dedication of St Odilo, see *De Gallica Petri Damian profectione*, MGH SS 30, 16, 1044. Damian references the *tollite portas*, a moment not found in every dedication liturgy, suggesting that wherever this dedication was the rite may have included that psalm and its typical encircling of the church. See the excellent study of Didier Méhu on Cluniac dedications, 'Les Cercles de la domination clunisienne', *Annales de Bourgogne* 72 (2000): 337–96. Méhu observes nicely the relationship between the expansion of construction, the execution of the rites and the granting of greater privileges. Susan L. Boynton notes that Damian could have been part of Nicholas II's dedicatory entourage in July of 1060 (bringing new texts and hymns), see Boynton, 'Liturgy and History at the Abbey of Farfa in the Late Eleventh Century, Hymns of Peter Damian and Other Additions to BAV Chigi C.VI.177', *Sacris Erudiri* 39 (2000), 317–44, at 334–5.

46 On these matters, Cowdrey, *Desiderius*, 73–79. See also Bloch, *Monte Cassino*, 1: 54, 91–3, 96–7. Whether Desiderius introduced Byzantine artists onto the peninsula and whether these were the source of artistic revival, or if he drew instead upon local or regional artists in executing his artistic programmes, is a subject of some debate. Most historians appear to be drawn to the latter position. The current trend is to view the artistic and architectural revival of the eleventh century as an extension of reforming ideologies.Toubert, 'Didier du Mont-Cassin', 17–106; Speciale, 'Montecassino, Il classicismo', *Desiderio di Montecassino*, 107–46; Gunhouse, 'Fresco Decoration of Sant'Angelo in Formis'; Speciale, *Montecassino e la Riforma Gregoriana*; Toubert, *Un art dirigé*; Cowdrey, *Desiderius*, 1–45; Krautheimer, *Rome: Profile of a City*, 170; Glass, *Studies on Cosmatesque Pavements*. On St Angelo in Formis and the Byzantine question, see Bloch, *Monte Cassino*, 60–5. Likewise St Martin's in Lucca may be seen within the context of *renovatio*; Romano Silva, 'La Ricostruzione della Cattedrale di Lucca (1060–1070): Un Esempio Precoce di Architettura della Riforma Gregoriana', in Violante, *Sant'Anselmo Vescovo*, 297–309.

47 Cowdrey, 15, n. 73. A sentiment much like Damian's own sense of the cardinalate as a '*renovatio* of the senate'; idem, 74.

48 Haec domus est similis Synai sacra iura ferenti/ Ut lex demonstrat, hic que fuit edita quondam./ Lex hinc exivit, mentes quae ducit ab imis,/ Et vulgata dedit lumen per clymata saecli. *Chron. Cas.*, MGH SS 34, 3.28, 397; see Bloch, *Monte Cassino*, 1: 53. The comparison with Sinai is rich: it was there that the cult was established, the Israelites consecrated and the law given. See also comparison to the law at Chiusa (as discussed above in Chapter 2).

49 Although what is being brought forth here is *sacra iura*, it is rightly equated with the gospels (i.e., evangelisation) because it is playing on the contrast between the 'old law' of the Jewish faith and the 'new law' of Christianity.

50 Ecce, Casinus abundat eis,/ mons venerabilis, aula Dei,/ mons Sion altera, dux
    fidei,/ mons ubi iura Deus populo/ scripta suo tribuit digito. Alfanus of Salerno,
    I carmi di Alfano I, Arcivescovo di Salerno, eds Anselmo Lentini and Faustino
    Avagliano, *Miscellanea Casinese* 38 (Montecassino, 1974), 173.

51 Haec domus est similis Sinai sacra iura ferenti/ Ut lex demonstrat, hic que fuit
    edita quondam./ Ut, duce te, patria iustis potiatur adepta./ Hinc Desiderius pater
    hanc tibi condidit aulum. *I carmi di Alfano I*, 139.

52 Most recently by Toubert, 'Didier du Mont-Cassin', 17–105.

53 Ibid., 75.

54 G.A. Loud, *Church and Society in the Norman Principality of Capua, 1058–1197*
    (Oxford, 1985), 49.

55 This antipathy also explains why Henry IV would turn to this same Hildebrand
    for support against Gregory VII in 1081; Cowdrey, *Desiderius*, 149. It is remark-
    able that Desiderius, then Abbot of Montecassino, would use Capua as the loca-
    tion for the council that would elect him pope in 1087. This signals perhaps both
    the dominance of Cassino and the importance of Norman Capua. Ibid., 201–4.
    That Montecassino produced nine episcopal appointees for the principality
    of Capua between 1059 and 1115 without ever claiming the metropolitan see of
    Capua might also suggest the vigorous independence of Capua. Loud, *Church
    and Society*, 46–7.

56 Loud, *Church and Society*, 49–53.

57 G.A. Loud, 'Nunneries, Nobles and Women in the Norman Principality of
    Capua', *Annali Canossani 1, Reggio Emilia* (1981), 45–62; reprinted in *Conquerors
    and Churchmen in Norman Italy* (Aldershot, 1999), 57.

58 Loud, 'Nunneries, Nobles', 50.

59 Discussed below in Chapter 5. For a full discussion, see Hamilton, 'Desecration
    and Consecration', 137–50.

60 I would like to thank Didier Méhu for this observation.

61 See Gabrielle M. Spiegel, 'Political Utility in Medieval Historiography', *History
    and Theory* 14 (1975): 314–25, esp. 321. Compare with Bede, *Homilia* 21 (PL 94:
    243–9 at 247D–9A), who is content mainly to retell the story of the rebuilding of
    the temple while only very indirectly implying a need for reform.

62 *Sermones*, 72, 1. 6–9. Thus also the *Quid significent*: Repsher, *Rite of Church
    Dedication*, 114, provides its origins; and also Bede, *Homilia* 21(PL 94: 244A–B),
    picking up an ancient topos.

63 *Sermones*, 72, 1.9–17 and also at 8.186–92. The reference to a mere 'game' may
    intend the *ludi* or plays composed to illustrate the historical narrative of a given
    feast.

64 As described in Robinson, 'Political Allegory', 84. For imperial use of Old
    Testament imagery, see Beryl Smalley, 'Ecclesiastical Attitudes to Novelty:
    *c.*1100–1250', in Smalley, *Studies in Medieval Thought and Learning from
    Abelard to Wyclif* (London, 1981), 97–115, at 113; Uta-Renate Blumenthal,
    'Canossa and Royal Ideology in 1077: Two Unknown Manuscripts of *De
    penitentia regis Salomonis*', *Manuscripta* 22 (1978), 91–6; Eugen Zweig, 'Zum
    christlichen Königsgedanken im Frühmittelalter', *Das Königtum, seine geistigen*

und rechtlichen Grundlagen, Vorträge und Forschungen 3 (Lindau, 1956): 7–73; J. Funkenstein, *Das Alte Testament im Kampf von regnum und sacerdotium zur Zeit des Investiturstreits* (Dortmund, 1938). See also Gerard E. Caspary, *Politics and Exegesis: Origen and the Two Swords* (California, 1979).

65 *Sermones*, 72, 2.18–30.

66 Ibid., 3.31–43, esp. 32–6.

67 Here Damian, who views the Abecedarium as the revival of the law, differs sharply from the *Quid significent*, which views it as a metaphor for the proclamation of ecclesiastical doctrine; Repsher, *Rite of Church Dedication*, 127–30. As examined below, Damian has other ambitions for allegorising preaching.

68 *Sermones*, 72, 3.43–7.

69 Ibid., 3.48–56.

70 Ibid., 4.57–88, esp. 69–88.

71 *Chron. Cas.*, MGH SS 34, 3.28, 397, as discussed above.

72 *Sermones*, 72, 4.79–81.

73 The *Laudes regiae* were part of the liturgical sacralising of king/queenship, though it would have lent its prestige to the ruling household as well; see Kantorowicz, *Laudes Regiae*. The parallels between supplication to a lord and to the Lord would also tend to reinforce the quasi-sacral character of lordship in general; see Geoffrey Koziol, *Begging Pardon and Favor: Ritual and Political Order in Early Medieval France* (Ithaca, 1992), esp. 77–103.

74 Some form of direct address was most likely expected by the lay leadership (though probably not so pointed) and was incorporated into the Romano-Germanic Pontifical; see Vogel and Elze, *Le Pontifical*, 40.129 (1: 169); and Repsher, *Rite of Church Dedication*, 86, 295.

75 Ps. 23 (24): 7. See Vogel and Elze, *Le Pontifical* 40.14 (1: 131–2); Repsher, *Rite of Church Dedication*, 61, 242; *Sermones*, 72, 4.57–88, esp. at 77–87.

76 Repsher, *Rite of Church Dedication*, 116–8.

77 As it is presented in *Quid significent*; Vogel and Elze, *Le Pontifical* 35.5 (1: 91–2); Repsher, *Rite of Church Dedication*, 33, 36 and 307.

78 *Sermones*, 72, 5.89–94.

79 Ibid., 6.106–10.

80 Ibid., 5.100–5.

81 Ibid., 5.103–5. The manuscripts of Damian are unanimous in recording 'Fecisti nos Deo nostro regnum et sacerdotes, et regnabunt super terram'. Most of the manuscripts listed in the critical edition of the Vulgate read: 'fecisti eos'. Hence, that is the reading chosen by the editors. However, several read 'fecisti vos', including the *Fuldensis* vel *Victoris* (Fulda, Landesbibliothek, Bonifatianus 1, a. 547) from Capua; see *Biblia Sacra Iuxta Vulgatam Versionem*, ed. Robert Weber (Stuttgart, 1983). The Vetus Latina also reads 'fescisti nos'. Damian's version of the texts is, therefore, in keeping with the immediacy of 1 Peter 2, 9: vos autem genus electum regale sacerdotum gens sancta. It is interesting to note that this older reading from the Vetus Latina is used by at least two of the so-called 'Giant Bibles' produced between 1065 and 1075. These are Admont, Stiftsbibliothek C–D, E; and Vatican City, Biblioteca Apostolica Vaticana Pal. lat., 3–4–5. The

former appears to have originated in Salsburg and the latter is described as 'certainly' from Germanic territory. Guy Lobrichon notices this variant reading and its import in his 'Riforma ecclesiastica e testo della Bibbia', in Marilena Maniaci e Giulia Orofino (eds), *Le Bibbie atlantiche, il libro delle Scritture tra monumentalità e rappresentazione* (Rome, 2000), 15–26 at 22–3.

82 It is interesting that Damian does not retain the first-person plural, but returns to the text when it becomes more openly political, '*they* will reign upon the earth'. [Emphasis mine.] It would seem that he is, again, trying to deliver a strong message, subtly. He may be consciously avoiding the charge of chiliasm, while trying to make an immediate call for reform.

83 *Sermones*, 72, 4.77.

84 Ibid., 7.125–6: tam profunda mysteria; 8.156: breviter perstringendo transcurrimus.

85 Compare with Archivio S. Pietro F 37 (thirteenth century?) at fol. 192r discussed in Chapter 1.

86 *Sermones*,, 8.162–7.

87 Augustine, *In iohannis evangelium tractatus cxxiv*, CCL 36 (Turnhout, 1954), Tract. IX. 2–5. (I am grateful to Susan L. Boynton for pointing me in the direction of this text.)

88 *Sermones*, 72, 8.167–76.

89 Ibid., 8.177–8. Pliny, citing Hypocrates, noted that a brew of hyssop in conjunction with other herbs (either nettles and pepper or bugloss) could loosen the bowels, purge the uterus and rid the body of tapeworms. Pliny, *Naturalis historiae*, Lib. XXII, par. 33–4 (XV) and par. 52 (XXV). Compare with the *Quid significent* for which hyssop represents humility; Vogel and Elze, *Le Pontifical* 35.26 (1: 104); Repsher, *Rite of Church Dedication*, 326; *Sermones*, 72, 8.179–81; and 3.48–56, as discussed above. On the purifying aspect of hyssop, see Eric Palazzo, 'Le Végétal et le sacré: l'hysope dans le rite de la dédicace de l'église', in Kathleen G. Cushing and Richard F. Gyug (eds), *Ritual, Text and Law: Studies in Medieval Canon Law and Liturgy Presented to Roger E. Reynolds* (Aldershot, Hampshire, 2004), 41–50.

90 *Sermones*, 72, 8.179–80.

91 Ibid., 8.182–5. This may be a visual allusion within the church being dedicated, as it is not at all otherwise clear as to what the *rubeum fragmen* refer. They may be the ubiquitous porphyry fragments of eleventh-century Italian paving. Perhaps the reference is to glowing pieces of burning incense, which would better explain why they burn with the fervour of charity. There are not many red fragments in Latin literature. Of possible interest is Pliny's reference to the red fragments produced when the authentic (*sincerus*) type of 'fragrant rushes' (*odorati iunci*) are rubbed: sincerus in confricando odorem rosae emittit rubentibus fragmentis. Pliny, *Naturalis historiae*, Lib. XXI, par. 120 (LXXII). The phrase is used by Aldhelm, Bishop of Sherbourne (C. 640–709) in his *De laudibus virginum*, PL 89, 269A.

92 *Sermones*, 72, 8.186–92.

93 Since we can not know precisely where and when this sermon was delivered, it is necessary to explore such allegory in broad terms. On the significance of a

new church to local aristocracy for religious insurance, income, social prestige and family cohesion around the memory of the founder, see Giovanni Tabacco, 'The Churches as Instruments and Active Centres of Political Power', in his *The Struggle for Power in Medieval Italy: Structures of Political Rule* (Cambridge, 1989), 166–76, at 167.

94 *Sermones*, 72, 9.193–7.

95 Ibid., 9.205–9.

96 Ibid., 9.214–16.

97 Andrea Strumi, *Vita sancti Arialdi*, c.4, 1052. See Cinzio Violante, *I Laici nel movimento Patarino*, Studi sulla cristianità medioevale (Milan, 1972), 212–13.

98 Hamilton, 'Sexual Purity', 237, 249–51.

99 PL 144, 465c; see Geary, *Furta Sacra*, 67. See also Patrick Healy, *The Chronicle of Hugh of Flavigny: Reform and the Investiture Contest in the Late Eleventh Century* (Aldershot, 2006).

100 Tabacco, *Struggle for Power*, 175. For a concise summary of the shift between personal and institutional charisma see Howe, *Church Reform*, 161. The line between ecclesiastical structures and military fortifications was often a blurred one, especially through the Romanesque period. This is especially true of monastic foundations; for example, Sancti Quattro Coronati in Rome was intended as a papal fortress, as well as a church – in the summer of 1999, in fact, workers discovered a tunnel connecting Sancti Quattro to the Lateran Palace – and the Codex Benedictinus (Vat. Lat. 1202, discussed in Chapter 1) depicts Maurus' monastic foundation as having crenellated walls (fol. 151v).

101 On political imagery of the body, see the classic study by Ernst Kantorowicz, *The King's Two Bodies: A Study in Mediaeval Political Theology* (Princeton, 1957).

102 *Sermones*, 72, 9.208–9.

103 Ibid., 9.220–4. This parallels the experience of the old law in general for Damian, as discussed above; ibid., 2.18–30. Damian is concerned to defend the *novus ordo* of the cardinalate against the challenges of the schism of 1061, hence his insistence on reading spiritually, in accordance with the new law, throughout; Robinson, 'Political Allegory', 84.

104 *Sermones*, 72, 10.234–40; at 240, . . . denuo per summi sacerdotis officium necesse est instauretur. Here too the liturgy is seen as a metaphor for reform.

105 Ibid., 10.245–9. See Mary Douglas, *Purity and Danger: An Analysis of Concepts of Pollution and Taboo* (New York, 1966) for a discussion of the use of disease and cleanliness in creating community. Although Damian has in mind here broader notions of sin and purity than clerical celibacy, helpful discussions of ritual purity are found in Michael Frassetto (ed.), *Medieval Purity and Piety: Essays on Medieval Clerical Celibacy and Religious Reform* (New York, 1998), esp. Paul Beaudette who observes that questions of clerical purity arise in the eleventh century as the clergy appear to be increasingly involved in 'the world' and, so, need to establish their otherness more distinctly: '"In the World not of It": Clerical Celibacy as a Symbol of the Medieval Church', 23–46, 29. Ritual purity aided ritual legitimacy within Christianity in no small part because it was seen as more Christ-like behaviour: see Phyllis G. Jestice, 'Why Celibacy?

Odo of Cluny and the Development of a new Sexual Morality', in ibid., 81–115, 81.

106 *Sermones*, 72, 11.250–5. On Temple imagery in the eleventh century and on Bernard of Clairvaux's incorporation of the imagery at a dedication, see Jennifer A. Harris, 'The Body as Temple in the High Middle Ages', in Albert I. Baumgarten (ed.), *Sacrifice in Religious Experience* (Leiden, 2002), 233–56, at 245, and 248–9.

107 *Sermones*, 72, 4.76–88, as discussed above.

108 Ibid., 11.256–72.

109 Ibid., 11.272–5.

110 Referencing Haggai 2, 8. *Sermones*, 72, 11.276–7.

111 Ibid., 12.288–92.

112 Ibid., 12.283–7, 300–4.

113 Ibid., 12.278–83.

114 Ibid., 12.304–8.

115 2 Cor 6: 16 (Lev 26: 12); Damian, *Sermones*, 72, 12.309.

116 On tensions between episcopal authorities and lay magnates, see Elisabeth Magnou-Nortier, 'The Enemies of the Church: Reflections on a Vocabulary, 500–1100', in Head and Landes, *Peace of God*, 58–79, at 62–3.

4

Anselm of Lucca, Urban II and the invention of orthodox dedication

> That the Roman church obtained its primacy from the Lord himself, and both Peter and Paul consecrated it by their death on the same day, and that it is the first see, Alexandria the second, and Antioch the third.
>
> Anselm of Lucca, *Collectio canonum*, Bk. V, c. 66.

A reformer practically from birth, Anselm II of Lucca would take up Gregory VII's charge to create a new form of canon law. In Anselm's hands the canons would be carefully selected and edited to reflect the ideals of Gregory VII. His canon collection would assert regulations for the dedication of churches and employ it as a broader metaphor in order to assert a papally centred ecclesiology. Born around 1036, Anselm was the nephew of the bishop of Lucca, Anselm I.[1] The latter would take the name Alexander II as pope, but would retain his episcopal see and title until his death in 1073. Nephew and uncle were by birth part of the new Milanese nobility that was rising from notarial and judicial circles in the late tenth and early eleventh centuries.[2] It was from this group, in part, that the Patarine movement formed, though Alexander II was a late supporter of the cause.[3] Alexander II regularly visited Lucca during his pontificate, reorganised its chapter and rebuilt and dedicated the cathedral of St Martin in 1070. While the physical remains reveal an active Lucchese clergy, their religiosity might be fairly described as conventional.[4] Lucca, under Alexander II, was neither distinguished by religious fervour nor marred by the urban strife of the religious conflicts found in contemporary Milan to its North or Florence to the East. Alexander appears to have trodden lightly where his nephew would not.[5]

Anselm II succeeded his uncle as bishop in 1073. He had pursued his

studies in Milan, though possibly elsewhere as well.[6] After much discussion with Gregory VII, Anselm chose to delay receiving his investment from Henry IV, who was tainted by association with his excommunicant advisors. Anselm was then invested by Henry and consecrated by Gregory in late 1074 or early 1075. Following the Lenten Synod of 1075, Anselm retired to a monastery. Gregory recalled him to his see later that year.[7] The sort of academic scrupulosity Anselm exhibited in the matter of his investment seems to have been a hallmark of his personality. He was as rigid concerning the liturgical form for the Mass as he was for his own investment.[8] It is not surprising, then, that Anselm was supposed to have continued to wear his monastic habit beneath his episcopal vestments.[9] Anselm's devotion to the monastic life was typical of the reformer's interests in reforming the bishop and his chapter according to monastic ideals.

Locally, however, these efforts at reform may have associated Anselm even more directly with the comital court at Canossa that was actively founding monastic communities in Tuscany. Matilda's monastic foundations not only fostered religious zeal but also promoted its authority. They posed a potential threat to the authority and financial basis of the canons of St Martin, as well as the independence of Lucca and other Tuscan cities.[10]

Anselm's efforts to reform the canons of St Martin and the subsequent controversy are best understood in light of the tension between Matilda and Lucca. Anselm was never able to convince more than a loyal minority of the canons to live the common life; in part, because the common life would have given greater control of the Cathedral's property to the bishop than he had held at Lucca at the time.[11] The canons remained staunch in their resistance, and Anselm's appeal for support to Matilda, countess of Tuscany, would have only confirmed their fears.[12] Matilda went so far as to offer to compensate the families of whatever Lucchese canons would agree to be reformed. The offer illustrates both the gravity of their defection and the value of their properties.[13] The person and letters of Gregory VII did not prevail upon the canons, nor did their excommunication in 1079, nor its reiteration in 1080.[14] Without strong local support for his reforms, Anselm was effectively stymied by the cathedral canons. Capitalising on this tension, in 1081 Henry IV granted the city its privilege and elevated one of the canons, named Peter, to the see.[15] Anselm fled to Mantua.[16] In turn, the city gave its support to Henry's papal candidate, Guibert of Ravenna. Anselm remained at Matilda's court from his exile in 1081 until his death in 1086.

Anselm's life and extant writings make clear his position as a staunch ally of Gregory VII and supporter of Gregory's vision of ecclesiastical reform. Anselm's most important work, apparently compiled at the behest of Gregory, is his *Canons Collected in Thirteen Books*.[17] His was one of the new type of canon collections being promoted by the reforming papacy that emphasised papal prerogatives and jurisdiction, and that depended not on the collections of the immediate past but on carefully sifted selections from among patristic texts, earlier canons and papal decretals. Such collections ought to be considered among the many literary strategies being marshalled to support the reforming popes.[18] At Mantua, Anselm would have been exposed to the kinds of allegorical reading of scripture that Peter Damian had helped innovate, since Matilda was promoting such literature.[19] Anselm's own polemic against Guibert of Ravenna was written as a commentary on the Psalms and so typifies the political allegory espoused by Peter Damian and later Bruno of Segni.[20] This was the environment in which Anselm's canons were compiled. It was also the environment in which Anselm attempted to give the dedication legal significance, and in which the dedication played a central role in the consolidation of power around the papacy and papally sanctioned bishops. Anselm's *Collectio canonum* invented a tradition of papal regulation of all church dedications, from great to small, not previously considered by scholars.[21]

Anselm's collection was an important source for the *Polycarpus* of Gregory of S. Chrisogono, Rome, compiled during the papacy of Paschal II. Through the *Polycarpus* and independently, Anselm's collection appears to have been the only Italian collection of the second half of the eleventh century used by Gratian in compiling his *Concordia disconcordiae canonici*.[22] Although there has been some question as to whether or not the collection bearing his name is properly attributed to Anselm, as it is only so attributed in a later manuscript, consensus continues to favour Anselmian authorship.[23] Current scholarship leaves little doubt that the canons can be understood as suitable for Anselm's milieu.

The canon collection of Anselm of Lucca

Despite the debate concerning how much of the collection ought to be attributed to Anselm, even the most radical abridgements in search of an Anselmian form include the first seven of the thirteen books in the collection.[24] That is, no one contests that Book V (*de ordinationibus ecclesiarum et de omni iure ac statu illarum*) was part of the original compilation.

This book contains the vast majority of the materials dealing with the occasion of the dedication of a church, establishing dedications as central to any original Anselmian form.[25] As Paul Fournier and Gabriel LeBras long ago argued, however, the fullest and earliest copy of the collection, Vat. lat. 1363, is best understood as a literary whole.[26] Their work, and that of Alfonso Stickler, demonstrated convincingly that Books XI (the Carolingian *Capitula iudicorum*), XII (concerning ecclesiastical censure and its application to heretics and schismatics, *de excomunicatione*), and XIII (on legitimate vengeance and repression, *de iusta vindicta*) were necessary to the religious aims of the entire collection.[27] It is within the full context of Vat. lat. 1363, therefore, that the canons for the dedication of a church ought to be understood.

The *Collectio canonum* boldly proclaimed the Gregorian position from its very outset: *de primatu Sancte Romane ecclesie*. Book I, in 89 chapters, established the primacy of Rome as the basis for all other canons. The second book (*de libertate appellationis*, in 82 chapters), began with a selection from Deuteronomy (Deut. 17, 8–13) and proceeded smoothly to the rights of judicial appeal and the rights of clergy. Book III (*de ordine accusandi testificandi et iudicandi*, in 114 chapters) moved from that ideal to procedural questions stemming from the ideal hierarchy urged by the previous books.

Book IV (*de privilegiorum auctoritate*, in 55 chapters) listed the privileges of churches and monasteries and how they ought to be observed.[28] Book V (*de ordinationibus ecclesiarum et omni iure et actu illarum*, in 69 chapters) contained the bulk of the material concerning the dedication of churches. Book VI (in 189 chapters) dealt with bishops: their election, ordination and every power or rank (*de electione et ordinatione ac de omni potestate sive statu episcoporum*). Book VII proceeded to discuss the lesser clergy, with an emphasis on the common life (*de communi vita clericorum et de omni actu eorum*, 174 chapters), and Book VIII the disciplining of lapsed clergy (*de lapsis*, 34 chapters).

Book IX (in 69 chapters) addressed baptism, the Eucharist, confirmation and the significance of sacraments administered by heretics and simoniacs. Marriage and sexuality was the subject of the briefest book of the collection, Book X (*de coniugiis*, 46 chapters).[29] Book XI (*de poenitentia*, 152 chapters) was derived from the Carolingian *Capitula iudicorum*.[30] Books XII and XIII (*de excommunicatione*, in 72 chapters; and *de iusta vindicta*, in 29 chapters respectively) formed something of a unit on the use of corrective powers of the Church and the censuring of heretics and simoniacs.[31]

Old texts with new contexts

Since they were built through the compilation of legal precedent, it is easy to overlook the creative dimension of canon-law collections, but the discussion and investigation of their genesis remains essential to assessing their significance.[32] Canon-law codices, as some liturgical texts, pseudonymous texts and scriptural commentaries of the Middle Ages, gained their authority by working in the medium of tradition, by receiving texts handed down from previous generations of ecclesiasts and legal experts. The author's art, however, was the skilful and all-but-imperceptible discrimination among, and organisation of, that tradition by the canonist. The final work, seemingly *ad naturam*, was in reality the fruit of the numberless decisions a master makes to include or exclude particular canons.[33] In this sense, the compiler of the collection acted with authorial intent.

The *Collectio canonum* of Anselm of Lucca presented the dedication as an integral part of the governing structure of the reform Church and close to the centre of its ideal episcopate. The organisation of Anselm's collection and the dedication's place within that organisation is essential to the meaning of the collection. Not only was the dedication of a church incorporated into the larger vision of an idealised Church as presented by the canons, but liturgical texts themselves become part of the basis for the canons.[34] By compiling selections from papal epistles, selections divorced from their original circumstances and whose significance was interpreted by rubricated chapter headings, Anselm attempted to create a tradition of papal authority over church dedications. This authority was justified not only by precedent, but also through the metaphor of church construction and dedication. The Roman Church was preeminent in its foundation in Peter and its dedication with the relics of Peter and Paul. Rome was, thus, the ultimate centre of the cult, on which all churches depended. In this manner the liturgy for the dedication would serve to reinforce and solemnise the ancient authority of the Roman precedent.[35]

From the outset the canons were concerned to assert the primacy of the Roman Church. Indeed, Book I was entitled 'On the primacy of the Roman Church', and commenced the first of its 89 chapters with the heading 'Quod in novo testamento post Christum dominum a Petro sacerdotalis coeperit ordo'.[36] What followed was a letter attributed to Anacletus I, outlining the significance of the commission: 'Tu es petrus et super hanc petram aedificabo ecclesiam meam' (Mt 16: 18). (The canons repeated that reform mantra so often that by the eleventh chapter of the first book the tiring scribe began to abbreviate it: 'Tu es p. et s. h. p. e. eccl[esi]am

mea[m] Et. p. i. n. p. a. u. s. ea[m] & cet[er]a'.[37] By means of this oft-repeated biblical metaphor of church construction, papal authority will be continuously asserted. The second and third chapters waste no time in drawing out the appropriate conclusion:

2. That the Roman Church is the head of all the Churches and it obtained primacy from the Lord himself and not from another.

3. Where the blessed Peter transposed to his successors the right of binding and loosing conceded to him.[38]

This was the refrain of the first book. The *Collectio canonum* was from its very outset, as others have described it, a legal defence of the reform efforts of Gregory VII.[39] That this was the appraisal of the text by contemporaries may be evinced by the *Vita Anselmi*, in which the bishop was described as having 'compiled an *Apology* from the diverse volumes of the holy fathers, by which all of the sentences, actions and even precepts of the Lord Pope could be defended by reasons and supported by orthodox authorities'.[40] Of all Anselm's work, this seems most likely a reference to the canon-law collection. Indeed, one manuscript of the *Collectio canonum* suggested that the collection may have been written at the behest of Gregory himself.[41]

The second book, *de liberatione appellationis*, established an ideal and imagined Church structure of defined rights and prerogatives, and of historical precedents for royal deference to papal authority.[42] It reminded the reader that Constantine himself had insisted that the bishops of Ravenna and Milan follow Roman discipline.[43] It was a legal brief attempting to demonstrate through precedent that all matters of doubt between bishops ought to be submitted to the Apostolic See (cc. 8 and 54); that the Apostolic authority governs all bishops (cc. 7 and 41); that all oppressed can appeal to the pope (c. 6); that the pope ought to have *cura* (care: with its implications of concern and management) for all the churches (*omnium ecclesiarum*, c. 22); that the Roman Church was the primary Church to which all must be obedient (c. 42); and all were to follow its example (c. 44). In short, Book II presented all of the arguments, greatly elaborated and carefully researched, that one would expect from a devotee of the Gregorian party, and a man with a strong faith in the inherent goodness of Roman pastoral authority.[44] It expressed neatly the ideal Church of the papal party without concession to the harsh realities of the early 1080s: bishops, lords and emperor in open, unapologetic conflict with the papacy; rival claims to the Apostolic See; and Gregory VII along with many of his supporters (including Anselm) living as exiles from their own bishoprics.

Nor were the third and fourth books any less bold. Book III, concerning legal procedure, was especially interested in the relationship between ecclesiastical and lay jurisdictions and authority. To provide only a few examples of these kinds of concern: clerics not to be tried by lay people without the permission of their bishop (cc. 23, 24); the manner in which bishops were rightly to be accused (cc. 56, 59, 60); lessers not to accuse their superiors (c. 58); the precedent for the condemnation of a bishop by a pope in council, from Chalcedon (c. 91). This concern for jurisdictional boundaries and proper procedure extended to the very highest elements of society: the Apostolic See may call councils for the purpose of condemning heresy (c. 99), while emperors could only convene councils in order to confirm the faith and not for the display of power (*non ad potentiam ostendam*, c. 104).

Book IV went on to describe the privileges and rights of churches and monasteries (cc. 1–2, 14–17) and assign penalties for those who violate those rights (cc. 18, 41, 52). Interestingly, Anselm asserted here, just prior to his discussion of the dedication of churches, the inviolability of monastic and ecclesiastical privileges (c. 1). Indeed, monasteries were to be allowed to remain at peace (*quies*) and their privileges were not to be challenged in such a way as to threaten that peace (c. 5). Book IV returned to the regular refrain of defining ecclesiastical rights against competing imperial interests. At chapter 11, *Ut imperatores obediant episcopis*, Anselm returned to the bold proclamation of what was not the actual but the ideal practice.[45] Book IV, Chapter 12, likewise presented an uncompromised Gregorian legal ideal, *Ut imperatores habeant privilegia legis publicae et sacerdotes habeant dispositiones universarum ecclesiarum.*[46] It presented an ideal of ecclesial-imperial relations completely opposite to the contemporary reality: 'Not by public laws, not by secular powers, but by pontiffs and priests does God almighty wish the clerics and priests of Christian religion to be ordained, and those remaining [ones] to be shaken and brought back from error.'[47] The theme of the inviolability of sacred space was then directly connected to the sanctity of its privileges in Chapter 15, 'That the defenders of sacred spaces are not to endure any harm (*nullam molestiam sustineant*)', and Chapter 16, 'That the privileges of churches are made inviolate'. (The theme was then carried through chapters 17–24.)[48] In fact, this discussion built up to perhaps the greatest privilege of them all, that given by Constantine to Sylvester, brought forward in Chapter 33, 'That the emperor Constantine conceded to the Pope the crown and all royal dignity in the city of Rome and in the western parts'. Chapter 33's assertion of the Donation of Constantine was followed

by Louis I's confirmation for Paschal I of the territorial authority of the Papacy, and further confirmations by Otto I and Henry I (cc. 34-36). A brief canon from Gregory VII himself that no one ought to compromise the property of the blessed Peter (c. 37) concluded the section.

As was the case with the Roman ecclesiastical architecture emerging in the same decades as Anselm's *Collectio canonum*, the collection presented the Constantinian precedent as exemplary.[49] Constantine was presented as solicitous of the Christian clergy and people (c. 13: 'That clerics ought to enjoy freely things pertaining to them' and c. 14: 'That faithful Christians should be placed in perpetual security', both from Constantine; and c. 40, from Constantine and his mother).[50] The Emperor Justinian (r. 527-565) was also presented as a defender of ecclesiastical privilege (cc. 19-20), along with imperial decrees collected in his *Digest* (cc. 53, 55).[51]

Skipping ahead, the sixth book dealt explicitly with the investment of bishops (*de electione et ordinatione ac de omni potestate sive statu episcoporum*), the issue around which the controversies between papacy and emperor would congeal. Book VII concerned the common life of clerics, and contained regulations asserting that the Mass was to be sung only in places consecrated by bishops (cc. 117-120), as was clearly not the uniform case on the Italian peninsula.[52] The dedication of churches, as presented by Anselm, was a central element to the discipline and structure of the Gregorian ideal of the Church. In essence, these enforced the common life of clerics by rooting their most basic activity, the Mass, under the direct control of the bishop.

Anselm placed the major discussion of the dedication in Book V, in the midst of elaborating the relationship between bishops and pontiff, pontiff and emperor, bishops and monks, clerical and lay jurisdictions. This suggested that the dedication of churches was understood as a principal mechanism for the promotion of this idealised ecclesiastical structure. Without first asserting strict papal-episcopal control over sacred places, the *loci* of the sacramental and ritual life of the Church, Anselm could not assert papal-episcopal control over the other sacraments (the subject of Books IX-XI), nor could the papal-episcopal structure have exercised coercive authority through excommunication and discipline (the subject of Books XI-XIII).

The consecration of churches

The chapters of Book V can be divided into three major categories: apostolic approval of all new churches, the circumstances under which

churches or altars may be reconsecrated, and the definition and control of the *res ecclesiae*. The first is the most prominent feature of this book and demonstrates a strong desire to create unity within the Church through the strict hierarchical control of ecclesiastical construction. The pope was the ultimate authority for the construction of all basilicas, churches and chapels. The term 'basilica', however, lacks a strict legal meaning and can be used for any major church, and further obscures the ambiguous boundary between papal and local episcopal authority. It is clear that popes did not have such strict control over church construction before Anselm, and they would not immediately after Anselm either. Thus, the first twelve chapters of Book V, as well as several later chapters, brought ecclesiastical consecration under strict, albeit hypothetical, apostolic control.[53]

The ambiguous nature of papal control over dedications may be exemplified in the case of S. Matteo in Salerno. After taking the city, Robert Guiscard appealed to Montecassino for relics of St Matthew but made no official request for papal approval of the construction of his basilica. In fact, he took the city against Gregory's expressed will and was briefly excommunicated for it. Strong overlordship of churches by their patrons was the custom in southern Italy, as had certainly been the case previously for S. Matteo.[54] Gregory's ultimate consecration and endorsement of the basilica was again also a product of shifting circumstances rather than legal nicety.[55] The complex dynamic between papal, episcopal, monastic and lay authorities was changing in the eleventh century, and so was especially fluid in our period of ecclesiastical controversy and legal revolution. An additional difficulty for the papacy would be the regulation of encastled churches.[56] In general, ecclesiastical historians have begun to address the assumptions of a normative, centralised ecclesial structure.[57] While the eleventh-century papal reformers such as Anselm were asserting this structure as the norm, it was not the reality. Thomas Noble's observations of the early mediaeval papacy are still germane for the period of the late eleventh and early twelfth century; while the popes were, in theory, the leading religious authority of the Latin West, that did not translate into simple, direct rulership (as the complaints of the emperor and the anti-popes make plain).[58]

Given the complexity of articulating Roman prestige as actual regulatory power, one must understand the consecration of churches as presented in Anselm's canons as an expression of ecclesiastical unity under the Apostolic See. The first three chapters of Book V moved from an emphasis on the Church as one with many members to an assertion of apostolic authority: 'That the Church or house of God is called a dove

or bride and that it has received the power of binding and loosing'. Most tellingly, however, chapter two declares profane 'whoever does not serve the unity of the Church'.[59] Thus, unity was asserted as the divide between that which was sacred and profane. It was then only a small and, by this logic, necessary step to assert a centralised authority for the creation of sacred space. So it began, at chapter four: 'That new basilicas ought not to be consecrated without the authority of the Apostolic See'. The prerogative of consecration flows out from the papacy. This was more than a figurative unity: it was intended as an institutional one, as exhibited by the requirement of direct apostolic approval of consecrations. The letter of Gelasius I, as reproduced by Anselm in chapter four, made plain the supremacy of the Apostolic See and its role in maintaining peace within the body of the Church.

> Let no one dare to dedicate newly established basilicas if they have not sought the customary indults of the Apostolic See . . . And since the Apostolic See, having been favoured by the Lord, should be superior to all these which have been set up before by the canons of the fathers, let it be zealous to hold to that which is proposed piously and devoutly; it is sufficiently unworthy that anyone, either a pontiff or [someone] of lesser order, refute this observance which the See of the blessed Peter appears to follow and teach; and coming together enough that the whole body of the Church be united in this observance that it might be seen to flourish, where the Lord has placed the beginning of all the Church.[60]

It is noteworthy that the idea that the Church was founded on Peter was here directly connected to the ideal that all church foundations should, therefore, defer to that Petrine foundation. It is worth comparing this text with the *Diversorum patrum sententiae*, also known as the *The Collection in Seventy-four Titles* (74T), a collection that Anselm had at his disposal. This collection may be Italian in origin and was composed some time before 1076, the date of the first reliable reference to it.[61] The 74T also cites the Gelasian epistle but much more succinctly:

> C. 209. On the consecration of churches. Gelasius to all bishops.

> Let no one dare to dedicate newly established basilicas if they have not sought the customary indults of the Apostolic See, nor let bishops seek to appropriate to themselves clerics from another's jurisdiction.[62]

Anselm, without informing his readers, eliminated the material concerning episcopal jurisdiction over clerics from the 74T and added material that

emphasised the importance of respecting all the canons of the Apostolic See.[63] The rubric also summed up the new canon quite nicely, emphasising papal control over the dedication of basilicas.

Chapter 5 added more to this discussion by continuing the same letter and expanding this control from basilical consecrations to church dedications in general.[64] Anselm left out the letters addressing Bishop John of Ravenna as *fratris et coepiscopi nostri, Iohannis Ravennatis*, perhaps to avoid dignifying Gregory's papal rival Guibert of Ravenna.[65] It is clear that Anselm saw an opportunity here that the author of the 74T did not. Anselm imagined a Roman authority that could be liturgically enforced through the dedication. By means of dedications Rome could ensure that reform ideals would be enforced not only among bishops, but even at the most humble level of Christian society. While the 74T only imagined papal approval of basilicas, and only addressed the matter in one chapter, Anselm emphasised this message in several chapters.

Book V, c. 6, 'That public Mass is not to be held in a church that was dedicated without the consent of the pope' was a Gelasian confirmation of a dedication that reaffirmed papal authority to regulate dedications in general. The *papa* in the title of chapter 6 was intended as the Apostolic See.[66] These broad powers would ultimately be taken over directly from Anselm by Gratian.[67] Their collection in the 1080s ought to surprise us because these canons presumed a sophisticated capacity to regulate church construction and dedication on the local level, not just in parts of Italy (the audience for Gelasius' letters) but for all the churches (*omnium ecclesiarum*, c. 12). Thus, the basilica of St Michael the Archangel in Capua, the original subject of Gelasius' letter, was transformed by Anselm's rubric in c. 11 into simply another church requiring licence from the pope for dedication ('That the pope gives a church licence to be consecrated'). This basilica itself would later come into conflict in the question of dedication. This bland title combined with c. 12 to expand papal prerogative over all churches, 'That the pope, whose concern ought to be all the churches . . .'[68] In fewer than a dozen canons Anselm has moved from a sense that major church building and dedication ought to be under the supervision of the Roman pontiff to a much more general supervision of all church dedications. The Roman pontiffs even had the authority to control the consecration of oratories, at least in the Anselmian rubric: 'That an oratory is not to be consecrated without the authority of the apostolic see'.[69] The canon itself referred to an oratory whose presence was disputed by another bishop as an infringement upon his territory. Gregory the Great ruled against the infringing bishop. The case reveals

how Anselm worked; here, a dispute settlement over boundaries became, in the Anselmian rubric, a broad papal authority to regulate the construction of oratories. Anselm moved from the bishop's right of appeal to the papacy in a dispute over prerogatives within an episcopal see to a sweeping papal authority necessary to the dedication of even an oratory.[70] In fact, within a generation, the reformers employed this new reading of the canon when Bruno of Segni appealed to Paschal II to dedicate an oratory in Capua.[71]

Such an authority, if it existed as presented here, would have meant that every encastled chapel, every village church, would have been neatly recorded and dated in the papal registers. They were not. These canons, however, illustrate that Gregory VII's closest advisors saw an opportunity to expand Roman authority through a close editing of Gregory the Great's letters and to enforce their ideals by means of the consecration of churches. It is surprisingly ambitious. While it did not mean that every church dedication was registered with the pope, it asserted the pope's right to delegate that authority to bishops or abbots as he saw fit. These dedications were also an opportunity not only to extend authority but to bring reform ideals to fundamental levels of ecclesiastical life: the peace of the Church, and the liberation of Church and its property from lay political and economic ambition.[72] Nor did the canons leave any doubt that the properly administered episcopal liturgy was itself the source for the sacred nature of a place. The common property of the church was also maintained through proper dedication.

> Those things are sacred that have been consecrated to God rightly and by pontiffs, such as sacred buildings and gifts which are dedicated to the service of God, which also we have forbidden by our order to be alienated or mortgaged, except for the redemption of captives. If someone will establish of his own authority a place for himself as sacred, it is not sacred but profane. The place, however, in which sacred buildings have been built, even after it has been destroyed, remains sacred.[73]

Since the metaphor of ecclesial baptism defined the consecration of churches in the *Quid significent*, it is no surprise that the question of when it might be appropriate to rebaptise churches consumes much of this book. It was a serious concern given the prohibitions against rebaptism stemming from the Donatist controversy and their extensions into the Gregorian controversies over licit investment.[74] These chapters, by granting the possibility of reconsecration of churches (if an altar was moved, c. 13; if consecrated by heretics, cc. 21–2; if its consecration was doubted,

c. 23), created two potentialities: a great increase in the use of the liturgy for the dedication (by liberating the liturgy from construction, or using it in cases of potentially minor construction), and greater papal prestige (by giving the papacy a tool for the disciplining and shaming of heretical or schismatic bishops: i.e., the reconsecration of their churches).[75] These canons, discussed below, help explain the increased dedications of the late eleventh and early twelfth centuries in the aftermath of schisms.

Several of the remaining chapters in Book V deal largely with defining the ecclesiastical and lay rights (or rather, the lack of the former) concerning the property of a church.[76] That the laity could not build or retain control over churches independently, even churches they founded, was also asserted (cc. 7–10).[77] These chapters, as those already discussed, gave legal solemnity to the sacred space of the church and enforce the peace of the Church. They also attempted to remove church property from dynastic concerns. Like clerical celibacy, they were an effort to prevent alienation, devolution and disintegration of ecclesiastical property.[78] But perhaps more to the point, these chapters restraining the lay founders of the church were placed in the midst of the discussion of papal authority over dedications and so not only enforced a clerical hierarchy, but also directly addressed the contemporary crisis between emperor and pope. The clergy was not to be subordinated to laypeople, even to those who founded a church. Indeed, two of these chapters (cc. 8 and 9) limited the rights of the laity to build in a church, and added that they do not have the right to ruling over something done in the church (*non auctoritas imperandi*).[79] In this way, these chapters pointed directly to a restraint on imperial power in particular, but seigneurial authority in general.

These broader ecclesiological concerns, and the reform interest in distinguishing between the sacred and secular, explain why the bulk of the chapters were committed to the protection of ecclesiastical possessions and enforcing the peace. It would be of no small importance to distinguish the ecclesiastical construction of a great (possibly episcopal) family while circumscribing the family's rights over such a donation or the episcopal property a relative may control. Thus, control over the income of donations was of primary importance: tithes were not to be controlled by the laity (c. 45), and unless authorised by a pope or appropriate bishop, not to be controlled by monastics (c. 48); and the possessions of a church were not to be alienated (cc. 19, 32–33, 35, 38, 40–41, 43–44, and 46), thereby limiting episcopal control over a local church and connecting that church to a more permanent Church. These canons also established rules for punishing offenders of the sanctity of ecclesiastical property (cc. 18, 27,

42, 52, and 59). That the church building had its own set of appropriate conduct would have fostered a sense of its sacrality.

Although this concern for a church's property may seem to us a rather base anxiety for the reforming pro-papal episcopate, it is clear that these same concerns were connected – both in the manuscripts and, it seems, in the minds of the reformers – to the highest demands of their pastoral office. The canons bind inextricably the consecration of a sacred space and its economic administration: to violate either was to be outside the *ecclesia*. Not only were the canons concerned to protect episcopal control of tithes, they were concerned to protect pious donations from familial ambition, and they instructed the reader on the proper episcopal use of tithes.

29. How ecclesiastical money might be preserved.

30. How religious are to be provided for in order that they might have a suitable place [to live], that they not suffer want or idleness.

31. Augustine. That tithes are to be distributed to needy souls.

. . .

40. That the possessions of the church are divided into four parts: one is for the bishop, another for clerics, a third for the poor, and the fourth for restoring churches.[80]

These chapters, along with chapters 28, 61, 62, and 64, outlined the appropriate use of tithes and set budgetary priorities.[81] Chapter 60, in particular, committed one quarter of episcopal resources to the episcopal household, one quarter to clerics, one quarter to the poor, and one quarter to the repair of churches (una videlicet episcopo et familiae eius propter hospitalitem atque susceptionem, alia clero, tertia pauperibus, quarta ecclesiis reparandis). As Damian had observed, charity in this sense truly keeps the walls of the Church standing.[82] Chapter 31, from Augustine, further urged charity to the poor through priests.[83] It is not necessary to re-establish here the primary role of ecclesiastical charity and distribution of wealth in providing for the poor and shaping mediaeval society.[84] It is important, however, to observe that such generosity was placed by Anselm within the context of the dedication of the church. In a sense, Book V became an elaboration of the dedication's capacity to establish sacred, juridical and charitable structures within a community. Here, as in Anselm's *Sermo de caritatis*, charity was institutional and at the heart of the Apostolic Church.[85] The care and upkeep of the physical church

was here an equal part of proper episcopal responsibilities. Such broader implications of consecration were repeated throughout Anselm's *Collectio canonum*.

In fact, Anselm drew upon tradition and the imagery of the liturgy for the dedication to strengthen the claim to Roman Apostolic authority from the outset of the collection. The Roman Church was consecrated by the deposition of Peter and Paul in the soil of Rome after their martyrdom.[86] Thus Rome itself became the high altar for all other churches. As relics might be brought from a greater church in dedicating another church, so Rome would become the source for the consecration of all other altars. It was this deposition of relics, this consecration of Rome that was the basis of its authority. Rome's dedication preceded all others; the dedication of Rome was the consecration from which all consecrations proceeded. Damian had been at pains to observe this at Venice.[87] Referring the reader to Anacletus I, Book I, chapter 66 asserted a similar claim to authority through consecration, as stated in Anselm's rubric, 'That the Roman church obtained its primacy from the Lord himself, and both Peter and Paul consecrated it by their death on the same day, and that it is the first see, Alexandria the second and Antioch the third'.[88]

The claim was elaborated in this long canon, with special attention paid to Christ's naming of Peter and his authority to loose and bind. Then Anselm invoked the authority of the relics to judge the churches that contain them.

> The first see therefore is by heavenly benefit the Roman Church, which, as is remembered, the most blessed Peter and Paul consecrated by their martyrdom. The second see was consecrated at Alexandria, honoured and even consecrated in Peter's name by his disciple, the evangelist Mark. The third see at Antioch is considered honourable with respect to blessed Peter, who lived there before he came to Rome and who made Ignatius bishop, and there first began the name of Christians.[89]

Chapter 66 thus makes explicit what was only implicit in the 74T. Title 2 of that work stated tersely, 'Concerning the Same [Roman primacy] and that Peter and Paul suffered on the same day'.[90] The 74T then referenced the very beginning of the letter of Anacletus including the consecration metaphor. Anselm, however, made plain how the consecration affects Rome's status both through his more overt rubric and by expanding the Anacletan citation.

The dedication was the basis for the evangelical authority of the Roman Church as well in chapter 67. Anselm again made explicit the metaphor

of the dedication that was implicit in T. 2, c. 2 of the 74T by means of the rubric, 'That the Roman Church, where Peter and Paul were killed on the same day, *is first* owing to evangelical authority [emphasis mine]'.[91] This selection (from Gelasius) reiterated Matthew 16: 18 (Tu es Petrus . . .) and adds that, by their martyrdom, Peter and Paul consecrated the Roman Church to Christ. Likewise, the *Collectio canonum*, Bk. I, cc. 68–69 provided additional texts to direct and expand upon those presented in the 74T.[92] Chapter 70 of Book I then described the deference appropriate to the relics of St Paul.[93]

While it is no surprise that the basis for Rome's claims to authority were the martyrdoms of Peter and Paul at the hands of Nero, what has been overlooked is that this claim gains its credibility from the dedication liturgy. That Peter was Rome's first bishop was of secondary importance to the broader metaphor of church construction and dedication. Rome's authority rested on the power of that image. Peter was the rock upon which the Roman Church and the entirety of the Church was to be built. In this metaphor, Peter and Paul's martyrdom serve as the deposition of their relics into that Church of Rome (relics deposited by themselves as bishops). Authority flowed out from Rome as relics might from a major to a minor church, as St Matthew had from Montecassino to Salerno, as the chains of Peter were distributed throughout Europe and the Mediterranean world. Unless one understood the communal significance of the construction and dedication of a church, this metaphor would have had little appeal. It was the deposition of relics that makes an altar holy, and it was this initial consecration that gave Rome ultimate authority. Alexandria was second in rank because it was consecrated in the name of Peter by Mark, the evangelist and Peter's disciple.

Even as Peter Damian had in Venice and Milan, Anselm used the liturgical metaphor of church construction and dedication to explain not only why Rome was unique among Churches but even why it had power and authority over worldly rulers.[94] The assertion formed the organisational basis for chapters 71 and 72, 'That the world is ruled by the authority of popes and the power of kings but the royal power ought to be subjected to the pontiffs'; 'That emperors ought to obey priests not judge them'.[95] The eleventh-century papal claim to authority over emperors is, of course, famous. The canonical claim here was based, in part, on Anselm's use of an alternate source to the 74T that enabled him to expand upon the letter from Gelasius to the Emperor Anastasius in chapter 71. The Anselmian rubric further expanded the authority of the Gelasian letter by replacing the priests of the 74T with the pontiff in the rubric.[96] As Cushing observed,

'With such modifications, Anselm truly transformed the "Gelasian ideal" into a concrete manifesto for his time'.[97] If the Gelasian ideal was the Anselmian manifesto, it was carefully edited and built upon the metaphor of church construction and dedication.

Thus, Anselm's collection both used the imagery of the dedication to establish papal authority and also asserted stricter, Rome-centred control over dedications, with the intention of promoting papal authority and Gregorian ideals. In short, Anselm tapped into the powerful imagery and experience of the dedication in order to advance the reforming papacy. Were these canons to be obeyed or were they possible to enforce, the papacy would reconfirm its control over local potentates, ecclesiastic or lay, with every new dedication. Simultaneously, every dedication would be confirming the basis of Roman authority: the superior dedication of Rome through the martyrdom of Peter and Paul. By the late eleventh century, therefore, the dedication was seen as a critical element for the promotion of religious reform by those closest to the papacy. The canonical significance of the dedication could thus become an important subtext when popes dedicated churches in the next generation.

Theory into practice: dedication of churches under Urban II

The death of Gregory VII in 1085 was nearly coterminous with a significant dedication: Gregory himself dedicated the cathedral church of S. Matteo in Salerno in July of 1084. For Guiscard, the dedication marked the culmination of his long campaign to wrest the southern peninsula from German imperial, Byzantine, Lombard and Saracen overlords. In May he had frightened off Henry IV, punished the rebellious citizens of Rome and re-enthroned Gregory at the papal palace on the Lateran Hill, and the two had proceeded, in triumph, toward Benevento and, finally, Salerno.[98] The dedication of the basilica itself was marked by the official reconciliation of Jordanus of Capua and Guiscard, a peace carved in stone on the architrave of the *porta leoni* of the basilica.[99] That inscription, with its emphasis of the subordinate status of Jordan, revealed as much as it concealed the recent conflict between the two men. It also marked the dramatic change in relations between the papacy and the Normans within less than two decades, since Alexander II had excommunicated Guiscard's brother, Count William, in 1067 for his 'depredations at the expense of Salerno cathedral'.[100] It was a ritual marking and reinforcing the new legitimacy of Robert Guiscard.[101] Gregory would find his final resting place in the Cathedral.

While Gregory had hoped that Anselm would succeed him, the canon-ist would not long survive him, and Desiderius became Victor III, albeit briefly. The next significant opportunity for papal dedications came under Urban II who, by the time he came to power in 1088, had inherited a growing tradition of papal dedications, an increasingly sophisticated legal tradition and exegetical strategies that incorporated the dedication into an ecclesiology centred on the papacy. Even as Anselm had been fostering this legal rationale, contemporary popes were employing the dedication with greater frequency. Recent work on southern Italy has revealed that bishops rarely dedicated churches prior to the reforming period, as they rarely went to Rome for consecration.[102] The reforming popes were encouraging greater attention to the pontifical liturgy as part of their agenda. But the lack of prior dedications also provided the oppor-tunity to employ the rite, as did the overall increase in church construction during the later eleventh century. The factors of reform and expansion explain the increasing number of papal dedications to a great extent. The pattern of papal dedications under Urban II and Paschal II, however, also suggests an increasing sophistication in the use of the rite to enhance papal authority. The *Liber pontificalis* took particular note of the surprising dedicatory activity of Paschal II.[103]

Urban II spent most of his papacy travelling outside of Rome, largely because he was not in control of the city. He used these itineraries of necessity as occasions to build support along the Italian peninsula and in France. These dedications provided an opportunity for him to complete an elaborate pontifical rite before large crowds, including local lords, bishops and abbots, and this reinforced his position as the true pope. Three of Urban's best recorded and most significant dedications deserve closer attention than they have received thus far (see Chapter 2 above), namely to S. Nicola in Bari, to Santissima Trinità in Cava and to Saints Peter and Paul at Cluny.

San Nicola di Bari

In order to understand the potential meaning of the rite of dedication in Bari, it is essential to understand how the construction of that church came about. If the dedication of San Nicola is placed within the broader context of the theft of the relics of St Nicholas from Myra and the creation of the church, it becomes clear that the rite presented an opportunity for Urban and Roger I to place themselves at the front of what would become a cult of pan-European repute. In so doing, they were endorsing, not

opposing, quasi-communal activities very much at the expense of local episcopal authority (albeit out of necessity). A close examination of the theft of the relics makes the complexity of the situation plain. There are four accounts of primary importance. Two of them, the account attributed to Niceforo and that of John the Archdeacon, date from around the time of the translation. There is also an anonymous Franco-Latin source.[104] The narrative of John the Archdeacon was written at the behest of the Archbishop Urso and hints at, but glosses over, the full extent of his conflict with the factions of the city.[105] The remaining source is a Russian account of the theft and translation which appears to date to the decades immediately following the dedication.[106] The creation of these texts is one example of how the translation and dedication could give rise to the process of writing histories.

The texts, written so close to the events, were in agreement on most of the details, though they differ in the amount of detail they offer. In the spring of 1087, a group of men left Bari in three ships to trade grain and other merchandise in the Byzantine-ruled Mediterranean (the north-eastern corner of the sea). The group was a diverse one including sailors and merchants and also a handful of priests. They sailed with funding from the members of the urban elite of Bari: nobles and several of the so-called 'good men' who earned status and wealth as judges or notaries, or through trade (see Appendix A).[107] Their travels would take them as far as Lycia in modern Turkey, north and just west of the Island of Cyprus. It seems that prior to leaving the port of Bari, the group had agreed upon a daring plan. Knowing that the region had been raided regularly and recently by Turkish forces, this mixed group of Barese decided to steal the remains of the famous wonder-worker St Nicholas located in Myra.[108] Some sources suggested that the theft was inspired by a rumour that the Venetians were planning to steal the relics, but the presence of clergy on the ships implies a premeditated theft – although certainly inspired by the ongoing rivalry with Venice.[109] The city of Bari had been governed by the Byzantine Emperor as recently as 1071 when it fell to the Norman Robert Guiscard after a three-year siege. The Barese knew well the difficulty of the Emperor, as the success of the siege of their own city was, in part, also the result of Turkish raiding and the shifting of Byzantine defences and resources to counter them. Bari had been a comparatively low priority for the Emperor and by 1087 when their ships set sail the city was under ostensible Norman control. The Barese were thus determined to steal a jewel from the crown of their former emperor.

When they arrived in Myra, they approached the monastery of St

Nicholas and asked to see the sacred relics. At first the monks acquiesced, but, growing suspicious, they soon began to cry for help. Matteus Sparro, a sailor, grabbed one of the monks and threatened him with his sword demanding to be shown the relics. Matteus then took a hammer to the pavement, quickly finding the relics themselves. Giving a cry the Barese raced for their boats with the remains, leaving the people of Myra shouting on the docks and beating the monks for their negligence.[110]

Hearing advance word of the arrival of the relics, a large and excited crowd gathered at the harbour in Bari. A group of the Cathedral clerics vested themselves and processed to the harbour singing hymns and prepared to receive the body of St Nicholas. Archbishop Urso, however, was not at Bari at this time but rather in Canosa di Puglia (some fifty miles north of the city). But instead of giving over the relics to the Cathedral clerics, the sailors, merchants and priests on the ship instead informed their 'fellow citizens' that they wanted to keep control of the relics themselves and build a new church for them at the site that included the former Byzantine governor's palace.[111] Some people in the crowd sided with the cathedral clergy and urged the men to place the relics immediately in the cathedral of S. Maria, and a debate ensued aboard ship. The sailors then requested that Elias, abbot of the urban monastery of St Benedict in Bari (an important Latin monastery in the Byzantine city), should board the ship.[112] After revering the remains, Elias offered to hold the relics at his monastery until the citizens reached an agreement as to what they wanted to do with them – at which point, he promised, he would return them to the citizens. As part of this agreement the citizens received from Elias a series of hereditary privileges in relation to the relics, including among others support in the event that they or their heirs should fall into poverty, a percentage of the oblations offered on the feast of the translation, special burial privileges, seating within the church, a place in the church without further donation if they wished to become clergy, and a percentage of the donations made at the feast of the translation.[113] At least one member of the society secured not only the right for him and his wife to have seats within (while living) and tombs (ultimately) outside the church but also the right to take up the clerical life and a benefice from the church. These privileges were in clear violation of the canons enumerated by Anselm of Lucca and discussed above; lay donors were clearly not to retain privileged rights vis-à-vis the church they helped construct.[114] In essence, the 'society of St Nicholas' was most likely formed on these boats: a sworn society with distinct privileges within the city, one that would undertake the city's largest building programme. This posed a clear challenge to local seigneurial authority and canon law.

Once the terms were agreed upon, Abbot Elias and the citizens of Bari processed through the city singing hymns and bearing the relics to St Benedict. There they were deposited within the altar and the monastery was placed under armed guard. Once Urso, the archbishop, received word of the event he raced back to the city and went directly to the remains, 'both to pay homage to them and also to take possession of them with all zeal'.[115] This led to further, but fruitless, arguement as Urso attempted to gain the relics for the cathedral. The Archbishop, according to Niceforo and repeated by the Franco-Latin source, then sent some of his soldiers to remove the body by force.[116] Supporters of the merchants were met in the streets by the troops and three of the Archbishop's men were killed in the ensuing fight. The Archbishop's supporters retreated and the Society of St Nicholas won the day. It is important to note that the violent urban conflict was not caused by the theft of the relics, but over where to place the body; in other words, the conflict was over sacred space within the community, its relative sacrality and whether one particular group should be allowed to create that new sacred space. The theft of the relics was uncontroversial in Bari, indeed it was greeted with universal delight, according to the Franco-Latin account, and some called it a 'victory for the people'. [117] The conflict was specifically over who controlled the body (the bishop, the group who stole it or the local abbot) and where it should be placed (the cathedral, the abbey or a new space). If the theft was a point of excitement, the creation of sacred space was a point of violent conflict.

After the scuffle, the relics were then carried to within the former Byzantine compound. This area included religious, domestic and Byzantine official buildings.[118] The relics were placed on an altar inside the compound with an armed guard 'of all the citizens' while work commenced on the crypt of the new church. This work required not only the seizure of what would be regarded as the property of the Norman Dukes by right of conquest but also the destruction of three chapels and a small church, all ostensibly under the control of the archbishop. John the Archdeacon states that Urso entrusted the matter of the construction (and demolition) to Elias, and places this observation immediately after the violent conflict with Urso's men (which he chooses to pass over in silence). Niceforo and the anonymous Franco-Latin source concur in this, but if Urso did agree to this construction he was making what he could of a very bad situation.[119] It seems improbable that Urso, having lost men in the conflict with the citizens of Bari, would then support the demolition of these buildings willingly. Two years later, after the death of Archbishop Urso, Urban II accompanied the Norman Dukes Roger and Boemond to

Bari, entering the city in September of 1089 to dedicate the new church of San Nicola. Urban himself led the elaborate rite of dedication and also consecrated the Abbot Elias, now also rector of San Nicola, as the new Archbishop. A large feast was held in celebration, the poor of Bari were fed and numerous miracles were recorded.

The historiography on Bari has confined itself largely to the narrative of the translation or theft of the relics and has failed to carry the story through to its natural conclusion at the construction and dedication of the new church. Patrick Geary's famous analysis of the event glossed over the later portion of the narrative, as his interest was exclusively in the theft, and hence downplays the significance of the event for the civic life of Bari.[120] Such a focus allowed the earlier portion of the narrative to be described in terms of a ritual of community. That is, historians of the cult of the saints have been interested largely in how the cult fostered communal identity, as the cult of San Nicola certainly did in Bari.[121] But the tendency of the historiography to focus on the formation of communal identity has over-shadowed the extent to which the dedication of churches and the initia-tion of the cult could lead to conflict. In most modern accounts, after the relics were stolen, the ensuing cult brought wealth, identity and prestige to the city of Bari.[122] If the dedication was discussed at all, it was only as an alliance between papal and feudal lords to display their power and control over the city, placing Bari into the narrative of rising papal and seigneurial authority.[123] Closer reading of the event must reject this and observe that at Bari, the theft of the body of St Nicholas led to conflict within Bari. This dedication may best be understood, as others have done in the context of contemporary Iberia, in the context of the important activity of early Italian civic assemblies, whereby the events leading up to the construction and dedication of the church asserted new civic authority over and against episcopal and seigneurial authorities (here personified by the archbishop Urso, a Norman *familiaris* appointed by Gregory VII at the behest of Robert Guiscard).[124] The episcopal and monastic authorities opposed or supported the society of St Nicholas respectively, most likely because of their own ongoing rivalry and interest in controlling the relics, rather than for any predisposition toward the citizens of Bari.

The conflict over access to and possession of the sacred relics once they had been stolen was overlooked in the older version that emphasised com-munal identity formation in the events at Bari. Conflict occurred because placing the relics in a particular sacred space, whether the cathedral, abbey or communally built church, gave those responsible for that sacred space control over access to relics that were broadly desired. Not only did

the relics become an immediate sensation in the city, but the events were recorded in chronicles across Italy, Europe and the Mediterranean.[125] Bari became the centre of pan-European and Mediterranean pilgrimage. Therefore, control over access to the saint's body would inescapably result in the realignment of political authority within Bari. It is clear that the group involved in the theft of the relics recognised this as they resisted the initial lay and clerical pressure to bring the saint's body to the cathedral. Indeed, it was broadly recognised that the placement of the relics was significant for the entire city – hence the debate within the crowd and the arrival of the cathedral clergy in vestments at the harbour. This also explains the Abbot's interest in the negotiations, his desire to guarantee the safety of the relics vis-à-vis his monastery, and his generous terms to the 'Society of St Nicholas' which had stolen the relics. This lay-monastic partnership was one of mutual benefit at the expense of the bishop (unlike at Capua where laity and bishop would oppose local monastic authority; discussed in Chapter 5).

The 'Society' wanted to place the relics in a new church to be built in the area of the city that had housed the Byzantine governmental buildings. This compound still housed a number of chapels and small churches of varying significance.[126] Therefore, after the relics were temporarily deposited in the main altar of the monastic church of St Benedict, they were removed for safest keeping to an altar within the fortified zone of the governor's palace (in the church of S. Eustazio). Niceforo claimed that the crowds were chanting the *Kyrie*, which would be their appropriate liturgical role if this were a dedication.[127] What the 'Society' chose to do, in essence, was to tear down and rebuild the sacred and, by extension, political topography of Bari.[128] Its members thus transformed not only the central symbol of Byzantine dominance but also its sacred space, destroying four churches or chapels, and by extension the sacred authority on which it rested. All of this was accomplished to the exclusion of their episcopal and Norman overlords who ostensibly held control over the churches and the former governing compound.[129] In turn, the heavy walls of the new church of San Nicola itself revealed the real power it exerted; indeed the remaining Byzantine tower, the so-called tower of the catapan from the ninth century, reminds one of the military capacities of the site.[130] The physical and spiritual strengths of the site reinforced each other, thus enabling it to become the core of a 'proto-communal' movement in Bari between 1089 and 1139, when Roger II definitively conquered the city.[131]

This brings us to the moment of dedication of the incomplete church of San Nicola in 1089. When Urban II arrived in the city earlier in that

year, his own position was a very tenuous one. While this dedication would mark the high point of Urban's first southern Italian itinerary, this was an itinerary driven by necessity. The city of Rome was at this point predominantly under the control of the so-called 'antipope' Guibert of Ravenna. Guibert's fortunes rose and fell with those of his patron, the Emperor Henry IV, and these fortunes had reached one of their peaks just prior to this time.[132] In September, when Urban arrived in the city, he had just held a significant Council at Melfi (September 10), which is thought to have been attended by some seventy bishops and twelve abbots and so, while regional in scope, must certainly have been part of the agenda of the itinerary.[133] It has been suggested that the assembly at Melfi sought a *modus vivendi* between the Greek and Latin clergy in southern Italy.[134] If so, the dedication of San Nicola would have been an inflammatory concluding gesture, given that at its heart lay the famous and stolen remains of a Greek bishop. The dedication of San Nicola made plain that the official *modus vivendi* would be Latin dominance. It also allowed the pope to be visible in an area that had previously looked to emperors East or West to guide and protect their churches.[135]

While there is no complete record of Melfi, two things are of particular note: the council appears to have declared a truce, and Roger swore an oath to Urban II. The texts of both are missing, but the council stands out in its prohibitions of violence against the clergy and against bishops in particular.[136] This provision may hint at the strife in Bari, as might other canons from Melfi, as Canon 6, 'No abbot . . . should presume to receive from the laity things which belong to ecclesiastical law without concession from the bishop'. It may have simply been a timely reminder of a Gregorian canon, or it may have signalled a deeper concern with the then Abbot Elias' initiative concerning the relics of St Nicholas.[137] The dedication of San Nicola was, for Urban, an opportunity to punctuate his council with a major public liturgy. Urban followed this dedication with another at Brindisi in the next month.[138] He would repeat this practice throughout his pontificate, the most obvious example being his dedication of the great abbey church of Cluny followed almost immediately by the Council of Clermont in October and November of 1095 respectively. Thus, these dedications, when taking place at the papal level, could intersect with local, European and Mediterranean political conflict (as at Bari). Since all dedications were to be done by bishops, however, even the simplest of dedications had not only local but also regional import.

So it was also at Bari that while conflict did not emerge at the dedication itself, a deadly conflict did emerge over the location of the sacred space;

hence, the visual frame and possible meaning of the dedication. Were the body of St Nicholas to be deposited in the Cathedral, then Archbishop Urso, a Lombard but also a Norman *familiaris*, would have had the opportunity to hold an elaborate dedication for the altar. This would certainly have meant processing with the relics through the streets of the city, an event which would enhance his position within the city, and subordinate the Society who stole the body.[139] The Society would not be so subordinated, however, and fought and killed the bishop's men. Further conflict was avoided by the convenient death of the bishop and Urban II's appointment of the Abbot Elias as the new archbishop.[140] Some historians have read this as a 'reform' appointment on the part of Urban, as Elias appears to fit the papal preference for monastic bishops; but it seems instead to reveal sensitivity to the political realities of Bari on the part of Urban.[141] In fact, Elias' activity in negotiating with the Society of St Nicholas reveals him to be a practical religious leader rather than a staunch reformer. Thus, Urban arrived in Bari in 1089 for a variety of reasons. The first was the simple veneration of the relics. The second was to reinforce his own authority through the dedication of San Nicola immediately after a council held in southern Italy and by extension, possibly, his authority over the Greek Church as well. The dedication of San Nicola was part of a strategy of securing his own tentative position as pope by reinforcing the positions of the reforming papacy over and against Henry IV. Third, and related to the previous reason, the dedication reinforced the sacrality of his person as the one effecting the consecration of the church. Fourth, it offered him the chance to consecrate Abbot Elias as archbishop.

The dedication could not have been intended to lend his support to the Normans Roger and his brother Boemond who tentatively controlled the city of Bari; in consecrating the space and consecrating the Abbot Elias as Archbishop, Urban was quite literally blessing the actions of a usurping civic association over and against their ducal lords Boemond and Roger and their previous bishop, Urso. Such a blessing also complicates the historiography of hostility between pope, bishops and urban liberties. This dedication happened because the Society of St Nicholas held the upper hand; they controlled the body of the saint and so dictated the terms of, and fashioned the meaning of, the rite. Urban gained much needed prestige by this valuable association. The festivities recorded in our sources mask some very grave disputes within the community which had been put aside for the moment but would erupt again later. The dedication took place peacefully, but it was preceded by violence both in the Norman siege and in the battle with the Archbishop. Its subtext was also one of conflict:

conflict between bishop and lords with lay society and abbot, conflict between pope and emperor for prestige in Europe, conflict between Normans and Byzantines in the Mediterranean. Ultimately it would lead back to violent conflict between Roger II and the citizens. To put all of this more concretely, rather than viewing the dedication of 1089 as an assertion of papal and feudal authority as previous historians have, the papal dedication marks a success in a battle for early urban liberties, even if only for a generation until Roger II would put his decisive stamp on the basilica.[142] Further, the Abbot Elias, whose prestige was enormously advanced by the events, used it to heighten his own authority, adding the relics of S. Sabino to the altar in 1091, emphasising his unique role in regards to San Nicola and within the region as well as 'for the salvation of the commune'.[143]

Santissima Trinità, Cava

One of the few exceptions to Urban's broader pattern of using dedications to mark the activities of a council is Urban's dedication of Santissima Trinità at Cava in 1092.[144] In essence, though, it is an exception that proves the general rule that Urban employed the dedication to assert a papal order to the Church. Cava had, under its Abbot Peter (abbot from 1070–1123), taken on a self-consciously Cluniac style of monasticism and, like Cluny, came to dominate its environs.[145] Moreover, at Melfi a committee of bishops (made up of Cardinal-bishops Hubald of the Sabina and John of Tusculum, Bishop Bruno of Segni, Archbishop Arnald of Acerenza, Bishops Herve of Capua and Saxo of Cassano, and Bishop-elect Balbuin of Telese) was created to decide the case between Bishop Marald of Paestum-Cappaccio and Abbot Peter concerning the disputed jurisdiction over religious houses in Cilento.[146] Their decision in favour of Cava also placed the abbey directly under the protection of the papacy.[147] Three of those bishops who decided in favour of Cava were among those present at its dedication (Hubald of the Sabina, John of Tusculum and Bruno of Segni). According to the longer narrative, Bruno of Segni dedicated the Abbot's chapel, while Rangerius, Cardinal and Bishop of Reggio, dedicated a church in the nearby town of Casale.[148] Therefore, the dedication reflected the local conflict over ecclesial jurisdiction and the assertion of papal authority both in reforming the spiritual life of the Church and as the head of a new ecclesiastical order. In a broader sense it reflected the new canon law compiled under Anselm, in that it placed the papacy at the centre of legitimate dedications in an era when the dedication rite was not commonly practiced by the bishops of southern Italy.[149]

From the vantage of the monks of Cava itself, however, the dedication suggested their reflection of the ideal, heavenly community and of the Temple itself. As discussed in Chapter 2, the dedication at Cava was recorded as a quasi-miraculous event (*mira ratione*). It was also presented as the mountain where Moses encountered God and received the Law. Similarly it was like the Tabernacle; heavenly in form, it reminded the monastic author of the *Historia consecrationis* that the poor in spirit were to inherit the kingdom of heaven.[150] In this sense, the dedication was an eruption of the heavenly into the earthly and so, from the vantage of the monastic chronicler, an endorsement of the order created through monastic and papal reforms. This expanded authority, however, was at the expense of other regional monasteries and the archbishop of Salerno (itself a strong papal ally).[151] For his part, Urban, after confirming the privileges and liberties of Cava, is said to have addressed the monks and Duke Roger:

> Have you seen, dearest ones, how many portions of sacred oils, how many rites of ceremonies, and how many intercessions [*suffragiis*] of prayers we have used, while we thus dedicated the house through ministry of our humility to the Lord? Which all were done without doubt on account of you and for everyone everywhere even who will be to the end of time, in which they were spiritually completed, which happened today visibly in these walls. These things indeed which we have visibly done in this house, Jesus Christ works daily in the souls of the faithful. That is truly and rightly known to be the temple of the Holy Spirit. You, o sons, are the Temple of the living God, just as the Apostle has said, 'The Holy Temple of God is what you are'. Act therefore, brothers, as much as might be deemed worthy of a religious monk, whom God has freed from the tide of the world and has led out in the most peaceful port [*sinum*] of religious life, so that the eye of the mind, purged by monastic discipline, might easily be able to understand how much human affairs might be ever difficult, perishing, most full of error and emptiness. And even if it [the Temple of God] dwells on the earth, nevertheless it holds the laws of heaven, and now, in a manner, it is placed among the Blessed number. These indeed are the true ornaments; these are the worthy insignia of Monks. Wherefore, hold on to what you have, so that no one might take your crown; and grieve, for my fate, our burden carried by your prayers and piety, dearest brothers, because [the monastic life] is not permitted to authority.[152]

In this sermon attributed to Urban, the reformation theme of renewal of the inner self to monastic standards was held up as the heavenly ideal. The

consecration of society was to begin with the ornamentation of the self in monastic ideals. The consecrated site was a reflection of the consecrated self, and the monastic community was the Heavenly Jerusalem present on this earth. Similar themes may have also been preached by Bruno of Segni on this occasion (see Chapter 5). The congruity of those themes adds a sense of authenticity to the sermon.[153] The request for prayers from the brothers also reveals the tension between Urban consecrating the church in his official capacity as bishop of Rome and the preacher's own awareness of the threat to the inner consecrated life such a public office entails. (This was especially poignant for Urban as a monk turned pontiff.)

The Council of Troia in March of 1093 was followed in August by the dedication of the monastery of S. Maria in Banza, a dependency of Cassino, and Urban assured Cassino that his dedication and confirmation of their privileges was not meant to curtail their own rights vis-à-vis S. Maria.[154] In July, Urban had won the renunciation of simony and clerical concubinage (this being a particular concern of Troia) from Bishop Gerewin of Amiens.[155] So this dedication, too, was within a broader context of reforming the peninsula to the new Gregorian ideals, from both the vantage point of the Council at Troia and the application of those ideals. Urban would soon after call upon Duke Roger and Boemond to protect the church of S. Maria from the predations of Godfrey, and emphasised that he himself had consecrated the church.[156]

Sts Peter and Paul, Cluny

The most famous of Urban II's dedications was that of the great altar at Cluny on October 25, 1095 containing the relics of Sts Peter and Paul. This consecration took place during Urban's itinerary through the territories that the papal records refer to as Francia and Gaul.[157] Because of its association both with the dedication of Cluny and with the Council of Clermont (and hence the initiation of the 'First' Crusade) this itinerary has long received significant scholarly attention.[158] Usually, however, the transalpine portion of this itinerary has been considered independently of Urban's activities on the Italian peninsula.[159] Nor have his transalpine activities been considered in the larger context of Urban's use of the dedication. Neglect of this aspect of Urban's role results in part from his astounding activity once north of the Alps, where he consecrated some twenty-one churches and/or altars. But prior to crossing the Alps he held an important council at Piacenza, followed by the dedication of a church in Asti. The matter is somewhat confused, since Urban was consecrating

a variety of things as he came upon them: altars, churches, a building site, stones for use in future building and the entire island of Maguelone (a papal stronghold). Certain patterns can be identified, however, indicating the significance of these dedications.

While his southern itineraries were often driven by political necessity, his northern itinerary beginning in 1094 arose from opportunity: Henry IV and Guibert had been put to flight. It has long been recognised that the purpose of his northern itinerary was to create 'ecclesiastical discipline and order', and similar objectives had already been part of the activity of dedicating churches.[160] As with his southern itineraries, it was marked by grand liturgy, and Bernold of Constance partisanly noted that Urban set out from Rome, celebrating the Nativity of the Lord, 'most gloriously', in Tuscany.[161] The immediate primary objective was to be a council at Piacenza so large and well attended it was held in an open field outside of the city. In addition to condemning simony and nicolaitanism (Henry and Guibert), the council was famous for having heard the plea of a legation from Constantinople for help against the Turks, though it was not the first time the subject was considered.[162] The request seems to have generated little support at this stage. Three liturgical matters were also addressed. The first concerned the appropriate period for Ember Days as established by Gregory VII, confirmed at both Piacenza and Clermont.[163] The second, according to Bernold, was the condemnation of Berengar of Tours and the confirmation that 'when consecrated on the altar the bread and wine, not only figuratively but also truly and essentially, are converted into the body and blood of the Lord'.[164] Finally, the collection of fees for anointing with chrism (pro chrismate), baptism and funerals (sepultura) was prohibited.[165] A fourth might be added in that the Council at Piacenza originated a preface for the Mass offered to the Blessed Virgin Mary.[166] Thus, it is clear from the council's activities at Piacenza that the sacramental life of the Church was to be understood within the same context as that of simony and concubinage and the dedication of churches alongside these (as with other rites requiring chrism). Finally, if the goal of Piacenza was, as Orderic Vitalis summarised it, the re-establishment of the peace within the Church, then the dedication of a church, which formally established a space governed by the Peace of God, and the activities of council must be considered linked.[167] After Piacenza, Bernold of Constance tells us, Urban dedicated the church of an Augustinian abbey to Pope Leo IX, emphasising the continuity of reform through dedication.[168] The first dedication after Piacenza, however, was on 3 June, the basilica of S. Abbondio in Como, and then in July he dedicated the Duomo of S. Maria

in Asti.[169] (This latter dedication may have been especially poignant as it marked the triumphal homecoming of Bruno of Segni, a native, educated in Asti, as part of the papal entourage.) Thus, Piacenza followed a pattern already established by Urban in southern Italy, the punctuation of councils that confirmed Gregorian principles with the dedication of churches. In the particular example of the city of Piacenza, which had a rather turbulent relationship with reforming bishops, most notably Bonizio of Sutri, the elaborate rite of the dedication may have provided an opportunity for Urban to attract support to his cause.[170] Either this itinerary or that of Paschal II in 1106–07 may have motivated a series of dedications and the initiation of the new *duomo* once the reformers had control of the city.[171] In another sense, this combination of dedication and reforming councils was an attempt to extend the notion of the ideal Church (as at Cava) from the sacred space of a church to that of the heavenly city, and from the ideals of the reformers to a Church purified of simony and concubinage. He pursued this pattern across the Alps and into France.

Urban's itinerary north of the Alps has been closely studied. Here, the dedication of the high altar of the remodeled Cluny, dedicated to the Apostles Peter and Paul, has appropriately drawn the most attention.[172] It has been seen as the normative dedication or rather the dedication by which to judge all of his other consecrations on this itinerary. The dedication of Cluny was set not only within the general context of reforming dedications, but within the particular context of the itinerary that combined the consecration of sacred space with councils long since established and employed again on the cisalpine leg of this itinerary as well. One of the earliest studies of this itinerary noted some twenty-nine sites of various types of consecration.[173] From the consecration at Asti, Urban proceeded through Gap to Valence, where he consecrated the cathedral.[174] From there he travelled to Romans and Le Puy. At the Cluniac monastery of la Chaise-Dieu he dedicated the Church in honour of Saints Vitalis and Agricola on 18 August and confirmed their privileges.[175] From there he proceeded toward Chirac and dedicated another monastic church.[176] From Chirac he went on to Millau, Nîmes, St Giles and Tarcason where he was supposed to have blessed the land that was to be used for a church and cemetery.[177] He then proceeded to Avignon and from there due north to Cluny with several stops along the way.

At Cluny, on 25 October, Urban dedicated the great altar of the new church and the matutinal altar. The near-contemporary record of his sermon on this occasion certainly suggests that his overriding understanding of the dedication was one of Church organisation, confirming

the privileges of monastery, its direct obedience to Rome and creating the famous 'sacred ban' of exclusive juridical privilege in a quasi-circle around Cluny.[178] Radiating out from the major altar of Cluny itself, side altars were dedicated by Hugh, Archbishop of Lyons, the Archbishop of Pisa, and Bruno, Bishop of Segni, a pattern not unlike that at Cava, where Bruno had dedicated the Abbot's chapel and another cardinal and bishop, Rangerius, had dedicated a nearby church. As Didier Méhu has stated, 'The consecration instituted a new social and spatial organisation around the poles of the consecrated place and the men who served it. The articulation of this new society at Cluny in 1095 is very clear.'[179] It is, as Méhu implied, an asserted ideal; such an ideal can be asserted without being actualised, as the case of Bari makes plain.

The dedication at Cluny was novel in its coherent use of the dedication rite. In part, this coherence was because of the relationship between these two most preeminent Latin Christian institutions, the papacy and the monastery of Cluny. If that relationship is no longer considered unique, its closeness was especially pronounced in this period.[180] This close relationship, especially in the person of Urban II, allowed the significance of church consecration to be readily projected. Cluny, dedicated to St Peter as it was, was also directly subordinate to St Peter, whose living remains lay in the church of the same name in the city of Rome. Indeed the church building itself echoed that of St Peter's in Rome.[181] For these reasons the dedication rite had a very distinct meaning at Cluny that it could not have had at Bari. At the same time, that meaning was not so very novel. Urban's preaching on the privileges of Cluny was rooted in the dedication rite itself that gave the dedicating bishop the opportunity to instruct lay authorities on their appropriate relation to the space. It was also part of a longer tradition of immunities and privilege within Europe, as Barbara Rosenwein has demonstrated.[182] What was unique about the dedication of Cluny, the coherence of its meaning, was precisely the result of the efforts of contemporaries to direct the meaning of the rite, including one of the participants in the dedication, Bruno of Segni, considered at length in Chapter 5.

After the consecration at Cluny, Urban proceeded to Sauvigny and from there to Clermont, where the Council was opened on 18 November.[183] It is well beyond the scope of this book to review the enormous historiography on the Council of Clermont as it relates to the so-called First Crusade. It is clear, however, that the large public liturgies of Urban II before and after Clermont, as with his other councils, helped reinforce the authority of the council. Moreover, the language of the dedication rite and its sermons, emphasising sacred space as a metaphor for the Church as both

the Temple and the Heavenly Jerusalem, must have helped to reinforce the message of an armed pilgrimage to the Holy Land.[184] The conciliar activity reflected a significant effort at ecclesiology along reform lines. His activities, such as the excommunication of Guibert of Ravenna and Henry IV and the structuring of the relationships between various local churches and episcopacies and Cluny, including consecrations at La Chaise-Dieu and Maguelone, reinforce a reform ecclesiology. Also suggestive of the manner in which the consecrations of churches and councils were linked was the excommunication of Bernard Girlandi and his sons for seizing the church of St Martin at Chaudes-Aigues, a possession of the Cluniac priory of Saint-Flour (which Urban would in turn consecrate) and of Elbo for seizing the church on the island of Oléron. The council also resolved the conflict between the Count of Clermont, the cathedral canons and the Abbot of St Alyre at Clermont.[185] Thus, the Council of Clermont needed to reinforce the sacred space that the dedication rites created as well as the ecclesiology the reformers were promoting. These examples serve as a healthy admonition against overemphasising the effective separateness of sacred space and of the power of the ban of Cluny.

After Clermont, Urban dedicated Cluniac churches at Sauxillanges, at Saint-Flour and at Aurillac. Conflict again followed the dedication rite, as Urban was not able to dedicate Sainte-Croix at Uzerche due to the objections of the Bishop of Limoges, Humbald of Sainte-Sevère.[186] Urban replaced Humbald with the prior of St-Martial and consecrated the cathedral of St Stephen and abbey church of St-Martial.[187] On 10 January 1096, when he dedicated the abbatial church of the Holy Saviour in Charroux, not only were the Italian bishops Dambert of Pisa, Rangerius of Reggio and Bruno of Segni still part of his entourage, but so was John of Gaeta (the future Gelasius II).[188] So it continued, in a tour of consecrations and dedications, at Vendôme, St-Eutrope des Saintes, Bourdeaux, Moissac and Toulouse. Two of these altars and one church were dedicated to the Holy Cross.[189] At Angers he dedicated an abbey-church to St Nicholas.[190] The monks of St-Aubin, however, refused the papal consecration. While the exact reasons are unknown, the refusal suggests an awareness that the papal dedication came with the kind of significant ecclesiological implications seen in Anselm and in the ban of Cluny.[191] At Poitiers, however, the community tore down an altar to have Urban consecrate the new one and to have the privilege and indulgences of St Peter.[192] In a telling moment he consecrated the entire island of Maguelone, an important papal stronghold. Returning to St-Gilles, he consecrated the altar of the new basilica.

While the consecration of the high altar at Cluny and its concomitant

elaboration of the sacred ban is striking in its coherence, the remainder of Urban's itinerary of 1095–96 has an ad hoc quality to it: responding to opportunities and invitations for dedications, consecrations and blessings of churches, altars, stones, land (for cemeteries and churches) and an entire island. The coherent logic of Cluny and the opportunism of the remainder of the itinerary suggest both the emerging significance of the reforming ideal of the dedication and the attractive power of the dedication rite. It is clear that many, though not all, sought out these papal dedications and with them the reform ecclesiology they suggested.

If Urban was building upon Anselm of Lucca's efforts, he did not have to rely solely upon his canonical collection, as Anselm was not alone among eleventh-century intellectuals in creating a pro-papal assessment of the liturgy for the dedication. Such an approach to the dedication liturgy was also manifested in the commentaries and letters of the leading liturgical exegete, Cardinal and Bishop Bruno of Segni. Even if they could have overlooked its significance in earlier canon collections, contemporaries could not have mistaken that Anselm was reconstructing the significance of the dedication rite and its new importance for the papacy. The young bishop from Segni had been among Gregory's closest advisors and was a keen observer of the broader ramifications of the liturgy; now in his middle age, he participated in all of Urban II's major dedications on the Italian peninsula and across the Alps. The significance of the dedication was not wasted on him. Bruno offered his own pro-papal interpretation of the dedication, and he would employ dedications as a strategy to promote his and papal authority through the reign of Paschal II. The ambitions of his youth, however, would need to be adjusted to the disappointments of his later years.

Notes

1 The most recent study of Anselm's work on canon law, which includes an overview of his career, is Cushing, *Papacy and Law*.

2 H. Keller, 'Le origini sociali e famigliari del vescovo Anselmo', in Violante, *Sant'Anselmo Vescovo*, 27–50, at 32.

3 Cowdrey, *Gregory VII*, 68–70.

4 M. Giusti, 'Le canoniche della città e diocesi di Lucca al tempo della Riforma Gregoriana', *Studi Gregoriani* 3 (1948): 321–67; E. Kittel, 'Der Kampf um die Reform des Domkapitels in Lucca im 11. Jahrhundert', in L. Santifaller (ed.), *Festschrift Albert Brackmann* (Weimar, 1931), 207–47. On the expansion and renovation of the Lucchese churches, see Maria Teresa Filieri, *Architettura Medioevale in Diocesi di Lucca: Le Pievi del Territorio di Capannori* (Lucca, 1990).

5   In this regard Alexander seems to exemplify the pattern of reform in Salerno, where Alfanus, also a vocal supporter of the reform movement, did not force the reform of his canons, see Ramseyer, *Transformation of a Religious Landscape*, 153–4.

6   There has been much speculation on whether Anselm studied with Lanfranc at Bec or Caen, or even the Benedictine abbey at Polirone, summed up by Cushing, *Papacy and Law*, 44–5.

7   The subject of Anselm's retirement and recall is much confused by his anonymous hagiographer to emphasize Anselm's Gregorian partisanship, as skilfully reconstructed by Cushing, *Papacy and Law*, 52–5.

8   *Vita Anselmi*, 37.

9   Ibid., 5, 40.

10 W. Goez, 'Reformpapsttum, Adel und monastiche Erneuerung in der Toscana', in J. Fleckenstein (ed.), *Investiturstreit und Reichsverfassung* (Sigmaringen, 1973), 205–39.

11 Cowdrey, *Gregory VII*, 304–5.

12 For example, the abbots of Montecassino had been expanding their control in the Lucchese since 1056 and the acquisition of the cloister of St George. It is telling that it was to the prior of St George, Bonomo, that Bruno of Segni, then abbot of Montecassino, would send his blunt criticisms of Paschal II for abandoning the reform position in 1111. Bloch, *Monte Cassino*, 428–32. Hansmartin Schwarzmaier, 'Das Kloster St Georg in Lucca und der Ausgriff Montecassinos in die Toskana', *Quellen und Forschungen* 49 (1969): 145–85.

13 *Vita Anselmi*, 7. On the early complexity of the Lucchese canons' economic life see Duane J. Osheim, 'The Episcopal Archive of Lucca in the Middle Ages', *Manuscripta* 17 (1973): 131–46.

14 *Vita Anselmi*, 8; Gregory VII, *Das Register Gregors VII*, ed. E. Caspar, MGH *Epistolae Selectae* 2 (1920–3), 5. 1, 6. 11, 7. 2. On these developments, H. Schwarzmeier, *Lucca und das Reich bis zum Ende des 11. Jahrhunderts* (Tübingen, 1972), esp., 13, 66–71, 400–12. Cowdrey, *Gregory*, 304–5.

15 Charles Buchanan, 'Spiritual and Spatial Authority in Medieval Lucca: Illuminated Manuscripts, Stational Liturgy and the Gregorian Reform', *Art History* 27(5), 723–44, at 729.

16 *Vita Anselmi*, 9–11.

17 Anselm of Lucca, *Anselmi episcopi Lucensis Collectio canonum una cum collectione minore*, ed. F. Thaner (Innsbruck, 1906–15). On Gregory VII and the creation of canon law, see the helpful overview of Uta-Renate Blumenthal, 'The Papacy and Canon Law in the Eleventh-Century Reform', *Catholic Historical Review* 84 (1998), 201–18.

18 Paul Fournier and Gabriel Le Bras, *Histoire des collections canoniques en Occident depuis les décrétales jusqu'au décret de Gratien*, 2 Vols (Paris: Recueil Sirey, 1932); James Brundage, *Medieval Canon Law* (London, 1995), 35–43.

19 Iohannis Mantuani, *In Cantica canticorum et De sancta Maria tractatus ad Comitissam Matildam*, ed. B. Bischoff and B. Taeger (Frieburg, 1973). Robinson, 'Political Allegory'.

20 Anselm of Lucca, *Liber contra Wibertum*, ed. E. Berheim, MGH Libelli de Lite (LdL) (Hanover, 1897), I. 517–28.

21 See Eric Hobsbawm, 'Introduction: Inventing Traditions', in Eric Hobsbawm and Terrence Ranger (eds), *The Invention of Tradition*(Cambridge, 1983), 1–14. Anselm is inventing a tradition of an actively regulatory papacy. On the papacy in the Carolingian period, see Thomas F.X. Noble, *The Republic of St Peter: The Birth of the Papal State (680–825)* (Philadelphia, 1984).

22 A brief overview may be found in Roger E. Reynolds, 'Law, Canon: To Gratian', in Strayer, *Dictionary of the Middle Ages*, 7: 395–413, 410; for comparative texts see Gratian, *Decretum*, ed. A. Friedberg, in *Corpus Iuris Canonici* (Leipzig, 1879), 2 Vols, 1: XLIX–LIII.

23 Gérard Fransen, 'Anselme de Lucques Canoniste?', in Violante, *Sant'Anselmo Vescovo*, 143–55.

24 Ibid., 153.

25 For a vigorous defense of Anselm's authorship of the collection, see Giorgio Picasso, 'La "Collectio Canonum" di Anselmo nella storia dell collezioni canon-iche', in Violante, *Sant'Anselmo Vescovo*, 313–21.

26 Fournier-Le Bras, *Histoire des collections canoniques*, 28–9.

27 Alfonso Stickler, 'Il Potere Coattivo Materiale dell Chiesa nella Riforma Gregoriana Secondo Anselmo di Lucca', *Studi Gregoriani* 2 (1947): 235–85, esp. at 281–2 and 285.

28 Fournier-LeBras, *Histoire des collections canoniques*, 28.

29 Folios 177r–185r, less than half of Book VIII (161r–176v), though rivalling Book V (88r–98v). While sex receives the fewest number of folios, the penitential that follows takes up more than twice as many (186r–207r). Fournier-LeBras, *Histoire des collections canoniques*, 28. Though content is most important it is interesting to consider the hierarchy of concerns that might be revealed by the use of materials.

30 Ibid., 31. Cushing, 'Anselm of Lucca and Burchard of Worms: Re-thinking the Sources of Anselm II', *De Penitentia*', in Cushing and Gyug, *Ritual, Text and Law*, 225–40.

31 These Books were the basis of Stickler's thesis in, 'Il Potere Coattivo', indirectly, a powerful argument for the coherence of the collection, and for its Anselmian authorship.

32 So, for example, John Gilchrist, 'Gregory VII and the Juristic Sources of His Ideology', *Studia Gratiana XII* (1967): 3–37, compares Gregory's *Registra* to other contemporary canon collections, without noting that Gregory was promoting the use of select canons, and, so, interpreting or creating law, not simply reflecting upon canon collections. The method employed (examining the *Registra* on issues of reform 'ideology' and searching for citations from precedent and canon collections) presumes continuity. In his comparison of Gregory's *Registra* with Anselm's collection in order to demonstrate that Gregory was relying on canonical sources (when Anselm used Gregory's own missives as a source for canon law, and clearly composed his collection in support of Gregory's reform efforts), the creative approach to the tradition is missed, as is Gregory's role in creating that tradition.

33 An appreciation of the creative nature of these collections may be found in Cushing, *Papacy and Law*, 29. See also Uta-Renate Blumenthal, 'Fälschungen bei Kanonisten der Kirchenreform des 11. Jahrhunderts', *Fälschungen im Mittelalter, Internationaler Kongreß der Monumenta Germaniae Historica, München, 16.–19. September 1986*, MGH SS 33, t. 2: *Gefälschte Rechstexte der bestrafte Fälscher* (Hanover, 1988), 241–62. Some modification to Cushing's study has been suggested, especially in regard to the relative importance of the *Collection in Seventy-Four Titles*, by Szabolcs Anzelm Szuromi in *Anselm of Lucca as a Canonist* (Frankfurt am Main, 2006), at 69–70, 79–91.

34 Anselm, *Collectio canonum*, Bk. VI, cc. 43, 44, 166, and 167; VII, cc. 43 and 44. Thaner, 289–91, 345–6, 381–3. This is not surprising, given the growing concern to reform the liturgy; Enrico Cattaneo, 'La liturgia nella riforma gregoriana', 169–90.

35 In this sense it is an 'invented tradition', Hobsbawm, 'Inventing Traditions', 8–9.

36 Incipit Liber I de primatu Sce Romane ecclesie QUOD IN NOVO TESTAMENTO POST XPM DNM A PETRO SACERDOTALIS COEPERIT ORDO; Vat. lat. 1363, fol. 3v, the capitalised clause being in rusticated capitals. Cushing prefers the reading *De potestae et auctoritate apostolicae sedis* from later manuscripts; this heightens the gap between Anselm and Deusdedit unnecessarily; *Papacy and Law*, 100.

37 Vat. lat. 1363, fol. 5r.

38 Ibid.

39 Picasso, 'La "Collectio Canonum"', 314. Also, E. Pásztor, 'Una fonte per la storia', 32. Stickler describes it as a most faithful reflection of the ideals of Gregory VII himself; Stickler, 'Il Potere coattivo', 282.

40 *Vita Anselmi*, 21.

41 Picasso, 'La "Collectio Canonum"', 315. Vat. Barb. lat. 535: facta tempore VII Gregorii sanctissimi pape a beatissimo Anselmo Lucensi episcopo eius diligenti imitatore et discipulo, cuius iussione et praecepto desiderante consummavit hoc opus. Thus the work is not only an apology for Gregory VII but was by his commission: 'iussione et praecepto'. On Hildebrand's unsuccessful efforts to enlist Peter Damian's assistance in creating a collection of canon law and the *Dictatus Papae*, see Cowdrey, *Gregory VII*, 40.

42 Anselm, *Collectio canonum*, Bk 2, c. 2. Thaner, 76.

43 Ibid., Bk. 2, c. 79. Thaner, 112–13.

44 For the resources Anselm may have had at his disposal, see Giuseppe Motta, 'I codici canonistici di Polirone', in Violante, *Sant'Anselmo Vescovo*, 349–71.

45 In this sense, canon law of the reforming type is always 'aspirational'. I would like to thank one of the anonymous readers of Manchester University Press for suggesting the phrase.

46 There is much discussion in the literature of the possible significance of *regalia* and *ecclesiastica*, especially in the context of Sutri. See Uta-Renate Blumenthal, 'Patrimonia and Regalia in 1111', in K. Pennington and R. Somerville (eds), *Law, Church, and Society: Essays in Honor of Stephan Kuttner* (Philadelphia, 1977), 12–16. See also Anselm, *Collectio canonum* Book IV, c. 19. Thaner, 198–9.

47 Anselm, *Collectio canonum*, Bk. IV, 12. Thaner, 196–7.

48 This is of particular interest, as scholars have seen Urban II's dedication as innovative in establishing a sacred ban around Cluny, but the connection between dedication and privileges is made overt here by Anselm just prior to Urban's papacy. See Rosenwein, *Negotiating Space*; Iogna-Prat, *Order and Exclusion*; and Méhu, *Paix et communautés*. Rosenwein sees the critical link as the consecration of cemeteries by Urban II as much as churches, *Negotiating Space*, 179. Here, in Anselm, the concern is with the dedication of churches.

49 Toubert, *Un art dirigé*.

50 The sources for these were *Codex Theodosianus*, ed. Theodore Mommsen (Berlin, [1955]) 16 2, 1.8; *Constitutum Silvestri*, c. 20, in *Epistolae Romanorum pontificorum*, ed. P. Coustant, Appendix 52, n. 27.

51 The sources for these were *Digesta Iustiniani Augusti*, ed. Theodore Mommsen, 2 Vols (Berlin, 1870), I 2, 1.22; I 3, 1.32; and I 2, 1.12; I 3, 1.34.

52 Anselm, *Collectio canonum*, Bk. VII, cc. 117–119; Thaner, 413–14. Ramseyer, *Transformation of a Religious Landscape*, 61.

53 Anselm, *Collectio canonum* Bk. V, cc. 1–12, 38, 50–51; Thaner, 229–30.

54 Ramseyer, *Transformation of a Religious Landscape*, 75.

55 Cowdrey, *Desiderius*, 40–1.

56 See Aldo A. Settia, 'Églises et fortifications médiévales dans l'Italie du nord', in his *L'Église et le château: Xe–XVIIe siècles* (Bordeaux, 1988), 81–94; '*Ecclesiam incastellare*: Chiese e castelli nella diocesi di Padova in alcune recenti pubblicazioni', in his *Fonti e studi di storia ecclesiastica padovana* (XII) (Padua, 1981), 47–75; 'Chiese e fortezze nel popolamento delle diocesi friulane', in *Il Friuli dagli Ottoni agli Hohenstaufen, Atti del convegno internazionale di studi* (Udine, 1984), 217–44. All reproduced in his *Chiese, Strade e Fortezze nell'Italia Medievale*, Italia Sacra 46 (Rome, 1991), 47–130.

57 See the essays collected in R.N. Swanson (ed.), *Unity and Diversity in the Church*, Studies in Church History 32 (Cambridge, 1996) and in Christopher M. Bellitto and Louis I. Hamilton (eds), *Reforming the Church* (Aldershot, 2005).

58 Noble sums up the matter nicely when he states, 'That the Roman Church was the largest landholder in Italy . . . is beyond dispute. That the possession of land in the early Middle Ages translated directly into power and influence is also beyond dispute. Unfortunately, the perfectly accurate qualitative judgements cannot be exchanged for equally accurate quantitative ones', *Republic of St Peter*, 244. As Noble points out, the gap between the rhetoric of papal authority and the reality of papal control is considerable (giving the examples of papal claims to control Venice, Istria, Benevento or Spoleto): ibid., 241–2. This earlier model of the papacy is changing but still predominant in the eleventh and early twelfth centuries. Ramseyer's *Transformation of a Religious Landscape* is excellent at capturing the complexity of religious power as practised.

59 Book V, cc. 1–3; Thaner, 231–2. Overall this approach is distinct from that of Burchard of Worms or Ivo of Chartres who emphasised the precedent of the dedication of the Temple. See Ziolkowski, *Consecration and Blessing*, 6, citing PL 160, 686 and PL 161, 1085.

60 Anselm, *Collectio canonum*, Bk. V, c. 4; Thaner, 232–3.

61 The date and origin of the 74T has been the subject of ongoing scholarly debate, summarised in *Diversorum patrum sententiae sive Collectio in LXXIV titulos digesta*, ed. J.T. Gilchrist, Monumenta Iuris Canonici Ser. B, v. 1 (Vatican City, 1973), xxi–xxxi.

62 74T, c. 209.

63 Cushing, *Papacy and Law*, 172. For an overall discussion of the multiple ways in which Anselm's reorganisation and emendation of his sources, and his addition of rubrics, serves to emphasise the ideals of the papal reformers, see the appendices in ibid., 147–200; see also Blumenthal, 'Fälschungen bei Kanonisten'.

64 Anselm, *Collectio canonum*, Bk. V, c. 5; Thaner, 233.

65 Jaffé, 636.

66 Anselm, *Collectio canonum*, Bk. V, c. 6; Thaner, 233–4.

67 Gratian, *Decretum*, III, D. 1, cc. 5–7.

68 Anselm, *Collectio Canonum*, Bk. V, c. 11; Thaner, 235.

69 Ibid., Bk. V, c. 26: Ut oratorium non consecratur absque auctoritate sedis apostolicae. Thaner, 241.

70 Ibid.

71 See below, Chapter 5.

72 On the *pax ecclesiae* and the Peace of God, see Magnou-Nortier, 'Enemies of the Church', in Head and Landes, *Peace of God*, 59–60.

73 Anselm, *Collectio Canonum*, Bk. V, c. 46; Thaner, 249. For examples where this is not the norm, see David Foote, *Lordship, Reform and the Development of Civil Society in Medieval Italy* (Notre Dame, 2004), 52–4. See Barbara Rosenwein, *To be the Neighbor of St Peter: The Social Meaning of Cluny's Property, 909–1049* (Ithaca, 1989) on the earlier, more fluid nature of donations of property.

74 Anselm, *Collectio Canonum*, Bk. V, cc. 13–14, 21–3; Thaner, 236, 238–40.

75 As may well have been the case in Parma in 1106, when Paschal II dedicated the basilica, built by Bishop Cadalo, who had been established as a rival pope.

76 Anselm, *Collectio canonum*, Bk. V, cc. 17–19, 27, 32–8, 40–8, 52, 58; Thaner, 237, 241, 244–51, 256.

77 Anselm, *Collectio canonum*, Bk. V, cc. 7–10; Thaner, 234–5.

78 Magnou-Nortier, 'The Enemies of the Church', 79; Goetz, 'Protection of the Church', in *Peace of God*, 259–79.

79 Anselm, *Collectio canonum*, Bk. V, cc. 8–9; Thaner, 234.

80 Anselm, *Collectio canonum*, Bk. V, 29–31, 40: Thaner, 242–4, 246–7.

81 I.e., Anselm, *Collectio canonum*, Bk. V, c. 64 in Thanner, who transposes chapters 63 and 64 from Vat. Lat. 1363, where 60 through 64 form a discrete unit on the division of income through tithing: Thaner, 257–58.

82 See above, Chapter 3.

83 Anselm, *Collectio canonum*, Bk. V, c. 31; Thaner, 243–4.

84 John Hine Mundy, *Studies in the Ecclesiastical and Social History of Toulouse in the Age of the Cathars* (Aldershot, 2006); Lester K. Little, *Religious Poverty and*

the Profit Economy (Ithaca, 1983); Michel Mollat, *The Poor in the Middle Ages: A Social History*, trans. Arthur Goldhammer (New Haven, 1986).

85 *Sermo Anselmi episcopi de Caritate*, ed. E. Pásztor, in 'Motivi dell'ecclesiologia di Anselmo di Lucca in margine a un sermone inedito', *Bulletino Istorico Italiano* 77 (1965): 45–104. Cushing, *Papacy and Law*, 113–16.

86 Anselm, *Collectio canonum*, Bk. I., cc. 67–69; Thaner, 35–7.

87 As discussed in the preceding chapter.

88 Anselm, *Collectio canonum*, Bk. I, c. 66; Thaner, 34–5.

89 Ibid.

90 74T, 30. Cushing notes the relationship between the 74T and *Collectio canonum*, Bk. I, cc. 67 and 68, but overlooks 66. In fact, Anselm is drawing upon and elaborating the 74T on this specific point of Roman primacy and the metaphor of construction and dedication.

91 Anselm, *Collectio canonum* Bk. I, c. 67; Thaner, 35.

92 Ibid., Bk. I, cc. 68–9; Thaner, 35–7.

93 Ibid., Bk. I, c. 70; Thaner, 37–8.

94 Damian, *Sermones* 14–16, *Die Briefe*, n. 65, 233–4 as discussed in Chapter 3.

95 Anselm, *Collectio canonum*, Bk. I, cc. 71–2; Thaner, 38–48.

96 74T, 41, De auctoritate sacerdotali et potestate regali.

97 Cushing, *Papacy and Law*, 171.

98 Gregory was led to Salerno *cum magno honore* according to the *Annales Benevantani*, ed. G.H. Pertz, Monumenta Germaniae Historica, Scriptores (MGH SS) 3, a. 1084, 182; Gaufredus Malaterra does not seem to think Gregory in a weakened position either: *De rebus gestis Rogerii Calabriae et Siciliae comitis et Roberti Guiscardi ducis fratris eius*, ed. R. Pontieri, Rerum italicarum scriptores, n. s. (RIS) 3.37, 80; *Chronica monasterii Casinensis*, ed. Hartmut Hoffmann, MGH SS 34 (1980) 3.58, 438. H.E.J. Cowdrey observes that it would not have been in Guiscard's own interest to lead Gregory defeated or imprisoned back to Salerno to dedicate his new basilica, as this would only undermine the significance of the dedication: Cowdrey, *Gregory VII*, 438–9.

99 A duce Roberto donaris, Apostole, templo;/ pro meritis regno donetur et ipse superno./ Dux et Iordanus, dignus princeps Capuanus,/ regnent aeternum cum gente colente Salernum; Alfanus, *I carmi*, *Carme* 53, 20, ll. 7–10.

100 Graham Loud, *The Age of Robert Guiscard: Southern Italy and the Norman Conquest* (Harlow, 2000), 252.

101 Loud, *Robert Guiscard*, 264.

102 Ramseyer, *Transformation of a Religious Landscape*, 61.

103 *Liber pontificalis*, ed. Louis Duchesne and Cyrille Vogel, 3 Vols (Paris, 1955 [1886–92]), II, 305.

104 Pasquale Corsi, *La traslazione di San Nicola: le fonti* (Bari, 1988), 7–11. F. Nitti di Vito, 'La Traslazione di S. Nicola di Bari (1087 o 1071?)', *Iapigia*, n.s 10 (1939), 374–82; F. Nitti di Vito, 'Leggenda di S. Nicola', *Iapigia*, n.s. 8 (1937), 265–74; F. Nitti di Vito, 'La traslazione delle reliquie di S. Nicola', *Iapigia*, n.s. 8 (1937), 295–411; F. Nitti di Vito, *La Leggenda della Traslazione di S. Nicola di Bari, I Marinai* (Trani, 1902).

105 Corsi, *Traslazione di San Nicola*, 62–3.

106 Cioffari, *Leggenda di Kiev*, 43.

107 Francesco Babudri, 'Sinossi critica dei traslatori Nicolaiani di Bari', *Archivio storico Pugliese* (1950), an. 3, 3–94, at 90–4.

108 Loud, *Robert Guiscard*, 134–5.

109 Orderic Vitalis, *Ecclesiastical History* IV, 56, 206–7; Corsi, *Traslazione di San Nicola*, Niceforo, 16; the Kiev Legend also contains this (Cioffari, *La Leggenda di Kiev*, 93) but it is an additional element of a premeditated plan conceived by a cleric (Cioffari, *La Leggenda di Kiev*, 87) that seems more credible.

110 Corsi, *Traslazione di San Nicola*, Niceforo, 31.

111 Ibid., 35.

112 Houben, 'La Chiesa di Bari alla fine dell' XI secolo', in Salvatore Palese and Giancarlo Locatelli (eds), *Il Concilio di Bari del 1098: Atti del Convegno Storico Internazionale e celebrazione dei IX Centenario del Concilio* (Bari, 1998), 91–107, 97–8.

113 Nitti di Vito, *La Leggenda*, 6–7; Babudri, 'Sinossi critica', 63–8; Donald Matthew, *The Norman Kingdom of Sicily* (Cambridge, 1992), 101.

114 As noted above concerning Anselm, *Collectio canonum* Bk. V, cc. 7–10.

115 Gustav Anrich, *Hagios Nikolaos: Der heilige Nicolaos in der Griechen Kirche: Texte und Untersuchungen*, Vol. 1 (Berlin, 1913), 435–49. The translation is by Eugene R. Whitmore, *St Nicholas, Bishop of Myra (Saint Nicolas of Bari): The Genesis of Santa Claus* (1944), 28–36, reproduced by Gerardo Cioffari, 'The Translation of Saint Nicholas, an Anonymous Greek Account of the Transfer of the Body of the St Nicholas from Myra in Lycia to Bari in Italy', *Bollettino di S. Nicola* 10 (1980), 2–18, at (17), 12.

116 Corsi, *Traslazione di San Nicola*, 'Niceforo', 37, 'Leggenda Gerosolimitana', 77; *Analecta Bollandiana* IV (1885), 169–92.

117 Corsi, *Traslazione di San Nicola*, 'Gerosolimitana', 77.

118 These would be the palace of the catapan, S. Gregorio, S. Eustazio, S. Basilio, and S. Demitrio, perhaps S. Sofia and S. Stefano. See Gerardo Cioffari, *Storia della Basilica di S. Nicola di Bari*, I: *L'Epoca Normanno Sveva* (Bari, 1984), 69.

119 Corsi, *Traslazione di San Nicola*, 'Niceforo', 37, John the Archdeacon, 62–3.

120 Geary, *Furta Sacra*, 94–103.

121 On a cult that fostered multiple communal identities and met multiple needs, see Sharon Farmer, *Communities of St Martin: Legend and Ritual in Medieval Tours* (Ithaca, 1991).

122 'The acquisition of Saint Nicolas meant more to Bari than mere one-upsmanship. From the saint's first arrival he was intended to attract pilgrims . . . Obviously the Bari efforts were a success . . . throughout Europe, from the Mediterranean to the Baltic, merchant communities envied the success of the *Societas Sancti Nicolai*', Geary, *Furta Sacra*, 103.

123 Orderic Vitalis, *Ecclesiastical History*, concludes that the appointment of Elias as archbishop was a great success for the reformers, IV, 353; Franco Schettini, *La Basilica di San Nicola di Bari* (Bari, 1967), 15.

124 Loud, *Robert Guiscard*, 243.
125 This includes a very long description by Orderic Vitalis, *Ecclesiastical History*, IV, 54–70, and a very important Russian account in Kiev. For the primary sources, see Cioffari, *Storia della Basilica*, 41–8.
126 Cioffari, *Storia della Basilica*, 68–9. Nino Lavermicocca, 'Il Pretorio Bizantino di Bari', in Michele D'Elia (ed.), *Città della Nicoliana: Un progetto verso il 2000* (Bari, 1995), 25–31, at 26–7; Angelo Ambrosi, 'La Basilica di San Nicola, Sito e Architettura', *Città della Nicoliana*, 33–46; Schettini, *Basilica di San Nicola*, 35–40.
127 Corsi, *La Traslazione di San Nicola*, Niceforo, 39.
128 Lavermicocca, 'Il Pretorio Bizantino di Bari', 25–6.
129 It has been suggested that Robert Guiscard may have given control of the area to Urso; although this is uncertain, if he had, it would only heighten the rebelliousness of the Barese who stole the relics; Cioffari, *Storia della Basilica*, 61.
130 Schettini, *Basilica di San Nicola*, 28 and 36.
131 H. Houben, *Roger II of Sicily: A Ruler between East and West*, trans. Graham A. Loud and Diane Milburn (Cambridge, 2002), 115–17.
132 Robert Somerville, *Pope Urban II, The* Collectio Britannica *and the Council of Melfi (1089)* (Oxford, 1996), 177; Robinson, *Papacy*, 124–5, 374.
133 Somerville, *Council of Melfi*, 178.
134 Alfons Becker, *Papst Urban II (1088–1099)* (Stuttgart, 1964) MGH, Schriften 19, t. 1–2, t. 2, 80–5, esp. 82–5; Somerville, *Council of Melfi*, 180; Matthew, *Norman Kingdom of Sicily*, 29.
135 For the slow acceptance of papal over imperial authority in the Abruzzi, see Graham Loud, 'Monastic Chronicles in the Twelfth-Century Abruzzi', *Anglo Norman Studies* 24 (2004), 101–31, esp. 115–17.
136 Somerville, *Council of Melfi*, 228, 258–9 and 294–8.
137 Somerville, *Council of Melfi*, 254 and 279.
138 Jaffé, 4514; MGH SS V, 62.
139 Loud, *Robert Guiscard*, 265–6.
140 Elias appears to have been an abbot whose savvy could match Desiderius', transitioning between Byzantine and Norman overlordship without difficulty: Houben, 'Chiesa di Bari', 100–1.
141 Loud, *Robert Guiscard*, refers to it as 'a centre for reforming ideals', 228, but is much more cautious at 265–8. Becker, *Papst Urban II*, 2.74–75.
142 Houben, *Roger II*, 115–17.
143 Houben, 'Chiesa di Bari', 105, n. 84 citing the *Anonymus Barensis*, 182.
144 Melfi was followed by the dedication of Bari (1089); the Council of Benevento (1091) was not associated with a dedication; Cava (1092) was not associated with a Council, but Cava was the subject of dispute at Melfi as discussed; Troia was followed in the summer, but as part of the same itinerary with a dedication at S. Maria, Banza; Piacenza was followed by the dedication at Asti (1095) and the very many dedications prior to Clermont and Cluny.
145 They had a copy of the customs of Cluny in the twelfth century. 'Although the exact meaning of "Cluniac rule" is unclear, and most likely the abbey of Cava did

not adopt Cluniac customs whole cloth, nonetheless Cava became the first large Benedictine abbey in the principality whose monastic community led a strictly controlled common life and engaged in a daily round of offices and prayers, often said in commemoration for donors', Ramseyer, *Transformation of a Religious Landscape*, 167-9, at 167.

146 I am following Somerville, *Council of Melfi*, 245.

147 Ramseyer, *Transformation of a Religious Landscape*, 149-50. Somerville, *Council of Melfi*, 246.

148 *Historia consecrationis*, RIS, VI, pt. V, 47. The shorter version states that these were dedicated by Oddo, Cardinal and Bishop of Albano and Berardo of Palestrina respectively at 48.

149 Ramseyer, *Transformation of a Religious Landscape*, 61.

150 Giles Constable, 'The Dislocation of Jerusalem in the Middle Ages', in Alois Hahn, et al. (eds), *Norm und Krise von Kommunikation, Inszenierungen literarischer und sozialer Interaktion im Mittelalter* (Berlin, 2006), 355-70; Harris, 'Body as Temple', 236-54; VQPAC, RIS, VI, pt. V, 19.

151 Somerville, *Council of Melfi*, 245; Ramseyer, *Transformation of a Religious Landscape*, 149-51.

152 RIS VI, 5, 47-8.

153 In addition to the discussion of Bruno of Segni's eleventh-century commentary on the dedication discussed below, see also Harris, 'Building Heaven on Earth', 131-51. For the relationship between Bruno of Segni and Urban II, see Becker, *Papst Urban II*, 2.42-7. Becker sees Bruno's Eucharistic commentary as especially centred on Roman primacy.

154 Jaffé, 5487, 5488; Bloch, *Monte Cassino*, 270, 694-95.

155 Jaffé, 5485, 5486; Somerville, *Council of Melfi*, 127-8, 304-5.

156 Jaffé, 5537; PL 151, 394. On Troia: Jaffé, 5481-2; Becker, *Papst Urban II*, t. 1, 120.

157 Alfons Becker, 'Le Voyage d'Urbain II en France', in *Le Concile de Clermont de 1095 et l'appel à la croisade*, Collection de l'École Français de Rome (236) (Rome, 1997), 127-40, 132.

158 See also Becker, *Papst Urban II*, t. 2, 435-58. Méhu, *Paix et communautés*, 152-4. Élisabeth Zadora-Rio, 'Lieux d'inhumation et espaces consacrés: le voyage du Pape Urbain II en France (août 1095-août 1096)', in André Vauchez (ed.), *Lieux sacrés, lieux de culte, sanctuaires, approches terminologiques, méthodologiques, historiques et monographiques* (Rome, 2000), 197-213. René Crozet, 'Études sur les consécrations pontificales', *Bulletin Monumental* 104 (1946), 5-46, at 24-30; 'Le Voyage d'Urbain II et ses négociations avec le clergé de France (1095-1096)', *Revue Historique* 179 (1937), 271-310 (hereafter, 'Le Voyage'); Crozet, 'Le Voyage d'Urbain II en France (1095-1096) et son importance au point de vue archéologique', *Annales du Midi* 49 (1937), 42-69.

159 With the notable exception of Somerville, *The Councils of Urban II*, Vol. 1, *Decreta Claromontensia* (Amsterdam, 1970), 3-6.

160 Somerville, *Claromontensia*, 5; Becker, *Papst Urban*, 214-19.

161 Bernold, *Chronicon*, MGH SS, V (Hanover, 1844), 461.

162 Ibid., 461; Urbani II, Concilium Placentium, MGH, *Leges* 4, *Constitutiones* 1, 560–3. Frederic Duncalf, 'The Councils of Piacenza and Clermont', in Marshall Baldwin (ed.), *A History of the Crusades*, Vol. 1, *The First Hundred Years* (Philadelphia, 1955), 220–52, on Piacenza at 228–230. See also Cowdrey, 'Pope Urban II's Preaching of the First Crusade', *History* 55 (1970), 177–88, reprinted in Thomas F. Madden (ed.), *The Crusades: The Essential Readings* (Oxford, 2002), 15–30.

163 Susan L. Boynton, 'The Customaries of Bernard and Ulrich as Liturgical Sources', in Susan Boynton and Isabelle Cochelin (eds), *From Dead of Night to End of Day: the Medieval Customs of Cluny* (Turnhout, 2005), 109–30, at 113.

164 Bernold, *Chronicon*, 462.

165 Ibid.; Urbani II, Concilium Placentium, 563.

166 Somerville, 'The French Councils of Pope Urban II: Some Basic Considerations', *Annuarium Historiae Conciliorum* 2 (Augsburg, 1970), 56–65, at 63, reprinted in Somerville, *Papacy, Councils and Canon Law in the 11th–12th Centuries* (Aldershot, 1990); Urbani II, Concilium Placentium, 563.

167 Orderic Vitalis, *Ecclesiastical History*, V, 9.

168 Bernold, *Chronicon*, MGH *Scriptores*, V, 463.

169 S. Maria, Jaffé, 5569; PL 158, 150–1. Furio Ricci (ed.), *La Basilica di Sant'Abbondio in Como: IX centenario della Consecrazione* (Como, 1996).

170 For an excellent synopsis of the situation in Piacenza on the eve of the council, see Dorothy F. Glass, 'The Bishops of Piacenza, their Cathedral, and the Reform of the Church', in John S. Ott and Anna Trumbore Jones (eds), *The Bishop Reformed: Studies in Episcopal Power and Culture in the Central Middle Ages* (Aldershot, 2007), 219–36, at 219–23.

171 Glass, 'Bishops of Piacenza', 223–5.

172 Most recently by Didier Méhu, *Paix et communautés*, 151–66.

173 Crozet, 'Le Voyage', 271–310. I will follow Becker's revised itinerary, *Papst Urban II*, t. 2., 458.

174 Becker, *Papst Urban II*, t. 2, 435; Jaffé, 5569; PL 151, 155; Crozet, 'Le Voyage', 275. R. Crozet, 'Études', 5–46, at 24.

175 Becker, *Papst Urban II*, t. 2, 436; PL 151, 157; Jaffé, 5571, 5575; Crozet, 'Le Voyage', 277.

176 Becker, *Papst Urban II*, t. 2., 436–7; Crozet, 'Le Voyage', 278.

177 Becker, *Papst Urban II*, t. 2, 437; Zadora-Rio, 'Lieux d'inhumation et espaces consacrés', 204–6; Becker, t. 2, 437–8; Jaffé, 5583; PL 151, 158; Crozet, 'Le Voyage', 279.

178 The most complete treatment is Méhu, *Paix et Communautés*, 151–65.

179 Ibid., 154. See also Harris, 'Building Heaven on Earth'.

180 On the complexity of that dynamic see Rosenwein, *Negotiating Space*, 157–68.

181 Arturo Carlo Quintavalle, 'Figure della Riforma in occidente', in Quintavalle (ed.), *Il Medioevo delle Cattedrali, Chiese e Impero: la lotta delle immagini (secoli XI e XII)* (Parma, 2006), 239–90, 239. K.J. Conant, *Cluny, les églises et la maison du chef d'ordre* (Mâcon, 1968).

182 Rosenwein, *Negotiating Space*, 183.

183 Somerville, 'The Council of Clermont (1095), and Latin Christian Society', *Archivium Historiae Pontificiae 12* (1974), 55–90, reprinted in Somerville, *Papacy, Councils and Canon Law*, 61.

184 Harris, 'Building Heaven on Earth', 140–7, 150–1; Iogna-Prat, *Order and Exclusion*, makes the connection between Cluny and anxiety over non-Christians explicit; on the consecration and the sacred ban, see 169–71.

185 Somerville, 'Council of Clermont', 88.

186 Crozet, 'Consécrations pontificales', 25; 'Le Voyage', 293; 'Le voyage ... archéologique', 63.

187 Geoffrey de Breuil describes Urban as having been received in triumph and even describes the outline of the dedication rite at St Stephen, MGH SS 26, 199–200. Crozet, 'Consécrations pontificales', 26; Jaffé, 5604–6; Somerville, 'French Councils', 59–60.

188 Becker, *Papst Urban II*, t. 2, 443; Jaffé, 5613.

189 Crozet, 'Consécrations pontificales', 26–8.

190 Ibid. 26; Jaffé 5616.

191 Crozet, 'Le Voyage', 296; 'Le Voyage ... archéologique', 63–4.

192 Becker, 'Le Voyage d'Urbain', 135; Jaffé, 5613.

Bruno of Segni and Paschal II: from coordination to conflict

Are you then, in this council, in our hearing, calling the Roman Pontiff a heretic?

John of Gaeta to Bruno of Segni[1]

The career of Bruno of Segni marked the high point of the use of the dedication rite, in both its practice and its interpretation. Peter Damian fostered a papally centred ecclesiology by means of his sermons at dedications, and Anselm creatively collected, edited and organised materials into a code of canon law that codified Damian's ideas, but Bruno extended both the moral and the eschatological meaning of the rite while participating in its careful use with two popes. Urban II relied heavily on Bruno, who accompanied him on itineraries in southern Italy and France, and when Paschal II became pope in 1099, he likewise came to rely upon Bruno while he pursued an active campaign of papal dedication. Despite having been at the centre of the papal reforms from the reign of Gregory VII to that of Paschal II, Bruno remains an enigmatic figure. Born near Asti in the Piedmont region in the mid-eleventh century, Bruno was educated first at a local monastery and then perhaps at Bologna.[2] He became a canon in Siena in the early 1070s, and in 1078 or 1079, in Rome, Bruno is supposed to have made his reputation in the Berengarian debate and was rapidly elevated to the episcopal seat of Segni.[3]

Bruno was part of the entourage of Gregory VII, and in the summer of 1082 was imprisoned by a partisan of Henry IV.[4] In 1084, he waited out the imperial siege of the city of Rome with Gregory VII in Castel Sant'Angelo.[5] He continued to serve the *curia* under Victor III, was an elector of and counsellor to Urban II, served as Papal legate and travelled with him regularly. Bruno composed his *Libellus de symoniacis*, an attack

on the imperially supported pope Guibert of Ravenna, probably in the latter part of Urban's papacy and, as will be argued below, likely composed the *De laudibus ecclesiae* at this time.[6]

In 1103, after an illness, Bruno entered the abbey of Montecassino; in 1107 he was elected its abbot. Still, Bruno continued to travel extensively in the service of the pope. When consecrating Bruno abbot of Montecassino, Paschal II 'announced in an assembly of the brethren that not only would he be a worthy abbot, but he would be a worthy successor to himself in the apostolic see'.[7] That was not to be, as he would have a famous falling out with Paschal II in 1111 over the privileges of investiture (the so-called *pravilegium* dispute) that Paschal granted to Henry V under duress in that same year. Paschal rebuilt his authority despite Bruno's opposition and had Bruno removed from Montecassino. Bruno, still Bishop of Segni, made a brief appearance at the Lenten synod of 1116 where John of Gaeta defended Paschal against Bruno's continued hostility. John would ultimately succeed Paschal as Gelasius II, and Bruno would leave few traces in the historical record before dying in 1123. Bruno's second commentary on the liturgy, the *De sacramentis ecclesiae*, was likely written during this final period of his life.[8] The *Vita* written for his canonisation by clerics of Segni was not filled with miracle stories; but the canons did record a miracle he accomplished while dedicating a church and his amazing ability to understand scripture.[9]

Bruno's first commentary on the dedication: the *De laudibus ecclesiae*

There are no critical editions of any of Bruno's extant books, homilies or letters save one: a letter in the *Libelli de lite*. The *Patrologia Latine* reproduced the two-volume *Opera* initially published in 1791.[10] It gave the *De laudibus* the title *Libri sententiarum* following Montecassino, Archivio dell'Abbazia 196 (s. XII), which entitled the work *Liber sententiarum Bruni: De laudibus ecclesiae in dedicatione templi*. Most extant manuscripts that offered a title preferred some form of *De laudibus ecclesiae* and no other manuscript employed the title *Liber sententiarum*.[11] Two of the manuscripts (Cava, Abbazia 6 and Rome, Biblioteca Angelica 362) were certainly made during Bruno's lifetime, the former possibly while Bruno was at Cava, either in 1092 with Urban to consecrate its church or in 1099. They differ slightly in their organisation and content, suggesting that Bruno revised and added to the work in his lifetime.[12]

Most scholars have treated Bruno's exegetical and allegorical texts

synthetically, in part because these works are not easily dated. Other readers of the *De laudibus* have isolated specific chapters of interest. Ian Robinson has attempted to place Bruno more properly in the reform context.[13] Robinson has described the *De laudibus* as 'six books of sermons', and this typifies the scholarly approach to the text, which has been to divide it into discrete units to exemplify themes from the rest of Bruno's corpus.[14] The work of István Bejczy has rightly pointed to the originality of Bruno's comments on the cardinal virtues as an address to princely authority. Bejczy addressed only isolated chapters within the *De laudibus*, reading them across Bruno's other works that involve the virtues more or less.[15] The *De laudibus* should be read as a complete work in its own right.[16] It is a mistake to conflate it with his later liturgical commentary, the *De sacramentis*, which is a distinct text with a specific audience.[17] The failure to recognise the *De laudibus* as a coherent work has meant that it has largely been ignored by scholars of twelfth-century liturgical commentary.[18]

Since the *De laudibus* has never been studied as a complete work, it requires closer examination. The text is self-referential throughout. For example, in Book III, chapter 6, *On the new animals*, Bruno noted, 'We have explained [the wild ass] above in the sermon published as "On abstinence"'.[19] In Book VI, chapter 3, sermon ii, *On the Apostles, Evangelists and Doctors*, the reader was instructed, 'See in the Book, *De novo mundo*, who is considered the new sea and the new fishermen. This was titled, *Hoc est mare magnum* [III, 8].'[20] This also supplied the proper title for Book III, missing in the Bruni edition – that is, *De novo mundo*. Understanding Book III was dependent on a reading of Books I and II, as Bruno referred explicitly to both in Book III. At Book III, chapter 5, *De arboribus novis*, a reading for the feast of a dedication, he stated 'but because it seems to us that we have said enough about good and bad trees above, namely in that place where the Lord speaks of good and bad trees . . . it does not seem necessary to repeat the same here, and it is easier to turn pages than to write the same thing again'.[21] Other references were internal to the same book, as in Book III, 9, *De avibus novis*, where he abbreviated his comments on fish, observing that he has said enough about these above (meaning Book III, 8).

Given this internal coherence, it is clear that when Bruno introduced the elements involved in dedicating a church, but then postponed interpreting, he was thinking strictly in terms of the *De laudibus*.[22] In fact, he returned to the subject and its particulars at Book I, 7, *De basilicis quae ab episcopis dedicantur*. This is an especially important detail, as Grégoire

had assumed the reference pointed ahead to Bruno's treatise *De sacramentis ecclesiae.*[23] It is improbable, however, that Bruno intended here to point his reader any further than a few chapters ahead where he addressed the postponed images directly and in detail. Most tellingly, in Book VI, *On the feast of a Martyr*, the reader was likewise informed about halfway through the sermon that '[t]hese things have been explained in that sermon entitled *De pace*. See above in the book *De ornamentis ecclesiae.*'[24]

Despite these references to an anticipated reader, the predominant internal evidence tended toward an anticipated auditor. Bruno referred to these chapters as sermons, and the overall impression is of a collection of sermons intended to be either delivered as is or used as the basis for creating sermons, but one that represented a coherent ensemble for Bruno.[25] As such, the work existed on the boundary between a theological treatise and a sermon collection. These chapters-cum-sermons are distinctly directed *ad cleros*, first, because they were intended as a tool for preaching. Second, their subject matter and its treatment were aimed at a religiously trained audience. The materials that Bruno regularly exhorted his audience to read alone certainly suggests a clerical audience: 'read the Gospels', 'read Moses, Isaiah and Jeremiah', 'read Paul', 'the Acts of the apostles', 'the Passions and the Lives of the Saints', 'Leviticus', 'all the Scriptures of both Testaments', 'the Song of Songs' and 'the books of the Prophets'.[26] All of these are in the imperative, *lege*. Nor is the reading list solely Scriptural. In one chapter, on the Trinity, Bruno points out that the term 'substance' was properly defined by Aristotle, and he also uses the term 'syllogism' without feeling obliged to define it.[27] In another sermon he cautioned his audience that he is not concerned with the wisdom of Plato and Aristotle, but that of Peter and Paul.[28] Other offhand references to 'the blessed' Dionysius the Aereopagite's 'in libro De hierarchia' (most likely the *De caelesti hierarchia*), Diogenes the Cynic's encounter with Alexander (from Plutarch's *Lives*) or his description of the use of magnets in an ancient automaton seem aimed at the educated few.[29] The audience for these sermons organised as a complete work was clearly an educated clergy. That audience may have included monks but was more often bishops and their clergy.

The date of the *De laudibus ecclesiae*

Although it is impossible to date the composition of the *De laudibus* with certainty, a date prior to 1100 is most likely. The *De laudibus* exists in two late eleventh- possibly early twelfth-century copies (Cava 6 and Bibl. Angelica 362).[30] While the dating of Cava 6 has been recently reconsidered

as 'presumably' of the first decade of the twelfth century, Angelica 362 remains attributed to the eleventh century.[31] Cava 6 is a densely written and unadorned manuscript that alternates between multiple hands writing in Beneventan and Caroline minuscules, suggesting a team of copyists from different *scriptoria* that worked quickly.[32] Commencing toward the end of folio 176v, and in a separate hand from the rest of 176, is Bruno's sermon honouring St Michael the Archangel. This is significant because there was a local devotion to St Michael in Cava. It was typical, also, of monastic homily collections to end with the feast of St Michael. It was also remarkable because the more elegant manuscript Biblioteca Angelica 362 (eleventh century) lacks this sermon.[33] That this sermon was added at the very end of Cava 6 suggests the possibility that it joined the *De laudibus* here for the first time. It would make sense that Bruno would have delivered this sermon in Cava, or offered it for inclusion in the *De laudibus*, for any number of reasons.[34] Montecassino also had a chapel dedicated to St Michael, and if the *De laudibus* were composed there, it would seem odd that Bruno would not have included the homily from the outset.[35] That both Angelica 362 and Cava 6 were copied out sometime around 1100, and that these already represented two distinct versions, suggests that the *De laudibus* was composed prior to 1100. Since Angelica 362 is considered an eleventh-century manuscript, it seems most likely that the text was composed prior to 1100.

The audience of the *De Laudibus*

The only reason to date the composition of the work later than 1100 is the argument presented by Grégoire, who assigned the *De laudibus* to Bruno's years as abbot of Cassino, 1107–1111, because Bruno referred to 'pater noster Benedictus' twice in the *De laudibus*.[36] The sentiment was particularly monastic and Cassinese and only appeared in this one text of Bruno's.[37] One significant reference to Benedict as 'our father' was contained in Book II, c. 12, *Ubi, id est in quibus, ecclesia ornatur*. Here, Bruno continued his description of the virtues as ornaments of the Church:

> But when the children of the Church put on the ornament of humility, then all pride will be confounded . . . Then you may see the choirs of virgins and the armies of monks clothed in wool and skins, by which garments humility is greatly glorified, and among these our Father Benedict, sitting on an ivory *cathedra*, dividing the entire ornament of humility into twelve parts.[38]

There was much ivory furniture in the exegetical decor of Bruno; there were ivory steps, ivory beds, ivory seats and the ivory *cathedra*. Ivory, in the *De laudibus*, represented chastity, but ivory steps represent both chastity and the apostles. Here again, the twelve parts of this ivory *cathedra* (and numerous late eleventh-/early twelfth-century Italian churches still exhibit a white marble *cathedra* in their apse), as well as its relation to the ivory steps, made Benedict a particularly Apostolic rather than strictly monastic figure. Bruno may well have had in mind the so-called 'Cathedra of St Peter', an ivory-panelled throne used in the ninth century for the imperial coronation of Charles the Bald and in the eleventh century used in papal ceremony. By the twelfth century the Cathedra was venerated as an apostolic relic.[39] Benedict was here seated in a *cathedra* dividing the garments of humility into twelve parts, the former a commonplace for episcopal authority and the apostles. The division of the garments of humility into twelve parts echoed the twelve steps of humility in the *Rule*.[40] If this were written during the papacies of Gregory VII, Victor III or Urban II, the references would be entirely understandable. Benedict was then seated on the apostolic throne. This monastic status was important in the polemical literature of the period, and Gregory VII's monasticism was attacked by the imperial partisans calling him a 'false monk', and a 'devil in a cowl'.[41] Given the polemical controversy around Gregory's monasticism, and the role of the monastic ideal in the reform, if Bruno were writing during or soon after the reign of Gregory VII, this reference to Benedict as 'our father' certainly would have had a pro-Hildebrandian intent even if it was not directly referential. Considered another way, the text might also read 'Our blessed father sitting on an ivory throne'. This reading might refer to Christ or the pope or both, and the pun might have even included all three, Christ, Pope and Benedict. If so, it would have been entirely coherent with a late eleventh-century reformers' vision of the papacy. This possibility was all the more probable given that this particular sermon was concerned with heresy and the peace of the Church and the material was clearly rhetorical. Bruno made clear here that whatever virtues 'heretics, pagans, philosophers and Jews' might have appeared to have, they were false since they lacked 'apostolic doctrine'.[42] Moreover, the true virtues led to the peace of the Church and the confounding of its enemies.[43]

Other descriptions of Benedict pointed likewise to his virtue, Apostolic authority and the fight against heresy. Benedict, 'whose authority is the greatest', offered instruction on the temperate exercise of fortitude, as did Paul. This assertion of Benedictine authority occurred during a chapter

on the cardinal virtues, and Bruno moved from this into direct address: 'Act, o prince, whoever you are, so that you have and hold justice'.[44] Bruno then compared the cardinal virtues of various biblical characters to the four loops by which the ark of the Testament ('which is the Church') were supported. The two bars (inserted through the loops) with which the ark was then carried are Peter and Paul and the rest of the saints, 'without which the Church of God cannot be lifted, carried or ruled'.[45] This was always a great concern to bishops and priests because 'without [these] bars, heretics bear the ark of God'.[46] This sermon will be considered further below, but for now it is necessary to observe that the Benedictine reference was in the broader context of Apostolic authority and the episcopal duty to oppose heresy. Benedict's feast day was the occasion for another sermon, but that feast was relegated to a common of confessors and observed only toward the end of the sermon.[47] There the high praise offered Benedict was brought back to the context of the cardinal virtues and the greater rulership of Benedict (who more perfectly exhibited the cardinal virtues), as a servant of God, when compared to Solomon.[48] In the final direct reference to Benedict in the *De laudibus*, the context was still the opposition of heresy and apostolic doctrine.[49]

Bruno held the monastic life in high esteem and saw it as integral to the reform of the self (which may partly explain Bruno's decision to enter Montecassino). Such references were not surprising for a reforming bishop, educated in a monastery as a youth and appointed by and serving under several monks turned pope, who was preaching a reform of the clergy to monastic habits (chastity and common property in particular). Nor do they demonstrate an intended monastic audience or composition. In fact, Alexander II, Urban II, Paschal II and Calixtus II all referred to Benedict as 'our father'. This was often, but not always, when they addressed monastic audiences.[50] Therefore, while the reference may suggest that a particular chapter had its origin in a sermon addressed to a monastic community, it does not evince that Bruno was himself a member of a monastic community at the time it was written. Most of Bruno's references to Benedict were aimed beyond the monastery and directed at the broader ecclesial problems of heresy and princely authority. The seven direct references to Benedict and the twelve to monks pale in comparison to the forty references to Peter, scores of references to the apostles and, most importantly, the fifty direct references to bishops and episcopal authority, and more than that number to priests and priestly authority. It is these more numerous references that make clear the import of the monastic and Benedictine comments found in the *De laudibus* that, in the

end, must be considered as part of an effort to reform a bishop and his clergy.

Just as the direct references to Benedict occurred in the context of the ecclesiastical orders, other evidence suggests a general clerical audience.[51] Book I, 2, seems to have been delivered just prior to the dedication of a church.[52] Bruno commenced the second part of the sermon saying that '[y]ou see today what the bishop will do, when he will undertake consecrating this hall. First before everything, he does the litanies . . .'[53] When describing the dedication of this church, therefore, he was explaining what his audience would see: 'Now we approach the altar and we see what the bishop is doing there.'[54] The deposition of relics and the consecration of the altar were typically carried out by the bishop only in the presence of assisting clergy. If Bruno expected his audience to see this on that day, his audience was a clerical one. The sermon, even though it directly addressed an anonymous Christian, was aimed at a clerical audience assisting the bishop at a dedication.[55]

Bruno not only discussed episcopal and priestly concerns at length, but most often discussed them in a way that seems to be addressed to bishops and priests as readers or auditors. He observed, for example, that it was the duty of priests and bishops to cook and remove the hard shell of the literal sense of scripture for the benefit of the young.[56] Bishops and priests were called to the mountain of the virtues, and they needed to ascend that mountain before they preached.[57] The command to preach the Gospel to the entire world was pointed directly at bishops: 'Bishops hear this, whoever hears this, takes up the office; neither does he presume to evangelise before he ascends the mountain of peace and mercy.'[58] This combination of a concern for bishops, their authority and morality, for the clergy in general, for preaching in particular and the obvious literacy of his audience, suggested that Bruno had before him a cathedral clergy and that this work was intended for cathedral use. Therefore, by the later part of Urban's reign or the very beginning of Paschal II's the reforming papacy had in Bruno's work a coherent consideration of the dedication and of sacred space as both ecclesiologically and morally reforming.

Themes: moral reform and the Church triumphant

An examination of the structure of the *De laudibus* reveals its themes. The work was divided into two halves; Books I to III set out allegorical motifs and Books IV to VI recapitulate those throughout the liturgical cycle. The first presented the biblical and liturgical types that described the Church.

Bruno was concerned with both ecclesiology and with the true eschatological Church; from the Prologue, he connected these themes directly
to the dedication of churches. Book II described the virtues as a means
of describing the saints, that is, the true members of the Church and
employed the image of virtues as the ornament of the body. Book III then
described the Heavenly Jerusalem, the eschatological, renewed world,
with a significant and subtle Gregorian dimension. Book IV addressed
the temporal cycle, Book V, the Marian feasts, and Book VI the sanctoral
cycle. But more importantly, Books IV through VI described the life of
the realised Church and praised the ruler and prominent citizens of the
Heavenly Jerusalem. Since the eschatological Church was also engaged in
the liturgy (as in Revelation) this structure had the effect of further diminishing the boundary between the heavenly and earthly liturgies.[59] That is,
the allegorisation of the Temple liturgy from the first books and the eschatological perspective of the last books conflated the historic, present and
future liturgies of the Church. In fact, Book VI contained the most direct
references to the Apocalypse.

Bruno offered a brief Prologue at the very outset of Book I:

> While there might be many and almost innumerable things in the
> divine volumes that signify the Bride of Christ, the Holy Church, there
> are certain ones nevertheless, where its praises and its greater sacra-
> ments seem to be contained more fully and more manifestly, such as,
> for example, paradise with its trees and rivers, or the ark which Noah
> built according to God's precept. Similarly, there is the tabernacle
> that Moses constructed and the Temple that Solomon built. The
> Church is also figured through a woman, as the Song of Songs clearly
> demonstrates. The Holy City of Jerusalem and the basilicas which
> are now everywhere dedicated by bishops openly signify the Church
> of God. With God's help, we will expound in the following on these
> things according to the order in which they are set down, indeed not
> all things, but those things and that of the material which accords to the
> season.[60]

If Bruno intended this as an introduction to Book I, a discussion of the
figures of the Church, then only the last sentence might have implied the
rest of the *De laudibus*: that is, a working out of that symbolism in
the order of the liturgical season. The reference to the Holy City of
Jerusalem and the practice of bishops dedicating churches everywhere,
however, revealed the eschatological import of the dedication. Given this,
and that the rest of the work was structured as a whole, however, it might

be better to read this as the Prologue to the entire *De laudibus*. When Bruno stated that his topic will be those Biblical references to 'the Bride of Christ, the Holy Church', he was referring to the true, eschatological Church, the subject of the entire volume. Thus, the second part of that first sentence, 'where its praises and greater sacraments seemed to be contained more fully and more manifestly', referred to the two-part division of the *De laudibus* into a section of praises (allegory) and sacraments (allegory in the liturgical sense – i.e., the mysteries of the Church). That the imagery of the dedication of a church dominated the first book of the *De laudibus* might have reflected the characteristic of at least some contemporary Italian pontificals that begin with the dedication of a church.[61] In this reading, the whole work was both liturgical and focused on the idealised Church. The sections that seemed more allegorical (Books I to III) were as rooted in the ritual life of the Church as are those more clearly focused on the calendar (Books IV to VI), and the allegorical themes of the first book persisted throughout the entirety of the work. Having said this, a two-part division that governed the entire work was intended as part of a coherent strategy. Bruno had little patience for those stuck on the literal sense of scripture, and pointed out that there were 'many other things in Scripture which if understood literally appear to be pointless'.[62] In fact, the first three books of the *De laudibus* began with the allegorical understanding of the Church, focusing on Old Testament prefigurations (especially the Temple and its dedication) in Book I. He proceeded then to offer a moral, or tropological, understanding of the Church through an examination of Temple images and church architectural images in Book II. Book III placed the auditor firmly in the eschatological or anagogical sense of the Church, in *De novo mundo*. Books IV through VI then remained within the eschatological Church contemplating the Trinity. Book IV, as Book III, might well have taken its title from its first chapter, *De trinitate*. Book V then considered Mary as Queen of Heaven and Book VI focused on the saints.[63] This reading is consistent with the sermon associated with Urban II at the dedication of Cava; the reform of the self transformed one into a citizen of the Heavenly Jerusalem. Similarly, Bruno noted here, both the image of the dedication and the image of Jerusalem always represented the true Church[64] – a theme he asserted in the Prologue's observation that 'The Holy City of Jerusalem and the basilicas which are now everywhere dedicated by bishops openly signify the Church of God'.[65] Thus, throughout the entirety of the work there was a regular connection between the creation of sacred space through the dedication of churches and the creation of the true eschatological Church through reform.

The meaning of the Church: liturgy, architectonics and ecclesiology

The liturgical and architectonic context Bruno provided for his sermons lent an originality and particular spirit to the *De laudibus*. The context was created through scriptural and liturgical exegesis and was essential to understanding both. From the outset beauty also pervaded the work: there were the beautiful trees of paradise, beautiful to see and sweet for eating.[66] Later, the 'Church of God' was described via the Marian image of the woman clothed with the sun because the Church was decorated by every clarity and all beautiful things.[67] Mary was compared to the citron tree (Book II, c. 5 and Book V, c. 5); that is, as beautiful as the citron, in its fruit, and leaves and flowers, in its odour and its taste.[68] At a common of confessors, the people of God were seen to be worthy of their saintly guardians if they imitated their odour and beauty. All of the Church was fecund and no part of it unfruitful.[69] Elsewhere, the reader was instructed to look at the chest of the pontiff and see the beauty of its ornaments, its gold, its stones and its colours of sapphire, purple, scarlet and white.[70]

The reader or auditor was meant to engage his senses actively. Odours permeated the text from beginning to end: the odour of the trees of paradise, the odours of life and death, the odour of sacred oils, the aroma of the virtues and the odour of sanctity.[71] Likewise the entirety of the *De laudibus* resounded with the thumping of the bishop's staff on the doors of a church, the sounds of preaching, of water, cymbals, drums and horns, and the joyous and frightening sounds of the Apocalypse.[72] Bruno routinely exhorted his listeners to use their eyes: 'Look at Peter, James and John',[73] 'Look at Stephen and Laurence',[74] 'Look at the mouth, listen to the words',[75] 'See the new clouds and the new doves',[76] 'Look at the Tabernacle of the testament, look at the Temple of Solomon',[77] 'Look at the apostles and martyrs . . . at the confessors and doctors of the Church',[78] 'Look now at the chest of the pontiff',[79] 'See how much blood flows out when Solomon dedicates the Temple'[80] and 'See the abundance of sacred oils'.[81]

The imagery provided the sense of a church without presenting a specific church. The wise architects of this Church were the apostles, no less capable than Bezalel and Oholiab who were appointed by God as sculptors, carpenters, embroiderers and craftsmen of the tabernacle (Ex. 31: 6; 35: 34; 36: 1–3; 38: 23).[82] To begin at the gates: while considering the woman of Revelation 12: 1 as a figure of the Church, Bruno moved quickly to the wise laws that govern the Church and Proverbs 31: 23, 'Her husband is noble in the gates, when he sits among the elders of the land.'

While portions of this recalled Bede's commentary on Proverbs, Bruno distinguished his reading by considering the elders (senators) as the apostles who could open the gates of heaven and hell.[83] He continued this idea in the next chapter on the Heavenly Jerusalem which had twelve gates. Here the apostles were both the gates and the foundation of the Heavenly City: 'They are the true gates because no one is joined to the society of the Church except through them – that is, through their faith and doctrine, they themselves are the gates and the doorkeepers.'[84] Again in the next chapter, *On Basilicas which are dedicated by bishops*, the apostles were the gates and windows of the Church, the ways one might enter the Church. With this comment he made the Petrine reference explicit: 'You are Peter and upon this rock I will build my church and the gates of hell shall not prevail against it.' He also connected this directly to the gates of the Psalm from the dedication rite: 'Lift up your gate o you princes, be lifted up eternal gates, so that the king of glory may enter.' This was the moment, initiated by the Bishop, when the Holy Spirit entered the new church.[85] This same theme of the apostles as gates to the Church (with its element of Petrine authority) was revisited throughout the *De laudibus*.[86] Similar imagery taken from Noah's ark and the Heavenly Jerusalem allowed the apostles also to be the door. Finally, the apostles were windows letting in the light of doctrine and keeping out heretics who tried to sneak into the Church by way of its windows, or, in a related manner, as the apostles were the windows of the Church, the clear glass of the Heavenly Jerusalem was wisdom.[87]

Once past the doors and windows, the pavement of the Church was inscribed by the bishop in the dedication rite, an act that represented the effect of preaching on the heart.[88] Moving from the pavement to the walls, Bruno drew attention to the walls of the Heavenly Jerusalem which was the Church. These walls, Bruno observed, were precious stones; they were the apostles and martyrs furnished in wisdom and virtue and anyone else who through faith and holy conversation pleased the Lord.[89] By drawing attention to the virtues as the precious stones in Book I, chapter 6, Bruno was anticipating the subject of Book II, where the virtues would be described as the ornaments of the Church.

Bruno pointed his audience to the walls of the dedicated church which were the members of the Church.[90] Book III, which considered the renewed earth, would return to the jewelled walls.[91] They were the walls of the Heavenly City, seen again in the person of Mary in Book V, where the walls of her virgin mind and body kept her safe from libidinousness and the enemies of her virginity and purity.[92] These walls were

re-established again in Book VI, chapter 3. But these impregnable walls were contrasted with the walls of Jericho brought down by faith, the first ornament of Book II.[93] The reader is reminded of them in turn within the context of the power of consecration and by means of the metaphor of the dedication of a church at the feast of Pentecost in Book IV, chapter 13.[94] These were stone walls, and Peter was presented as the rock and foundation of the Church in Book I, chapters 6, 7 and 8: that is, at the heart of the overt ecclesiological imagery in the *De laudibus*. While *lapides pretiosi* represented the apostles, martyrs and holy Christians, Bruno did not neglect the cornerstone that is Christ.[95]

The columns of the Temple of Solomon and the columns of the dedicated Basilica were allegorised by Bruno in a similar manner as for the apostles. In Bk I, c. 4, *De templo Salomonis*, Bruno discussed the columns of the Temple as the patriarchs Abraham, Isaac, Jacob, Moses, Joshua, David and Daniel.

> Such [columns] were also many others who conquered kingdoms through faith, and because they were firm and robust neither by the violence of storms nor by the entrance of winds could they be separated them from justice and truth. In another sense, I see [the columns as] the apostles, martyrs, confessors and bishops whose actions reveal clearly how strong they were. Look at Peter, James and John who are called the pillars of the Church. Look at Stephen and Laurence; look closely also at the confessor, the bishop Martin and our father Benedict, and soon you will be able to see that which they signify. Nor is it fitting that someone enters the temple, unless he first understands these things.[96]

While this identification of the columns with the pillars of the Church – Peter, James and John – was ultimately from Galatians, and others such as Bede used this imagery when interpreting the Old Testament, Bruno carried the image further to include a series of ideals for the reformers and described two exemplary deacons, an exemplary bishop and an abbot: i.e., Stephen, Laurence, Martin and Benedict.[97] The imagery was brought into the interior of the basilica where the columns were once again the apostles.[98]

Beyond these allegorical columns, the reader entered the Temple: 'Nothing is seen except gold.' 'None of this', Bruno assured the listener, 'is without cause, without mystery, without significance . . . [because] [t]his refers to the whole Church, which is entirely gold, free of all corruption of vice, more white than snow.'[99] Further, 'The virtues are this gold by which every member of the Church is gilded. If we hold faith, hope and charity

we are golden; without these, even the angels are not beautiful . . .'[100] He explained this further under the allegory of the Church as a strong woman: 'We offer gold to God if our minds and hearts are pure', and the offering of incense represented the virtues.[101] Virtue was the liturgical sacrifice. The listener was also warned that many were cursed by the Lord and thrown outside of this Church.[102]

Book II, *De ornamentis ecclesiae*, took up the discussion of the virtues as the ornaments of the Church. Bruno addressed first each of the theological virtues, and these were ornaments that the reader was to put on. Likewise, concerning the cardinal virtues, he noted:

> Such is wisdom among all virtues, as gold among other metals. Therefore it is not without merit that wisdom is often signified through gold on the divine page. Behold the tabernacle of the covenant, behold the Temple of Solomon and you will see that nearly all is made of the most pure gold, then you will finally understand that the greatest decor and the greatest beauty of the saints is wisdom.[103]

This imagery of ecclesiastical architecture was complemented by another architectonic image, that of Noah's ark, which completed Bruno's ideas for this set of images. In Book I, chapter 2, ostensibly on Noah's ark, Bruno immediately drew the listener's attention to the dedication of a church: 'It is fitting that a crowd of people drawn from everywhere comes to the dedication of churches, if indeed the Holy Church is signified in that ark in which an innumerable multitude of animals comes together.'[104] The very structure of the ark suggested to Bruno the Church as a whole, a strictly hierarchical Church with the papacy at its head. Contemplating the ark's pyramidal construction he observed:

> If someone wished to consider the orders of the Church, how clerics are seated above laics, priests above clerics, bishops above priests, archbishops over bishops, and patriarchs over them, and then, finally, one sees how the Roman pontiff sits above all, one would also be able to understand the manner in which the ark of God is wide in its lower parts and now by gradually narrowing itself it ends in a cubit.[105]

While no animal can enter the ark except through the door that is Christ, 'Simoniacs and heretics struggle to enter the Church through other means. They do this because they are thieves and brigands. The windows are those who give light to the Church'.[106] Therefore the entire clerical, hierarchical structure of the ark was designed to keep out those who would threaten it and, while the door was secure, the onus was on

the windows, the ministers of the Church, to keep it safe. Its structure reflected the structure of the Church wide in its number of believers, but culminating in a point, 'in one father and teacher'.[107] Thus the peak of this pyramidal ark was both Christ and the pope. Outside of the ark, all was lost: 'Whoever is afraid to die and desires to be saved should not leave the unity of the Church.'[108] The papal hierarchy was the only safe transport of the Church to the Heavenly City. Combined with the strong emphasis on apostolic authority, the exemplars of the Christian faith and the use of the Petrine imagery, it is clear that the architecture of the *De laudibus* was, overall, in the service of a Gregorian, papally-centred ecclesiology.

Once Bruno drew his audience inside this Church, they were directed to consider its activity and its furnishings. Here, as well, Gregorian ideals asserted themselves. Book I was especially interested in liturgical activity and in the imagery of the dedication of churches. While this theme was overt in Book I, chapter 7, it wove its way in and out of each of the other chapters. Just as the discussion of Noah's ark in Book I, chapter 2 began with a dedication image, so too the dedication was present in the image of the Temple, the Tabernacle of the Law and even the last chapter, *De evangeliis*. *De evangeliis* was the one chapter of Book I that was not directly named in the Prologue. Chapter 8 did not address the Gospels directly; rather it took as its basis Matthew 7: 17: 'No good tree bears bad fruit, nor is there a bad tree that bears good fruit.' This was the reading for the anniversary of the dedication of a church. He developed this in part by observing, 'Bonae arbores, boni homines sunt'. These were also the good trees of Paradise that produced the Church: that is, he allegorised the passage in terms of two other important themes (dedication and Paradise) of the prologue. The old fruit was the prophets and patriarchs and the new fruit was the apostles and doctors of the Church. These were cultivated by the bishops and priests who interceded daily on behalf of the listener and so ought to be attended lest the listener or reader be cut down and thrown into the fire.[109] In chapter 8, therefore, the reader encountered both a liturgical subtext and a strong sense of the ecclesiology of the Church.

Likewise for Bruno, the Petrine commission of Matthew 16: 18 was an occasion to think about the foundation of a church which was the Church in Book I, 7, *De basilicis quae ab episcopis dedicantur*. But it was also the occasion to think about the gates of hell versus those of the Church, which were the gates of Zion, the Heavenly City.[110] The Petrine commission made the apostles the foundation (placed on Christ) of the Heavenly Jerusalem.[111] The image of the apostles as the Church's columns and its windows was sustained as the basis of the virtues in Book II. When

Bruno considered the first ornament of the Church, faith, from which all virtues follow, he observed that believers approached the Church, asked for baptism and, if they held the catholic faith, were baptised; if they did not, they were thrown outside. 'To these', Bruno observes, 'the gates of the Church are closed, nor does Heaven accept them. As the Lord said to Peter, "I give to you the keys to the Kingdom of Heaven."'[112] Thus, Petrine authority was at the very foundation of the Church, the first step of the life of faith and the entrance to the virtues.

Book II continued the discussion of the virtues as the ornaments of the Church and by the conclusion, at chapter 12, 'Where, that is in which things, the Church is adorned', it culminated in a Gregorian ecclesiology tending toward the eschatological.

> Indeed heretics, pagans and Jews often appear to have the same orna-
> ments . . .; however, the difference is this, they are not gold though
> they seem to be gold. No other wisdom is gold except that which is
> confirmed by evangelical and apostolic doctrine. Therefore, whatever
> faith, charity, humility, mercy, peace, patience, justice or obedience
> there might be, if it is not shining in golden apostolic doctrine, it is false,
> it is corrupt, it is unclean and to be feared as death and destruction.[113]

Thus, not only was Petrine authority the first step of faith, but apostolic teaching gave the virtues their authentic beauty. He assured his reader that although one did not always see all of faith's ornaments, they were present. 'When, however,' he continues, 'the faith appears to grow, then you will see wonders, fleeing demons, the dead rising . . . and other miracles which those who are not dressed in the ornaments of faith believe to be impossible.'[114] Bruno then reiterated the transforming effect of each virtue. The penultimate virtue discussed here, humility, led to the vision of Benedict seated in an ivory *cathedra* dividing the garments of the virtue of humility into twelve parts. Thus, the combination of a strong Petrine and a strong Benedictine image, with Benedict in a bishop's seat, reinforced the notion that Bruno might have intended here one of the late eleventh-century popes or possibly Paschal II who had monastic backgrounds.[115] Within this strong papal context, however, apostles could have both an explicitly papal dimension for Bruno or could refer more broadly to the orthodox episcopate. The theme of the virtues continued throughout the *De laudibus*, and in Book VI he observed that the bishops were 'overseers' and 'attentive' because they were seated on the mountain that was not only the Church but also the virtues.[116]

Bruno's interest was in the current Church as a reflection of the future,

eschatological, Church. The apostles were the foundation of the Heavenly
Jerusalem, and apostolic authority was rooted not only in the historic
Church but also in the not-yet-realised Church of eternity. In the chapter
De civitate sancta Jerusalem (Book I, 6), Bruno explained that the Petrine
commission was both the foundation of the Church and of the Heavenly
Jerusalem; he also employed a metaphor based on the dedication of a
church to explain citizenship in that truly eternal city.

> Let us be elevated along with the blessed John onto the great and high
> mountain, so that having been raised up in ecstasy (*in mentis excessu*),
> we understand these things not according to the letter but spiritually.
> This city is the holy Church; these walls and these precious stones are
> people: noble and bright people endowed with virtues and wisdom,
> such were the apostles and martyrs and others who through faith and
> holy conversation pleased God . . . The gold, stone and wood by which
> the temple of God is constructed are not born there but they are trans-
> lated there from elsewhere. Thus therefore even the Church has been
> built by all the people and all the nations it has received; no one coming
> to it is rejected.[117]

The image was based on the construction of a church and the translation of relics. These were represented by the gold and stone (the saints)
translated to the temple of God, as the relics were translated into a church
for deposition into an altar at either the consecration of the church or of
an altar within the church. Thus, the image was ecclesiological on two
levels. First, it was a straightforward statement about the true citizens
of the true Church, the saints and martyrs of the Heavenly Jerusalem,
described in *Revelation*. Second, it was a more complex statement about
how one became a member of the Heavenly Jerusalem. Specifically, while
no one was turned away, the believer needed to be translated to the heavenly Church. In the earthly Church it was the bishop and his clergy who
translated the saints into the church being dedicated. By extension, the
liturgical metaphor became a strong statement of the role of bishops and
priests in creating the citizenry of the Heavenly Jerusalem. It also helped
explain how, for Bruno, the apostles were both citizens of the eternal city
and its very foundations.

Book III, *De novo mundo*, was taken up entirely with the eschatological understanding of the Church, as Bruno made abundantly clear in the
preface to that Book:

> By which world he shows also the third world, for which we under-
> stand the Church, which is chosen from the world but which now is

not of the world . . . If in this world all things are made new, the Church has a new sky, new earth, new sun, new moon, and new stars, clouds, rains, lightning, thunder, mountains, forests, and all new things which were signified by that old world, and have a certain [meaning] by that similitude . . . Behold we come upon a new world which alone by definition ought to be called clean, by water and the Holy Spirit it is made clean from the unclean. Here is material for us to speak about and for composing sermons in praise of God.[118]

Bruno connected Book III to the larger project of the *De laudibus* and explained that project in part. The 'praises' that were the subject of these first three books are of that eternal Church which was the true Church.[119] Bruno proceeds to explain how each of these new natural elements signified an ecclesiastical reality here in the present. The eschatological nature of the Church was also the overt topic of Book V, 1, *De laude beatae Mariae civitatis Dei* which was perhaps also best thought of as a preface connecting Book V to the larger project.[120] The last three sermons of the *De laudibus* emphasised the eschatological Church.[121]

Ecclesiology and political society

It is in the context of this ecclesiology which was thoroughly focused on the eschatological that the reader was presented with some of the other important themes of the Gregorian era.[122] Most notably, Bruno employed the 'political allegory' to which I.S. Robinson first directed our attention.[123] Stern warnings against lay authorities who would undermine the Church could be found in the central books of the *De laudibus*. One of the more striking moments in the *De laudibus* comes in Book II, 7 when Bruno is discussing cardinal virtues. Bruno's comments in this chapter are not only considered the first commentary on the cardinal virtues since the Carolingian era but are unique for envisioning them as a guide to princely rule.[124] But these guidelines came in a very specific context within both the chapter and the *De laudibus*. Bruno equated *sapientia* and *prudentia* and observed that true wisdom that pertained to the soul '[is] not that which the philosophers and orators teach, but is that which the apostles and doctors preach'.[125] Bruno shifted into direct address:

Such is wisdom among all virtues, as gold among other metals . . . Behold the tabernacle . . . behold the Temple . . . and you will see that nearly all is made of the most pure gold, [and] then you will finally understand that the greatest decor and the greatest beauty of the saints

is wisdom. Where [wisdom] is absent, all things are uncertain, dark and obscure. Who will be able to govern his kingdom, his province, his land, his family or even himself without it? Understand, you powers of this age, and do the work of wisdom. How very necessary justice is, the laws themselves of the emperors, and the canons, and the decrees of saints show well enough which are made in order to be the guard of [justice] itself. Take away justice and the world is lost.[126]

Bruno made explicit the political nature of the cardinal virtues. Within those politics he made it clear that the sources of wisdom are the apostles, doctors and saints, and that without their guidance all was lost in darkness. Justice was presented as an extension of wisdom via the law which was the act of governing.

Likewise the other cardinal virtues were intertwined. After dismissing the philosophers a second time Bruno pointed to Benedict as the highest authority and prime example of fortitude.[127] The interconnectedness of these four principal virtues returned Bruno to the direct address of lay powers:

Act, o prince, whoever you are, so that you have and hold justice. This seems to be most necessary for you, and soon through this virtue you will appear to all as wise, strong and well-moderated. See that you who do justice to others are not indifferent to the same, and you who exercise justice on people, exercise it also on yourself.[128]

The chapter concluded with the apostles as the poles used to carry the Church (as ark), saying that

the two poles I understand as Peter and Paul and the other saints without which the Church cannot be lifted up, carried or ruled. And these are of gold because they are glowing with the light of the immaculate life and wisdom . . . By these therefore the ark is carried because the holy Church is governed by the faith, doctrine and example of these and raised up to heaven by the steps of virtuous bishops and the ministries of priests.[129]

In this role the bishops and priests protected the Church from falling into the hands of heretics.[130] Bruno added an additional warning to them as well.

But rightly is this always frightening to bishops and priests, lest they attempt to bear the ark without the poles. Indeed, heretics who, preaching their foolishness (naenias), flee the authority of the apostles and withdraw from catholic faith and doctrine, bear the ark of God without poles.[131]

This regular shift between strong affirmations of apostolic and episcopal authority and stern warnings and imperative instruction to lay rulers reflected the tension within the Church under the reformers and was a clear example of 'political allegory'. Bishops and priests returned at the end of the chapter as the primary focus, and apostolic authority opposed to unjust princes and heretical preaching were the proper guidance of the Church.

This was a strong assertion of apostolic authority. In Bruno's address to the unnamed princes, he likened the Church to the ark carried by the bishops and priests by means of the poles of apostolic authority; he noted further that unnamed heretics attempted to carry the ark without those apostolic poles. Finally, in the chapter on the cardinal virtues he lamented the state of the Church. He compared the heretics to Phinehas and Hophni (1 Sam., 4: 4–11) who had dared to carry the ark into battle against the Philistines, losing the ark and their lives in the process. Then he observed:

> For it is not fitting that one takes up governing the Church of God who is mute and does not yet have feet shod in preparation of the peace of the Gospels. Such therefore have seized the Church of God and through evil spirits have handed it over into bondage; they themselves have died in battle who ought to free others from death.[132]

While Bruno may have had someone precisely in mind in this lament, it was aimed in a general way at the contemporary state of ecclesial affairs. The very ecclesiology of the treatise drew Bruno into the contemporary conflicts and gave it a polemical undertone that came to the fore periodically, as it did here.

His direct address of an unnamed prince in Book II, chapter 4, *On the Cardinal Virtues* was one of the more overtly politicised moments in the *De laudibus*. The *De laudibus'* overall structure, however, revealed how these political themes, overt here, found their way into nearly the entire *De laudibus*. First, Bruno engaged the notion of the four virtues, 'by which all the world is ruled . . . Whoever has one, has them all; whoever is missing one, has none'.[133] This led Bruno to a discussion of wisdom – not the wisdom of the philosophers, 'but that which the apostles and doctors preach. These indeed have understanding of divine things . . . which is the true wisdom and without which there is no wisdom'.[134] This wisdom was 'among all virtues, like gold among all metals'. This was the gold inscribed on the divine page, and on the tabernacle and Temple of Solomon.[135] This apostolic wisdom immediately became the absolute

foundation, the *sine qua non*, for society and politics, 'Who would be able to rule or govern his kingdom, his province, his land, his family or even himself without it?'[136] Thus, wisdom was elided into justice by Bruno as an expression of the interconnectedness of all four cardinal virtues. In so doing, he had articulated in a novel manner a particularly Gregorian vision of the world. It has been observed that Bruno's assertion of the cardinal virtues as ruling the world echoed the Gelasian expression of the two powers, sacred and secular, that ruled the world.[137] What has not been appreciated is that the logical structure of the chapter on the cardinal virtues made the Gregorian point explicitly: apostolic authority was the root of every sound society, since it was the source of wisdom and justice.

After introducing this theme and addressing briefly the remaining virtues of fortitude and temperance, Bruno concluded with a caveat.

> Look, enough has been said briefly of the four principle virtues, how and why they are especially necessary to every potentate to whom the governments of the world have been given . . . Act, o prince, whoever you are, so that you have and hold justice . . . See that you who do justice to others are not indifferent to the same, and you who exercise justice on people, exercise it also on yourself.[138]

Thus, the political content was set within a discussion of virtue and personal reform ('exercise it also on yourself') that was in keeping with the broader moral reform of the clergy that the *De laudibus* entailed. That this statement initiated a series of biblical *exempla* of just rulers (Abraham, Joseph and Solomon), the discussion of the ark and the poles of Peter and Paul, revealed that the entirety of this chapter, with its political force, was framed by discussions of apostolic authority. The apostles and doctors were the source of true wisdom that is the foundation of society and just rulership and they were that which carried the Church properly. The ecclesial and secular powers were held distinct by Bruno in this chapter (i.e., he addressed the secular powers distinctly as *saeculi potentes*), but the latter were subsumed within the context of the former and both were rooted in the apostles (hence, canon law and the saints were equally subject to the virtues, as were the laws of emperors). In both cases, whether ruling a kingdom or bearing the Church, legitimate authority was rooted in the virtues, which were in turn rooted in the apostles. This chapter reveals how inextricable the critique of secular power is from Bruno's ecclesiology and from his ideals of personal morality. This observation exposes the weakness of the notion of a separate 'political' allegory

in Bruno: there was no true boundary between political, biblical, moral or ecclesial within his thought. This moment in Book II should not be isolated from the rest of the *De laudibus*. In Book III, whose broad theme is the eschatological renewal of the world, Bruno returned overtly to the theme of political power in chapter 7, *De potestatibus novis*: 'The new world has a new emperor, new kings, new dukes, new princes and new judges. The new kings, dukes, princes and judges are the apostles'.[139] The implicit new emperor was Christ. This blunt eschatological statement was meant to reinforce and build the ecclesiology and political ideals elaborated in the previous discussion of the cardinal virtues, and the audience was reminded that these apostolic potentates were, 'more wise, more powerful, more enduring [*fortiores*], more just and more wealthy' than the powers of this age.[140] Again, apostolic wisdom became the basis of the virtues of justice and fortitude and ultimately of real power and wealth. That greater, apostolic power and fortitude was cast, by Bruno, in terms of the Petrine commission without directly quoting it: 'They have the power to close and to open; they take up whom they will; they exclude whom they will . . ., evil spirits . . . coming to them, flee, and cannot stand in the presence of them'.[141]

Apostolic ecclesiology, overtly political in chapter 7, was built slowly over the course of Book III through a series of seemingly innocuous images of the renewed created world. In chapter 3, *On the new clouds*, he stated flatly, 'The new world is the Church . . . and what do we understand by the new clouds except the apostles?'[142] Their preaching was the rain that made everything fertile: 'they wash our body and soul'.[143] But as the south wind put to flight the north wind, certain people fled these apostolic clouds, those 'who persecute the saints, who banish the apostles from the cities of the unfaithful and force them to flee to other cities'.[144] This was a moment that resonated with the difficulties of the papacies of Gregory VII, Victor III and Urban II, who could not safely reside in the city of Rome for much of their pontificates. Indeed, there were 'evil clouds that are heretics and schismatics'. The new mountains of the next chapter were the patriarchs, prophets, apostles and doctors to whom the reader was to look for help. These were the mountains that rejoice, '[n]ot as wolves and lions and other beasts exult, who take joy in blood and live on cruelty. Such is the exultation of tyrants and heretics; but these [others] exult as doves and lambs and gentle and immaculate things do'.[145] The patriarchs, prophets, apostles and doctors may seem to be threatened but, Bruno noted, 'we will not be afraid while the earth is shaken and the mountains tossed into the heart of the sea'.

> What is to be understood by 'the heart of the sea' except the kings and princes, and other powerful people of this age . . . When, therefore, our mountains, our eternal mountains, the holy apostles seem to be tossed into the heart of the sea . . . when they are dragged before kings and princes and the frightened Church trembles, then we will not be afraid because the Lord is our refuge.[146]

Certainly, this echoed the conflict between imperial and papal supporters, but more importantly it was plain that Bruno's concern with heresy and schism was rooted in those same contemporary ecclesiological debates.

The theme of conflict between secular and ecclesiastical power was sustained and built throughout Book III. While Bruno saw in the new clouds of chapter 3 the stormy conflict between bishops and local urban elites, and saw in the mountains of the apostles the tremors of conflict between royal and papal authority, the matter took a pointedly imperial turn when Bruno considered the eschatological animals. Bruno concluded chapter 6, *On the new animals*, by considering Isaiah 60: 7, and in the context of Isaiah's praise of the restoration of Jerusalem, posed a rhetorical question: 'Who are these rams, who minister to the Lord and are not afraid to fight against kings? Peter and Paul are such rams who, having put on the sword of the spirit, overcame King Nero, the worst, most cruel of all, and they cast Simon Magus from the sky.'[147] It was the apostles who opposed the emperor and simony fearlessly who shall lead the Heavenly Jerusalem. This pointed reference to Nero concluded chapter seven and introduced the chapter *On the new powers* where Bruno asserted the rulership of the apostles.

Book III, chapter 8, considered the winds and the sea. The image here was of Christ commanding the sea to be still (Matthew 8: 26). The structure, like that of chapter 6, concluded with a Roman emperor; the emperor was now Constantine. Thus the chapter *On the new powers* was framed by the worst and best of Roman emperors. Likewise the imagery of the winds and the sea had been transformed from one of the Church persecuted by kings and princes to an image of the Church at peace.

> This immense disturbance of these seas immediately disturbed the holy Church from the times of the apostles to the time of the emperor Constantine, and with difficulty at that time he pacified [it]. After that true peace and tranquility was made, the fishermen of the peaceful Christ and of untroubled fishing began to draw the net about the earth . . . But the net is not full . . . and when the evil fish have been rejected, the good will be led to eternal life.[148]

This was a portrait of the eschatological Church in the process of being realised. It suggested a social organisation and an ecclesial authority that pointed toward the heavenly kingdom. Book III concluded by pointing to the bishops as having apostolic wisdom and as preaching against errors.[149] Specifically, he considered an elaborate vestment that, for Bruno, was both liturgical and eschatological: the pontiff's *rationale*.[150] Bruno's description of the *rationale* here was similar to that of the extant fourteenth-century *rationale* now located in the Regenzberg Domschatzmuseum. While a contemporary example of this episcopal vestment remained from Bamberg Cathedral, the vestment is something of a mystery, but in Bruno's it was worn over the vestments of the bishop with four medallions (two on the shoulders, and one on the front and the back of the vestment).[151] The first reference to it in Italy was from the papacy of John XIX (1024–32). Bruno allegorised the four medallions and the colours of his described *rationale* as pointing to the wisdom in the heart of the bishop. In so doing, Bruno reasserted a clear ecclesiology with social implications: the wisdom that was the basis of a peaceful and just society was rooted in the apostolic authority. It should be noted that while imperial conflict, particularly in Book III, marked the heart of the *De laudibus*, Bruno did not transform the totality of the work into a political treatise.[152] Rather, Bruno's ecclesiology was rooted in his sense of apostolic authority, and that authority was the basis of the just society for Bruno.

A strikingly pro-papal and sustained interpretation of the liturgy and church architecture in general (but the dedication in particular) pervaded the *De laudibus* and represented Bruno's understanding of the rite in the last decade of the eleventh century. It accorded well with Anselm's canonical approach to the dedication, with which it was a near contemporary. In images such as Noah's ark, the ark of the Covenant and the architecture of the basilicas dedicated by bishops, Bruno repeatedly asserted in an innovative manner a coherent and reforming ecclesiology that included personal reform, scriptural exegesis and liturgical meaning. It was this coherent vision that he brought to the papacy of Paschal II (1099–1118).

Paschal II and Bruno of Segni: coordinated dedications and the itinerary of 1106–07

Paschal II is often considered the weakest of eleventh- and twelfth-century papal reformers. He has been characterised as lacking 'sufficient doctrinal sagacity and political acumen to be equal to the task of carrying on successfully the work of his predecessors', Gregory VII and Urban II.[153]

Compared to the extensive studies of those two reformers, Paschal has been largely ignored by historians. At the beginning of his pontificate, Paschal and Bruno shared an understanding of the importance of liturgy in general and the rite of dedication in particular. Paschal would dedicate sixteen churches outside of Rome, and also initiated a significant building programme within Rome. Taking his name from a Carolingian pope (Paschal I, 817–824) who was famous in the *Liber Pontificalis* for having interred the relics of the catacombs into, and re-ornamented the churches of Rome, and who had built the church of S. Cecilia, the site of six Roman dedications by the eleventh-century popes, Paschal II chose to define his papacy in terms of a building programme.[154] At least nine Roman churches were dedicated by Paschal II, and many more were restored or rebuilt during his papacy.[155] Put briefly, the verifiable dedications of Paschal's 19-year papacy in the city rival the total for the entire eleventh century. In addition, Paschal's building activity would have had a much broader influence within the city itself than the previous dedications, which had been concentrated on the crypt of S. Cecilia. Given the developments of the preceding generation of reformers and the increasingly pro-papal meaning they gave to the dedication, this programme is not surprising. Paschal's dedications reflected a strategy of advancing the cause of reform through a liturgy he would have understood as a symbol of papal authority.

Paschal's northern itinerary of 1106 and 1107 employed a careful and coordinated use of the dedication rite.[156] His rapprochement with Philip I of France and strong stand against Henry V of Germany, the two elements that constituted the culmination of the itinerary, were made possible in large part through his successful liturgical programme of 1106–07: a series of elaborate ceremonies that increasingly drew upon imperial imagery were at their most elaborate just prior to his meeting with Philip I, and then promptly ceased. These leave the impression of a deliberate liturgical diplomacy.

In 1105, just prior to Paschal's itinerary, the pan-European political situation was both complex and volatile. In 1104 and 1105 Paschal II began to rebuild strained relations with Philip I. Meanwhile, the Emperor Henry IV's son, King Henry V, was in open revolt. The rebellious king sought and received Paschal's support in February of 1105 against his notorious father. King Henry also depended on the strong support of the anti-imperial Bishop of Mainz, Rothard.[157] Henry IV had destroyed the city walls of Mainz and flushed Rothard out of his see in 1097.[158] The young King Henry was able to use these alliances to create a coalition against his father, the emperor. According to the *Annales Hildesheimenses*, Paschal

then made overtures to the young Henry that he would have his support were he to prove a more just ruler of the Church than his father. With the aid of Rothard of Mainz and Bishop Gerhard of Constance, King Henry began to reconcile the Saxon princes to the Roman see.[159] With this coalition in place, events unfolded quickly. By the spring of 1105 almost all the bishops of Germany had been reconciled to Paschal; by December, the young Henry V held his father unbathed and without communion in captivity, and had restored Rothard to Mainz. By January of 1106 the emperor was deposed and Henry V ruled in his own right, invested by Rothard. While Paschal may have been happy to be rid of Henry IV, he appears to have been wary of Henry V from the outset. The young king had no more intention of giving up the imperial right to invest bishops than had his repeatedly excommunicated father.[160]

Thus, in November of 1105, when Paschal sent a letter to Rothard it should be read not only as an attempt to make plain the papal position to the rapidly progressing king, but also to set the agenda for his itinerary of 1106 and 1107. He laid out three points: (first) that princes were meant to defend the Church, not appoint its clerics; (second) that bishops who had received their office by the imposition of the hands of the excommunicant Henry IV were to be judged by Paschal's council in Italy (or by his legates in Germany); and (third) that the churches of schismatic bishops were to be reconsecrated.[161] This letter established Paschal's intention to use the liturgy as an instrument of his diplomacy. He planned from the outset of his itinerary to assert his authority through the dedication of churches.

On 7 October 1106, Paschal dedicated the church of S. Geminiano in Modena, a stronghold of the most important papal ally, the Countess Matilda of Canossa. That dedication is well documented and rewards closer attention. The story begins in 1099 when, 'not only the clergy' but the *plebs*, prelates, citizens and knights of the church, in the absence of a bishop, had demanded, 'with one will and voice, one desire and clamor', the renovation of the cathedral in Modena.[162] The citizens and the people helped to select the location of the new basilica, and at the blessing of the foundation a 'multitude of men and women' processed to the site. By the spring of 1106, the cathedral was complete enough for the relics of the saint to be translated and the main altar consecrated and the bishop of Modena, Dodo, set the date for the 'translation'.[163] Although the church was ready to be dedicated (translation of the relics into a newly built church accompanied by the consecration of its altar), the *Relatio translationis corporis Sancti Geminiani*, written in the first half of the twelfth century, did not use the term *dedicare*, but here used *translatio* (*consecratio* is used in the

title).[164] This is not surprising as *dedicare* or *consecrare ecclesiam* was not consistently used in this period. (That the church was incomplete would not preclude a dedication, as in Bari.) Technically, what followed both was and was not a dedication. It was a dedication in that it was a translation of relics and consecration of the altar that initiated the use of a newly built church space. It technically was not a dedication in that it was not referred to as such in the *Relatio* and the events that unfolded did not reveal an entire dedication rite, but were highly irregular in the context of a true dedication.

The earliest extant copy of the *Relatio* was preserved in a thirteenth-century (second half) manuscript (Modena, Archivio capitolare, O.II.11) thought to be a copy of a much earlier text produced nearer the events themselves.[165] That manuscript entitled the events 'A relation or description of the renewal of the church of S. Geminiano, Bishop of Modena, and of the translation or revelation or rather the consecration of his most blessed body carefully celebrated by the Lord Paschal supreme Pontiff of the Holy Roman See'.[166] The title suggests the complexity of how best to describe what precisely took place in 1106, as it called the event either a *translatio*, a *revelatio* or a *consecratio* of the body of the saint at the *innovatio ecclesie*, and by noting that this was done *diligenter* by Paschal.[167] The confusion of the description might have been a result of the the later (1184) dedication of the *duomo* by Lucius III. The later dedication may have required the 1106 dedication to be described as something other than a dedication when the *Relatio* was copied.

Either as a dedication of the church or as the consecration of an altar (albeit the consecration of the primary altar of a newly constructed church), the event was surprising. As the day of the translation approached, a large number of bishops, clerics, abbots, monks, a *congregatio militum* and a *conventus populorum* of both sexes formed a crowd of a size that had never been seen before.[168] The *conventus populorum* appeared to refer to the combination of the *cives* and *plebs* named previously as separate groups. Moreover, Matilda of Canossa and her army were also present and 'all were unanimously awaiting the translation and revelation of the great father with joy. But because, as we said, an infinite crowd of people had come together from everywhere it seemed hard, nearly impossible, to put a hand to such a task. So, the most spacious place of the fields was sought where the crowd might gather'.[169] The locale itself was redolent of the earliest communal gatherings and the makeup of the crowd is likewise suggestive; the event was a critical moment in the early history of the communal movement.[170] It is striking that, just as the sermons on

the dedication of Peter Damian, Urban II and Bruno had all urged the audience to think of themselves as citizens of the Heavenly Jerusalem and thereby had politicised the meaning of the rite, so too the Modenese saw themselves as members of a political unit in regard to the church building. The *Relatio* recorded that because of the lengthy preaching of the bishops and the size of the crowd the decision was made to postpone the translation until the next day, 30 April 1106. From the outset the very size of the attendant crowd (the number of the crowd characterising the nature of its viewing) reshaped the event.

But what actually happened on 30 April is not entirely clear. While the *Relatio* noted that the translation was done 'most gloriously', it also made clear that problems emerged:

> Concerning the consecration of the altar, also of the body of the most holy prelate, no small dispute arose between the bishops and citizens of Modena; because the bishops wanted to uncover his relics, the citizens and all the people wholly renounced this. The opinion of Prince Matilda was therefore sought who indeed . . . announced that the apostolic see was expected: declaring that in this year [the pope] would be coming to Italy. And so, a counsel having been undertaken, and the sedition of the people calmed, this dispute between bishop and citizens was appeased.[171]

The liturgy inspired opposition. The *Relatio* revealed the capacity of a rite to create tension within a community. Conflict centred on the viewing of the relics. Those observing the liturgy not only changed the date of the initial event based on their number, they also objected to an element of the rite and further delayed the dedication. The relics were transferred but the altar was not consecrated. After some debate it was agreed to delay the event until the arrival of Paschal II. The ritual was not the negotiation of power within the community; it was the source and focal point of the conflict. Paschal's arrival was described as an *adventus* and 'abundant pomp was prepared [for it]'.[172] The pope arrived with a 'great crowd of bishops and cardinals, abbots, monks and other clerics and laics'. Matilda arrived with a large army.[173]

> It was deliberated concerning the dedication of the altar before the Apostolic See, between the bishops, cardinals, clerics and the people, and concerning the revealing of the holy body. The judgement of these things, as is the will of people, is divided into many [parts]. Finally, after a decision was made concerning the order of the knights or the citizens, they demanded many to affirm by swearing an oath to guard and to

protect [the body] lest in the revealing some rash person presume to violate the relics of such a Father. Six men, therefore, from the order of the knights swore and twice six from the citizens swore. Therefore the stone and altar [*mensa*] on top were raised with great reverence; and another altar [*mensa*] was found placed beneath with great care. Thus, many [people] made one decision not to scrutinise the relics further.[174]

The *Relatio* intended for the reader to view the experience as ultimately unifying and eliminating the doubt of the citizens (*ne alicui infido . . . ad unum redeunt favorem*); it was misleading in this regard. The *Relatio* also stated clearly that the body had already been translated to an altar, hence an altar and stone needed to be opened. That the translation took place to an altar that had to remain unconsecrated due to the objections of a portion of the lay participants was both highly irregular and made clear. The obvious scepticism of the citizens seemed to have focused on the unseen activity of the bishops while handling the relics, as the initial dispute arose during their translation and interrupted the consecration of the altar. Only once it had been determined by the Pope, in consultation with the clergy and laity, that a delegation of knights and citizens could be given access to the rite was the rite allowed to proceed. (In some, but not all, of the PRXII *ordines* there was an explicit opportunity for a viewing of the relics before their deposition.)[175] Furthermore, while the *Relatio* presented a peaceful conclusion to this strife it is also clear that the resolution to the problem resulted from the discovery of the second stone (*mensa*) concealing the relics, the removal of which apparently satisfied the viewers that the relics were safe. The relics were exposed and scrutinised by the citizens, by the attendant clergy and, curiously, by the Bishop of Reggio Bonisenior (1101–1129) but not, it seems, by Paschal II or Dodo, although the pope and Dodo were present at the event.[176] According to the text, before the exposition of the relics a crowd began to gather and Paschal II gave a 'full sermon' to the gathered assembly. Crowds came to see the exposed relics and some brought gifts.[177] This suggests that the *Relatio* was misleading in the notion of communal unity around the relics, and that the decision to reveal the relics was made without the acquiescence or despite the resistance of the Pope, Matilda or Dodo (absent from the exposition).

It should be noted here that although the extant copy of the *Relatio* was made during the age of the commune, the original text – most likely written by the *magister scholarum*, the canon Haymo soon after the events took place – was not predisposed to represent the lay intervention in a

positive light.[178] The thirteenth-century manuscript (Modena, O.II.11) is considered a reproduction of the twelfth-century original and, it has been argued, its illuminations were also copies of a twelfth-century manuscript now lost; they were careful to specifically identify the participants in the events.[179] The *Relatio* comprises folios 1–10v (9v according to the erroneous foliation of the manuscript in red ink). The two very interesting miniatures at folios 1v (1r is blank) and 9r (folio 8 is blank) are reproduced here as Figures 1 and 2.[180] Each miniature was framed and subdivided into two scenes, for a total of four scenes, each captioned. The figures within each of the four scenes images were labelled.[181]

At folio 1v, the top image was captioned 'Anno Dominice Incarnationis Domini nostri Ihesu Christi millesimo XC.VIIII. Ind. VII. sub die decimo Kalendas iunii incepta est fossio fundamenti huius nostre ecclesie Mutinensis'. Identified within the first scene were 'Lanfrancus architector' and 'Operarii'. The bottom image at folio 1v was captioned, 'Eodem anno V idus Iunii ceptum est cementari fundamentum prefate Ecclesie Mutinensis.' Labelled in this scene are 'Lanfrancus', 'Artifices' and 'Operarii'. This latter group was presented as vulgar with ill-kempt hair, large noses and odd expressions.

The official event and a liturgical rite were presented at folio 9r. The top image here was captioned 'Anno dominice incarnationis millesimo centesimo sexto, pridie Kalendas maii, facta est translatio patronis nostri Beatissimi Geminiani'. Here, importantly, only 'Matildis comitissa' was identified. This left three unidentified bishops standing before her, two of whom were identified in the frame below, but the third gesturing as if in dialogue with Matilda must be Pope Paschal II, who was present at and concluded the deliberations at Matilda's request. The bottom image at folio 9r was the culmination as it is the most detailed, and it also revealed a close connection to the narrative: 'Eodem anno VIII. idus Octubris dedicatur et consecratur corpus et altare ipsius confessoris'. Many people and much activity were identified for the viewer: 'Matildis, Lanfrancus, lapis monumenti, Eps. Reginus, Dodo Eps. Mut', are well identified at the top of the frame.[182] In the centre of the lower image the tomb/altar of S. Geminiano was identified as a 'Monumentum'. While S. Geminiano's enshrouded body was clearly visible, he was not identified. In the lower portion of the image the 'Custodes Monumenti' were also identified.

The illumination noted the presence of the *populus*, Matilda, Dodo, Bonisenior, Lanfranc the architect and the six armed knights and twelve armed citizens. Matilda was shown presenting the pallium, Dodo offering his chalice, and Bonisenior removing the stone to reveal the body

Figure 1:   Construction of S. Geminiano, Modena, Archivio capitolare,
O.II.11, folio 1v. Photograph by Roberto Bini, Il Bulino edizioni d'arte.

Figure 2: Exposition of S. Geminiano, Modena, Archivio capitolare, O.II.11, folio 9r. Photograph by Roberto Bini, Il Bulino edizioni d'arte.

(here with the aid of Lanfranc). It is surprising to see Matilda, a lay lord, presenting the pallium to the dead bishop, a post-mortem investment that certainly appears to conflict with a central reform tenant but that reflected her exalted status within papal circles. It is probably best to imagine this as the donation of a liturgical vestment rather than a direct investment. All of this was recorded in the *Relatio*. The knights and citizens were depicted as bearing arms in the presence of the relics, a situation that hardly bespoke a peaceful moment within an (albeit unconsecrated) church and pointed to the explicit threat of violence at this dedication (whether these armed men were meant to protect the relics against violence or were themselves the potential source of violence). The body of the saint was visibly represented. The visibility of the saint would have had the effect of making clear to the viewer the sacred character of the moment and could have heightened the viewer's awareness of the inappropriate and violent activity of the knights and citizens. It is also important to note here that the people were presented in a vulgar manner with large hooked noses and expressive faces quite distinct from the presentation of the bishops, Matilda or Lanfranc who retain a sense of *gravitas* in expression and whose features were well-proportioned. The slightly grotesque features of the gathered crowd reveals the illuminator's and, therefore (assuming a close relationship between a twelfth-century illuminator and chronicler), the chronicler's lack of sympathy for the crowd. It seems most likely that the crowd's presence was recorded in this thirteenth-century copy of the text not to lionise the *populus* but rather in spite of a suspicion of its presence (as articulated in the effort to make the crowd appear ridiculous via slacked jaws and hooked noses). In addition, the failure to identify Paschal II in the top image of folio 9r might suggest a desire to minimise the need for intervention between the city and the countess; it also minimised Paschal's having absented himself from the exposition of the relics in the presence of an armed crowd. The *Relatio* revealed the striking behaviour of the crowd and the gravity of the conflict over the rite despite the author's transparent preference for Paschal, Matilda and their episcopal supporters.

The cleric who produced this manuscript depicted a crowd with which he was not pleased, and presented somewhat foolishly. He also recorded several breaches of liturgical decorum: the presence of armed knights, swords drawn, and most importantly what appears to have been a fragmentation of the rite into a series of disjointed events (translation to an altar, followed weeks later by the consecration of the altar) in order to reveal the relics to a group of laity (citizens, knights and Matilda) that

involved a breaking open of the altar table. This then had to be conse-crated and so, 'the holy body and altar of the most blessed Geminiano was dedicated and consecrated'.[183] The dedication at Modena confirms the real and problematic presence of 'the crowd' at these rites. Far from passive observers absorbing a message of hierarchy, the people were actively altering the rite by the act of observation. While Bruno thought it fitting that large crowds attended the dedication, this was not the role he envisioned for them. This tense dynamic both reflected and lent power to the dedication rite. As at Bari, the dedication of S. Geminiano at Modena enhanced the authority of the *cives* and restrained the authority of pope, bishop and countess alike.

While the dynamic of the rite reflected the fluidity of meaning, Paschal was attempting to apply the rite in the manner of his predecessors: as a ritual reinforcement of a papally centred ecclesiology, as an event that reinforced the authority and sacrality of the pope. From Modena, Paschal proceeded to hold Council at Guastalla on 22 October. The Council of Guastalla was motivated to reiterate 'Gregorian' positions regarding control of churches and reconcile, if possible, bishops who had been supporters of Henry IV. Thus, among the canons issued at Guastalla was the following:

c.3 – Let no laic dispose of, or occupy churches or the goods of churches . . .

c.6 – That clerics, abbots, monks who obtain churches from laity . . . are excommunicated.

c.7 – Following the customs of the holy canons, we declare that any member of the clergy who accepts the investiture of the church or ecclesiastical dignity from the hand of a lay person and the one who imposes his hand, let his rank be reduced and let him be deprived of communion.[184]

This last canon, 7, was an attempt to accommodate Henry V's treatment of his father in December of 1106 (but reminiscent of Matilda's dona-tion of a palium to S. Geminiano).[185] (The emperor had complained of having been deprived not only of his crown but also of the sacraments during Christmastide.)[186] More generally, the canons reasserted ecclesias-tical control over the physical space of churches as well as their temporal goods. The Council also condemned multiple German bishops and the bishop of Padua. However, those bishops who sought it were reconciled within a few days to weeks of the Council.[187]

Most interestingly, the Council at Guastalla also reconciled the City of Parma that had supported as antipope their Bishop Cadalus, appointed by Henry IV and taking the name Honorius II from 1061 until his death in 1072.[188] Cadalus had begun to rebuild the Basilica of St Mary in the late eleventh century.[189] Construction continued well into the twelfth century, prolonged by fires, earthquakes and the crisis of 1104.[190] That crisis had been provoked when the papal legate Bernard (with the support of Matilda and the wealthier landed citizens) arrived in the city in 1104 to preach against heresy and error.[191] On the feast of the Assumption, the Cardinal legate said Mass at the Basilica and, true to his mission, he preached against the heresy of Henry IV. According to Donizio, in the midst of the Eucharistic Prayer, just after he lowered the chalice (a very dramatic moment in between the consecration and fraction of the Eucharist) the people began to murmur against Bernard's condemnation of Henry. The literary nature of this presentation, associating Bernard with Christ in the Eucharist and directly connecting the crowd with the Jews who verbally abused Christ on the cross, makes one dubious as to the authenticity of the moment.[192] The story demonstrates that the Basilica was in use in 1104. The crowd drew weapons in the church and Bernard received a small wound. They dragged him away from the altar and out of the church, imprisoning him. They then proceeded to destroy a chapel Matilda had built in the basilica; this provoked a strong and rapid military response from the countess. The citizens of Parma acquiesced, releasing Bernard and paying for the damaged chapel.[193] It is important to note that the crowd expressed their displeasure not only by accosting Bernard, but also by damaging the sacred space created by Matilda, thereby attempting to efface her symbolic presence within the Basilica. The desecration of the chapel reveals that for some, this sacred space was offensive within the Basilica.

Having reconciled Parma at Guastalla in 1106, Paschal took the opportunity to proceed to Parma in the company now of Bernard, Bishop-elect of Parma, and Matilda. Parma presented an opportunity for Paschal and he seems to have taken advantage of that liturgical moment to assert his authority, as Urban had in 1095 and 1096. According to the *Vita Mathildis*, 'He consecrated there the temple of the mother of Christ, giving a decree, that [the cathedral] be subject to no one except Peter, who holds the keys to heaven, and likewise to the chair of [Peter]'. Matilda, in turn, marked the occasion by making a large donation to the church, 'such that it pleased the people greatly'.[194] Having done this, he consecrated Bernard as bishop. The dedication at Parma, thus, reinforced a network

of Papal support through the assertion of sacred authority, as well as through lay donation and episcopal submission. By placing Parma under the direct control of St Peter, Paschal was removing it from the control of the Bishop of Ravenna. This was a slap at imperial pretensions to appoint popes, weakening the independence of both Parma, seat of the papal pretender Cadalus, and of Ravenna, seat of Guibert. Therefore the meaning of the dedication at Parma was entirely distinct from that of Modena. Here the dedication marked absolutely the authority of the reform party and of Paschal II. It reasserted that authority in the face of the desecration of the chapel. The consecration of the Basilica was of a church already in use, and so very likely already consecrated while the bishops of the city were in conflict with Rome. Thus, the re-consecration here emphasised the role of Paschal, the true pope, in consecrating things and persons, as the source of true sacrality. The dedication provided him the opportunity to directly address the community about the relation of the church to its bishop and to lay authorities (if his, Bernard's and Matilda's actions had not spoken eloquently enough). The *Vita* also recounted that Paschal then went to France, 'making fruitful many spaces . . . there'.[195] This remark echoed the dedication's capacity to create sacred space, and Paschal's effective use of it in France.

As had Urban II, Paschal punctuated his itinerary with dedications and important liturgies. On 4 January 1107 he dedicated the church of S. Evasio in Casale Monferrato. On 29 January he dedicated St Martin d'Ainay in Lyons.[196] Hugh, Archbishop of Lyons and a staunch Gregorian, had died on his way to Guastalla in October of 1106.[197] This dedication served to reinforce the relationship between Lyons and Rome; it may have also been the occasion to install his successor. At Cluny in February Paschal confirmed its privileges and possessions, and settled the dispute between a local count and the archbishop of Narbonne.[198]

On 16 February Paschal dedicated St Maurice in Dijon.[199] After this, the papal entourage met with and granted the episcopacy of Laon to Gaudry, a former chancellor of Henry I of highly dubious character, whose appointment was opposed by Anselm of Bec.[200] Members of the papal court, most notably Peter of Cluny, the Papal *camarerius* (treasurer), ultimately prevailed upon Paschal. After the appointment, Peter warned Gaudry that he should 'obey [Paschal's] orders in all matters'.[201] Thus, the appointment of Gaudry allowed Paschal not only to collect much-needed funds, but also to insert a loyal dependent into the episcopacy.

Two days later, 18 February, Paschal dedicated the church of St Pierre de Bèze.[202] On 9 March 1107 he dedicated the Cluniac church

of La Charité-sur-Loire in Niève.[203] Here, Suger of St Denis joined the entourage, participating in the dedication, as did the 'noble magnates' of France, including the seneschal Guy the Red, count of Rochefort, who was to 'serve the pleasure of the pope throughout the kingdom'.[204]

With this expanded entourage, Paschal proceeded to another dedication at Dole and then to St Martin of Tours to celebrate the fourth Sunday of Lent, the so-called *Laetare Jerusalem* liturgy.[205] This provided an important moment for the papacy: it was a Sunday when the popes process wearing the *frigium* (the papal head gear supposed to have been given by Constantine to Sylvester) and carrying the golden rose to present to a city official as a sign of papal favour. Paschal was following the pattern of Urban II's itinerary of 1096. The use of the *frigium* would have heightened the imperial imagery Paschal had been deploying throughout this ceremonial itinerary through regular processions for the dedication and at least one Papal *adventus* in Modena. The ceremony of the golden rose provided Paschal with yet another opportunity to display the imperial finery of the papacy, here before the citizens of Tours. Thus, Paschal's deployment of Papal liturgy and imperial symbolism appears to have culminated at Tours.

The dénouement would be his meeting with Philip I and Louis VI at St-Denis. Philip and Louis rendered Paschal imperial homage, 'the royal majesty bowing at his feet, for the love of God, following the custom of kings at the tomb of the fisherman Peter lowering their diadem'.[206] Thus they conceded the Gregorian position that kings and emperors should humble themselves before the feet of the pope. Afterward, Paschal raised the king and his son to their feet, sat them before himself, especially and 'conferred with them closely . . . on the state of the Church'. According to Suger, Paschal asked that they follow their predecessor, Charlemagne, and defend the Church against Henry.[207] This was no small thing. Paschal appears to have implied that the kings of France were the rightful heirs to the imperial crown, not Henry V. It was, as Suger noted with the eye of hindsight, 'flattery', but it formed the alliance that would allow Paschal to confront the imperial party at Châlons effectively.

Two weeks after Easter, on 11 May, at the town of Châlons-sur-Marne, Paschal met with emissaries of Henry V. As a result of the recent rapprochement with the King of France, Philip, Louis VI and a large body of the highest-ranking French ecclesiastics, as well as members of the papal curia and Roman nobility, accompanied Paschal at the meeting. Paschal's entourage stated their case baldly: he would not tolerate lay investiture, not even by the emperor. 'If hands consecrated for the body and blood of

the Lord are placed in obligation beneath a layman's hands bloodied from a sword, it degrades his holy orders and sacred anointing.' The German delegation 'gnashed their teeth violently, like typical Germans', and said prophetically, 'Not here, but in Rome, with swords this quarrel will be settled.[208]

The rebuff of the imperial party at Châlons marked the diplomatic high point of Paschal's 17-month northern itinerary of 1106 and 1107. It was a carefully planned moment, culminating with Paschal's comment on the nature of consecration, in particular the sacerdotal consecration of the bread and wine in the Eucharist, but also, more broadly, 'sacred anointing' which would include the dedication of churches. Paschal was taking up the rigorous Gregorian position on the relation between simony, imperial investiture and the purity or pollutedness of sacred rites as Peter Damian had observed on the consecration.

This same position was maintained at the Council of Troyes on 23 May. The fifth canon deposed any bishop accepting 'investiture of churches or ecclesiastical things' from the hands of the laity.[209] The council also reiterated the extension of the Peace to ecclesiastical persons and things, merchants and pilgrims, as well as reasserting positions on clerical marriage and the sale of benefices typical of the reform.[210] It was the relationship between the assertion of the sacrality of space via the Peace, its prohibition of sale, and the ban on lay investiture that was reinforced by the dedication rite and that made the regular dedication of churches so apt a way to frame these councils.

Most striking about Paschal's liturgical itinerary and expressing most eloquently the strategic use of the rites preceding the meeting with Henry's delegation is that once their purpose had been accomplished the dedications ceased. The pope celebrated Easter in Chartres, held Council at Troyes in May and continued to confirm rights and privileges, but he did not dedicate another church until after his return to Rome in November of 1107. Once the most challenging portion of his diplomacy was over, the intensive displays of papal liturgy and imperial symbol stopped, suggesting that these were deployed from the outset in a premeditated manner that reflected Paschal's experienced papal court.

While Paschal's northern itinerary has heretofore been described largely as an imitation of Urban II's itinerary, no similarly clear pattern can be discerned in Urban's use of papal ceremony.[211] Urban's more numerous dedications came both before and after councils, are at times incomplete, and give the overall impression of being opportunistic and ad hoc. Paschal, however, was able to maximise the diplomatic impact of

the papal liturgy, in part because he was supported by highly seasoned advisors (including Bruno) who were familiar with the opportunities of papal ceremony abroad and who had been considering the significance of these rites for two generations, and in part because Paschal had stronger support in Rome than his predecessors.

Paschal and Bruno in southern Italy

In southern Italy, Paschal likewise employed the dedication rite in a deliberate manner (albeit more chronologically diffuse), dedicating nine churches. In 1101 he dedicated the high altar of the abbey of Mileto and St Sabinus of Canossa; St Dominic at Sora in 1104; the Cathedral of Gaeta in 1106; St Benedict in Capua in 1108; St Mennas at Sant'Agata dei Goti in 1110; S. Vincenzo al Volturno in 1115; and the cathedrals of Siponto in April of 1117 and of Palestrina on 16 December.[212] Paschal died on 21 January 1118. While he dedicated churches to the very end, it is important to note that his dedicatory activity in southern Italy declined after the crisis with Henry V of 1111, the so-called 'pravilegium' dispute.

The clearest example of the coordinated use of the dedication in southern Italy was in the company of none other than Bruno of Segni. Bruno, already bishop and cardinal, took the monastic habit at Montecassino in 1103. In the spring of 1106, Bruno was asked to dedicate a new chapel at Sant'Angelo in Formis to the honour of St Nicholas. The dedication at Sant'Angelo may have also honoured the memory of Desiderius, who had been consecrated as Pope Victor III on the very day the bones of St Nicholas arrived in Bari (9 May 1087). Perhaps because of this, by the early twelfth century the cult of Nicholas was associated with both Desiderius and the Gregorian cause, explaining why the dedication by the monk-bishop Bruno was so offensive to the Archbishop of Capua, Sennes, who likely saw in it the extension of Cassinese authority into his Metropolitan See.[213] With expanding Cassinese prestige could come reforming ideals and Roman influence: reforming ideals of clerical celibacy and common property that the Capuan canons did not share.[214] Sennes was already embroiled in ongoing disputes over the control of local churches.[215] He gathered a force of armed Capuans and sent them to Sant'Angelo where they destroyed the altar of San Niccolò and stole the relics. According to the Chronicle of Montecassino, Bruno denounced these actions at a Synod in Rome and the clerics and people of Capua were made 'to emend themselves in humility'.[216]

While the chapel of San Niccolò does not appear to have been rebuilt,

Bruno's subsequent actions left no room to doubt the strong connection between the liturgy of dedication and the Roman-Cassinese dominance of Capua. In 1108 he convinced Paschal II to travel to Capua, at the conclusion of a synod in Benevento, to dedicate the Cassinese dependency of San Benedetto.[217] The scene of Cardinal, Bishop and Abbot Bruno in procession with Pope Paschal II on the streets of Capua only two years after Archbishop Sennes had destroyed the chapel of San Niccolò at Sant'Angelo in Formis must have been a triumphant one. At least some of the viewers of the procession would have seen it this way. In fact, the previous dedicatory inscription on San Benedetto would have placed Bruno in a succession of abbots beginning with Benedict and re-emphasised the Desiderian link between Cassino and Rome through the presence of Paschal, also a successor of Desiderius (as Victor III).

Desiderius, known as Victor, bishop and abbot
Began this work; Oderisius, best abbot,
Completed it, o Benedict, decorating it to your honour.[218]

Fragments of the eleventh-century frescoes reveal images of monks in the manner of those at Sant'Angelo; these fragments strongly suggest that the abbatial line of succession was represented from Benedict through the eleventh century.[219] Thus, in 1108, the consecration of San Benedetto was pitted against the desecration of 1106, and papal authority and Cassinese honour were pointedly reasserted in the very centre of the city of Capua.[220]

Other dedications in southern Italy followed familiar patterns for Paschal. The dedication at Canosa in Apulia in 1101 followed closely on the heels of a revolt by the citizens against the Normans in the previous year. Two weeks after this dedication Paschal and Roger entered Benevento in triumph.[221] The dedication of the cathedral at Siponto in 1117 may have marked a synod of that same year in the region.[222] This fits the pattern of dedication that Paschal had inherited and deftly continued.

Bruno's final commentary: the *De sacramentis* and the '*pravilegium*' dispute

While Bruno was with Urban II in France in 1096 he probably first met a cleric in the episcopal household of Maguelone named Walter. Walter, who would have witnessed the consecration of Maguelone by Urban, became bishop of Maguelone in 1104 or 1105 and would need to lead the pontifical rites. Bruno addressed him as bishop in his second commentary

on the dedication, his *De sacramentis ecclesiae*, and thus the work was written some time after 1104. Although Bruno worked closely with Paschal II during the first decade of the twelfth century, the events of 1111 changed Bruno's relationship to the papacy. In 1111, Henry V approached Rome with a large army and, after an abortive coronation ceremony, met with Paschal in February at Sutri, about thirty miles northwest of Rome. Recent scholars have shown that despite a reputation for weakness and the criticisms of the other reformers, Paschal at first presented a strong, reform-minded position to Henry that ultimately resulted in the failure of the coronation and Henry's seizure of Paschal. In Paschal's original position, Henry would have lost the right to invest bishops and the bishops would have given up their regalia. This last term caused much confusion at Sutri and subsequently, but Paschal appears to have meant that bishops would no longer hold royal or civil offices while retaining their *ecclesiastica*, i.e., the churches and lands donated to them.[223] However, by April 1111, after several months of captivity, Paschal granted Henry the right to invest bishops elected without simony.

In a letter to Bonomo, the prior of the Cassinese dependency of S. Giorgio, Bruno, who had not been at Sutri in February and had escaped imprisonment, accused Paschal of betraying the reform movement. Bruno's reaction helped give rise to the rumour that the synod to be held in 1112 would depose Paschal and elect a new pope.[224]

> First, you should know this: that the lord pope neither loves me nor my counsel. However, a good purpose ought not to be modified. And I say this which I have indeed said [before], and I adhere most firmly to the position of Gregory and Urban, and I hope for the mercy of almighty God because I will persist in this purpose until the very end.[225]

Nonetheless, in another letter written to Paschal himself, even as Bruno condemned lay investiture as heresy he attempted to assure Paschal of his ultimate loyalty:

> Certainly I so love you as I ought to love a father and lord and, with you living, I wish to have no other pope, just as I along with many others promised you . . . I ought to love you, but I ought to love more the one who has made you and me.[226]

Despite this tempered show of respect, Bruno argued that the *privilegia* of April 1111 did violence to all religion and piety, and reminded Paschal that the pope himself had declared lay investiture heretical. Bruno urged the pope to confirm lay investiture as heresy so that peace might reign in the Church.[227]

In 1112, after Paschal renounced the *privilegium*, Bruno remained unconvinced of the pope's commitment because Paschal refused to excommunicate Henry. Paschal, in response to this criticism and *schismatis et discordiae metuens*, recanted his decision to allow Bruno to be abbot, and compelled him to return to Segni.[228] If Bruno had thought that the abbacy of Montecassino placed him closer to attaining the office of pope, this certainly put an end to that ambition. In any case, this must have come as a terrible blow to Bruno and done little to endear Paschal to him.[229]

This was the context that best explains Bruno's *De sacramentis ecclesiae*, although the exact date of the composition of the document is unknown. It was written after 1104, however, as it was addressed to *fratri Galterio, Magalonensi episcopo*, and Walter was elevated to the episcopate no earlier than that year.[230] Bruno referred to himself only as bishop, and not as abbot, which could imply that it was written after he had been removed from Montecassino; however, Bruno rarely used the title of abbot.

The *De sacramentis* was a belated reply to questions Walter had posed to Bruno while in Rome in 1104-1105 concerning the tabernacle and the vestments of Aaron and 'things that are figurative and that signify a great mystery . . . [that] we might find in the church'.[231] Bruno had set aside these questions, as he apologised to Walter, because 'other matters impeded us'.[232] It was not until later, when a hermit priest named Helbertus arrived from Walter, that Bruno was reminded of Walter's questions, probably no earlier than 1106.[233] Even if Bruno's response were written as early as 1106, his decision to comment on the dedication was telling. For, as he told Walter, 'There are many things in the dedication of churches, many even in the other sacraments of the Church, which no less than those, appear to be done under a shadow and a figure'.[234] Walter's questions to Bruno reflected the complexity of the dedication liturgy that Bruno and Paschal were so frequently conducting; filled as it was with imagery and liturgical activity from Exodus 25–30, from the anointing of the altar (Ex. 29: 36–37) to the purple robes of the pontiffs (Ex. 28: 15–30). These were confusing symbols whose significance seemed to imply a direct correlation between Christian and Old Testament priests, the very interpretation of the pro-imperial bishops. If the bishops were recapitulating the old law of Exodus in the dedications of temples, ought not they likewise be subject to the authority of kings?

When we were together in Rome on the island, at the house of the bishop of Porta, and when we read in the book of Exodus, in the

account of the tabernacle of the covenant and the vestments of Aaron, certain things that are figurative and that signify a great mystery, you (and then I) began to wonder what others like these we might find in the Church, as now these old things have passed away and have all been made new.[235]

This was the same framework that Damian had used in the sermon on the dedication where he vigorously defended sacerdotal authority against princely authority. It was the same metaphor that Anselm had already developed into a vigorous defence of papal authority; it was an argument that Bruno himself had employed in the *De laudibus ecclesiae*. It is important to note that this introduction was well suited to the material contained in the *De laudibus* where he treated the subject of Aaron and the bishop's liturgical vestment, the *rationale*, at length.[236] That material on the dedication not only helps us understand Bruno and Walter's conversation on the Tiber Island, how their discussion of the liturgical vestments and pontifical rites dovetailed with a discussion of Exodus, but it also raises the problem of why Bruno chose to create a new commentary for Walter, rather than refer him to the *De laudibus*. Moreover, when Bruno arrived at the question of Aaron's vestments in the *De sacramentis*, he chose to be brief, referring Walter to his commentary on Exodus.[237] Like Damian, Bruno promised to interpret the rite according to the new law. Unlike Damian's sermons, however, Bruno's *De sacramentis* lacks a vigorous defence of papal prerogative. This silence is surprising given the career and writings of Bruno and given Paschal's extensive dedications in conjunction with Bruno. The kind of commentary Bruno chose to create in this climate of intense papal dedications is surprising because it has few papal references and offers a very tepid vision of papal symbolism.

Damnatio memoriae: the silences of the *De sacramentis*

Bruno's *De sacramentis ecclesiae* offered three major themes: it moved from the consecration of a church, to baptism and confirmation, and finally to the significance of priestly and episcopal robes.[238] Thus, by its very structure, it was also a commentary on the major issue of the late eleventh-century reform: the significance of the episcopate and of episcopal investment. It was addressed to a bishop, concerned pontifical rites, and discussed the significance of episcopal vestments. Through the rhetorical structure of the text Bruno asked his reader to think about the consecration of a church in terms of the question of investiture and the

nature of the episcopacy. Bruno's rhetoric is most understandable in the context of his troubled relationship with Paschal after 1112.

If the *De sacramentis* were written after the events of 1112 its most perplexing feature would be resolved: the almost complete lack of reference to the papacy or to Petrine authority. It offers a portrait of the episcopate as the principal mechanism of reform while scarcely referring to the relationship between reforming bishop and Roman pontiff. In this latter characteristic the *De sacramentis* diverges sharply from the 'Gregorian conception of episcopacy' – an ideal, found in the writings of the reformers of the late eleventh century and early twelfth century, including Bruno, of both reforming zeal and strong papal discipline of the episcopate.[239] Such an absence is extraordinary in a text written by one of the leading reformers of the Gregorian party as a type of handbook of pontifical liturgical significance. It is all the more striking given Bruno and Paschal's coordinated approach to and extensive employment of the dedication prior to 1110.

While composing the *De sacramentis*, Bruno confined even his use of the word 'pontiff' to three of the final sections on priestly vestments: *Quid pallium significet*, *De vittis*, and *De summo pontifice*. In the section on the *pallium* Bruno distinguished between the title *pontifex* referring to all bishops, and *summus pontifex*. For bishops in general the *superhumerale* referred to the grave burden they bore: carrying the weak and the sinful. The bishops carried the burden of the whole Church.[240] In contrast, in the *De laudibus*, the ark of the Covenant, which for Bruno represented the Church, was borne by means of the poles that are Peter and Paul and no one dared carry that burden without them.[241] That apostolic intermediary was strikingly absent from the *De sacramentis*. In other words, the burden of carrying the Church had shifted directly onto the shoulders of the bishops who, in the *De laudibus*, had only carried the Petrine and Pauline poles that bore the Church.

Bruno prefaced his reference to *summus pontifex* by noting that those bishops who did not lift a finger to bear the burden of others did not truly bear the *pallium*. Bruno observed that the *summus pontifex* (Christ) was the one who, on being ornamented with the *pallium*, left the ninety-nine sheep to seek out the one stray. *Summus pontifex* in this section was left as an episcopal reference in that Christ, as the highest pontiff, set an example of caring for his flock.[242]

In the very brief, three-sentence-long section *De summo pontifice*, Bruno asserted that he did not believe that the pope wore purple robes because of his royal power but because Constantine once gave to Pope

Sylvester all the imperial insignia, and so popes wore what was once worn by emperors.[243] These few direct references to the papacy are ambivalent at best, and may, in fact, suggest a contrast between the earlier reforming papacy, and a ceremonial papacy in the hands of the emperor. Indeed, Bruno's cool treatment of this subject implied that the royal ceremonial garb of the papacy had no temporal significance and did not point to a territorial authority, but simply referred blandly to a historical event. By thus limiting the significance of papal vestments to their historical, literal sense, Bruno took a position on the regalia that may have reflected Paschal's original position of 1111 (i.e., that bishops would give up their regalia). He was making a direct comment on the significance, or more precisely the lack of significance of the vestments worn by the pope on the most important occasions in Rome. Whereas Constantine was held up as an ideal, almost eschatological figure and the subject of the 'new powers' in the *De laudibus*, here he was reduced to a simple historical anecdote. In the *De laudibus*, Bruno addressed the princes of the world directly; here he chose silence. In fact, of the four manuscripts that contain Bruno's dedicatory letter, one (Vat. Lat. 1254, s. XIII) titled this section *De imperio summo*.[244] Even if this manuscript cannot be established as the most primitive exemplar and thus may not represent a sentiment of Bruno himself, it does establish that on the subject of papal primacy the section was confusing enough to at least one mediaeval copyist who read this section as pro-imperial.

The relative absence of papal language also stood out when the *De sacramentis* was placed alongside the Carolingian *Quid Significent*, which made strong assertions of Petrine authority and used the title *pontifex* as an episcopal title throughout.[245] In one instance, the anonymous commentator of the *Quid Significent* interpreted the bishop's staff as representing *sacerdotis potestas*.[246] This priestly power stems from Christ's commissioning the apostles to go out and preach the gospel taking only a staff with them (Mt 10: 10, Mk 6: 8, Lk 9: 3). Later, when the pontiff rapped the staff three times on the lintel of the church building the act was taken to represent Petrine authority over heaven, earth and hell. The commentator quoted Matthew (16: 18–19), 'Tu es Petrus et super hanc petram edificabo ecclesiam meam'.[247] These two references combined to make the pontiff's staff a strong symbol of Petrine authority, both doctrinal and juridical.

Bruno likewise connected the *virga pastoralis* with *sermo divinis et praedicatio evangelica*. Bruno, however, did not link these to Christ's commissioning of apostolic authority; rather, he made his point more obliquely by referring to Isaiah 11: 4: *percutiet terram virga oris sui, et*

spiritu laborium suorum interficiet impium. This reference allowed Bruno to retain the sense of teaching authority from the *Quid Significent* without introducing its understanding of apostolic authority. This reference allowed Bruno to note that the bishop knocking three times on the door represented the Trinity evoked in the sacraments, and the bishop's preaching knocked on the ears (the doors) of the faithful.[248] An episcopal reader, however, familiar with the pontifical and the *Quid Significent*, would have had to ask himself why Bruno, previously so concerned with asserting apostolic authority, avoided the opportunity to assert that authority here by choosing such a relatively obscure reference.

Further, the *Quid Significent* referred a second time to the passage (*Tu es Petrus*) in order to make the analogy between Petrine authority and the strong walls of the Church.[249] Bruno, when confronted with the *lapides* of his church, chose to ignore the more obvious reference used in the *Quid Significent* and preferred to see them as signifying the Church built from 'living stones' (*vivis lapidibus aedificatur*) joined and united by charity.[250] The *Lapis altaris* was Christ and all his limbs, and so it was appropriate to put relics in the altar.[251] Bruno had directly connected the rite of dedication to the foundation of the Church Petrine commission of Matthew 16: 18 in the *De laudibus*.[252]

In the *De sacramentis*, Bruno again chose a more enigmatic reference over an obvious Petrine one when he discussed the use of hyssop in the dedication. He began this section by observing, *Hyssopus naturaliter in petra nascitur.*[253] Here Bruno chose *petra* over *saxa*. The anonymous commentator of *Quid Significent* had said *Ysopus . . . est humilis, quae radicibus suis saxorum dicitur penetrare duritiam.*[254] For the anonymous commentator hyssop represented the humility which entered our hardened hearts. Bruno chose *petra*, but was not at all interested in connecting this with Petrine authority, choosing instead a more obscure scriptural allusion:

> Hyssop is naturally born in rock [petra]: 'The rock [Petra], however,' as the Apostle said, 'was Christ'. The Hyssop is the good herb which is born, reborn and rooted in Christ. Although through this indeed all the multitude of the faithful can be understood, nevertheless especially those are figured in the hyssop who, rooted and founded in the faith of Christ, are not able to be torn away from or separated from his love. Through which [hyssop] what better are we to understand than the bishops and priests, who, to the extent that they obtain a greater dignity within the Church, ought to adhere more firmly to faith in Christ?[255]

In this passage Bruno's choice of *petra* and preference for *episcopus* requires an explanation. Bruno's question was a rhetorical one. Who had greater dignity within the Church than priests and bishops? Who ought to be more firmly rooted in the rock (*petra*) which is Christ? Bruno answered, 'bishops and priests', but obviously the one with the highest dignity in the Church, the pope, could best be understood here, since he sat in the chair of St Peter: who better to be rooted in *petra*?

By choosing *petra* over *saxa*, Bruno called his readers' attention to the appropriate answer to his rhetorical question. What is more, if Bruno had followed the style more typical of the commentaries and referred to all bishops as *pontifex* rather than as *episcopus*, he would not have been able to make his point. Without directly attacking the papacy, Bruno was critical of the papacy and emphasised the role of bishops and clergy within the Church at the expense of the papacy. It would be hard to imagine this choice passing unnoticed either by Bruno or his audience. While Bruno cannot be said to have been rigid in his other uses of Petrine metaphors, he had been a firm advocate of the reform position. Anselm and Damian had already elaborated papal prerogative in terms of the metaphor of the dedication, and Bruno himself had invoked Matthew 16: 18–19 in defence of papal prerogative when exposing the mystical significance of other Old Testament texts, as he was here for Walter.[256]

The rhetoric of the *De sacramentis* is only fully appreciated if it is read as composed after 1112. Were it written after 1112 the reader can easily imagine Bruno shifting his attention to the role of the episcopate *in consecratione ecclesiae*. Bruno was out of favour with the papacy, perhaps with his own papal ambitions scuttled, and certainly did not trust Paschal II or John of Gaeta (Paschal's successor) to continue with the reforms he held dear.[257] The episcopal rite of making holy (*consecratio*) a new church provided an established means to promote the reforming ideals while shifting the burden of reform on to the bishops (such as Bruno and Walter) and away from the papacy, or rather, away from those popes – Paschal and his successor John of Gaeta (Gelasius II) – whom Bruno felt had betrayed the Gregorian cause.

There could be few pretenses better for undermining Paschal than an exegesis of the rite of church dedication, given his extensive building programme and a ceremonial life unlike anything Rome had seen, or the popes had attempted, in the eleventh century. Bruno himself was acutely aware of the violent controversy and miraculous power that could erupt around the dedication of a church.[258] For Bruno to have written a commentary on the episcopate and the significance of the rite of church

dedication with slight and diminishing reference to the papacy, when the pope was embarked on a significant building and liturgical campaign, would have been a clear diminution of Paschal's efforts. To undermine the liturgical import, the symbolic meaning, of the rich ceremonial life Paschal was constructing in Rome was to undermine Paschal's own authority. It would have been a rhetorical strategy not wasted on Walter, bishop of a papal stronghold, who knew Bruno personally.

Returning to the broader context of the *De sacramentis*, Bruno contemplated not only liturgical symbolism but such symbolism as it related to the investiture controversy. An examination of these sources reveals how Bruno's thought changed after 1112. Bruno had given much thought to the symbolism of different liturgies and liturgical elements by 1112. Enclosed within Bruno's letter to Bonomo of 1111/12 (to whom Bruno observed that the pope neither loved him nor his counsel) was a letter addressed to the 'cardinals and bishops of the holy Roman Church'.[259] Bruno informed Bonomo that he would follow the 'sentences' of Gregory VII and Urban II, and asked Bonomo to pass along a 'little work' to the bishops of Lucca and Parma, both communities that knew at first hand the struggle between their bishops and the papacy over the question of reform. In that enclosed epistle, Bruno equated the significance of the consecration of churches with that of bishops, connecting many of the same sacramentals he would interpret for Walter in the *De sacramentis* (*anulus, virga, aqua, sal, oleum* and *crisma*) directly to the investiture controversy.

> When, however, the ring and staff are given by whom they ought to be given, and when and where and how they ought to be given, they are sacraments of the Church, just like water and salt, oil and chrism, and all the other things without which the consecrations *of people and churches* can not be made.[260]

While Bruno was careful not to accuse Paschal of heresy directly in this 'little work' addressed to the bishops and cardinals, and even referred to a signer of the *privilegium* (Bishop Peter of Porto) as his 'most beloved friend', the letter to Bonomo made clear that Bruno saw himself splitting from a papacy with which he was now at odds.[261]

These two letters demonstrate that Bruno was at odds with the *privilegium*'s position on lay investiture and viewed this matter as akin to the proper consecration of a church. It is clear from this letter that this change in Bruno's thought occurred after the *privilegium* and contained all of the elements (de-emphasising the papacy while still pursuing the themes of reform) of the *De sacramentis*.[262] Therefore, the tools for the ministration

of those sacraments were the exclusive domain of the Church, upon which true 'consecrations of people and churches' depend. This letter to the bishops and cardinals of Rome lends further credence to interpretation of the *De sacramentis* as a contribution to the investiture debate after the so-called *pravilegium* dispute. In that context, Bruno, disenchanted with Paschal and out of favour with the papacy after the compromise of 1112, re-envisioned for himself and his fellow bishops a means to continue the reform of the Church. It would be the responsibility of the bishops to make the Church holy, to make the institution a sacred place. This is the consistent metaphor of the *De sacramentis*: episcopal consecration of the Church, and Bruno put forth this metaphor by describing and interpreting the liturgy of a bishop consecrating a church.

More specifically, Bruno made this point within the individual analogies of his commentary. By combining a discussion of the greater significance of a bishop's vestments with a discussion of the duties of a bishop, he placed his polemic within the context of the investiture controversy. Salt, placed in a child's mouth at baptism, represented the rudiments of faith contained in the baptismal creed the bishop put to the faithful.[263] The bishop's staff represented his authority and responsibility to preach to his flock.[264] Water also represented the bishop preaching to his congregation.[265] In a strong reforming key, the bishop's humeral represented his chastity as did his mitre and gloves.[266] The *orarium* represented the yoke and burden of Christ which the bishop bore.[267] The tunic, which was sky-blue in the Old Testament, represented the celestial focus of the bishop, his ability to provide heavenly nourishment, and that he ought to be pure.[268] The maniple represented the good works of the bishop, and the ring marked the bishop as both the Vicar of Christ and as representative of the Bride of Christ, the Church.[269]

Finally, the bishop was anointed on his hands, and this should remind him of his responsibility to be merciful and generous to the poor.[270] This last analogy came at the very end of the work, *De consecrationibus episcoporum*. While both kings and bishops were anointed on the head, 'according to the ancient custom', it was from the anointing of the hands that consecration was given: 'that whatever they bless, is blessed, and what ever they sanctify is sanctified' (drawing from the dedication rite). The unanointed hand was greedy; the anointed hand was open to all in charity. Bruno distinguished sharply between bishops and kings: only bishops were anointed on the hands and had the power to consecrate. This concluding section mirrored the opening section, *De consecratione ecclesiae*. The very structure of the commentary united the holiness of the

church to the holiness of the bishop. Concerned with the moral meaning of pontifical rites, in particular the dedication, it operated on the level of 'political' allegory in its silences.[271] While the *De sacramentis* stood at the end of a reforming tradition of exegesis of the consecration that had emerged with Damian and the reformers of the late-eleventh century, it set about to restrain that tradition in the face of the crisis of 1111 and Bruno's disillusionment with Paschal II, and to focus the liturgical allegory on the person of the bishop.[272]

Paschal's final dedication was at Palestrina on 16 December 1117, about twenty-five miles from Rome. It was of the upper church of S. Agapitus, the crypt having been dedicated the prior year.[273] This dedication with Conus, the cardinal and bishop of the city, marked perhaps a memorial of Paschal's early glory: a major dedication in a stronghold of one of his old Roman nemeses, the Colonna family. But it paled in comparison with the significance of the far-flung rituals of his early papacy. In little more than a month Paschal would be dead, having survived the crisis of 1111, but never having fully restored his personal authority. His successors, however, would continue to employ the dedication and liturgy in a manner that was developed in the eleventh century. While it is possible to see Bruno's conflict with Paschal as part of a larger disenchantment among some papal reformers with the emerging papal rapprochement with the imperial party, by the 1120s the ritual life of the papacy had become too central an expression of its religiosity and authority, thanks to the efforts of the eleventh-century reformers, to be contained. Papal ritual would become increasingly sophisticated and continue to expand in the twelfth century, although not primarily via the dedication.[274] Likewise, the eleventh-century tradition of allegorical readings of the liturgy would increase dramatically and the twelfth century would emerge as one of the leading eras of liturgical commentary.[275] The expanding understanding of the liturgy in the twelfth century was begun and fostered in the reforming efforts of the eleventh.

Notes

1   Ekkerd of Aura, *Chronicon*, ed. F.-J. Schmale, *Ausgewählte Quellen zur deutschen Geschichte. Freiherr vom Stein Gedächtnisausgabe* 15 (Darmstadt, 1972), 189. See the presentation of these events in William North, 'In the Shadows of Reform: Exegesis and the Formation of a Clerical Elite in the Works of Bruno of Segni (1078/9–1123)' (PhD diss., University of California Berkeley, 1998), 101–6. Bernhard Gigalski, *Bruno, Bischof von Segni, Abt von Monte-Cassino (1049–1123): sein Leben und seine*

Schriften: ein Beitrag zur Kirchengeschichte im Zeitalter des Investiturstreites, und zur theologischen Litteraturgeschichte des Mittelalters (Münster, 1898).

2 Réginald Grégoire, Bruno de Segni: exégète médiéval et théologien monastique (Spoleto, 1965), 16-19.

3 Grégoire, Bruno, 24-7, from Bruno's commentary on the Apocalypse (PL 165, 605A-B) we know he was a canon at Siena, and from the Chronica monasterii Casinensis, IV, 31 we know of his birth in Asti, Die chronik von Montecassino, ed. H. Hoffman, MGH Scriptores 32.

4 Ibid., 30.

5 See North, 'Shadows of Reform', 74-5. This commentary needs and would reward close scrutiny. A. Amelli, Spicilegium Casinese complectens Analecta Sacra et Profana III/1 (Montecassino, 1897). E. Mégier, 'Otto of Freising's Revendication of Isaiah as the Prophet of Constantine's "Exaltation of the Church" in the Context of Christian Latin Exegesis', Sacris erudiri 42 (2003): 287-326, 302-14.

6 I.S. Robinson, Authority and Resistance in the Investiture Conflict: The Polemical Literature of the Late Eleventh Century (New York, 1978), 174.

7 Chronica Casinensis, IV, 31.

8 As discussed below and in an earlier form in Hamilton, 'To Consecrate the Church', 123-7.

9 AASS 31, Jul., t. 4, 481, ss 17-18.

10 Bruni's edition is based on the 1521 printed edition of Grenoble, Bibliothèque publique 345, a manuscript of the twelfth century that Bruni compared to Vatican City, Biblioteca Apostolica Vaticana, Vaticanus Latinus 994 (s. XII) and 1254 (s. XIII), Torino 787 (s. XIV [destroyed in 1904 by a fire]); Florence, S. Marco 13 (s. XIII); and Rome, Vallicelliana, F. 36 (s. XII). He also consulted Montecassino, Archivio dell'Abbazia 196 (s. XII) and 619 (s. XVII) to make his argument concerning the authorship of the text, and references to them appear in Bruni's notes to Book VI of the De laudibus. I have consulted the following additional mss: Bologna, Biblioteca Universitaria di Bologna 1494 (s. XVI); Cava, Abbazia 6 (s. XI); Rome, Biblioteca Angelica 362 (s. XI ex.); Vatican City, Biblioteca Apostolica Vaticana, Archivio S. Pietro F. 37 (s. XII); BAV, Urbinate Latino 59 (s. XV); Paris, Bibliothèque Nationale de France latin 579 (s. XIII ex.); and Turin, Biblioteca Nazionale Universitaria 574 (s. XIII).

11 Grégoire, Bruno, 99-100. Based upon my initial survey of the manuscripts, a critical edition will not significantly change the text as much as it will nuance our understanding of the process of the De laudibus' composition, shed light on the organisation of the last three books and perhaps help date its composition. Grégoire himself thought the edition of Bruni found in the PL adequate but also thought that of all Bruno's works, the De laudibus was most deserving of an edition as it most typified his thought: Grégoire, 99.

12 Grégoire lists twelve fragmentary copies, 99-101.

13 Robinson, "Political Allegory," 69-98. North, 'Shadows of Reform'.

14 Robinson, Papal Reform, 93; the synthetic approach is employed by Giuseppe Ferraro, Lo Spirito Santo nei commentari al quarto vangelo di Bruno di Segni, Ruperto di Deutz, Bonaventura, e Alberto Magno (Vatican City, 1998).

15 István Bejczy, 'Kings, Bishops, 267–86.

16 For an extended discussion, see Louis I. Hamilton, 'Decor et decorum: Reforming the Episcopacy in Bruno of Segni's *De laudibus ecclesiae* (Eleventh Century)' (LMS diss., Pontifical Institute of Mediaeval Studies, 2007).

17 Hamilton, 'To Consecrate the Church', 123–7.

18 Christina Whitehead, for example, seems unaware of Bruno, 'The best and earliest locus [for architectural allegory] appears to be a series of Latin liturgical handbooks composed between approximately 1120 and 1290'. Christina Whitehead, 'Columnae . . . sunt episcopi', 30.

19 Bk. III, c. 6, PL 165, 959C. Grégoire discusses some of the following examples at 95–6, n. 66. These and the examples given below can also be found in Cava 6.

20 Bk. VI, c. 3, PL 165, 1070C–D.

21 Bk. III, c. V, PL 165, 956C.

22 Bk. I, c. 3, PL 165, 884C: sed hic alio tempore exponenda servamus.

23 If this were correct it might suggest that the *De laudibus* and *De sacramentis* were composed approximately at the same time as Grégoire argued: Grégoire, *Bruno*, 61–2.

24 Bk. VI, c. 1, PL 165, 1035C. See also Book V, chapter 5, *On the Assumption of the Blessed Virgin Mary* (PL 165, 1032C) where the reader is instructed to see the sermon on humility in the second book *De ornamentis ecclesiae* (that is, Book II, chapter 5 [PL 165, 915–19]). Other references might be internal to a single book or even within a sermon as the reference in *De templo* to *De arca testamenti* at Bk. I, c. 4, PL 165, 887C.

25 Bk. II, c. 4, PL 165, 913A. Other examples can be found at 911B, 935D, 964B and 977B.

26 Gospels: Bk. I, c. 6; Bk. II, c. 1; Bk. IV, c. 8; Bk. VI, c. 3, PL 165, 894C, 904B, 1000D, 1075C. Moses, etc.: Bk. I, c. 6; Bk. VI, c. 3, PL 165, 894C, 1071D. Paul: Bk. I, c., 6, PL 165, 894C. Acts: Bk II, c. 1; Bk. II, c. 8; Bk. IV, c. 8, PL 165, 904B, 927B, 1000D. Passions: Bk II, c. 1; Bk. II, c. 8; Bk. IV, c. 8, PL 165, 904B, 927B, 1000D. Leviticus: Bk. II, c. 5, PL 165, 918B. Both Testaments: Bk. IV, c. 5, PL 165, 989A. Song: Bk. IV, c. 6, PL 165, 991B. Prophets: Bk. IV, c. 8, PL 165, 1000D.

27 Bk. IV, c. 2, PL 165, 978B, 978D.

28 Bk. VI, c. 2, PL 165, 1047C.

29 Bk. VI, c. 3, PL 165, 1076B; Bk. III, c. 7, PL 165, 961A. Plutarch, *Lives, Alexander*, XIV, 3 in J. Henderson, ed. *Plutarch's Lives* (Cambridge, MA, 1919), Loeb Classical Library, vols 241–51, Vol. 247, 258; and Bk. IV, c. 3, PL 165, 983D–4A.

30 Grégoire, *Bruno*, 99.

31 Maria Galante, 'Esperienze Grafiche a Cava nel XII secolo, Il Cod. Cav. 6', *Archivio Storico per le Province Napoletane* ann. 21 (1982), 7–25, at 22.

32 The manuscript appears to change hands, on average, every other folio; for a complete discussion see Galante, 'Esperienze Grafiche a Cava'.

33 Rome, BAV, Archivio S. Pietro F37 also belongs to the tradition that lacks the sermon honouring St Michael.

34 Reasons may include that there were important patrons of the abbey who were devoted to St Michael, or that Cava had a claim on Sant'Arcangelo in Perdifumo, or that it would conform to their monastic liturgical norm. John, son of Pandulf VI, donated property to the abbey while Bruno and Paschal II were on their way to Salerno in 1100. It would seem that Paschal confirmed the dedication of churches (with Bruno present) in honour of St. Sophia and St Michael in 1100 and relevant property donations; Ferdinando Ughelli, *Italia Sacra*, 10 Vols (Venice, 1717–22), v. 7, 395–6. See Ramseyer, *Transformation of a Religious Landscape*, 186–7.

35 In the tower to the right of the propylaeum of the atrium; Bloch, *Montecassino*, 119, 1425.

36 Grégoire, *Bruno*, 49. North assumes the *De sacramentis* and the *De laudibus* are near contemporaries (following Grégoire) and so does not distinguish them from each other; at North, 'Shadows of Reform', 340 and 341. He is correct to point out that Bruno never reduces scriptures or the liturgy to a mere tool of immediate political concerns. Neither Gigalski, Grégoire nor North considers why Bruno, having written extensively on the dedication, would compose an entirely new treatise for Walter. Bk. I, c. 4; Bk. II, c. 12, PL 165, 886A, 942B.

37 Bruno also compared Benedict to Sts Stephen, Laurence and Martin: Bk. I, c. 4, PL, 165, 885D. Similarly Benedict is mentioned in a list (Anthony, Paul, Hilary and Benedict) of monastic examples of abstinence (Hilary being an example of a monastic bishop as his disciple Martin). Bk. II, c. 11, PL 165, 937C.

38 Bk. II, c. 12, PL 165, 942BC.

39 Herbert L. Kessler, 'On the State of Medieval Art History', *Art Bulletin* 70 (1988), 166–87, at 175. M. Maccarone, 'La Storia della Cattedra', in *La Cattedra Lignea di S. Pietro in Vaticano, Atti della Pontifica Academia Romana di Archeologia*, ser. III, Memorie X (Vatican, 1971), 3–70.

40 *Regula Sancti Benedicti* 7.10–64, ed. Timothy Fry, *RB1980: The Rule of St Benedict in Latin and English with Notes and Thematic Index* (Collegeville, MN, 1981), 41–9. Another possible comment on the *Rule* can be found at Bk. V, c. 3, PL 165, 1028A–B, compare with *Regula Sancti Benedicti* 58.17, Fry, *RB1980*, 106.

41 Robinson, *Authority and Resistance*, 33–4. Uta-Renate Blumenthal has recently questioned whether Hildebrand was in fact a canon rather than a monk. The confusion suggests the fluidity of the categroies of monk or reformed canon within the period; see Blumenthal, *Gregor VII: Papst zwischen Canossa und Kirchenreform* (Darmstadt, 2001), 30–8.

42 Bk. II, c. 12, PL 165, 940C.

43 Bk. II, c. 12, PL 165, 941C, 942B.

44 Bk. II, c. 4, PL 165, 913D. See Bejczy, 'Kings, Bishops', 274–6.

45 Bk. II, c. 4, PL 165, 914D.

46 Bk. II, c. 4, PL 165, 914D–15A.

47 Bk. VI, c. 2, PL 165, 1050C–4B, at 1053B.

48 Bk. VI, c. 2, PL 165, 1053C–D. See Bejczy, 'Kings, Bishops', 281–2.

49 Bk VI, c. 2, PL 165, 1057B for the singling out of Benedict for praise; but the opening context is the distinction between 'apostles, bishops and doctors' and the 'heretics, Jews and philosophers', 1054D.

50 PL 146, 1373A; PL 151, 292C; PL 163, 77C, 424D, 1181D, 1282B.

51 General references to a clerical audience include Bk. IV, c. 6; Bk. V, c. 1, PL 165, 992A and 1022C.

52 Bk. I, c. 7, PL 165, 896C–98D. The description contains many of the essential elements of contemporary dedication rites. The order of the events that he does record, however, does not match those of any extant pontifical that I know. The steps are (1) the litany, 896C; (2) blessing of salt and water for use on exterior of church, 896D; (3) triple circuit, aspersing exterior, with reference to *Asperges me hyssopo*, 897A; (4) bishop knocking on door with reference to *Tollite portes*, 897B (presumably punctuating circuits); (5) entering of church, preparation of Gregorian water, 897B; (6) inscription of alphabet on pavement, 897D; (7) consecration of altar, 898A; and (8) deposition of relics (898C).

53 Bk. I, c. 7, PL 165, 896C.

54 Bk. I, c. 7, PL 165, 898A.

55 Bk. I, c. 7, PL 165, 898A.

56 Bk. VI, c. 3, PL 165, 1071CD.

57 Bk. VI, c. 2, PL 165, 1049BC.

58 Bk. IV, c. 11, PL 165, 1014D.

59 Nor is this simply the unstated pattern: for example, PL 165, 882C, 1039B.

60 Bk. I, Prologue, PL 165, 875–6.

61 For example Rouen, Bibliothèque municipale, ms. 368 (A 27), as described in Palazzo, *L'Évêque et son image*, 136.

62 Bk. VI, c. 3, PL 165, 1071D.

63 Much work needs to be done on Bruno's influence on later commentators. Christina Whitehead, for example, ignored the *De laudibus* as discussed above in note 18; Whitehead, '*Columnae . . . sunt episcopi*', 30. While Ruth Horie notes Bruno's sermons she does not examine them in her *Perceptions of* Ecclesia, 107.

64 RIS VI, 5, 47–8 (as discussed above in Chapter 4).

65 Bk. I, Prologue, PL 165, 875–6.

66 Bk. I, c. 1, PL 165, 876A.

67 Bk. I, c. 5, PL 165, 888BC.

68 Bk. II, c. 5, PL 165, 918CD.

69 Bk. VI, c. 2, PL 165, 1054B.

70 Bk. VI, c. 2, PL 165, 1065D–6D.

71 For example Bk. I, c. 5; Bk. IV, c. 6, PL 165, 890C–D, 991C.

72 For example Bk. I, c. 7; Bk. III, c. 4; Bk. VI, c. 1; Bk. VI, c. 2, PL 165, 897A, 953C, 1044B, 1046D.

73 Bk. I, c. 4, PL 165, 885D; 'Look at Paul', Bk. I, c. 4, PL 165, 887A.

74 Bk. I, c. 4; Bk. II, c. 8, PL 165, 886D, 927B.

75 Bk. I, c. 8, PL 165, 900C.

76 Bk. III, c. 1, PL 165, 944B.

77 Bk. II, c. 4, PL 165, 911D.

78 Bk. II, c. 4, PL 165, 914C.
79 Bk. III, c. 10, PL 165, 972A.
80 Bk. VI, c. 1, PL 165, 1038D.
81 Bk. VI, c. 1, PL 165, 1042A.
82 Bk. III, c. 7, PL 165, 962D. Paul is directly referred to as an architect at Bk. III, c. 7, PL 165, 963A.
83 Bk. I, c. 8, PL 165, 889C. Compare with Bede on Proverbs CCCM 119B,158.
84 Bk. I, c. 6, PL 165, 892C.
85 Bk. I, c. 7, PL 165, 897B.
86 Bk. II, cc. 1 and 4; Bk. III, cc. 2, 6, 7, and 10; Bk. IV, c. 7; and Bk. VI, c. 3.
87 Bk. I, c. 2, PL 165, 879C–D; Bk. I, c. 6, PL 165, 892B.
88 Bk. I, c. 7, PL 165, 897D–8A.
89 Bk. I, c. 6, PL 165, 891D.
90 Bk. I, c. 7, PL 165, 896A.
91 Bk. III, c. 10, PL 165, 971A.
92 Bk. V, c. 1, PL 165, 1021A.
93 Bk. II, c. 7, PL 165, 923D; Bk. II, c. 1, PL 165, 904A.
94 Bk. IV, c. 13, PL 165, 1018D; also again at the feast of a martyr in Book VI, chapter 1 in order to describe the triumph of the city of God, Bk. VI, c. 1, PL 165, 1044B, sermon 5 is a reproduction of (or reproduced in) his commentary on Psalm CL, PL, 164, 1225A.
95 Bk. I, c. 7, PL 165, 895C.
96 Bk. I, c. 4, PL 165, 885D.
97 Bede, *De tabernaculo et vasis ejus, ac vestibus sacerdotium* PL 91, 448C.
98 Bk. I, c. 4, PL 165, 886A.
99 Bk. I, c. 4, PL 165, 886B.
100 Bk. I, c. 4, PL 165, 886BC.
101 Bk. I, c. 5, PL 165, 890D.
102 Bk. I. c. 8, PL 165, 899D.
103 Bk. II, c. 4, PL 165, 911D.
104 Bk. I, c. 1, PL 165, 879C.
105 Bruno, *Libri Sententiarum*, Bk. I, c. 2, PL 165: 881B.
106 Bk. I, c. 2, PL 165, 880D. It has been suggested that Bruno's depiction of Noah's ark is connected to the image of the ark on the Cathedral of Modena: initially by Francesco Gandolfo, 'Note per una interpretazione iconologica delle Storie del Genesi di Wilgelmo', in Arturo Carlo Quintavalle (ed.), *Romanico padano, romanico europeo* (Parma, 1982), 323–7, at 332 and more extensively by Glass, 'Revisiting the Gregorian Reform', 200–18. On the influence of Bruno at S. Clemente in Rome, see Riccioni, *Il Mosaico Absidiale*; on the possible use of Bruno's commentary on Genesis in Ceri see Nino Zchomelidse, *Santa Maria Immacolata in Ceri: pittura sacra al tempo della riforma gregoriana* (Rome, 1996).
107 Bk. I, c. 2, PL 165, 881A. This both builds upon and exceeds the image of the ark as developed by Origen and Augustine in its focus on the clerical hierarchy. In this regard it appears to stand apart from Hugh of St Victor's later treatise as well.

See Christina Whitehead, *Castles of the Mind, Studies in Medieval Architectural Allegory* (Cardiff, 2003), 39-48. However, this also means that the transformation that Whitehead posits in the twelfth century, architectural allegory removed from scriptural exegesis and placed into the centre of study, is properly Bruno's innovation. Whitehead, *Castles*, 42.

108 Bk. I, c. 2, PL 165, 882A.

109 Bk. I, c. 10, PL 165, 900A.

110 Bk. I, c. 7, PL 165, 895D-6A.

111 Bk. I, c. 3, PL 165, 892C-D.

112 Bk. II, c. 1, PL 165, 901C.

113 Bk. II, c. 12, PL 165, 940C-D.

114 Bk. II, c. 12, PL 165, 941A.

115 Mercy was considered as the command to wash the feet of others (an evocative image also of monastic import). Bk. II, c. 12, PL 165, 942CD. I would like to thank Susan Boynton for this observation.

116 Bk. VI, c. 2, PL 165, 1049B.

117 Bk. I, c. 6, PL 165, 891C-D, 893D. The phrase 'in mentis excessu' as *ekstasis* is derived from the Vulg. Act. 11: 5; Ps. 30: 22; Ps. 115: 2. This is the only occasion Bruno uses the phrase in the *De laudibus*.

118 Bk. III, c. 1, PL 165, 943C-4D.

119 This is rooted, in a broad sense, in the *De civitate dei contra paganos* of Augustine, with which Bruno is familiar.

120 That chapter emphasises the overall theme of praises of the Church (under the figure of Mary) as did the preface to *De novo mundo*. It is also the only chapter in Book V that is not given to a Marian feast. Bk. V, c. 1, PL 165, 1021A: Ad laudem Matris Domini invitat nos, dilectissimi, Spiritus sanctus per os David patris ipsius virginis, dicendo: 'Gloriosa dicta sunt de te, civitas Dei'; also, 1022C.

121 Bk. VI, 3, s. iii, *De evangelicae legis praedicatione*; s. iv, *De virginibus*; s. v, *De sancto Michaele archangelo*.

122 The connection between moral reform, ecclesiastical reform and eschatological ideal is a constant of reform movements: see Wayne J. Hankey, 'Self and Cosmos in becoming Deiform: Neoplatonic Paradigms for Reform by Self-knowledge from Augustine to Aquinas', in Bellitto and Hamilton, *Reforming the Church before Modernity*, 39-60.

123 Robinson, 'Political Allegory', 69-98.

124 Bejczy, 'Kings, Bishops', 275. Given Bruno's interest in the *De laudibus* they would only serve as a rather indirect 'piece of princely instruction', as Bejczy suggests they are, 'Kings, Bishops', 276.

125 Bk. II, c. 4, PL 165, 911C.

126 Bk. II, c. 4, PL 165, 911D-12A. In a broad sense, Bruno was probably influenced by Peter Damian's allegorisation of the Temple in moral terms, but Bruno was much more precise in detail of description: see Jennifer A. Harris, 'Peter Damian and the Architecture of the Self', in Gert Melville and Markus Schürer (eds), *Das Eigen und das Ganze: Zum Individuellen im mittelalterlichen Religiosentum*

(Münster, 2002), 131–57. For Damian and the Temple's gems as virtues, see PL 145, 209B.

127 Bk. II, c. 4, PL 165, 913A–B.

128 Bk. II, c. 4, PL 165, 913D.

129 Bk. II, c. 4, PL 165, 914D–15A.

130 Bk. II, c. 4, PL 165, 913B; 914D–15A, Bejczy, 'Kings, Bishops', 280. Bejczy also considers this sermon overtly political, but he considers the audience of the *De laudibus* to be, therefore, 'princely', but Bruno uses direct address elsewhere for bishops and priests. For 'the intended princely audience of his *Sententiae*', see Bejczy, 'Kings, Bishops', 281–2.

131 Bk. II, c. 4, PL 165, 914D–15A. See Susan Boynton's discussion of *nenia* in her *Shaping a Monastic Identity*, 217–18.

132 Bk. II, c. 4, PL 165, 915A–B.

133 Bk. II, c. 4, PL 165, 911B.

134 Bk. II, c. 4, PL 165, 911C. Bejczy has intriguingly suggested that Bruno 'indignantly rejected the idea that pagans had any familiarity with virtue', and that this idea met 'serious opposition' in the eleventh century. István P. Bejczy, 'The Problem of Natural Virtue', in István P. Bejczy and Richard G. Newhauser eds., *Virtue and Ethics in the Twelfth Century* (Leiden, 2005), 133–54, at 135–6.

135 Bk. II, c. 4, PL 165, 911D.

136 Bk. II, c. 4, PL 165, 912A.

137 Bejczy, 'Kings, Bishops', 274. Gelasius, Ep. 8, Eduard Schwartz (ed.), *Publizistische Sammlungen zum acacianischen Scisma* (Munich, 1934), 20. Bejczy correctly assesses the novelty of Bruno's project in this chapter and its overall import: 'Bruno, then, is not only one of the first authors since Carolingian times to present systematic discussion of the virtues, but also to conceive the virtues as *Herrschertungenden*, as the chief moral guidelines of princely rule . . . Bruno anticipates the scholastic authors of the thirteenth century who characterized the cardinal virtues as *virtutes politicae*', see Bejczy, 'Kings, Bishops', 275. Bruno's influence is suggested by Céline Billot-Vilandrau, 'Charlemagne and the Young Prince: A Didactic Poem on the Cardinal Virtues by Giles of Paris', in Bejczy and Newhauser (eds), *Virtue and Ethics in the Twelfth Century*, 341–54, at 342 n. 6, and 345. On the interconnectedness of the virtues see Cicero, *On Duties*, II: 35 (New York, 1913), 202.

138 PL 165, 913CD.

139 Bk. III, c. 7, PL 165, 960C.

140 Ibid.

141 Bk. III, c. 7, PL 165, 960D.

142 Bk. III, c. 3, PL 165, 949A.

143 Bk. III, c. 3, PL 165, 949B–D.

144 Bk. III, c. 3, PL 165, 950A.

145 Bk. III, c. 4, PL 165, 952C–D.

146 Bk. III, c. 4, PL 165, 953B.

147 Bk. III, c. 6, PL 165, 960A.

148 Bk. III, c. 8, PL 165, 967C.

149 Bk. III, c. 10, PL 165, 972A and D.

150 For an extended discussion of the *rationale* and its role in the *De laudibus* see Hamilton, '*Decor et Decorum*: Reforming the Episcopacy', 68–77.

151 Joseph Braun, *Die liturgischen Paramente in Gegenwart und Vergangenheit: ein Handbuch der Paramentik* (Freiburg, 1924), 235–6.

152 A similar pattern can be traced in Book IV where, interestingly, the apostolic fight is against Herod and apostolic preaching is against Jews and pagans. See for example Book IV, cc. 7, 10, and 13.

153 Robert E. Lerner, 'Paschal II, Pope', in Joseph Strayer (ed.), *Dictionary of the Middle Ages*, 13 Vols (New York, 1982–89), Vol. 9, 444–6, at 444.

154 *Liber Pontificalis*, 2: 430.3.22–7, 431.4.28–30, and 431.5.4–432.6.27 on Paschal I. See also Dorothy Glass, 'Papal Patronage in the Early Twelfth Century: Notes on the Iconography of Cosmatesque Pavements', *Journal of the Warburg and Courtauld Institutes* 32 (1969): 386–90. In addition to works cited above, see Uta-Renate Blumenthal, 'Opposition to Pope Paschal II: Some Comments on the Lateran Council of 1112', *Annuarium Historiae Conciliorum* 10 (1978), 82–98; her *The Early Councils of Paschal II: 1100–1110*, Studies and Texts 43 (Toronto, 1978); and her 'Paschal II and the Roman Primacy', *Archivum Historiae Pontificiae* 16 (1978), 67–92. Recent efforts at re-evaluating the papacy of Paschal II are from Glauco Maria Cantarella, *Ecclesiologia e politica nel papato di Pasquale II. Linee di una interpretazione*, Studi Storici 131 (Rome, 1982); Cantarella, *La Construzione della verità: Pasquale II, Un papa alle strette*, Studi Storici 178–9 (Rome, 1987); and Carl Servatius, *Paschalis II (1099–1118): Studien zu seiner Person und seiner Politik*, Päpste und Papsttum 14 (Stuttgart, 1979). See also Mary Stroll, *Symbols as Power*.

155 See Appendix B. In addition to the works cited in n. 10 above see Priester, 'Belltowers of Medieval Rome', 71 and 73.

156 This itinerary is discussed by Servatius as part of Paschal's northern Italian objectives and relationships, *Paschalis II*, 101–14.

157 I.S. Robinson, *Henry IV of Germany, 1056–1106* (Cambridge, 1999), 320–44.

158 For not effectively defending the Jewish population of Mainz from a violent crowd of Crusaders, see Robinson, *Henry IV*, 302–3.

159 *Annal. Hildesh.* MGH *Scriptores* 8 (Hanover, 1878), 52–3.

160 Robinson, *Henry IV*, 335.

161 Jaffé, 6050, Nov. 11, 1105. On reconsecration see Hamilton, 'Sexual Purity', 237–59.

162 *Relatio translationis corporis sancti Geminiani*, ed. Giulio Bertoni (Città di Castello, 1907), RIS, Vol. 6, 1, 4. The event is discussed in Giorgio Cracco, 'Cattedrale, città, territorio: l'esempio di Modena', in Augusto Bergamini (ed.), *Atti dell'VIII centenario della dedicazione del Duomo di Modena (1184–1984)*, 90–101. It is also discussed in terms of the construction by William Montorsi, *Il Duomo di Modena: 'Palinsesto' Lanfranchiano-Campionese, 1099–1999, Nono centenario della fondazione del Duomo 'di Lanfranco'* (Modena, 1999), 59–96. More generally discussed in Giuseppe Pistoni, 'Matilde di Canossa ed il Duomo di Modena', in *Studi Matildici, atti e memorie de convegno di studi Matildici*,

Modena and Reggio Emilia, 19–21 Ottobre 1963 (Modena, 1964), 104–9. Churches constructed during Matilda's reign are often perceived by art historians as having a pro-Gregorian iconography; see Glass, ' Bishops of Piacenza', 219–36; Christine Verzár Bornstein, *Portals and Politics in the Early Italian City-State: the Sculpture of Nicholaus in Context* (Parma, 1988); Massimo Mussini, 'Pievi e vita canonicale nei territori matildici: Architettura e riforma gregoriana nella campagne', in Quintavalle (ed.), *Romanico padano, romanico europeo* (Parma, 1982), 27–53; also in Quintavalle, Christine Verzár Bornstein, 'Matilda of Canossa, Papal Rome and the Earliest Italian Porch Portals', 143–58.

163 *Relatio*, 6: Anno igitur Dominice Incarnationis iam millesimo centesimo sexto, gubernante domno Dodone, Dei gratia venerabili episcopo, Mutinensium ecclesiam, datur huius translationis certissimus kalendarum maiarum terminus omnium cordibus gratissimus. Dodo appears to have been consecrated after 1102 and died in 1134. See, C. Frisone, 'Dodone', *Dizionario Biografico degli Italiani*, v. 40 (Rome, 1991), 355–7.

164 Pietro Galavotti, *Le più antiche fonti storiche del Sumomo di Modena* (Modena, 1972), 37–8. Golinelli, *Città e culto dei santi*, 73–4.

165 *Relatio*, ix–x. Franca Baldelli (ed.), *Inventario dei Manoscritti dell'Archivio Capitolare di Modena* (Modena, 2003), 77–8.

166 *Relatio*, 3: Relatio sive descriptio de innovatione ecclesie sancti Geminiani mutinensis presulis ac de translatione vel revelatione seu etiam consecratione eius beatissimi corporis a domno Paschali sancte romane Sedis summo Pontifice diligenter celebrata.

167 The version of the narrative contained in Modena, Biblioteca estense latini 388, c. 4 does not contain the title. *Relatio*, 3.

168 Cracco, 'Cattedrale, città, territorio', 93 is clear on this event.

169 *Relatio*, 6, lines 24–40.

170 Cracco, 'Cattedrale, città, territorio', 93–4. More broadly, see Gina Fasoli, 'La Cattedrale nella civiltà comunale', in *Atti dell'VIII centenario* (Modena, 1986), 114–30.

171 *Relatio*, 7.

172 Ibid.

173 Ibid.

174 Ibid.

175 Kozacheck, 'Repertory of Chant', 362–4 compares Biblioteca Apostolica Vaticana, Vat. lat. 4770 at f. 226, Tunc episcopus expandit velum & ponit ipsa [sic] reliquas super altare novum. & cantor. incip[it] antiphonam Ambulate sancti dei ad lo [sic]. Et antequam recludantur extensum velum. ante altare. Int[er] cantores et epicopus [sic]. et ibidem thianiterium cum primis accensis. et incensum desuper. et ponit chrisma intus in confessione. per angulos IIIIor. in cruce dicendo . . . with the relevant steps in Roman *Ordo XLII*, 9–10 (M. Andrieu, *Les Ordines*, Vol. 4, 400): Ipsa finita suscipit ipsas reliquias a presbitero et portat eas cum laetania ad altare intus in ecclesia et ponit super altare novo. Et antequam recludantur ponit chrisma intus in confessione per angulos quattuor in cruce. ita dicendo . . . The former referring to an exposition of the relics by

means of opening and closing of a curtain and the latter to the closing of the altar. The transcription of Vat. lat. 4770 is from Kozacheck, 'Repertory of Chant', 363. But the selection might better compare with *PRXII, Ordo XVII*, 48 (Andrieu, *Le Pontifical romain*, 186), Et cum intraverit, extenso velo inter populum et altare, pontifex recondat reliquias in capsa et . . . Here there is little opportunity for viewing the relics once inside the church.

176 *Relatio*, 7–8.

177 *Relatio* 8: Matilda dona ferens ingentia: aurum, argentum, pallia insignia. Sed et domus Dodo venerabilis pontifex calicem argenteum cum pathena ei obtulit optimum aureis signis intus forisque mirabiliter decoratum . . .

178 On the later commune see Michelle M. Fontaine, 'Back to the Future: Remaking the Commune in Ducal Modena', in Paula Findlen et al. (eds), *Beyond Florence: The Contours of Medieval and Early Modern Italy* (Stanford, 2003). On the duomo and reform see Dorothy F. Glass, 'Prophecy and Priesthood at Modena', *Zeitschrift für Kunstgeschichte*, 63 Bd., H. 3 (2000), 326–38; Anat Tcherikover, 'Reflections of the Investiture Controversy at Nonantola and Modena', *Zeitschrift für Kunstgeschichte*, 60 Bd., H. 2 (1997), 150–65; Arturo Carlo Quintavalle, *Wiligelmo e Matilde, L'officina romanica* (Milan, 1991), esp. 46–8; and his *La cattedrale di Modena: problemi di romanico emiliano*, 2 Vols (Modena, 1965). More generally, see Orianna Baracchi, *Modena: Piazza Grande* (Modena, 1981); Giuseppe Pistoni, *San Geminiano: Vescovo e prottetore di Modena nella vita nel culto nell'arte* (Modena, 1983).

179 Galavotti, *Più antiche fonti storiche*, 62.

180 Ibid., 22.

181 See Galavotti, Ibid., 63; and see *Relatio*, ed. Bertoni, RIS, Vol. 6, 1, 21–3.

182 It is possible to read the latter either as 'Dodo episcopus mutinensis' or as 'Dodo episcopus' and 'Mutinensium', the former seeming more likely.

183 It is not entirely clear what the consecration of the body entailed: it may simply be a manner of speaking about the dedication, or it may have been a separate anointing of the body.

184 Blumenthal, *Early Councils*, 69–71. Servatius, *Paschalis II*, 200–5

185 I would like to thank Susan Boynton for this observation.

186 Robinson, *Henry IV*, 335.

187 Aquileia, Halberstadt, Minden, Liège, Cambrésis, Trier and Augsburg were anathematised; Trier, Augsburg and Liège then reconciled. Blumenthal, *Early Councils*, 71–3.

188 Robinson, *Henry IV*, 42, 54.

189 Arturo Carlo Quintavalle, *Basilica, Cattedrale di Parma: Novecento anni di arte, storia, fede*, 3 Vols (Parma, 2005).

190 Quintavalle, *La Cattedrale di Parma e Il Romanico Europeo* (Parma, 1974), 15–16.

191 David J. Hay, *The Military Leadership of Matilda of Canossa, 1046–1115* (Manchester, 2008), 172–4; see the extended discussion by Reinhold Schumann, *Authority and the Commune, Parma 833–1133* (Parma, 1973), 321–33. Donizio II. 14, 11, 960–5.

192 Donizio II. 14, 11, 980-1: Dum calicem sancta vir mitis ponit in ara, Supplicet ut Christum pro cuncta plebe benignum, Hinc clamor multus . . . Adversus Christu ceu Iudei crucifixum. Plures dicebant: 'Moriatur pseudopropheta'. This, it seems, is the moment after the consecration when the priest returns the chalice to the altar and continues with the Eucharist prayer, but prior to the fraction, or it could be as Schumann thought at the beginning of the Liturgy of the Eucharist, assuming the chalice needed to be brought to the altar at that point. In either case, I doubt Donizio recorded these comments, as Schumann states, 'verbatim'. Schumann, *Authority and the Commune*, 324.

193 Hay, *Matilda*, 174; Donizio II. 14, 11, 995-1022.

194 Donizio II. 14, 11, 1114-20. Jaffé, 6094, Nov. 4, 1106.

195 Donizio II. 14, 11, 1122.

196 Jaffé, 6112, Jan. 4 and Jan. 29, 1106 respectively.

197 Blumenthal, *Early Councils*, 39. Robinson, *Papacy*, 155.

198 Jaffé, 6114-22.

199 Jaffé, 6124, Feb. 16, 1107. It is interesting that Suger observed that around this time, reports circulated that Henry V had forced his father Henry IV to give up the signs of imperium, including the lance of St Maurice. This might have given the dedication the tone of a celebratory gesture on the part of Paschal. Suger, *Vita Ludovici Grossi*, ed. and trans. Henri Waquet, *Suger, Vie de Louis VI Le Gros* (Paris, 1964), X, 50-2.

200 Guibert of Nogent, *De vita sua, sive monodiae*, ed. and trans. Edmond-René Labande, *Guibert de Nogent: Autobiographie* (Paris, 1981), Bk. III, c. 4, 282-4.

201 Guibert, Bk III, c. 4, 293.

202 Jaffé, 6125.

203 Jaffé, 6125, March 9, 1107.

204 Suger, X, 52: It is interesting to note that Suger suggests that his presence at the dedication seems to have helped St-Denis' case against the bishop of Paris.

205 Jaffé, 6127, April 24, 1107. *Laetare Jerusalem* gets its name from Is. 66, 10-11, 'Rejoice Jerusalem!' sung at the Introit. This fourth Sunday in Lent marks the shift from penance to the anticipation of Easter.

206 Jaffé, 6127, Suger, X, 54.

207 Suger, X, 54-6.

208 Suger, X, 56-60. Servatius, *Paschalis II*, 206-9.

209 This particular phrasing is in two of the four variants provided by Blumenthal, *Early Councils*, 92-3. Servatius, *Paschalis II*, 209-14.

210 Blumenthal, *Early Councils*, 91-5.

211 Blumenthal, *Investiture Controversy*, 166.

212 G.A. Loud, *The Latin Church in Norman Italy* (Cambridge, 2007), 211-12. Mileto: *Italia Pontificia* X, 145, no. 4; Canossa: Jaffé, 5871 Sept. 7, 1101; see also Ann Wharton Epstein, 'Date and Significance of Canossa Cathedral in Apulia', *Dumbarton Oaks Papers* 37 (1983), 79-90; Sora: Jaffé, 5977 Aug. 22, 1104; Gaeta: Jaffé, 6070 Feb. 1106; Paul F. Kehr, *Italia pontificia, sive, Repertorium privilegiorum et litterarum a Romanis pontificibus* (Berlin, 1906-), 88, 1; Capua: Jaffé, 6216, see discussion below; Sant'Agata dei Goti:

Jaffé, 6275, Ughelli, *Italia Sacra*, VIII, 346; Volturno: Jaffé, 6468 Sept. Oct. 1115; Siponto: *Italia Pontificia*, ix.241, no. 1; Palestrina: Jaffé, 6565, Ughelli, *Italia Sacra*, I, 198. He also dedicated an altar in the grotto at Subiaco, an important papal stronghold, in 1109, *Chronicon Sublacense*, RIS t. 24, pt. 6, 17; Jaffé, 6239, August 29.

213 Cowdrey, *Desiderius*, 212–13.
214 Loud, *Church and Society*, 235–9.
215 Loud, *Latin Church*, 206–8.
216 Chron. Cas. IV, 28.
217 Chron. Cas., IV, 33, 549.
218 Monachus, *Sanctuarium capuanum*, 165. See Speciale and Nardone, 'La Basilica e gli affreschi desideriani', 153. Speciale and Nardone do not suggest any construction that might have precipitated the 1106 dedication. If there were none, this would suggest that the motive for Paschal's 1108 dedication was the perceived importance of a papal dedication. It would be unsurprising if Oderisus' dedication of 1090 preceded the actual completion of the work. Bloch does not mention Oderisus' dedication. Bloch, *Monte Cassino*, 236.
219 Speciale and Nardone, 'La Basilica e gli affreschi desideriani', 177–9.
220 Sennes will be able to reassert his authority and reverse his relationship with Paschal II after Bruno was removed from Montecassino in 1111. From 1113 Sennes served as papal legate in the region. G.A. Loud, *Church and Society in the Norman Principality of Capua, 1058–1197* (Oxford, 1985), 102.
221 Epstein, 'Cathedral of Canossa', 83; Ferdinand Chalandon, *Histoire de la domination normande en Italie et en Sicile*, 2 Vols (Paris, 1907): I, 308. Jaffé, 5871.
222 Kehr, *Italia Pontificia*, IX, 241, no. 1.
223 See Robinson, *Papacy*, 424–9. Robinson depends on Uta-Renate Blumenthal's reading of Paschal's position at Sutri: Blumenthal, '*Patrimonia* and *Regalia* in 1111', in *Law, Church and Society*, 12–16. The crisis is discussed fully by Servatius, *Paschalis II*, 214–338.
224 Grégoire, *Bruno*, 52; Robinson, *Papacy*, 429; Bloch, *Monte Cassino*, 1: 431. See also H. Hoffman, 'Die Älteren Abtslisten von Montecassino', *Quellen und Forschungen* 47 (1967): 224–354 at 323–4.
225 Bruno, *Epistola 3* MGH LdL 2: 565. Grégoire, *Bruno*, 53.
226 Bruno, *Epistola 2*, MGH LdL 2: 564.
227 Bruno, *Epistola 2*, MGH LdL 2: 564–5.
228 Grégoire, *Bruno*, 54–5. For a detailed discussion of the relationship between Paschal II and Bruno, see Glauco Maria Cantarella, 'Bruno di Montecassino o il disagio del Primato Romano', in *L'età dell'Abate Desiderio*, ed. Guglielmo Cavallo, *Miscellanea Cassinese* 60 (Montecassino, 1989): 483–91.
229 Bruno's brothers at Montecassino appear to have been ambivalent at best about him while he was abbot; see Grégoire, *Bruno*, 55–6; and Heinrich Dormeier, *Montecassino und die Laien*, 112–13.
230 Gigalski, *Bruno, Bischof von Segni*, 282, places the commentary between 1106 and 1111. The earlier date is for the reasons given, but he does not fully explain his reasons for the later date.

231 Gigalski, *Bruno, Bischof von Segni*, 282. *De sacramentis*, PL 165: 1090C.

232 *De sacramentis*, PL 165: 1091A: aliis negotiis impeditus.

233 Following Gigalski's sequence based upon Walter's complaint of a delay in Bruno's response, and Bruno's admission of such a delay. If the request was made in 1104 or 1105, then 1106 seems a reasonable delay before sending a reminder: Gigalski, *Bruno, Bischof von Segni*, 282.

234 *De sacramentis*, PL 165: 1090C–1A.

235 *De sacramentis*, PL 165: 1089–90: Cum Romae quondam in Insula in domo episcopi Portuensis simul essemus; cumque in libro Exodi de tabernaculo testimonii, et de vestibus Aaron, typica quaedam, et magni mysterii significativa legeremus, coepisti mirari tu, coepi mirari et ego, quod aliqua illis similia adhuc in ecclesia fieri videamus, cum jam vetera transierint, et facta sint omnia nova.

236 Bruno, *De laudibus*, Bk. IV, c. 10, PL 165, 972A.

237 Bruno, *De sacramentis*, 1106A.

238 The *De sacramentis* opens with a description of the consecration of a new church (PL 165: 1091) and an extensive analysis and commentary on the elements of that consecration (165: 1092–1100). Following this is a brief exposition of baptism and confirmation (165: 1100–3), and an analysis and commentary on various sacramental elements and the liturgical vestments of a bishop (165: 1103–10); see Gigalski, *Bruno, Bischof von Segni*, 282. Bruno may have included a discussion of baptism as a result of reading the *Quid Significent*, in which the dedication becomes a type of baptism; see Repsher, *Rite of Church Dedication*, 181.

239 Robinson, *Authority and Resistance*, 163–9.

240 Bruno, *De sacramentis*, PL 165: 1106A.

241 Bruno, *De laudibus*, Bk. II, c. 4, PL 165, 914D–15A, discussed above.

242 Bruno, *De sacramentis*, 165: 1106A–B. At 1106B.

243 Ibid., 165: 1108B. The full section reads: Summus autem pontifex propter hac et regnum portat (sic enim vocatur) et purpura utitur, non pro significatione, ut puto, sed quia Constantinus imperator olim beato Silvestro omnia Romani imperii insignia tradidit. Unde et in magnis processionibus omnis ille apparatus pontifici exhibetur, qui quondam imperatoribus fieri solebat. Haec autem de vestibus sacerdotalibus dicta sint. Bruno's 'sic enim vocatur' certainly reflects the confusion over the meaning of regalia.

244 I have examined eight of the twenty-three extant manuscripts.

245 Amalarius of Metz (c.775–850/51) in his commentary *De Officio in Dedicatione Ecclesiae* had associated *episcopus* with *pontifex*, a commonplace that Bruno avoided here; Amalarii episcopi, *Opera Liturgica Omnia*, ed. John M. Hanssens, SJ (Vatican City, 1950), 3: 98–9. Hugh of St Victor (1096–1141) does not distinguish the two offices when considering the dedication of a church in *De sacramentis Christianae fidei* 2.5 (PL 176: 439–42).

246 Vogel and Elze, *Le Pontifical*, 35.7 (1: 93–4); Repsher, *Rite of Church Dedication*, 308–10.

247 Vogel and Elze, *Le Pontifical*, 35.7 (1: 93–94); Repsher, *Rite of Church Dedication*, 310.

248 *De sacramentis*, PL 165: 1094. Damian, *Sermo* 72, 4.79–81, used this image to declare boldly that the bishop was tearing down the walls of the haughty and elevated; see above.

249 Vogel and Elze, *Le Pontifical*, 35.47 (1: 114); Repsher, *Rite of Church Dedication*, 342. Damian allegorised these walls as the strong walls of a fortification bonded by charity, an extension of the *Quid Significent's* commentary.

250 *De sacramentis*, PL 165: 1092B. 'Living stones' references both the dedication hymn *Urbes beata Hierusalem* and *Revelation*. As does Damian; but unlike Damian, Bruno does not return to a reassertion of ecclesiastical hierarchy; instead he continues with the weak passage on *De summo pontifice*.

251 Ibid., 165: 1100B–C.

252 Bk. I, c. 7, PL 165, 895D–6A.

253 Bruno, *De laudibus*, 165: 1093.

254 Vogel and Elze, *Le Pontifical*, 35.26 (1: 104); Repsher, *Rite of Church Dedication*, 326. In the *Quid Significent* hyssop purifies the law, while for Damian it was the cross that established the new law, making sweet the bitter waters of the old; see above. For the hyssop's habitat they are probably directly or indirectly dependent on Isidore of Seville. See Joseph Hrbata, 'De expositione missae Walfradi Strabonis', *Ephemerides Liturgicae* 63 (1949): 146–7.

255 *De sacramentis*, PL 165: 1093–4; thus, choosing a third interpretation for the hyssop, distinct from Damian, for whom hyssop designates faith that purifies the secret heart (Damian, *Sermo* 72, 8.177–8) and from the *Quid Significent*, in which hyssop represents humility (Vogel and Elze, *Le Pontifical*, 35.26 [1: 104]; Repsher, *Rite of Church Dedication*, 326).

256 *Exposito in exodum* PL 164: 373D; *Expositio in psalmos* PL 164: 1032B, 1073A; *Commentaria in mattheum* PL 165: 212C, 213A, 213C; *Commentaria in lucam* PL 165: 342B, 368A; *Commentaria in joannem* PL 165: 459C, 459D; *De laudibus* PL 165: 892D, 895D; *De sacrificio azymo* PL 165: 1088A. Since scholars have not succeeded in creating a chronology of Bruno's works it is impossible to simply chart his use of this phrase; his *De sacrificio Azymo* and *Libri sententiarum* certainly predate 1111.

257 *De sacramentis*, PL 165: 1091.

258 Recall the incidents at Sant'Angelo in Formis (discussed above), and at St Thomas the Apostle, Vallemaio. The latter account is immediately followed within the same section by an apocalyptic vision, from Germany, of the demise of the king of the Christians and the spread of error (*Chron. Cas.* MGH SS 34, 4.41, 509). The juxtaposition of the miracle and the vision serves to heighten the relations linking Bruno, the rite of dedication and the politics of reform.

259 The complete text is found in Gérard Fransen, 'Réflexions sur l'étude des collections canoniques à l'occasion de l'édition d'une lettre de Bruno De Segni', *Studi Gregoriani* 9 (1972): 515–33.

260 [Emphasis mine.] Fransen, 'Réflexions', 532.

261 The comments on Peter are in letter four: Fransen, 'Réflexions', 528; of Paschal, Bruno states the situation flatly to Bonomo, 'dominus papa neque me diligat neque me consilium' (MGH LdL, 3: 565). North, who downplays the intensity

and significance of the conflict between Bruno and Paschal, refers to Bruno's implication, at the Lenten council of 1116, that the Pope was acting heretically in signing the *privilegium* as a 'major *faux pas*' in a moment of unguarded 'zeal': North, *Shadows of Reform*, 104. To the contrary, Bruno was consistent in his condemnation of the *privilegium* as heresy throughout the controversy. His expressed opinion at 1116 was, therefore, well known, and almost certainly anticipated at the council of 1116. When John of Gaeta stood and asked Bruno if he was accusing Paschal of heresy, he was seizing an opportunity, not reacting to a faux pas. John, a monk of Montecassino, may have been responsible for fomenting tensions between Bruno and Paschal earlier as well, and was soon to succeed Paschal as Gelasius II. Both of these men had grown old in the world of papal politics, and neither was likely to have been so unguarded and spontaneous at such a critical moment.

262 Fransen, 'Réflexions', 531–2.

263 *De sacramentis*, PL 165: 1093A–B.

264 Ibid., 165: 1094B–C.

265 Ibid., 165: 1098B–C.

266 Ibid., 165: 1103C–D and 1107A–B.

267 Ibid., 165: 1104B–C.

268 Ibid., 165: 1104D–1105A.

269 Ibid., 165: 1107C–1108AB.

270 Ibid., 165: 1110A.

271 For more on the legacy of Bruno see Barton Brown, '*Enigmata Figuram*: A Study of the Third Book of the Rationale Divinorum Officiorum of William Durandus and its Allegorical Treatment of the Christian Liturgical Vestments' (PhD diss., New York University, 1983), 160–1; and Grégoire, *Bruno*, 104.

272 Robinson, 'Political Allegory', 84–6.

273 Jaffé, 6566. Ughelli, *Italia Sacra*, I, 198.

274 Robinson, *The Papacy*, 67–73. For further discussion, see Twyman, *Papal Ceremonial*; Stroll, *Symbols as Power*.

275 Reynolds, 'Liturgical Scholarship at the Time of the Investiture Controversy', 109–24.

Conclusion: liturgy and history

Walk, o saints of God, enter into the city of the Lord, indeed a new church is built for you, where the people ought to adore the majesty of the Lord.

Antiphons from the Romano-Germanic Pontifical[1]

While historians often study the dynamics of reform as distinct religious, political or social phenomena, these characteristics did not exist as separate realities in the eleventh or twelfth centuries. This is not to say that religious history should be eliminated as an 'eighteenth-century creation . . . wholly innappropriate' to the Middle Ages, nor should it be reduced to a set of 'rules by which mediaeval society functioned'.[2] Rather, religious rites, sacred space and the desire to connect to them were not only integral to but formative of social norms and political authority. The dedication of churches shaped individuals and communities, positively and negatively, in a variety of ways. For the reformers of the eleventh century, religious reform was necessarily social because it was moral. The moral reform of the self thus required regulating social behaviour via the Peace and Truce of God, clerical celibacy or the sale of religious office. For men like Peter Damian and Bruno of Segni, the dedication rite was an occasion to consider (in sermons or commentaries) a personal reform, a reform that was both to be embodied and put on like new vestments, and was also to be transformative, intended to convert the Christian community into the heavenly reality. These moral reforms required individuals to accept them as personal ideals, to embrace them for themselves, and to be willing to hold others to that same standard. That this was never, in fact, fully accomplished does not mean that the reformers failed to promote them and have them accepted as new and bold ideals. The reforms were necessarily

political in part because bishops had long been essential to the governance of mediaeval society (hence Henry V's rejections of Paschal II's initial offer in 1111), but at least as importantly because the religious ideal fostered by the dedication of a church was itself cast in political terms: the church was the Heavenly Jerusalem, ruled by the true Emperor Christ. What was truly at issue was how to achieve that religious, political and eschatological ideal. The desire to create that ideal community resulted in a debate that was liturgical (concerning investment and consecration). A liturgical debate with such profound political and social implications cannot be properly understood apart from that broader eleventh-century context.[3] That eschatological ideal was paired, as is typical of reform movements, with the ideal Church of the apostles, at this time increasingly understood by the papal reformers in terms of the Petrine authority to bind and loose, and so to shape the Church.[4]

The liturgy for the dedication was symbolically rich enough to hold within it all of these tensions and ideals. It came to the fore in the eleventh century, in part because of the increased ecclesiastical building and rebuilding that was itself a product of a zeal for reform, and in part because the Peace of God placed a greater burden on the sacrality of churches. The liturgy focused reformers' attention on the purity of the Church and its sacraments, on who had the legal authority to consecrate people and objects, and on how a thing (building, bishop, water, wafer, emperor) came to be consecrated, if consecrated in different manners. It asserted a set of social norms for a community, a separate space where distinct behaviour was expected. The liturgy created the space that was to be, in its own words, 'the house of God, the gate of heaven'.[5] The liturgy did not simply reflect social rules, it created them. Participants in the rite did not merely absorb or necessarily obey those rules, they also challenged, modified or attempted to co-opt them.

That the consecrated church and its control were contested, that its norms were violated, and that its meaning was debated, reveals the complex, dynamic, but real power of the liturgy to create a separate space within a community and so to reshape that community. This ritual power was not easy to control and it could and did become explosive. As symbols become invested with meaning, as symbols gain power to shape people and places, they become volatile; they need to be defended or attacked. For example, a building is destroyed because it is understood to have power. Sometimes that power is overtly military, sometimes not, but it is always, in part, symbolic. If it did not represent power to the observer, no one would think to destroy it. In turn, if there is no evidence for an

attack (physical or otherwise) on a symbol, then the historian cannot be certain that it held any particular significance. The contestation of sacred space makes clear the importance of offering sermons, laws, commentaries and inscriptions on its significance. The list of those who attacked these sacred spaces is a surprising one. Sometimes it was the urban laity, as at Modena, Parma or Bari. Sometimes that laity acted in coordination with a local abbot and lesser clergy against their bishop, as at Bari. Sometimes it was the bishop who, in conjuction with local lay support, destroyed the sacred space of a monastery, as at Capua. At Venice, bishop and monk were subordinated altogether by the citizens, although Peter Damian, cardinal and monk, pushed back. Sometimes a pope blessed these activities (Bari, Modena); sometimes he opposed them (Capua, Parma). The dynamic cannot be reduced to one of general papal opposition to lay civic authority, let alone a coherent ecclesiastical resistance to lay power. The violence of many of these responses to the dedication, however, reflects the perception of the power of the consecrated space and the rite's ability to make that space powerful.

Moreover, while these moments of violence are the most striking examples of people shaping the rite, the liturgy did not need to be violently opposed in order to be refashioned or co-opted. The observer of the rite was always a participant, influencing the ritual in some manner. A sickly woman could steal water from the rite (as at Vallemaio or Lucca), employing it to her own ends. That woman, as a participant in the rite, proposed or confirmed a particular meaning for it – it had miraculous power. A crowd could form in enthusiasm, in expectation of miracles, signs or a feast, or fail to form through indifference. That crowd could be shaped or shape the liturgical moment in ways that are often now lost to the historian, but which are suggested by the many Italian examples considered, inserting themselves in violence, or supporting the rite as enthusiastic participants. Likewise, ecclesiastical leaders could be affected by the event.[6] The rite might present a moral ideal, or be made into a moral ideal for abbots or bishops via inscriptions (as at Montecassino or Salerno) or sermons. A monastic community could be transformed into a verdant heavenly ideal community by the liturgy (as at Rome, Cassino, Cava or Cluny) with a new, more forceful presence on the landscape. An urban community could likewise be reformed, could imagine themselves as civic actors needing to shape their ideal heavenly Church, and at Bari, Parma and Modena we see that possibility. Most obviously, the liturgy could be promoted as an occasion to reform the Church in head and members according to the ideals of a presiding bishop; or it could be reinterpreted

if those ideals were believed to be betrayed. Our eleventh-century sources present us with evidence for all of these activities, they reveal a reform movement and a society shaping and being shaped by a liturgy.

In the late eleventh century the act of consecration was frequently debated in a variety of ways, and the consecration of churches was employed as a metaphor for reforming the Church. Studying a period of intense cultural transformation by means of the liturgy offers the possibility to dissolve the anachronistic divisions of religion, politics and society. The dedication rite, in particular, provides a lens to reconsider the relationship between all three, and perhaps to consider them more completely. In order to create such a history, the liturgy should be considered as having a potential energy, not a fixed meaning. The liturgy did not exist for the purpose of announcing power or social rules. Rather its symbolic potential was an attractive force that drew people to it and that became kinetic as the liturgy was practised, participated in, commented on, co-opted and opposed. In that process it gained meaning, and new political, religious and ecclesiological forms were created and contested. Papal reformers of the eleventh century did not simply create the liturgy's meaning, or its authority, but they did attempt to direct and shape that meaning – as did many, from emperors and lords to the sickly, the plebs and the citizens of eleventh-century Italy.

Notes

1 PRG 40: 148, 173.
2 Iogna-Prat, *Order and Exclusion*, 4. Of course religious authorities did exercise coercive power, but the basis of that power was the capacity of religious forms (ritual, space and doctrine) to generate compelling meaning, which people (religious authorities and many others) attempted to direct.
3 That context has often been ignored despite the urging of Robinson, '"Political Allegory" in the Biblical Exegesis of Bruno of Segni', and so the eleventh-century commentaries have in turn often been ignored or dismissed, as in Whitehead, 'Columnae . . . sunt episcopi', or Horie, *Perceptions of* Ecclesia; while North, 'Shadows of Reform', denies the political allegory of Bruno's commentaries. Bejczy, 'Kings, Bishops, and Political Ethics', is exceptional in this regard.
4 On the creative tension between apostolic and heavenly churches in reformations, see Hamilton, 'Introduction', in Bellitto and Hamilton, *Reforming the Church before Modernity*.
5 For Maureen Miller, the episcopal architecture of twelfth-century Italy is comparable to fascism, '. . . in supporting the restoration of the medieval . . . bishop's palace, did [the fascists] intuit some of the historical and architectural messages in the structure . . .? These medieval episcopal residences were about power . . .

governance . . . order. Their rounded Romanesque portals represented an authority that resorted increasingly to repressive measures'. Miller, *Bishop's Palace*, 10. I am proposing a more complex dynamic where power was created in the symbolic capacity of the ritual, and we can recognise that power most clearly when people attend, attack or co-opt it. If religious space and ritual merely represented repressive authority, it would have been attacked or otherwise confronted as sometimes happened at dedications. At other dedications, the event was embraced by participants, suggesting the power was valued as positive ('heavenly', 'pure' or otherwise ideal).

6 Palazzo, *L'Évêque et son image*, notes that the representation of the bishops in the pontificals asserted episcopal authority. This may well be correct, but the primary audience for those images was the bishop, with only the smallest of clerical circles from the episcopal households also having access to them. Therefore, those images are aimed at shaping the bishop himself. Much of the liturgical commentary of the reformers examined in the previous chapters was likewise directed at regulating and changing the behaviour of the bishops.

Appendix A: Italian dedications with named participants

CHURCH, LOCATION SOURCE	DATE	PARTICIPANTS	NOTABLE EVENTS
S. MICHELE, CHIUSA *Chronica monasterii Sancti Michaelis Clusini*, ed. G. Schwartz and E. Abegg in MGH, SS, Vol. 30 (Leipzig, 1926), 963.	987	Iohannis Vincentius (hermit); famulus Domini Iohannem; omnes clerici et populi; hominum multitudo innumerabilis ex diversis urbibus, opidis et villis; praesul Amizo (of Turin)	Column of fire seen by bishop Amizo and people. People supplicate and beat breasts; Amizo responds with the antiphon, 'O quam metuendus est . . . ', 'This is another Mt Synai'. Following day: oil is seen flowing down on the church, bishop says Mass, grants perpetual privilege.
S. SALVATORIS, MONTE AMIATA *Notitia dedicationis ecclesiae Sancti Salvatoris in Monte Amiata*, ed. E.P. Schramm in MGH, SS, Vol. 30, 971–2.	1036	18 cardinals and bishops; Patriarch of Aquileia; comitatu clericorum et aliorum bonorum virorum	
VALLEMBROSIA *Vita Sancti Iohannis Gualberti*, ed. F. Baethgen in MGH, SS, Vol. 30, 1086.	1038, Feb/ Mar	Henricus rex Florentius; regina (not present but sends gift); Bp Rodulfus Patherbrunnensis; Iohannis Gualberti	'From virtue, in short, comes virtue', the priestly office is so highly regarded that no simoniac, nicolaitan, or anyone who

Source	Date		
		had lapsed into a crime after baptism dared approach the altar. This is then connected to following foundations by *viri nobiles et fideles de diversis partibus:* S. Salvus, S. Peter Apostle (Musceta), S. Paul (Razulum); S. Reparta (Romagna), S. Cassian (M. Scalario)	The octave to be observed within the walls of the city and an extra day to be observed by *plebs*; Alexander II compares dedication with Moses and Tabernacle, Solomon and Temple.
St Martin, Lucca Sermon, in Pietro Guidi, 'Per la storia della cattedrale e del Volto Santo', *Bollettino Storico Lucchese* (1932), 169–86, at 182–86.	1070	P. Alexander II; 22 bishops; numerous abbots; infinite multitude of clerics (qui non modo de vicinis urbibus sed ab usque ipsa Francia)	
St Benedict, Montecassino *Chronica Monasterii Casinensis*, ed. Hartmut Hoffman MGH, SS, Vol. 34 (Hanover, 1980), 398–400.	1 Oct., 1071	Alexander II; Desiderius; Hildebrand; Roman Cardinals, bishops and nobles; abbots, monks, magnates, lower clergy, and men and women of diverse	

Appendix A (continued)

Church, Location	Date	Participants	Notable Events
Source			
Narratio of Leo of Ostia, ed. T. Leccisotti, in Angelo Pantoni, *Le Vicende della Basilica di Montecassino, Attraverso la Documentazione Archeologica*, *Miscellanea Cassinese* 36 (Montecassino, 1973), 215–25.		condition. Abps of Capua, Salerno, Naples, Sorrento, Amalfi, Sipoto, Trani, Acereza, Otranto, Ora-Brindisi; Bps of Porto, Tusculum, Sabina, Segni, Anagni, Veroli, Terracina, Gaeta, Aquino, Sora, Marsica, Valva, Penne, Teano, Carinola, Roselle, Aversa, Nola, Avellina, Paestum-Capaccio, Troia, Florence, Melfi, Lucera, Dragonara, Civitate, Termoli, Guardialfiera, Larino, Ariano Irpino, Isernia-Venafro, Boiano, Salpi, Canne, Ruvo, Venosa, Minervino Murge, Bisceglie, Molfetta, Giovinazzo, Monopoli, Ostuni, Tarent, Perugiam Città di Castello. Magnates: Richard, Pr. Capua, his son Jordanus, brother Rainulf; Gisulf Pr. Salerno, his brothers Landulf Pr. Benevento, Sergius Dk. Naples, Sergius Dk.	

234

St Nicholas, Bari	Oct., 1089	Sorrento, Counts Marsorum, Balvensium, his son Borelli. Other innumerable powerful or noble people of the natives or Normans. A great crowd of people that could not be contained in the monastery.	P. 'Germanus' (Urban II); bishops and dignitaries; great multitude of people; all the citizens.	Group who stole relics able to resist bishop and build separate church. Abbot who supported them becomes bishop.
Gerardo Cioffari (ed.), *La leggenda di Kiev* (Bari, 1980).			Relics guarded by 'large crowd of citizens' until altar for St finished	
Cioffari; 'The Translation of Saint Nicholas, an Anonymous Greek Account of the Transfer of the Body of the St. Nicholas from Myra in Lycia to Bari in Italy', *Bollettino di S. Nicola* 10 (1980), 2–18.			Society that stole the relics: ALBERTUS, SHIPMASTER; **IOHANNACIUS DE CARO**; *ELIAS CRISTIANI*,	
Pronotuario del Secolo XII, Codice Benevento di Niceforo, Elenco del				

Appendix A (continued)

Church, Location	Date	Participants	Notable Events
Source			
P. Beatillo, ed. Francesco Babudri in 'Sinossi dei Traslatori delle Ossa di San Nicola da Mira a Bari', *Archivio Storico Pugliese* an. 3 (1950), 3–94, at 90–4.		*Shipmaster*; **Idelmannus di Polignano**; Sifandus di Ioannis de Argiro, cleric of San Nicola; *Benedictus Manicella; Nicolaus di Polignano;* **Stephanus Tarentino; Faracus;** Romano di Nicolò, cleric of S. Pelagia; **Mele di Caloioanni**; *Meliacca Boccalata;* **Simeone Dentica;** *Iohannis di Polignano; Bisantius di Monopoli;* **Kirizzius di Urania; Barda di Gisilfo;** *Miro di Polignano;* **Topazio;** *Elefantus;* **Mele, son of the priest Basilio;** *Disigius di Alberto, cleric; Summus;* **Urso, son of the priest Lupo; Mele di Germano;** Lupus, priest; **Stefanus Bos, son of Simeone;** *Mattheus Sparro;* **Romuladus Vulpagna; Bonus homo;** *Gittagno; Summissimo, shipmaster; Maraldizius; Iohannoccarus, shipmaster;*	

	Date		
		SIRE AZZO CABALLO; PETRACCA CAPERRONE; *Demetrius Bazzus;* **LEO DEL NOTARO GIACOMO** **DE GUISANDA;** *Iohannes de Polignano; Giovannoccaro;* **PETRACCA PILILLO; LEO PILILLO;** *Maione di Polignano; Leo di Lado; Pertacca di Rossemanno;* **LUPUS DI CHIUNATA;** <u>Grimualdus,</u> priest; *Michael di Zizula; Nicolaus d'Alba,* son of Albertus; **PETRUS DI SICHINOLFO;** *Stassius Scannoria; Maio di Adelfo;* **LEO DI SAPATICO;** *Pandulfus di Polignano; Stephanus de Cretazariis* di Bisceglie; **BISANTIUS BUCCONUS;** *Petronus Nasus; Dalfius di Monopoli;* **Leo, of the cleric Disiglio;** **MELICIACCA CORBARIO;** *Bisantius Saragolla*	Leo Pilillo sells his rights and privileges as negotiated with Elias to the Abbot Eustasius of San Nicola in 1105 (CDB, v.42) *SHIPMASTERS (FLEET COMMAND)* [4] **NOBILES, BONI HOMINES** [12] MERCHANTS [10] *Sailors* [26] <u>Clergy</u> [5] **Children of Clergy** [4]
ST MARK'S, VENICE Andrea Danduli, *Andreae Danduli, Ducis Venetiarum Chronica per extensum*	1089 or 1094	Doge, Primicerius, Procurator	Clergy, laity, *plebs* present just prior to and represented on tympanum of

Appendix A (continued)

Church, Location Source	Date	Participants	Notable Events
descripta (aa. 46–1280 d.c.), ed. Ester Pastorello (Bologna, 1938), RIS, Vol. 12, 1, 219.			S. Marco as present at dedication. Location of the body kept hidden.
St Martin, Vallecorsa Annales Ceccanensis, 281	1090	Iohannes Tuscolano; six bishops	
Santissima Trinitá, Cava *Historia consecrationis monasterii Sanctissimae Trinitatis Cavensis*, ed. Leone Mattei-Cerasoli, RIS, Vol. 6, 5, 46–7.	1092	P. Urban II; Abbot Peter; Dk. Roger; Bps: Alphanus, Salerno; Ubaldo, Sabina; Odo, Albano; Berardo, Praenest; Iohannes, Tuscolano; Bruno, Segni; Rangerius, Regitanus; Gerardus, Troiano; Iohanne, Rapollano; Card. Pr.: Hermannus, Quattro Coronati; Gregorius, S. Vitalis; Benedictus, S. Susanna; Card. D.: Gregorius, S. Maria Via Lata; Iohanne, S. Maria Schola Graeca; Petrus, S. Adriano; Iacobus, S.	Bp. Bruno of Segni consecrates the chapel (*sacellus*) of the abbot; Rangerius of Regitanus a nearby church.

Privileges granted by Roger in the hearing of princes and people. |

Source	Date	Persons	Description
Brevior Historia, ibid., 48.		Eustachio; Teutionus, S. Georgio Velabro; innumerable multitude of princes, clerics, laics Urban II; Dk. Roger; Abbot Peter; Bps: Ubaldo, Sabina; Odo, Albano Berardus Praenest; Bruno, Segni; Rangerius, Reginatus; Gerardus, Troianus; Iohannes, Rapollanus; Card. Pr.: Hermannus, Gregorius, Benedictus; Card. D.: Petrus, Iacobus, Teutio	Bp Odo of Albano consecrates the chapel (*capellus*) of the abbot to the Virgin; Berardus of Palestrina consecrates a church in nearby town.
St Thomas, Vallemaio *Chron. Mon. Cass.*, 509.	13 Apr 1111	Bp. Bruno of Segni; mulier	Woman is cured by water used by Bruno; boy in Germany has vision of death of King and error in diverse parts.
Vita Brunonis, AASS July, t. 4, 483A		Bruno; mulier arrepta	Woman is cured by using water used in the dedication (*aqua perfusionis ejus*).
S. Geminiano, Modena *Relatio sive descriptio de innovatione ecclesie sancti Geminiani mutinensis presulis ac de translatione*	8 Oct. 1106	Pope Paschal II; Abp Dodo; Matilda of Canossa with her army; Lanfrancus, architect; large crowd of bishops, cardinals, abbots, monks, other clerics	Decision to rebuild church in absence of Bp by counsel of clerics, citizens, representatives of the plebs and knights of the church who seek approval of

Appendix A (continued)

Church, Location Source	Date	Participants	Notable Events
vel revelatione seu etiam consecratione eius beatissimi corporis, RIS VI, t. 1, 3–8.		and laics; six sworn knights; twelve sworn citizens; innumerable people; Bp Bonisenior Reginus; laics and women	Matilda. Citizens of Modena and all people of the church select Lanfranc. Rite of consecration is paused after a dispute arises between clerics and laity over the exposition of the relics, and rite is deferred until the arrival of Paschal II who allows the presence of armed guards (six sworn knights and twelve citizens). Further debate ensues about the activity of the exposition.
S. Vincenzo al Volturno Falcone di Benevento, *Chronicon Beneventanum, città e feudi nell'Italia dei Normanni*, ed. Edoardo D'Angelo (Florence, 1998), 20–1.	1115	P. Paschal II; cardinals, archbishops, bishops, twenty abbots	Council meeting
Confirmation of privileges by Paschal of April 20, 1117, doc. 86 in ibid., at 170.		P. Paschal II; cardinal priests	

Appendix B: papal dedications (1009–1143)

POPE	Sergius IV (1009–12)	Bene VIII (1012–24)	Leo IX (1048–54)	Nicholaus II (1059–61)	Alexander II (1061–73)	Gregory VII (1073–85)	Victor III (1086–87)	Urban II (1088–99)	Paschal II (1099–1118)	Gelasius II (1118–9)	Calixtus II (1119–24)	Honorius II (1124–30)	Innocent II (1130–43)
YEAR	**1010**	**1020**	**1049**	**1059**	**1070**	**1073**	**1087**	**1089**	**1099**	**1118**	**1119**	**1128**	**1130**
	Rome #3969	Bamberg #4027	Cassino #4154	Lavello #4407	Lucca Gu	Rome Forcella XIII, 338–9	Pico #5345	Bari #5411	Rome Forcella I, 381 (year?)	Pisa #6651	Vienne #6684	Rome Forcella IV, 119	Porto-venere #7414
			Atina #4154	Venosa #4407	**1071** Cassino #4689	Rome Forcella XI, 137–8 (year?)		Brindisi #5414	Rome LP II, 305 (year?)	Genoa #6655	Nîmes Cr: 34		Cluny #7424
			Trier #4172	Melfi #4408	**1061–1072** Gubbio #4697	**1080** Rome #5171		**1092** Cava #5466	**1101** Canossa, Puglia #5871	Tavel Cr: 33	Toulouse Cr: 34		**1131** Soissons Cr: 41 #7440[a]

241

Appendix B (continued)

POPE	Sergius IV (1009–12)	Bene VIII (1012–24)	Leo IX (1048–54)	Nicholaus II (1059–61)	Alexander II (1061–73)	Gregory VII (1073–85)	Victor III (1086–87)	Urban II (1088–99)	Paschal II (1099–1118)	Gelasius II (1118–9)	Calixtus II (1119–24)	Honorius II (1124–30)	Innocent II (1130–43)
			Rheims #4175	**1060**		**1085**		**1093**	Rome LP II, 305	Estagel #6663	Fronton Cr: 36		Morigny Cr: 40
				Florence #4429		Salerno MGH SS III, 182		Banzi #5486-7					#7488
													Autun Cr: 41
			Verdun #4185	Farfa #4437[a]				**1095**	**1104**	Tillan #6663	Cahors Cr: 36[a]		**1132**
								Asti #5569	Rome #5977				Novara #7566
			Metz #4185					Valence #5569	**1105**	Tarnac #6664	Fauntevraud #6736		
									Rome #6054				
			Mainz #4193					Le Puy MGH V, 463	**1106**	Avignon Cr: 33	Angers #6737		Mortara #7566[a]
									Gaeta #6070				
			Andlau #4195					Chaise-Dieu #5575	Modena #6092	Avignon Cr: 33	Angers #6737		Pavia #7568

242

Reichenau, Insula #4204[a]	Chirac Be: 2,436	Parma #6098	Tours #6742	**1139** Rome Forcella VII, 535
Ottmar-sheim Cr: 20	Tarascon #5576 **1107** Casale #6112	Morigny #6746	**1141** Rome Forcella VI, 267
1050 Toul #4239[a]	Cluny #5583 Lyons #6112	Auxerre Cr: 38	**1143** Rome Forcella V, 517
Besançon Cr: 20	Sauxil-langes Cr:25 Dijon #6124	**1120** Volterra #6848	
Épinal Cr: 22	St.-Flour #5603 Bèze #6124	**1123** Rome #7006	
Remire-mont Cr:22	Limoges #5604–06 Nième #6125	Rome #7069[a]	

Appendix B (continued)

Pope	Sergius IV (1009–12)	Bene VIII (1012–24)	Leo IX (1048–54)	Nicholaus II (1059–61)	Alexander II (1061–73)	Gregory VII (1073–85)	Victor III (1086–87)	Urban II (1088–99)	Paschal II (1099–1118)	Gelasius II (1118–9)	Calixtus II (1119–24)	Honorius II (1124–30)	Innocent II (1130–43)
			1052					**1096**	Dole #6127				
			Trebur #4284ᵃ					Charroux #5613 #5627					
								Poitiers	**1108**				
								CrV: 296 #5638	Capua #6216				
									1109				
								Angers #5616	Subiaco #6239ᵃ				
								Vendôme Cr: 27ᵃ	**1110**				
									Rome Forcella X, 449				
								Tours #5618–9	S. Agata de'Goti #6275				

1112
Saintes
Cr: 27ª
Rome
#6309

Bour-
deaux
Cr: 27
#5644
Rome
Forcella
V,
117–18

1114
Nérac
#5644
Rome?
#6400

1115
Layrac
Cr:27
#5645
Volturno
#6468

1116
Moissac
Cr: 27ª
Rome
Forcella
VII, 389

1117
Toulouse
Cr: 27
#5648*
Castelli
#6556

Carcas-
sonne
Pallest-
rina

Appendix B (continued)

Pope	Sergius IV (1009–12)	Bene VIII (1012–24)	Leo IX (1048–54)	Nicholaus II (1059–61)	Alexander II (1061–73)	Gregory VII (1073–85)	Victor III (1086–87)	Urban II (1088–99)	Paschal II (1099–1118)	Gelasius II (1118–9)	Calixtus II (1119–24)	Honorius II (1124–30)	Innocent II (1130–43)
								#5649^s Maguelonne #5650^i Nîmes #5650	#6566				
Total	1	1	15	5	3	4	1	28	26	8	14	1	11
Rate	0.33	0.08	1.83	1.67	0.25	0.33	1	2.55	1.37	4	2.8	0.17	0.85
Max:	1: 1010	1:1020	9: 1049	3: 1059	—	—	1:	14: 1096	6: 1107	8: 1118	12: 1119	1: 1128	4: 1132
Yr							1087						

#Jaffé
^{a}altar dedication
Be: Becker, *Papst Urban II*
Cr: Crozet, 'Les Consécrations pontificales'
CrV: Crozet, 'Le voyage'
Gu: Guidi, 'Per la storia della cattedrale'
*reads 4648
^{i}Island of Maguelone
^{s}Pile of stones

246

BIBLIOGRAPHY

Manuscripts

Admont, Stiftsbibliothek C–D, E.

Bamberg, Staatsbibliothek, Cod. Lit. 56.

Bologna, Biblioteca Universitaria di Bologna 1494.

Cava, Abbazia 6.

Florence, Biblioteca Laurenziana, Acquisti e doni 84.

——, S. Marco 13.

Grenoble, Bibliothèque publique 345.

Lucca, Biblioteca Capitolare 607.

——, Biblioteca Capitolare codex P. †.

Modena, Archivio capitolare, O.II.11.

——, Biblioteca estense latini 388.

Montecassino, Archivio dell'Abbazia 196.

——, Archivio dell'Abbazia 619.

——, Biblioteca dell'Abbazia 359.

——, Biblioteca dell'Abbazia 451.

Paris, Bibliothèque Nationale de France latin 579.

Pistoia, Biblioteca Capitolare 141.

Rome, Biblioteca Alexandrina 173.

——, Biblioteca Angelica 362.

——, Biblioteca Vallecelliana D. 5.

——, Bib. Vall. F. 36.

Rouen, Bibliothèque municipale, ms. 368 (A 27).

Turin, Biblioteca Nazionale Universitaria 574.

Vatican City, Biblioteca Apostolica Vaticana, Archivio S. Pietro C 103.

——, S. Pietro C 105.

——, S. Pietro F 37.

——, Barberini latinus 535.

——, Barb. lat. 592.

——, Barb. lat. 631.

——, Chigianus A. V. 145.

——, Chig. P VIII.

——, Pal. lat., 3–4–5.

——, Reg. lat. 496.

——, Urbinate Latino 59.

——, Vaticanus Latinus 994.

——, Vat. Lat. 1202.

——, Vat. Lat. 1254.

——, Vat. Lat. 1363.

——, Vat. Lat. 3828.

——, Vat. lat. 4770.

——, Vat. lat. 5055.

——, Vat. lat. 8563.

Primary sources: printed editions

Aldhelm of Sherbourne, *De laudibus virginum*, ed. J.A. Giles, PL 89 (Paris, 1850).

Alfanus of Salerno, *I carmi di Alfano I, Arcivescovo di Salerno*, eds Anselmo Lentini and Faustino Avagliano, Miscellanea Casinese 38 (Montecassino, 1974).

Amalarii episcopi, *Opera Liturgica Omnia*, ed. John M. Hanssens, SJ (Vatican City, 1950).

Analecta Hymnica Medii Aevi, ed. C. Blume and G.M. Dreves, 55 Vols (Leipzig 1886–1922; repr. Frankfurt am Main 1961).

Andreae Danduli Ducis Venetiarum, *Chronica per extensum descripta aa. 46–1280*, ed. Ester Pastorello, RIS XII, pt. 1 (Bologna 1938).

Andrea Strumi, *Vita sancti Arialdi*, ed. F. Baethegen, MGH 30 (Berlin, 1929).

Andrieu, Michel (ed.), *Le Pontifical romain au Moyen-Âge*, 4 Vols, *Studi e testi* 86–8, 91 (Vatican City, 1938–41).

Annales Benevantani, ed. G.H. Pertz, MGH SS 3 (Hanover, 1838).

Annales Hildesheimensis, ed. G. Waitz, MGH SS 8 (Hanover, 1878).

Anselm, *Historia dedicationis ecclesiae S. Remigii*, PL 142, 1417–40.

Anselm of Lucca, *Sermo Anselmi episcopi de Caritate*, ed. E. Pásztor, in 'Motivi dell'ecclesiologia di Anselmo di Lucca in margine a un sermone inedito', *Bulletino Istorico Italiano* 77 (1965): 45–104.

——, *Anselmi episcopi Lucensis Collectio canonum una cum collectione minore*, ed. F. Thaner (Innsbruck, 1906, 1915).

——, *Liber contra Wibertum*, ed. E. Berheim, MGH LdL 1 (Hanover, 1897).

Arnulf, *Gesta archiepiscoporum Mediolensium*, ed. L.C. Bethmann and W. Wattenbach, MGH 8 (Hanover, 1826).

Augustine, *In iohannis evangelium tractatus cxxiv*, ed. R. Willems, CCL 36 (Turnhout, 1954).

Bedae Venerabilis, *Opera*, ed. D. Hurst, CCL 122 (Turnhout, 1955).

Bede, *De tabernaculo et vasis ejus, ac vestibus sacerdotium*, PL 91, 393–498.

Benevento, Falcone di, *Chronicon Beneventanum, città e feudi nell'Italia dei Normanni*, ed. Edoardo D'Angelo (Florence, 1998).

Bernold, *Chronicon*, ed. G.H. Pertz, MGH SS, V (Hanover, 1844).

Biblia Sacra Iuxta Vulgatam Versionem, ed. Robert Weber (Stuttgart, 1983).

Bruno of Segni, *Libri sententiarum*, PL 165, 875–1078.

——, *Tractatus de sacramentis ecclesiae*, PL 165, 1089–1110.

——, *Commentarium in Isaiam*, ed. A. Amelli, *Spicilegium Casinese complectens analecta sacra et profana* III/1 (Montecassino, 1897).

Caesarius of Arles, *Sermones*, ed. D. Germanus Morin, CCL 104 (Turnhout, 1953).

Chronica monasterii Casinensis, ed. Hartmut Hoffmann, MGH SS 34 (Berlin, 1980).

Chronica monasterii Sancti Michaelis Clusini, ed. G. Schwartz and Elisabeth Abegg, MGH 30, t. 2 (Leipzig, 1936).

Chronicon Sublacense, ed. R. Morghen, *RIS* 24, pt. 6.

Chronicon Vulternense del Monaco Giovanni, ed. Vincenzo Federici, *Fonti per la storia d'Italia*, Vols 58–60 (Rome, 1925).

Cicero, *On Duties* (New York, 1913).

Cioffari, Gerardo, *La Leggenda di Kiev: La traslazione delle reliquie di S. Nicola nel racconto di un annalista russo contemporaneo* (Bari, 1980).

Codex Theodosianus, ed. Theodore Mommsen (Berlin, [1955]) 16 2, 1.8.

Codice Diplomatico Barese, 19 Vols (Bari, 1897–1950).

Cronica gestorum ac factorum memoriabilium civitatis Bononie, ed. H. Bursellis, RIS 23, 2.

Digesta Iustiniani Augusti, ed. Theodore Mommsen, 2 Vols (Berlin, 1870).

Diversorum patrum sententiae sive Collectio in LXXIV titulos digesta, ed. J.T. Gilchrist, *Monumenta Iuris Canonici* Ser. B, v. 1 (Vatican City, 1973).

Donizio, *Vita Comitissae Mathildis*, ed. Ugo Bellocchi and Giovanni Morzi, *Matilda e Canossa: Il poema di Donizione*, Deputazione di storia patria per le antiche provincie modenesi, Monumenti, t. 24 (Modena, 1984).

Ekkerd of Aura, *Chronicon*, ed. F-J. Schmale, *Ausgewählte Quellen zur deutschen Geschichte: Freiherr vom Stein Gedächtnisausgabe* 15 (Darmstadt, 1972).

Epistolae Romanorum pontificorum, ed. P. Coustant (Farnborough, 1967 [1721]).

Eusebius, *Historia Ecclesiastica*, ed. Gustave Bardy, *Sources Chrétiennes*, Vols 31, 41, 55, and 73 (Paris, 1952–60).

Eusebius Gallicanus, *Collectio homiliarum*, ed. Iohannes Leroy, CCL 101A (Turnhout, 1971).

Gaufredus Malaterra, *De rebus gestis Rogerii Calabriae et Siciliae comitis et Roberti Guiscardi ducis fratris eius*, ed. R. Pontieri, RIS 3.

Gratian, *Decretum*, ed. A. Friedberg, *Corpus Iuris Canonici*, 2 Vols (Leipzig, 1879).

Gregory VII, *Das Register Gregors VII*, ed. E. Caspar, MGH *Epistolae Selectae* 2 (1920–3).

Guibert of Nogent, *De vita sua, sive monodiae*, ed. and trans. Edmond-René Labande, *Guibert de Nogent: Autobiographie* (Paris, 1981).

Hermiae Sozomeni, *Historia Ecclesiastica*, ed., J.P. Migne, *Patrologiae Graecae* 67.

Hildegard of Bingen, *Scivias*, ed. Adelgundis Führkötter, OSB and Angela Carlevaris, OSB, CCCM 43–43A (Turnhout, 1978).

Historia consecrationis sacri monasterii Sanctissimae Trinitatis Cavensis solemniter factae a beatae memoriae Urbano papa secundo, Anno Domini MXCII die quinta Septembris, RIS 6, 5.

Hugh of St Victor, *De sacramentis Christianae fidei*, PL 176.

Humberti Cardinalis Adversus Simoniacos, ed. F. Thaner MGH LdL 1 (Hanover, 1891).

Iohannis Mantuani, *In Cantica canticorum et De sancta Maria tractatus ad Comitissam Matildam*, ed. B. Bischoff and B. Taeger (Freiburg, 1973).

Jerome, *Tractatus in Psalmos 137*, ed. D. Germanus Morin, CCL 78 (Turnhout, 1958).

John of Lodi, *Vita sancti Petri Damiani*, PL 144, 114–46.

La leggenda di Kiev, La traslazione delle reliquie di S. Nicola nel racconto di un annalista russo contemporaneo, ed. and trans. Gerardo Cioffari (Bari, 1980).

Leo Marsicanus, *Narratio De Consecratione et Dedicatione Ecclesiae Casinensis*, ed. T. Leccisotti, 'Il racconto della dedicazione dell basilica desideriana nel codice Cassinese 47', *Miscellanea Cassinese 36* (1973): 215–23.

Liber Pontificalis, ed. Louis Duchesne and Cyrille Vogel, 3 Vols (Paris, 1955 [1886–92]).

Mommsen, Theodore and Paul Krueger (eds), *The Digest of Justinian*, trans. Alan Watson, 4 Vols (Philadelphia, 1985).

Monachus, M., *Sanctuarium capuanum* (Naples, 1630).

Notitiae dedicationis ecclesiae Sancti Salvatoris in Monte Amiata, ed. P. Schramm, MGH t. 30, pt. 2 (Leipzig, 1934).

Orderic Vitalis, *The Ecclesiastical History*, ed. Marjorie Chibnall, 6 Vols (Oxford, 1973).

Peter Damian, *Letters*, trans. Owen J. Blum (Washington, DC, 1989–2005).

——, *Die Briefe des Petrus Damiani*, ed. Kurt Reidel, 4 Vols, MGH (München, 1983–93).

——, *Sermones*, ed. Giovanni Lucchesi, CCCM 57 (Turnhout, 1983).

Pliny the Elder, *Naturalis historiae*, ed. H. Rackham, 10 Vols (Cambridge, MA, 1938–63).

Plutarch, *Lives*, ed. J. Henderson, 10 Vols (Cambridge, MA, 1919).

Regula Sancti Benedicti, ed. Timothy Fry, *RB1980: The Rule of St Benedict in Latin and English with Notes and Thematic Index* (Collegeville, MN, 1981).

Relatio aedificationis ecclesiae cathedralis Mutinensis et tranlationis Sancti Geminiani, ed. H. Bresslau MGH t. 30, pt. 2 (Leipzig, 1934).

Relatio translationis corporis sancti Geminiani, ed. Giulio Bertoni (Città di Castello, 1907), RIS, Vol. 6.

Sancti Leonis Vita, PL 143, 457–504.

Socrates Scholasticus, *Ecclesiastical History*, ed. Günther Christian Hansen, *Socrates Kirchengeschichte* (Berlin, 1960).

Suger of St-Denis, *Vita Ludovici Grossi*, ed. and trans. Henri Waquet, *Suger, Vie de Louis VI Le Gros* (Paris, 1964).

Urbani II, *Concilium Placentium*, MGH *Constitutiones* 1, 560–63.

Vita Anselmi episcopi Lucensis, ed. R. Williams, MGH SS 12 (1856).

Vita Brunonis, AA SS 31, t. 4.

Vita prima et secunda Bernardi episcopi Parmensis, ed. P. Schramm MGH t. 30, pt. 2 (Leipzig, 1934).

Vitae quatuor priorum abbatum Cavensum, RIS, VI, 5 (Bologna, 1941).

Vita sancti Iohannis Gualberti, ed. F. Baethgen, MGH t. 30, pt. 2 (Leipzig, 1934).

Vogel, Cyrille and R. Elze (eds), *Le Pontifical romano-germanique du dixième siècle*, 3 Vols, *Studi e testi*, 226, 227, 269 (Vatican City, 1963).

Secondary works

Ambrosi, Angelo, 'La Basilica di San Nicola, Sito e Architettura', in Michele D'Elia (ed.), *Città della Nicoliana: Un progetto verso il 2000* (Bari, 1995), 33-46.

Amelli, A., *Spicilegium Casinese complectens Analecta Sacra et Profana* III/1 (Montecassino, 1897).

Andrieu, Michel, *Les Ordines Romani du haut Moyen Âge*, 4 Vols (Louvain,1931-1961).

Anrich, Gustav, *Hagios Nikolaos: Der heilige Nicolaos in der Grieschen Kirche: Texte und Untersuchungen*, Vol. 1 (Berlin, 1913).

Avagliano, F. (ed.), *Desiderio di Montecassino e l'arte della Riforma Gregoriana*, Montecassino, 1997.

Babudri, Francesco, 'Sinossi critica dei traslatori Nicolaiani di Bari', *Archivio storico Pugliese* an. 3 (1950), 3-94.

Baldelli, Franca (ed.), *Inventario dei Manoscritti dell'Archivio Capitolare di Modena* (Modena, 2003).

Baracchi, Orianna, *Modena: Piazza Grande* (Modena, 1981).

Barbour, Ian, *Myths, Models and Paradigms: A Comparative Study in Science and Religion* (San Francisco, 1974).

Beaudette, Paul, '"In the World not of It": Clerical Celibacy as a Symbol of the Medieval Church', in Frasetto, *Medieval Purity and Piety*, 23-46.

Becker, Alfons, 'Le Voyage d'Urbain II en France', in *Le concile de Clermont de 1095 et l'appel à la croisade*, Collection de l'École Français de Rome (236) (Rome, 1997), 127-40.

——, *Papst Urban II (1088-1099)* (Stuttgart, 1964), MGH, Schriften 19, t. 1-2.

Bejczy, István, 'The Problem of Natural Virtue', in István P. Bejczy and Richard G. Newhauser (eds), *Virtue and Ethics in the Twelfth Century* (Leiden, 2005), 133-54.

——, 'Kings, Bishops, and Political Ethics: Bruno of Segni on the Cardinal Virtues', *Mediaeval Studies* 64 (2002): 267-86.

Bell, Catherine, *Ritual: Perspectives and Dimensions* (Oxford, 1997).

——, *Ritual Theory, Ritual Practice* (New York, 1992).

Bellitto, Christopher M. and Louis I. Hamilton (eds), *Reforming the Church* (Aldershot, 2005).

Benson, Robert L., Giles Constable, and Carol D. Lanham (eds), *Renaissance and Renewal in the Twelfth Century* (Oxford, 1985).

Billot-Vilandrau, Céline, 'Charlemagne and the Young Prince: A Didactic Poem on the Cardinal Virtues by Giles of Paris', in Bejczy and Newhauser, *Virtue and Ethics in the Twelfth Century*, 341-54.

Bloch, Herbert, *Monte Cassino in the Middle Ages*, 3 Vols (Cambridge, MA, 1986).

Blum, Owen J., *St. Peter Damian: His Teaching on the Spiritual Life* (Washington, DC, 1947).

Blumenthal, Uta-Renate, *Gregor VII: Papst zwischen Canossa und Kirchenreform* (Darmstadt, 2001).

——, 'The Papacy and Canon Law in the Eleventh-Century Reform', *Catholic Historical Review* 84 (1998): 201-18.

——, *The Investiture Controversy, Church and Monarchy from the Ninth to the Twelfth Century* (Philadelphia, 1988).

——, 'Fälschungen bei Kanonisten der Kirchenreform des 11. Jahrhunderts', *Fälschungen im Mittelalter, Internationaler Kongreß der Monumenta Germaniae Historica, München, 16.–19. September 1986*, MGH SS 33, t. 2: *Gefälschte Rechstexte der bestrafte Fälscher* (Hanover, 1988): 241–62.

——, 'Canossa and Royal Ideology in 1077: Two Unknown Manuscripts of *De penitentia regis Salomonis*', *Manuscripta* 22 (1978): 91–6.

——, 'Opposition to Pope Paschal II: Some Comments on the Lateran Council of 1112', *Annuarium Historiae Conciliorum* 10 (1978): 82–98.

——, *The Early Councils of Paschal II: 1100–1110*, Studies and Texts 43 (Toronto, 1978).

——, 'Paschal II and the Roman Primacy', *Archivum Historiae Pontificiae* 16 (1978): 67–92.

——, '*Patrimonia* and *Regalia* in 1111', in K. Pennington and R. Somerville (eds), *Law, Church, and Society: Essays in Honor of Stephan Kuttner* (Philadelphia, 1977), 12–16.

——, 'Eine neuer Text für das Reimser Konzil Leo IX. (1049)?', *Deutsches Archive für des Mittelalters* 32: 1 (1976): 23–48.

Bornstein, Christine Verzár, *Portals and Politics in the Early Italian City-State: The Sculpture of Nicholaus in Context* (Parma, 1988).

——, Matilda of Canossa, Papal Rome and the Earliest Italian Porch Portals', in Arturo Carlo Quintavalle (ed.), *Romanico padano, romanico europeo* (Parma, 1982): 143–58.

Bossy, John, 'The Mass as a Social Institution, 1200–1700', *Past and Present* 100 (1983): 29–61.

Bowen, Lee, 'The Tropology of Mediaeval Dedication Rites', *Speculum* (1941): 469–79.

Boyle, Leonard E., 'The Date of the Consecration of the Basilica of San Clemente', *San Clemente Miscellany II, Art and Archaeology* (Rome, 1978): 1–12, reprint of *Archivium Fratrum Praedicatorum* 30 (1960): 417–27.

Boynton, Susan L., 'The Customaries of Bernard and Ulrich as Liturgical Sources', in Susan Boynton and Isabelle Cochelin (eds), *From Dead of Night to End of Day: the Medieval Customs of Cluny* (Turnhout, 2005), 109–30, at 131–51.

——, *Shaping a Monastic Identity: Liturgy and History at the Imperial Abbey of Farfa, 1000–1125* (Ithaca, 2006).

——, 'Liturgy and History at the Abbey of Farfa in the Late Eleventh Century: Hymns of Peter Damian and Other Additions in BAV Chigi C.VI.177', *Sacris Erudiri* 39 (2000): 317–44.

Braun, Joseph, *Die liturgischen Paramente in Gegenwart und Vergangenheit: ein Handbuch der Paramentik* (Freiburg, 1924).

Brown, Barton, '*Enigmata Figuram*: A Study of the Third Book of the Rationale Divinorum Officiorum of William Durandus and its Allegorical Treatment of the Christian Liturgical Vestments' (PhD diss., New York University, 1983).

Brubaker, Leslie, *Vision and Meaning in Ninth-Century Byzantium: Image as Exegesis in the Homilies of Gregory of Nazianus* (Cambridge, 1999).

Brundage, James, *Medieval Canon Law* (London, 1995).

Buc, Philippe, *The Dangers of Ritual: Between Early Medieval Texts and Social Scientific Theory* (Princeton, 2001).

Buchanan, Charles, 'Spiritual and Spatial Authority in Medieval Lucca: Illuminated Manuscripts, Stational Liturgy and the Gregorian Reform', *Art History* 27(5): 723–44.

Buchowiecki, Walther, *Handbuch der Kirchen Roms: Der Romische Sakralbau in Geschichte und Kunst von der altchristlichen Zeit bis zur Gegenwart* (Vienna, 1967–74).

Burke, Peter, *The Historical Anthropology of Early Modern Italy: Essays on Perception and Communication* (Cambridge, 1987).

Callahan, Daniel F., 'The Peace of God and the Cult of the Saints in Aquitaine in the Tenth and Eleventh Centuries', in Head and Landes, *Peace of God*, 165–83.

Camille, Michael, *The Gothic Idol: Ideology and Image-making in Medieval Art* (Cambridge, 1989).

Cantarella, Glauco Maria, 'Bruno di Montecassino o il disagio del Primato Romano', in *L'età dell'Abate Desiderio*, ed. Guglielmo Cavallo, *Miscellanea Cassinese* 60 (Montecassino, 1989): 483–91.

——, 'La Construzione della verità Pasquale II: Un papa alle strette', *Studi Storici* 178–9 (Rome, 1987).

——, 'Ecclesiologia e politica nel papato di Pasquale II: Linee di una interpretazione', *Studi Storici* 131 (Rome, 1982).

Carruthers, Mary J., *The Book of Memory: A Study of Memory in Medieval Culture* (Cambridge, 1990).

Caspary, Gerard E., *Politics and Exegesis: Origen and the Two Swords* (Berkeley, CA, 1979).

Cattaneo, Enrico, 'La liturgia nella riforma gregoriana', in *Chiesa e Riforma nella Spiritualità del sec. XI: Convegni del Centro di Studi sulla Spiritualità Medievale VI, 1–16 Ottobre 1963* (Todi, 1968), 169–90.

Chalandon, Ferdinand, *Histoire de la domination normande en Italie et en Sicile*, 2 Vols (Paris, 1907).

Cioffari, Gerardo, *Storia della Basilica di S. Nicola di Bari*, I: *L'Epoca Normanno Sveva* (Bari, 1984).

——, 'The Translation of Saint Nicholas, an Anonymous Greek Account of the Transfer of the Body of St Nicholas from Myra in Lycia to Bari in Italy', *Bollettino di S. Nicola* 10 (1980): 2–18.

Conant, K.J., *Cluny: les églises et la maison du chef d'ordre* (Mâcon, 1968).

Constable, Giles, 'The Dislocation of Jerusalem in the Middle Ages', in Alois Hahn, Gert Melville and Werener Röcke (eds), *Norm und Krise von Kommunikation: Inszenierungen literarischer und sozialer Interaktion im Mittelalter* (Berlin, 2006), 355–70.

Corsi, Pasquale, *La traslazione di San Nicola: le fonti* (Bari, 1988).

'La coscienza cittadina nei Comuni italiani del duocento', *Convegni del Centro di Studi sulla Spiritualità Medievale* 11 (Todi, 1972).

Cowdrey, H.E.J., 'Pope Gregory VII and the Liturgy', *Journal of Theological Studies* 55(1) (2004): 55–83.

——, *Pope Gregory VII (1073–1085)* (Oxford, 1998).

——, *The Age of Abbot Desiderius: Montecassino, the Papacy, and the Normans in the Eleventh and Early Twelfth Centuries* (Oxford, 1983).

——, 'The Anglo-Norman Laudes Regiae', *Viator* 12 (1981): 37–78.

——, *The Cluniacs and the Gregorian Reform* (Oxford, 1970).

——, 'Pope Urban II's Preaching of the First Crusade', *History* 55 (1970): 177–88, reprinted in Thomas F. Madden (ed.), *The Crusades: The Essential Readings* (Oxford, 2002), 15–30.

——, The Papacy, Patarenes and the Church of Milan', *Transactions of the Royal Historical Society*, ser. 5, 18 (1968): 25–48.

Cracco, Giorgio, 'Cattedrale, città, territorio: l'esempio di Modena', in Augusto Bergamini (ed.), *Atti dell'VIII centenario della dedicazione del Duomo di Modena (1184–1984)*, 90–101.

Crozet, R., 'Etudes sur les consécrations pontificales', *Bulletin Monumental* 104 (1946): 5–46.

——, 'Le voyage d'Urbain II et ses négociations avec le clergé de France (1095–1096)', *Revue Historique* 179 (1937): 271–310.

——, 'Le voyage d'Urbain II en France (1095–1096) et son importance au point de vue archéologique', *Annales du Midi* 49 (1937): 42–69.

Cushing, Kathleen G., *Reform and the Papacy in the Eleventh Century: Spirituality and Social Change* (Manchester, 2005).

——, 'Anselm of Lucca and Burchard of Worms: Re-thinking the Sources of Anselm II, *De Penitentia*', in Cushing and Gyug, *Ritual, Text and Law*, 225–40.

——, *Papacy and Law in the Gregorian Revolution: The Canonistic Work of Anselm of Lucca* (Oxford, 1998).

Cushing, Kathleen G. and Richard F. Gyug (eds), *Ritual, Text and Law: Studies in Medieval Canon Law and Liturgy Presented to Roger E. Reynolds* (Aldershot, 2004).

Dale, Thomas E.A., 'Inventing a Sacred Past: Pictorial Narratives of St Mark the Evangelist in Aquileia and Venice, ca. 1000–1300', *Dumbarton Oaks Papers* 48 (1994): 53–104.

Dameron, George, *Episcopal Power and Florentine Society* (Cambridge, MA, 1991).

Demus, Otto, *The Mosaics of San Marco in Venice*, 2 Vols (Chicago, 1984).

DeRossi, G.B., 'Degli Alfabeti che il Vescovo scribe sulla Croce Decussata ne Consecrare le Chiese', *Bulletino di Archaeologia Cristiana* (1881): 140–95.

Dischner, Margit, *Humbert von Silva Candida: Werk und Wirkung des lothringischen Reformmönches* (Novotny, Starnberg, 1996).

Dormeier, Heinrich, *Montecassino und die Laien im 11. und 12. Jahrhundert* (Stuttgart, 1979).

Douglas, Mary, *Purity and Danger: An Analysis of Concepts of Pollution and Taboo* (New York, 1966).

Duffy, Eamon, *Stripping of the Altars: Traditional Religion in England, c.1400–c.1580* (New Haven, 1992).

Duncalf, Frederic, 'The Councils of Piacenza and Clermont', in Marshall Baldwin (ed.), *A History of the Crusades*, Vol. 1, *The First Hundred Years* (Philadelphia, 1955), 220–52.

Egidi, Pietro, *Necrologi e libri affini della provincia Romana, Fonti per la storia d'Italia* 44 (Rome, 1908).

Eisenhofer, Ludwig, *The Liturgy of the Roman Rite* (New York, 1961).

Epstein, Ann Wharton, 'Date and Significance of Canossa Cathedral in Apulia', *Dumbarton Oaks Papers* 37 (1983): 79–90.

Farmer, Sharon, *Communities of St. Martin: Legend and Ritual in Medieval Tours* (Ithaca, 1991).

Fasoli, Gina, 'La Cattedrale nella civiltà comunale', in Augusto Bergamini (ed.), *Atti dell'VIII centenario della dedicazione del Duomo di Modena (1184–1984)* (Modena, 1986), 114–30.

Fassler, Margot, *Gothic Song: Victorine Sequences and Augustinian Reform in Twelfth-Century Paris* (Cambridge, 1993).

Ferraro, Giuseppe, *Lo Spirito Santo nei commentari al quarto vangelo di Bruno di Segni, Ruperto di Deutz, Bonaventura, e Alberto Magno* (Vatican City, 1998).

Filieri, Maria Teresa, *Architettura Medioevale in Diocesi di Lucca: Le Pievi del Territorio di Capannori* (Lucca, 1990).

Flanigan, C. Clifford, 'The Apocalypse and the Medieval Liturgy', in Richard K. Emmerson and Bernard McGinn (eds), *The Apocalypse in the Middle Ages* (Ithaca, 1992), 333–51.

Fliche, Augustin, *La Réforme grégorienne*, 3 Vols (Louvain, 1924).

Fonseca, Cosimo Damiano, 'Il movimento canonicale a Lucca e nella diocesi lucchese tra XI e XII secolo', in Cinzio Violante (ed.), *Allucio da Pescia (1070 c.a.–1134): Un santo laico dell'età postgregoriana. Religione e società nei territori di Lucca e della Valdinievole*, Pubblicazioni del Dipartimento di Medievistica dell'Università di Pisa, 2 (Rome, 1991), 147–57.

Fontaine, Michelle M., 'Back to the Future: Remaking the Commune in Ducal Modena', in Paula Findlen, Michelle M. Fontaine, and Duane J. Osheim (eds), *Beyond Florence: The Contours of Medieval and Early Modern Italy* (Stanford, 2003).

Foote, David, *Lordship, Reform and the Development of Civil Society in Medieval Italy* (Notre Dame, 2004).

Forcella, Vincenzo, *Iscrizioni delle chiese e d'altri edificii di Roma dal secolo XI fino ai giorni nostri* (Rome, 1869–84).

Fornasari, Giuseppe, *Medioevo riformato del secolo XI: Pier Damiani e Gregorio VII* (Naples, 1996).

——, 'S. Pier Damiani e lo "sciopero liturgico"', *Studie Medievali*, ser. 3 an. 17, f. 2 (1976): 815–32.

Fournier, Paul and Gabriel Le Bras, *Histoire des collections canoniques en Occident depuis les décrétales jusqu'au décret de Gratien*, 2 Vols (Paris: Recueil Sirey, 1932).

Fransen, Gérard, 'Anselme de Lucques Canoniste?', in Violante, *Sant'Anselmo Vescovo*, 143–55.

——, 'Réflexions sur l'étude des collections canoniques à l'occasion de l'édition d'une lettre de Bruno De Segni', *Studi Gregoriani* 9 (1972): 515–33.

Frassetto, Michael (ed.), *Medieval Purity and Piety: Essays on Medieval Clerical Celibacy and Religious Reform* (New York, 1998).

Frazee, Charles A., 'The Origins of Clerical Celibacy in the Western Church', *Church History* 41(2) (June 1972): 149–67.

Frisone, C., 'Dodone', *Dizionario Biografico degli Italiani*, Vol. 40 (Rome, 1991), 355–7.

Funkenstein, J., *Das Alte Testament im Kampf von regnum und sacerdotium zur Zeit des Investiturstreits* (Dortmund, 1938).

Galante, Maria, 'Esperienze Grafiche a Cava ne XII secolo, Il Cod. Cav. 6', *Archivio Storico per le Provincie Napoletane* ann. 21 (1982), 7–25.

Galavotti, Pietro, *Le più antiche fonti storiche del Sumomo di Modena* (Modena, 1972).

Gandolfo, Francesco, 'Note per una interpretazione iconologica delle Storie del Genesi di Wilgelmo', in Arturo Carlo Quintavalle (ed.), *Romanico padano, romanico europeo* (Parma, 1982), 323–37.

Geary, Patrick, *Furta Sacra: Thefts of Relics in the Central Middle Ages* (Princeton, 1978).

Gigalski, Bernhard, *Bruno, Bischof von Segni, Abt von Monte-Cassino (1049–1123): sein Leben und seine Schriften: ein Beitrag zur Kirchengeschichte im Zeitalter des Investiturstreites, und zur theologischen Litteraturgeschichte des Mittelalters* (Münster, 1898).

Gilchrist, J.T., 'Gregory VII and the Juristic Sources of His Ideology', *Studia Gratiana XII* (1967): 3–37.

——, 'Humbert of Silva-Candida and the Political Concept of *Ecclesia* in the Eleventh Century Reform Movement', *Journal of Religious History* 2 (1962–1963): 13–28.

Giusti, M., 'Le canoniche della città e diocesi di Lucca al tempo della Riforma Gregoriana', *Studi Gregoriani* 3 (1948): 321–67.

Glass, Dorothy, 'Revisiting the "Gregorian Reform"', in C. Hourihane (ed.), *Romanesque Art and Thought in the Twelfth Century* (Princeton, 2008), 200–18.

——, 'The Bishops of Piacenza, their Cathedral, and the Reform of the Church', in John S. Ott and Anna Trumbore Jones (eds), *The Bishop Reformed: Studies in Episcopal Power and Culture in the Central Middle Ages* (Aldershot, 2007), 219–36.

——, 'Prophecy and Priesthood at Modena', *Zeitschrift für Kunstgeschichte* 63(3) (2000): 326–38.

——, *Studies on Cosmatesque Pavements* (Oxford, 1980).

——, 'Papal Patronage in the Early Twelfth Century: Notes on the Iconography of Cosmatesque Pavements', *Journal of the Warburg and Courtauld Institutes* 32 (1969): 386–90.

Goetz, Hans-Werner, 'Protection of the Church, Defense of the Law, and Reform: On the Purposes and Character of the Peace of God, 989–1073', in Head and Landes, *Peace of God*, 259–79.

Goez, W., 'Reformpapsttum, Adel und monastiche Erneuerung in der Toscana', in J. Fleckenstein (ed.), *Investiturstreit und Reichsverfassung* (Sigmaringen, 1973), 205–39.

Golinelli, Paolo, *Città e culto dei santi nel Medioevo italiano* (Bologna, 1996).

——, *Indiscreta sanctitatis: studi sui rapporti tra culti, poteri e società nel pieno medioevo* (Rome, 1988).

——, 'Dall'Agiografia all Storia: Le "Vitae" di Sant'Anselmo di Lucca', in *Sant'Anselmo, Mantova, e la Lotta per Le Investiture*, Atti del convegno internazionale di studi (Mantova 23-25 maggio 1986), ed. Paolo Golinelli (Bologna, 1987), 27-79.

——, *La Pataria, lotte religiose e sociali nella Milano dell'XI secolo* (Milan, 1984).

Grégoire, Reginald, 'Liturgia e agiografia a Lucca durante gli episcopati di Giovanni II (1023-1056), Anselmo I (1056-1073) e Anselmo II (1073-1086)', in Violante, *Sant'Anselmo Vescovo*, 273-82.

——, *Bruno de Segni: exégète mediéval et théologien monastique* (Spoleto, 1965).

Guidi, Pietro , (ed.), 'Per la storia della cattedrale e del Volto Santo', *Bolletino Storico Lucchese* (1932): 169-86.

Guidobaldi, Federico, *Il Complesso Archeologico di San Clemente: Resulti degli scavi più recenti e riesame dei resti architettonici* (Rome, 1978).

Gunhouse, Glenn, 'The Fresco Decoration of Sant'Angelo in Formis' (PhD diss., Johns Hopkins University, 1992).

Gyug, Richard F., 'The Pontificals of Monte Cassino', *L'Età dell'abate Desiderio*, Atti del IV Convegno di studi sul medioevo Meridionale (Montecassino – Cassino, 4-8 ottobre, 1987) (3 Vols), ed. Faustino Avagliano and Oronzo Pecere (Montecassino, 1992), Vol. 3, 413-39.

——, 'A Pontifical of Benevento (Macerata, Biblioteca Comunale "Mozzi-Borgetti" 378)', *Mediaeval Studies* 51 (1989): 355-423.

——,'The Milanese Church and the Gregorian Reform', *Scintila* 2-3 (Toronto, 1985-86): 29-65.

Hamilton, Louis I., 'Les Dangers du ritual dans l'Italie du XIe siècle: entre textes liturgiques et témoignages historiques', in Didier Méhu (ed.), *Mises en scène et mémoires de la consécration de l'église dans l'occident médieval* (Turnhout, 2007), 159-88.

——, 'Decor et Decorum: Reforming the Episcopacy in Bruno of Segni's *De laudibus ecclesiae* (Eleventh Century)' (LMS diss., Pontifical Institute of Mediaeval Studies, 2007).

——, 'To Consecrate the Church: Ecclesiastical Reform and the Dedication of Churches', in Christopher M. Bellitto and Louis I. Hamilton (eds), *Reforming the Church before Modernity: Problems, Patterns and Approaches* (Aldershot, 2005), 105-37.

——, 'Desecration and Consecration in Norman Capua, 1062-1122: Contesting Sacred Space during the Gregorian Reforms', *Haskins Society Journal* 14 (2005): 137-50.

——, 'Sexual Purity, "The Faithful", and Religious Reform in Eleventh-Century Italy: Donatism Revisited', in Kim Paffenroth et al. (eds), *Augustine and Politics* (Lanham, MD, 2005), 237-59.

——, 'Memory, Symbol and Arson: Was Rome "Sacked" in 1084?', *Speculum* (2003): 378-99.

——, 'The Power of Liturgy and the Liturgy of Power in Eleventh- and Twelfth-Century Italy' (PhD diss., Fordham University, 2000).

Hamilton, Sarah, *The Practice of Penance, 900-1050* (Woodbridge, Suffolk, 2001).

——, and Andrew Spicer, 'Defining the Holy: the Delineation of Sacred Space', in Andrew Spicer and Sarah Hamilton (eds), *Defining the Holy: Sacred Space in Medieval and Early Modern Europe* (Aldershot, 2005), 1-23.

Hankey, Wayne J., 'Self and Cosmos in becoming Deiform: Neoplatonic Paradigms for Reform by Self-knowledge from Augustine to Aquinas', in Bellitto and Hamilton, *Reforming the Church before Modernity*, 39–60.

Harris, Jennifer A., 'Building Heaven on Earth: Cluny as *Locus Sanctissimus* in the Eleventh Century', in Susan Boynton and Isabelle Cochelin (eds), *From Dead of Night to End of Day: the Medieval Customs of Cluny* (Turnhout, 2005), 131–51.

——, 'The Body as Temple in the High Middle Ages', in Albert I. Baumgarten (ed.), *Sacrifice in Religious Experience* (Leiden, 2002), 233–56.

——, 'Peter Damian and the Architecture of the Self', in Gert Melville and Markus Schürer (eds), *Das Eigen und das Ganze: Zum Individuellen im mittelalterlichen Religiosentum* (Münster, 2002), 131–57.

Haskins, Charles Homer, *The Renaissance of the Twelfth Century* (Cambridge, MA, 1927).

Hay, David J., *The Military Leadership of Matilda of Canossa, 1046–1115* (Manchester, 2008).

Head, Thomas and Richard Landes (eds), *The Peace of God, Social Violence and Religious Response in France around the Year 1000* (Ithaca, 1992).

——, 'Introduction', *Peace of God*, 3–9.

Healy, Patrick, *The Chronicle of Hugh of Flavigny: Reform and the Investiture Contest in the Late Eleventh Century* (Aldershot, 2006).

Hobsbawm, Eric, 'Introduction: Inventing Traditions', in Eric Hobsbawm and Terrence Ranger (eds), *The Invention of Tradition* (Cambridge, 1983), 1–14.

Hodges, Richard, *Light in the Dark Ages: The Rise and Fall of San Vincenzo al Volturno* (Ithaca, 1997).

Hoffmann, Hartmut, 'Die Älteren Abtslisten von Montecassino', *Quellen und Forschungen* 47 (1967): 224–354.

——, *Gottesfriede und Treuga Dei*, MGH Schriften 20 (Stuttgart, 1964).

Horie, Ruth, *Perceptions of Ecclesia: Church and Soul in Medieval Dedication Sermons* (Turnhout, 2006).

Houben, H., *Roger II of Sicily: A Ruler between East and West*, trans. Graham A. Loud and Diane Milburn (Cambridge, 2002).

——, 'La Chiesa di Bari alla fine dell' XI secolo', in Salvatore Palese and Giancarlo Locatelli (eds), *Il Concilio di Bari del 1098: Atti del Convegno Storico Internazionale e celebrazione dei IX Centenario del Concilio* (Bari, 1998), 91–107.

Howe, John, *Church Reform and Social Change In Eleventh-Century Italy: Dominic of Sora and His Patrons* (Philadelphia, 1997).

Hrbata, Joseph, 'De expositione missae Walfradi Strabonis', *Ephemerides Liturgicae* 63 (1949): 146–7.

Hülls, Rudolf, *Kardinal, Klerus und Kirchen Roms, 1049–1130* (Tübingen, 1977).

Hülsen, Christian, *Le chiese di Roma nel medioevo* (Florence, 1927).

Illich, Ivan, *In the Vineyard of the Text: a Commentary on Hugh's Didascalicon* (Chicago, 1993).

Iogna-Prat, Dominique, *Order and Exclusion: Cluny and Christendom face Heresy, Judaism and Islam (1000–1150)*, trans. Graham Robert Edwards (Ithaca, 2002).

——, 'Lieu de culte et exégèse liturgique à l'époque carolingienne', in Celia Chazelle and Burton Van Name Edwards (eds), *The Study of the Bible in the Carolingian Era* (Turnhout, Brepols, 2003): 215–44.

Jaffé, Philipp and Wilhelm Wattenbach et al., *Regesta pontificum romanorum ab condita ecclesia ad annum post Christum natum MCXCVIII*, 2 Vols (Leipzig, 1885).

Jensen, Brian Møller, *Tropes and Sequences in the Liturgy of the Church in Piacenza in the Twelfth Century: An Analysis and an Edition of the Texts*. Texts and Studies in Religion 92 (Lewiston, 2002).

Jestice, Phyllis G., 'Why Celibacy? Odo of Cluny and the Development of a new Sexual Morality', in Frassetto, *Medieval Purity and Piety*, 81–115.

Jones, Christopher A., 'The Book of Liturgy in Anglo-Saxon England', *Speculum* 73 (1998): 659–702.

Jones, Philip, *The Italian City-State: From Commune to Signoria* (Oxford, 1997).

Kantorowicz, Ernst, *The King's Two Bodies: A Study in Mediaeval Political Theology* (Princeton, 1957).

——, *Laudes Regiae: A Study in Liturgical Acclamations and Medieval Ruler Worship* (Berkeley, 1946).

Kehr, Paul F., *Regesta Pontificum Romanorum*, Vol. 1: *Roma* (Berlin, 1961 [1906]).

——, *Italia pontificia, sive, Repertorium privilegiorum et litterarum a Romanis pontificibus* (Berlin, 1906–).

Keller, H., 'Le origini sociali e famigliari del vescovo Anselmo', in Violante, *Sant'Anselmo Vescovo*, 27–50.

Kertzer, David I., *Ritual, Politics, and Power* (New Haven, 1988).

Kessler, Herbert L., 'On the State of Medieval Art History', *Art Bulletin* 70 (1988): 166–87.

Kinney, Dale., 'Fact and Fiction in the *Mirabilia Urbis Romae*', in Éamonn Ócarragáin and Carol Neman de Vegvar (eds), Roma Felix – *Formation and Reflections of Medieval Rome* (Aldershot, 2007), 235–52.

——, 'Rome in the Twelfth Century: *Urbs fracta* and *renovatio*', *Gesta* 45(2) (2006): 199–220.

Kittel, E., 'Der Kampf um die Reform des Domkapitels in Lucca im 11. Jahrhundert', in L. Santifaller (ed.), *Festschrift Albert Brackmann* (Weimar, 1931), 207–47.

Kitzinger, E., 'The Gregorian Reform and the Visual Arts: A Problem of Method', *Transactions of the Royal Historical Society*, 5th ser., 22 (1972): 87–102.

Klauser, T., *A Short History of the Western Liturgy* (Oxford, 1979).

Kosto, Adam J., 'Reasons for Assembly in Catalonia and Aragón, 900–1200', in P.S. Barnwell and M. Mostert (eds), *Political Assemblies in the Earlier Middle Ages* (Turnhout, 2003), 133–50.

Kozachek, Thomas Davies, 'The Repertory of Chant for Dedicating Churches in the Middle Ages: Music, Liturgy and Ritual' (Ph.D. diss. Harvard University, 1995).

Koziol, Geoffrey, *Begging Pardon and Favor: Ritual and Political Order in Early Medieval France* (Ithaca, 1992).

Krautheimer, Richard, *Rome: Profile of a City* (Princeton, 1980).

——, *Corpus basilicarum christianorum Romae: The Early Christian Basilicas of Rome (IV–IX Cent.)*, 5 Vols (Vatican City, 1937–77).

Ladner, Gerhart, *Theologie und Politik vor dem Investiturstreit: Abendmahlstreit/ Kirchenreform, Cluni und Heinrich III* (Brünn, 1936).

Lavermicocca, Nino, 'Il Pretorio Bizantino di Bari', in Michele D'Elia (ed.), *Città della Nicoliana: Un progetto verso il 2000* (Bari, 1995), 25–31.

Leone, Simone, 'La data di fondazione della Badia di Cava', in Simeone Leone and Giovanni Vitolo (eds), *Minima Cevensia: studi in margine al ix volume del* Codex Diplomaticus Cavensis (Salerno, 1983), 45–59.

Lerner, Robert E., 'Paschal II, Pope', in Strayer, *Dictionary of the Middle Ages* 9, 444–6.

Lewis, Gilbert, *Day of Shining Red: An Essay on Understanding Ritual* (Cambridge, 1980).

Little, Lester K., *Religious Poverty and the Profit Economy* (Ithaca, 1983).

Liturgie et musique (IXe–XIVe s.), Cahiers de Fanjeaux: Collection d'histoire religieuse du Languedoc au XIIIe et au début du XIVe siècles 17 (Toulouse, 1982).

Lobrichon, Guy, 'Riforma ecclesiastica e testo della Bibbia', in Marilena Maniaci e Giulia Orofino (eds), *Le Bibbie atlantiche: il libro delle Scritture tra monumnetalità e rappresentazione* (Rome, 2000), 15–26.

Lombardi, Ferruccio, *Roma: Chiese, Conventi, Chiostri. Progetto per un inventario, 313–1925* (Rome, 1993).

Loud, G.A., *The Latin Church in Norman Italy* (Cambridge, 2007).

——, 'Monastic Chronicles in the Twelfth-Century Abruzzi', *Anglo Norman Studies* 27 (2004): 101–31.

——, *The Age of Robert Guiscard: Southern Italy and the Norman Conquest* (Harlow, 2000).

——, 'Nunneries, Nobles and Women in the Norman Principality of Capua', *Annali Canossani 1, Reggio Emilia* (1981), 45–62; repr. in *Conquerors and Churchmen in Norman Italy* (Aldershot, 1999).

——, *Church and Society in the Norman Principality of Capua, 1058–1197* (Oxford, 1985).

Lucchesi, Giovanni, 'Il Sermonario di S. Pier Damian come monumento storico agiografico e liturgico', *Studi Gregoriani* 10 (1975): 7–67.

——, 'Per una vita di San Pier Damian', in *San Pier Damini nel IX centenario della morte (1072–1972)*, 4 Vols (Cesena, 1972–3), 1, 26–8.

Maccarone, M., 'La Storia della Cattedra', in *La Cattedra Lignea di S. Pietro in Vaticano: Atti della Pontifica Academia Romana di Archeologia*, ser. III, Memorie X (Vatican, 1971), 3–70.

Magnou-Nortier, Elisabeth, 'The Enemies of the Church: Reflections on a Vocabulary, 500–1100', in Head and Landes, *Peace of God*, 58–79.

Markus, Robert A., *The End of Ancient Christianity* (Cambridge, 1990).

Martimort, Aimé-Georges et al., *L'Eglise en prière: Introduction à la liturgie* (Paris, 1961).

Martini, Paola Supino, *Roma e l'Area Grafica Romanesca (Secoli X–XII)* (Alessandria, 1987).

Matter, E. Ann, *Voice of My Beloved* (Philadelphia, 1990).

Matthew, Donald, *The Norman Kingdom of Sicily* (Cambridge, 1992).

McGinley, J. and H. Mursurillo, trans., 'An Anonymous Greek Account of the Transfer of the Body of Saint Nicholas from Myra in Lycia to Bari in Italy', *Bolletino di S. Nicola*, N. 10, *Studi e testi* (Bari: October 1980): 3-17.

Mégier, E., 'Otto of Freising's Revendication of Isaiah as the Prophet of Constantine's "Exaltation of the Church" in the Context of Christian Latin exegesis', *Sacris erudiri* 42 (2003): 287-326.

Méhu, Didier (ed.), *Mises en scène et mémoires de la consécration de l'église dans l'occident médieval* (Turnhout, 2007).

——, *Paix et communautés autour de l'abbaye de Cluny, Xe–XVe siècles* (Lyons, 2001).

——, Les Cercles de la domination clunisienne', *Annales de Bourgogne* 72 (2000): 337-96.

Meyvaert, Paul (ed.), *The Codex Benedictus: An Eleventh-Century Lectionary from Monte Cassino, Vat Lat 1202*, Codices e Vaticanis Selectis Quam Simile Expressi Iussu Ioannis Paulus PP II Consilio et Opera Curatorum Bibliothecae Vaticanae, Vol. L (New York, 1982).

Miccoli, Giovanni, 'Chiesa Gregoriana: Ricerche sulla Riforma del secolo XI', *Storici antichi e moderni* 17 (Florence, 1966).

Miedema, Nine Robijnte, *Die 'Mirabilia Romae': Untersuchungen zu ihrer Überlieferung mit Edition der deutschen und niederländischen Texte* (Tübingen, 1996).

Miller, Maureen, *The Bishop's Palace: Architecture and Authority in Medieval Italy* (Ithaca, 2000).

——, *The Formation of a Medieval Church: Ecclesiastical Change in Verona, 950–1150* (Cornell, 1993).

Mollat, Michel, *The Poor in the Middle Ages: a Social History*, trans. Arthur Goldhammer (New Haven, 1986).

Montorsi, William, *Il Duomo di Modena: 'Palinsesto' Lanfranchiano-Campionese, 1099–1999, Nono centenario della fondazione del Duomo 'di Lanfranco'* (Modena, 1999).

Moore, R.I., *The First European Revolution, c.970–1215* (Oxford, 2000).

——, 'Postscript: The Peace of God and the Social Revolution', in Head and Landes, *Peace of God*, 308-26.

——, *The Formation of a Persecuting Society: Power and Deviance in Western Europe, 950–1250* (Oxford, 1987).

——, Family, Community and Cult on the Eve of the Gregorian Reform', *Transactions of the Royal Historical Society*, 5th Ser., 30 (1980): 49-69.

——, *Origins of European Dissent* (New York, 1977, repr. Toronto, 1994).

Morris, Colin, *The Papal Monarchy: The Western Church from 1050 to 1250* (Oxford, 1989).

Mosey, Douglas L., 'Allegorical Liturgical Interpretation in the West 800 AD to 1200 AD' (PhD diss., University of Toronto, 1985).

Motta, Giuseppe, 'I codici canonistici di Polirone', in Violante, *Sant'Anselmo, Vescovo*, 349-71.

Muncey, R.W., *A History of the Consecration of Churches and Churchyards* (Cambridge, 1930).

Mundy, John Hine, *Studies in the Ecclesiastical and Social History of Toulouse in the Age of the Cathars* (Aldershot, 2006).

Mussini, Massimo, 'Pievi e vita canonicale nei territori matildici: Architettura e riforma gregoriana nella campagne', in Quintavalle, *Romanico padano*, 27–53.

Neale, John Mason and Benjamin Webb, *The Symbolism of Churches and Church Ornamentation* (London, 1906).

Nitti di Vito, F., 'La Traslazione di S. Nicola di Bari (1087 o 1071?)', *Iapigia*, n.s 10 (1939): 374–82.

——, 'Leggenda di S. Nicola', *Iapigia*, n.s. 8 (1937): 265–74.

——, 'La Traslazione delle reliquie di S. Nicola', *Iapigia*, n.s. 8 (1937): 295–411.

——, *La Leggenda della Traslazione di S. Nicola di Bari, I Marinai* (Trani, 1902).

Noble, Thomas F.X., *The Republic of St. Peter: The Birth of the Papal State (680–825)* (Philadelphia, 1984).

North, William, 'Negotiating Public Orthodoxy in the "Pravilegium" Dispute of 1111/1112: The Evidence of Bruno of Segni', in S. Elm, E. Rebillard and Antonella Romano (eds), *Orthodoxie, christianisme, histoire = Orthodoxy, christianity, history* (Rome, 2000), 199–220.

——, 'In the Shadows of Reform: Exegesis and the Formation of a Clerical Elite in the Works of Bruno of Segni (1078/9–1123)' (PhD diss., University of California Berkeley 1998).

Orme, Nicholas, *English Church Dedications, With a Survey of Cornwall and Devon* (Exeter, 1996).

Osheim, Duane J., 'The Episcopal Archive of Lucca in the Middle Ages', *Manuscripta* 17 (1973): 131–46.

Palazzo, Eric, 'Le Végétal et le sacré: l'hysope dans le rite de la dédicace de l'église', in Cushing and Gyug, *Ritual, Text and Law*, 41–50.

——, *L'Évêque et son image: l'illustration du pontifical au Moyen Âge* (Turnhout, 1999).

Passarelli, G. (ed.), *Il santo patrono nella città medievale: il culto di s. Valentino nella storia di Terni* (Rome, 1982).

Pásztor, E., 'La "Vita" anonima di Anselmo di Lucca: Una rilettura', in Violante, *Sant'Anselmo Vescovo*, 207–22.

——, 'Una fonte per la storia dell' età gregoriana: la *Vita Anselmi episcopi Lucensis*', *Bolletino dell'istituto storico italiano per il Medio Evo e archivio Muraturiano* 72 (1960), 1–33.

Paxton, Frederick S., 'History, Historians and the Peace of God', in Head and Landes, *Peace of God*, 21–40.

Picasso, Giorgio, 'La "Collectio Canonum" di Anselmo nella storia dell collezioni canoniche', in Violante, *Sant'Anselmo Vescovo*, 313–21.

Pistoni, Giuseppe, *San Geminiano: Vescovo e prottetore di Modena nella vita nel culto nell'arte* (Modena, 1983).

——, 'Matilde di Canossa ed il Duomo di Modena', in *Studi Matildici, atti e memorie de convegno di studi Matildici, Modena and Reggio Emilia, 19–21 Ottobre 1963* (Modena, 1964), 104–9.

Priester, Ann Edith, 'The Bell Towers of Medieval Rome and the Architecture of *Renovatio*' (Princeton University: PhD diss., 1990).

Quintavalle, Arturo Carlo, 'Figure della Riforma in occidente', in Arturo Carlo Quintavalle (ed.), *Il Medioevo delle Cattedrali, Chiese e Impero: la lotta delle immagini (secoli XI e XII)* (Parma, 2006), 239–90.

——, *Basilica, Cattedrale di Parma: Novecento anni di arte, storia, fede,* 3 vols (Parma, 2005).

——, *Wiligelmo e Matilde: L'officina romanica* (Milan, 1991).

——, (ed.), *Romanico padano, romanico europeo* (Parma, 1982).

——, *La cattedrale di Parma e il romanico europeo* (Parma, 1974).

——, *La cattedrale di Modena: problemi di romanico emiliano,* 2 Vols (Modena, 1965).

Rabe, Susan A., 'The Mind's Eye: Theological Controversy and Religious Architecture in the Reign of Charlemagne', in Lizette Larson-Miller, *Medieval Liturgy: A Book of Essays* (New York, 1977), 235–66.

Ramseyer, Valerie, *The Transformation of a Religious Landscape: Medieval Southern Italy, 850–1150* (Ithaca, 2006).

Rappaport, Roy A., 'Veracity, Verity, and *Verum* in Liturgy', *Studia Liturgica* 23 (1993): 35–50.

Remensnyder, Amy G., 'Pollution, Purity, and Peace: An Aspect of Social Reform in the Late Tenth Century', in Cushing and Landes, *Peace of God,* 280–307.

Repsher, Brian Vincent, 'The Abecedarium: Catechetical Symbolism in the Rite of Church Dedication', *Mediaevalia* 24 (2003): 1–18.

——, *The Rite of Church Dedication in the Early Medieval Era* (Lewiston, NY, 1998).

Reynolds, Roger E., 'Les Cérémonies liturgiques de la cathédrale de Bénévent', in Thomas Forrest Kelly (ed.), *La Cathédrale de Bénévent* (Ghent, 1999), 167–205.

——, 'Law, Canon: To Gratian', in Strayer, *Dictionary of the Middle Ages* 7, 395–413.

——, 'Odilo and the *Treuga Dei* in Southern Italy: A Beneventan Manuscript Fragment', *Mediaeval Studies* 46 (1984): 450–62.

——, 'Liturgical Scholarship at the Time of the Investiture Controversy: Past Research and Future Opportunities', *Harvard Theological Review* 71 (1978): 109–24.

Ricci, Furio (ed.), *La Basilica di Sant'Abbondio in Como: IX centenario della Consecrazione* (Como, 1996).

Riccioni, Stefano, *Il Mosaico Absidiale di S. Clemente a Roma:* Exemplum *della chiesa riformata* (Spoleto, 2006).

Robinson, I.S., *The Papal Reform of the Eleventh Century: the Lives of Leo IX and Gregory VII* (Manchester, 2004).

——, *Henry IV of Germany, 1056–1106* (Cambridge, 1999).

——, *The Papacy, 1073–1198: Continuity and Innovation* (Cambridge, 1990).

——, '"Political Allegory" in the Biblical Exegesis of Bruno of Segni', *Recherches de théologie ancienne et médiévale* 50 (1983): 69–98.

——, *Authority and Resistance in the Investiture Conflict: The Polemical Literature of the Late Eleventh Century* (New York, 1978).

Robison, Elaine Golden, 'Humbert of Silva Candida', in Strayer, *Dictionary of the Middle Ages* 6, 329–30.

Rosenwein, Barbara, 'Worrying About Emotions in History', *American Historical Review* 107(3) (June 2002): 821–45.

——, *Negotiating Space: Power, Restraint, and Privileges of Immunity in Early Medieval Europe* (Ithaca, 1999).

——, *To be the Neighbor of St. Peter: The Social Meaning of Cluny's Property, 909–1049* (Ithaca, 1989).

Rubin, Miri, *Corpus Christi: The Eucharist in Late Medieval Culture* (Cambridge, 1991).

Schettini, Franco, *La Basilica di San Nicola di Bari* (Bari, 1967).

Schramm, Percy Ernst, *Herrschaftszeichen und Staatssymbolik: Beiträge zur ihrer Geschichte vom dritten bis zum sechszehnten Jahrhundert*, MGH Schriften 13 (1–3) (Stüttgart, 1954–6).

Schumann, Reinhold, *Authority and the Commune, Parma 833–1133* (Parma, 1973).

Schwartz, Eduard (ed.), *Publizistische Sammlungen zum acacianischen Scisma* (Munich, 1934).

Schwarzmaier, Hansmartin, *Lucca und das Reich bis zum Ende des 11. Jahrhunderts* (Tübingen, 1972).

——, 'Das Kloster St. Georg in Lucca und der Ausgriff Montecassinos in die Toskana', *Quellen und Forschungen* 49 (1969): 145–85.

Servatus, Carl, *Paschal II (1099–1118): 'Studien zu seiner Person und seiner Politik'*, *Päpste und Papsttum* 14 (Stuttgart, 1979).

Sessa, Michela, 'La condizione giuridica della donna nel sec. XI', in Alfonso Leone (ed.), *Appunti per la storia di Cava* (Cava dei Terreni, 1983), 15–20.

Settia, Aldo A., '"Ecclesiam Incastellare": Chiese e Castelli in Diocesi di Padova', in his *Chiese, Strade e Fortezze*, 67–97.

——, *Chiese, Strade e Fortezze nell'Italia Medievale*, Italia Sacra 46 (Rome, 1991).

——, 'Églises et fortifications médiévales dans l'Italie du nord', in Aldo Settia, *L'Église et le château: Xe–XVIIe siècles* (Bordeaux, 1988), 81–94.

——, 'Chiese e fortezze nel popolamento delle diocesi friulane', in Giuseppe Fornasir, *Il Friuli dagli Ottoni agli Hohenstaufen, Atti del convegno internazionale di studi* (Udine, 1984), 217–44.

——, '*Ecclesiam incastellare*: Chiese e castelli nella diocesi di Padova in alcune recenti pubblicazioni', *Fonti e studi di storia ecclesiastica padovana* (XII) (Padua, 1981), 47–75.

Sheerin, Daniel J., 'Dedication "Ordo" Used at Fulda, 1 Nov., 819' *Revue Bénédictine* (1982): 304–16.

Smalley, Beryl, 'Ecclesiastical Attitudes to Novelty: c.1100–1250', in Smalley, *Studies in Medieval Thought and Learning from Abelard to Wyclif* (London, 1981), 97–115.

Silva, Romano, 'La Ricostruzione della Cattedrale di Lucca (1060–1070): Un Esempio Precoce di Architettura della Riforma Gregoriana', in Violante, *Sant'Anselmo Vescovo*, 297–309.

Skinner, Patricia, *Family Power in Southern Italy* (Cambridge, 1995).

Smalley, Beryl, *The Becket Conflict and the Schools: A Study of Intellectuals in Politics* (Oxford, 1973).

Somerville, Robert, *Pope Urban II, The Collectio Britannica, and the Council of Melfi (1089)* (Oxford, 1996).

——, *The Councils of Urban II*, Vol. 1, *Decreta Claromontensia* (Amsterdam, 1970).

——, 'The Council of Clermont (1095), and Latin Christian Society', *Archivium Historiae Pontificiae* 12 (1974): 55–90, reprinted in Somerville, *Papacy, Councils and Canon Law in the 11th–12th Centuries* (Aldershot, 1990).

——, 'The French Councils of Pope Urban II: Some Basic Considerations', *Annuarium Historiae Conciliorum* 2 (Augsburg, 1970): 56–65, repr. in Somerville, *Papacy, Councils and Canon Law in the 11th–12th Centuries* (Aldershot, 1990).

Somigli, Constanzo, 'San Pier Damiano e la Pataria', *San Pier Damiano nel IX centenario della morte (1072–1972)*, 4 Vols, Centro studi e ricerche sulla antica provincia ecclesiastica ravennate (Cesena, 1972).

Speciale, Lucinia: 'Montecassino, Il classicismo e l'arte della Riforma', in Avagliano, *Desiderio di Montecassino e l'arte*, 107–46.

——, 'Montecassino e la Riforma Gregoriana: L'Exultet Vat. Barb. Lat. 592', *Studi di Arte Medievale 3* (Rome, 1991).

—— and Giuseppina Torriero Nardone, 'La Basilica e gli affreschi desideriani di S. Benedetto di Capua', in Avagliano, *Desiderio di Montecassino e l'arte*, 147–88.

Spiegel, Gabrielle M., 'Political Utility in Medieval Historiography', *History and Theory* 14 (1975): 314–25.

Stickler, Alfonso, 'Il Potere Coattivo Materiale dell Chiesa nella Riforma Gregoriana Secondo Anselmo di Lucca', *Studi Gregoriani* 2 (1947): 235–85.

Stock, Brian, *The Implications of Literacy: Written Language and Models of Interpretation in the Eleventh and Twelfth Centuries* (Princeton, 1987).

Strayer, Joseph (ed.), *Dictionary of the Middle Ages*, 13 Vols (New York, 1982–1989).

Stroll, Mary, *Symbols as Power: the Papacy following the Investiture Contest* (Leiden, 1997).

Swanson, R.N. (ed.), *Unity and Diversity in the Church*, Studies in Church History 32 (Cambridge, 1996).

Szövérffy, Josef, *Religious Lyrics of the Middle Ages* (Berlin, 1983).

Szuromi, Szabolcs Anzelm, *Anselm of Lucca as a Canonist* (Frankfurt am Main, 2006).

Tabacco, Giovanni, *The Struggle for Power in Medieval Italy: Structures of Political Rule* (Cambridge, 1989).

Taylor, Daniel S., 'Bernold of Constance, Canonist and Liturgist of the Gregorian Reform: An Analysis of the Sources in the *Micrologus de ecclesiasticis observationibus*' (PhD diss., University of Toronto, 1995).

Tcherikover, A., 'Reflections of the Investiture Controversy at Nonantola and Modena', *Zeitschrift für Kunstgeschichte*, 60 Bd., H. 2 (1997): 150–65.

Tellenbach, Gerd, *The Church in Western Europe from the Tenth through the Twelfth Century* (Cambridge, 1993).

——, 'La Città di Roma dal IX al XII secolo: Vista dai Contemporanei d'Oltre Frontiera', in Ottorino Bertolini, *Studi Storici in Onore di Ottorino Bartolini* (Pisa, 1972), 679-734.

Thompson, Augustine, *Cities of God: the Religion of the Italian Communes, 1125-1325* (State College, PA, 2005).

Töpfer, Bernhard, 'The Cult of Relics and Pilgrimage in Burgundy and Aquitaine at the Time of the Monastic Reform', trans. János Bak and Thomas Head, in Head and Landes, *Peace of God*, 41-57. Originally published as 'Reliquienkult und Pilgerbewegung zur Zeit der Klosterreform im burgundisch-aquitanischen Gebeit', in Hellmut Kretzschmar (ed.), *Vom Mittelalter zur Neuzeit: Zum 65. Geburtstag von Heinrich Sprömberg* (Berlin, 1956), 420-39.

Toubert, Hélène, 'Didier du Mont-Cassin et l'art de la réforme grégorienne: l'iconographie de l'Ancien Testament à Sant'Angelo in Formis', *Desiderio di Montecassino e l'arte della riforma gregoriana* (Montecassino, 1997), 17-106.

——, *Un Art dirigé: réforme grégorienne et iconographie* (Paris, 1990).

——, 'Le Renouveau paléochrétien à Rome au début du XIIe siècle', *Cahiers archéologiques fin de l'Antiquité et le Moyen Âge* 20 (1970): 99-154.

Toubert, Pierre, 'Pour une histoire de l'environnement économique et social du Mont-Cassin (IXe-XIIe siècles)', *Comptes rendus de l'Académie des Inscriptions et Belles-Lettres, nov.-déc. 1976* (Paris, 1976), 689-702.

——, 'Hérésies et réforme ecclésiastique en Italie au XIe et au XIIe siècles: à propos de deux études récentes', *Revue des études italiennes*, nouv. série VII (Paris, 1961): 58-71 and repr. in Toubert, *Études sur l'Italie médiévale (IXe-XIVe s.)* (London, 1976).

——, 'Essai sur les modèles hagiographiques de la réforme grégorienne', in *Les structures du Latium médiéval - Le Latium méridional et la Sabine du IXe à la fin du XIIe siècle*, Bibliothèque des Ecoles françaises d'Athènes et de Rome, fasc. 221 (Rome, 1973), 806-40.

Twyman, Susan, *Papal Ceremonial at Rome in the Twelfth Century* (London, 2002).

Ughelli, Ferdinando, *Italia Sacra*, 10 Vols (Venice, 1717-22).

Ullman, Walter, *The Growth of Papal Government in the Middle Ages: A study in the Ideological Relation of Clerical to Lay Power* (London, 1965 [1955]).

——, 'Cardinal Humbert and the *Ecclesia Romana*', *Studi Gregoriani* IV (1952): 111-27.

Van Dijk, S.J.P., *The Origins of the Modern Roman Liturgy: The Liturgy of the Papal Court and the Franciscan Order in the Thirteenth Century* (Westminster, MD, 1960).

Vauchez, André, *Lieux sacrés, lieux de culte, sanctuaires, approches terminologiques, méthodologiques, historiques et monographiques* (Rome, 2000).

Violante, Cinzio (ed.), *Sant'Anselmo Vescovo di Lucca (1073-1086) nel quadro delle trasformazioni sociali e della riforma ecclesiastica (atti del convegno internazionale di studio, Lucca 25-28 settembre 1986)* (Rome, 1992).

——, *I Laici nel movimento Patarino: Studi sulla cristianità medioevale* (Milan, 1972).

——, 'I laici nel movimento Patarino', in *I laici nella 'societas christiana' dei secoli XI e XII*, Atti della terza settimana internazionale di studio, Mendola, 21–27 agosto 1965, Publicazioni dell'Università Cattolica del S. Cuore, Contributi – serie terza, *Miscellanea del Centro di studi medioevali*, V (Milan, 1968), 597–687. Repr. in Cinzio Violante, *Studi sulla cristianità medioevale: Società, istituzioni, spiritualità* (Milan, 1972).

——, *La Pataria Milanese e la riforma ecclesiastica* (Rome, 1955).

——, *La Società Milanese nell'età precomunale* (Bari, 1953).

Vogel, Cyrille, *Medieval Liturgy: An Introduction to the Sources* (Washington, DC, 1986).

Volpe, G., *Movimenti religiosi e sette ereticali nella società medievale italiana* (Florence, 1922).

Waddell, Chrysogonus, 'The Reform of the Liturgy from a Renaissance Perspective', in R.L. Benson and Giles Constable (eds), *Renaissance and Renewal in the Twelfth Century* (Cambridge, MA, 1982), 88–112.

Walter, Christopher, 'Papal Political Imagery in the Medieval Lateran Palace', *Cahiers archéologiques fin de l'Antiquité et le Moyen Âge* 20 (1970): 155–76.

Ward, Benedicta, *Miracles and the Medieval Mind, Theory, Record and Event, 1000–1215* (Philadelphia, 1982).

Webb, Diana, *Saints and Cities in Medieval Italy* (Manchester, 2007).

——, *Patrons and Defenders: The Saints in the Italian City States* (London, 1996).

Werner, Ernst, 'Pietro Damiani ed il movimento popolare del suo tempo', *Studi Gregoriani* (1975): 289–314.

——, *Pauperes Christi, Studien zu Sozial-Religiösen Bewegungen im Zeitalter des Reformspapsttums* (Leipzig, 1956).

Whitehead, Christina, 'Columnae . . . sunt episcopi. Pavimentum . . . est vulgus: The Symbolic Translation of Ecclesiastical Architecture in Latin Liturgical Handbooks of the Twelfth and Thirteenth Centuries', *Medieval Translator/Traduire au Moyen Age* 8 (2003): 29–37.

——, *Castles of the Mind: Studies in Medieval Architectural Allegory* (Cardiff, 2003).

Whitmore, Eugene R., *St. Nicholas, Bishop of Myra (Saint Nicolas of Bari): The Genesis of Santa Claus* (1944).

Wickham, Chris, 'Il problema dell'incastellamento nell'Italia centrale: l'esempio di San Vincenzo al Volturno', in Federico Marazzi (ed.), *San Vincenzo al Volturno: Cultura, istituzioni, economia* (Abbazia di Montecassino, 1996).

Wilmart, A., OSB, 'La Trinité des Scots à Rome et les notes du Vat. lat. 378', *Revue Bénédictine* 41 (1929): 226–8.

Woody, Kennerly M., 'Damian and the Radicals' (PhD diss., Columbia University, 1966).

Wordsworth, John, *On the Rite of Consecration of Churches* (London, 1899).

Wright, Craig, *Music and Ceremony at Notre Dame of Paris, 500–1550* (Cambridge, 1989).

Zadora-Rio, Élisabeth, 'Lieux d'inhumation et espaces consacrés: le voyage du Pape Urbain II en France (Août 1095–Août 1096)', in André Vauchez (ed.), *Lieux sacrés,*

lieux de culte sanctuaires, approches terminologiques, méthodologiques, historiques et monographiques (Rome, 2000), 197–213.

Zchomelidse, Nino, *Santa Maria Immacolata in Ceri: pittura sacra al tempo della riforma gregoriana* (Rome, 1996).

Ziolkowski, Thaddeus S., *The Consecration and Blessing of Churches: A Historical Synopsis and Commentary* (Washington, DC, 1943).

Zumhagen, Olaf, *Religiöse Konflicte und Kommunale Entwicklung: Mailand Cremona, Piacenza und Florenz zur Zeit der Pataria* (Weimar, 2002).

Zweig, Eugen, 'Zum christlichen Königsgedanken im Frühmittelalter', *Das Königtum, seine geistigen und rechtlichen Grundlagen, Vorträge und Forschungen* 3 (Lindau, 1956): 7–73.

INDEX